BLACK SEPARATISM IN THE UNITED STATES

BLACK SEPARATISM IN THE UNITED STATES

RAYMOND L. HALL

Published for Dartmouth College

by the University Press of New England

Hanover, New Hampshire 1978

Copyright © 1978 by Trustees of Dartmouth College

All Rights Reserved

Library of Congress Catalogue Card Number 77-75515

International Standard Book Number 0-87451-146-1

Printed in the United States of America

The University Press of New England

Sponsoring Institutions:

Brandeis University

Clark University

Dartmouth College

The University of New Hampshire

The University of Rhode Island

The University of Vermont

2-26-79

TO TERRY

PREFACE

It is ironic that even today there is a paucity of serious works on black separatism in the United States. It stems, I suspect, from a general inclination to believe that black separatism is simply another irrational and misguided reaction to oppression. It may also be that most white and some black Americans think that black separatism is irrelevant, and some may never have heard of it.

More than anything else, I want to show that black separatism is complex, with deep historical roots into a part of the American character which many people would rather not see. It deserves better than to be effusively praised or rapidly or angrily or fearfully damned. It deserves to be thought about, especially in this decade of the 1970's when the recent past progress of black Americans seems to have slowed, as the majority turns to other concerns.

Data for the contemporary phases of the separatist organizations were gathered between 1968 and 1972 from the following sources: interviews with members in the five organizations, including personal interviews and correspondence with most of the leadership at different times; information gleaned from primary and secondary sources, such as intraorganization memoranda and other personal data; organization newspapers, pamphlets, and books written by leaders and by rank-and-file members; information gained from interviews with individuals who defected from certain organizations; as well as other forms of general and specific discussions with members and former members of the various organizations.

I was also fortunate enough to observe as well as to participate in some of the activities of these organizations. The members knew I was not a true believer but nevertheless allowed me to check out what was going on. They knew that if I ever wrote about them, I would have enough good sense to omit information that was meant only for the in-group.

In writing a book of this nature, one inevitably incurs all sorts of debts: intellectual, inspirational, clerical, even financial. Beginning with the intellectual, I wish to acknowledge especially the help of Stanley H. Udy, Jr., and Jere R. Daniell, who read several drafts of the manuscript. Special thanks are due Bernard E. Segal, who at the very beginning helped me to improve the manuscript, and Lewis M: Killian, for his critique of the manuscript at a critical stage of its development. Ronald Walters also read the initial version and made several useful suggestions. Full responsibility for the final product is, of course, mine.

I am grateful to Donna Musgrove for typing the manuscript and Judy Jones, Ann Fellows, Marilyn Dickinson, and Pat Bromley at Dartmouth College for other clerical assistance. David Horne, Director and Editor of the University Press of New England, patiently (and sometimes painfully) edited the manuscript and made other invaluable suggestions in guiding it to a finished book. I am grateful to the Department of Sociology and the Faculty Research Committee at Dartmouth College for financial assistance in defraying certain clerical expenses.

Finally, I want to thank Terry Tarun Hall for providing me comfort when I asked for it. She always knew when I needed it and was too up tight to deserve it.

Hanover, N.H.   *R.L.H.*
January 1978

CONTENTS

Preface   vii

1.   Introduction   1

I. Background

2.   The Roots   21

3.   Separatists in Disguise   38

4.   Militant Black Nationalism   58

5.   Subdued Separatism   75

II. The Contemporary Period

6.   Separatist Ideologies, I   97

7.   Separatist Ideologies, II   123

8.   Economic Programs   139

9.   Interrelations and Comparisons   166

III. In Perspective

10.   Change and the Movement Organizations   199

11.   Separatism: Catalyst for Change   225

12.   Conclusions   241

Appendix: Views on Five Issues 257

Bibliography 265

Notes 273

Index 291

BLACK
SEPARATISM
IN THE
UNITED STATES

1 INTRODUCTION

Although black separatism is deeply rooted in American history, its contemporary forms are both similar to and different from its historical expressions. Its contemporary inclusiveness, together with its tendency to confront authority directly by seeking a rearrangement of societal power relations favoring oppressed black Americans, make it possible to evaluate and redefine the black experience in the United States from this perspective. A redefinition from such a separatist perspective may be expedient in the enhancement of minimum dignified black survival, or, at most, of an opportunity for black people—individually and collectively—to play the social roles of their own choosing rather than those dictated by various modes of social, political, and economic inequality.

Black separatism is a subcategory of black nationalism. Black nationalism, stemming from the idea of racial solidarity, implies that blacks should organize themselves on the basis of their common experience of oppression as a result of their blackness, culture, and African heritage. Believing that organization is the first step to freedom, black nationalism incorporates complex and diverse political, cultural, territorial, and economic themes; it includes an almost bewildering variety of ideas about almost every aspect of social organization and belief. Cultural nationalism, religious nationalism, economic nationalism, bourgeois reformism, revolutionary black nationalism, territorial separatism —these are a few of the headings under which black nationalism can be discussed.

Cultural nationalism asserts that black people have distinctive culture, life-styles, values, philosophy, etc., which are essentially different from those of white people. According to some cultural nationalists, black culture is but one of the many subcultures that make up pluralistic American society. Another variation stresses the superiority of black culture over (white) Western culture.

Religious nationalism is closely related to cultural nationalism and is sometimes classified under it. It usually asserts that black people should establish, control, and run their own churches. The emphasis is usually Christian, but recent manifestations indicate that the Christian framework is no longer dominant. The Black Muslims, for example, denounce Christianity.

Economic nationalism is the trunk for two divergent branches, socialist and capitalist. Both branches assert that blacks should create and control a black segment of the economy. Socialists favor cooperatives; capitalists favor the establishment of black business and "buying black."

Bourgeois reformism is based upon a pluralistic America. Blacks could and therefore should use mechanisms provided by the present political system to win control over local areas where they are in the majority. To this extent the concept is straight out of high school civics, except that the bourgeois reformist separatists call for an all-black political party to ensure majority black control.

Revolutionary black nationalism burns the civic texts, contending that only the overthrow of the existing political and economic system can bring about the liberation of black Americans.

Nationalists who believe in territorial separatism within the United States hold that black people have a stake in American society because blacks, among other things, helped to build the country. But since they also hold that blacks and whites cannot live in the same society in mutual equality, blacks, they say, should have a separate territory, with all-black towns or all-black states—or preferably, an all-black nation. A better known urban variant of this form of separatism is "community control of black communities."[1]

The importance of these distinctions should not be minimized. At the risk of repetition, it should be made clear that black separatism is a subcategory of black nationalism, but black nationalism is not a subcategory of separatism: a cultural nationalist may believe in the uniqueness of black culture stemming from its African roots and may even believe it to be superior to Western culture, but a black nationalist may also believe that black and white geographical separation is unnecessary, accepting that cultural nationalism is a proper part of American pluralism. An economic nationalist may believe that blacks should strive to control their own economic destiny; political nationalists may believe that blacks should elect their own (black) officials and control politically where blacks are in the majority; other nationalists may believe in "community control," ranging from local control of primarily black communities in urban settings to the formation of all-black towns and cities. All of these facets of black nationalism reflect the number and diversity of views which may be placed under its umbrella, and all stem from the premise of racial solidarity. All of them have separatist overtones if stretched to their logical extremes, but that would not necessarily be so if total black and white separation were not insisted upon.

Black separatism in its purist form, as a subcategory of black nationalism, asserts that blacks and whites ideally should form two separate nations. Insofar as the ideal of black and white national separation has not become a reality, however, separatist sentiment is often manifested in one or more of the above forms of black nationalism. In short, a separatist is always a nationalist, but a nationalist is not always a separatist.

Separatist dimensions may be measured at the local or community level, later encompassing the concept of a black nation or nation-within-a-nation, and finally embracing Pan-Africanism as the ultimate expression of black nationalism/separatism. Pan-Africanism in this sense holds that all black peoples everywhere are of African descent and are therefore members of the African Diaspora. And all members of the Diaspora should return to Africa. This view, is, however, only one dimension of Pan-Africanism; the other is chiefly concerned with African unity on the African continent.

Some black separatists ultimately envision the revival of Mother Africa's power through the return of her skilled, trained, and technologically efficient Diaspora children. Others are content to regard Africa proudly as their ancestral homeland and, though not intending to return there, to replenish their "soul supply" with visits. Such recharges may be seen as serving to keep the fires of separatism burning in the United States; the anticipated Black Nation, once established, may base its sociocultural organization on an African model—Tanzania's Ujamaa, or some other ancient or current tribal system, usually one of the Western African variety. In short, the Black Nation would be located geographically in the United States (or somewhere in North America) but would receive its sociocultural sustenance from an African source.[2]

A comprehensive perspective of black separatism in the United States involves more than emphasis upon its historical dynamics. It is a contemporary phenomenon simultaneously causing angry concern over its potential for further fragmenting an already fragile pluralism along with providing fervid hope for many who do not have, but often angrily desire, self-determination.[3]

Though the contemporary loud cry for black separatism was muted and isolated until around the mid-1960's, even as early as the late 1950's revolutionary black nationalism was prominent in the action and rhetoric of Robert F. Williams and Malcolm X. Williams advocated armed self-defense and retaliation against Ku Klux Klan violence, and after he organized the black community in Monroe, North Carolina, for self-defense, the Klan ceased its wanton forays there. Malcolm X rose to prominence by criticizing the integration movement ("integrate into what?"). He was a minister of the Nation of Islam or Black Muslims, the largest black nationalist organization in the early 1960's and the Muslims' most effective spokesman for their program of separatism, self-defense, and liberation "by any means necessary."

The early successes of the sit-ins and boycotts in breaking down racial barriers in the early 1960's primed many black people to expect continued progress. The Deep South, with the Student Non-Violent Coordinating Committee (SNCC) in the forefront, became a battleground for attempts to organize blacks politically, and efforts were made by the Congress of Racial Equality (CORE), among other organizations, to deal with the problems of the urban poor in the North. Still, resistance to meaningful change was commonplace in both the North and the South. It is fair to say, in retrospect, that the March on Washington and the late Dr. Martin Luther King, Jr.'s "I Have a Dream" speech marked the end of the massive large-scale interracial demonstrations. Even at the time of the August 1963 March, the Freedom Now Party (which lasted from 1963 to 1964) and the Revolutionary Action Movement (RAM) were preparing for the emergence of all-black organizations.

Black reaction to the bombing of a church in late 1963 by white racists in Birmingham, Alabama—an act that killed three little black girls attending Sunday School—created doubts in the minds of many civil rights workers about the wisdom of the nonviolent direct-action approach. The rejection of the interracial Mississippi Freedom Party by the Democratic Party at the Democratic Convention in 1964, and the acceptance of the all-white, anti-black "regular delegation" (which conveniently forgot that Mississippi is nearly 40 percent black), along with black demonstrations in Harlem that same summer, led many blacks to believe that non-violence and integration were not the right methods and goals for achieving black freedom; and so-called riots in Rochester, New York, Watts, Harlem, and other large cities between 1964 and 1966 for the most part signaled an end to the interracial, non-violent, direct-action movement. By 1965 CORE had moved to eliminate whites from leadership positions; SNCC had elected Stokely Carmichael chairman in the process of becoming an all-black group, and had formed the Lowndes County, Alabama, Freedom Organization, which had as its symbol a Black Panther. SNCC's purpose then was to win political control in the areas of the South where blacks were a majority of the population.

In June 1966 James Meredith led the "Meredith Mississippi Freedom March," to show the people, especially black people, that one could walk the roads of Mississippi without fear. He was shot. Martin Luther King felt that the march had to continue "in order to demonstrate to the nation and the world that Negroes would never again be intimidated by the terror of extremist white violence."[4] The march did continue, under the auspices of CORE, SNCC, and the Southern Christian Leadership Conference (SCLC), with the understanding that all other civil-rights organizations would be invited to join. And so a national call for support and participation went out.

Prior to the Meredith incident, there had been incidents of violence during the Selma March in 1965, which resulted in the death of Jimmy Lee Jackson, a black, and James Reeb, a white minister. The public reaction to the news of the death of these two people could be regarded as the main factor underlying the final split between SNCC and SCLC. For many blacks it was no longer acceptable that whites often came down from the North, and then, because of their superior educational backgrounds and to no small degree the color of their skins, assumed leadership. Black people began to resent being mere aides and second-echelon leaders, regarding the process as a continuation of the same old system. Adding to their frustration was the sense that even when blacks and whites died together for the same cause, the whites got far more attention. After the fatal shooting of Jackson and the fatal clubbing of Reeb, President Johnson, in his eloquent "We Shall Overcome" speech, paused to mention James Reeb. He even sent flowers to the widow of the slain Unitarian minister. For some reason, he did not mention Jimmy Lee Jackson, who died first and for the same cause, and Jackson's parents got no presidential flowers. Similarly, when James Chaney, a black, was murdered in or near Philadelphia, Mississippi, the news media played up as a national tragedy the deaths of Andrew Goodman and Michael Schwerner, the two young white men who had been murdered with him.[5] What was news, apparently, was that whites were killing whites. It seemed to many young blacks that things were not really different after all: whites had always killed blacks in the South without causing much concern to other whites.

By 1966 it was clear to many blacks that if they were to be liberated from white oppression, they had to do it themselves. The old-line civil rights organizations, such as SCLC and the National Association for the Advancement of Colored People (NAACP), still believed that "integration" and "black and white together" would eventually bring to fruition the movements' main theme, "We Shall Overcome." But many blacks, young and old, North and South, militants and moderates, and some whites believed that white racism was too old and deeply entrenched in American society to be dislodged by temporary good will, integrated singing, and reform measures. Hence, many young blacks took the occasion of the Meredith Mississippi March, in defiance of Martin Luther King's and others' integrationist positions, to sing civil rights or protest songs. But they changed some of the lyrics to demonstrate their emerging ideological disagreement with integration as a proper goal for black people. Instead of "We Shall Overcome," they substituted "We Shall Overrun," and instead of Bob Dylan's "The Times They Are A-Changing," they might well have sung, had it been recorded then, James Brown's "I Got Soul and I'm Super Bad."

In any case, the foundation was laid, and the Meredith Mississippi March provided the opportunity for mostly young blacks to articulate alternatives to integration religiously adhered to by old-line civil rights organizations, first in sentiment and quite soon after in fact. On that march Stokely Carmichael, speaking for his organization (SNCC), defiantly cried, "What we need is black power." His cry was symptomatic of the many past and present varieties of organized and generalized black separatist thrusts. Though they frequently emphasize different methods and goals, they have all quickened and revitalized black consciousness, kindling a renewed interest in black self-determination.

Against this background, the present book analyzes several facets of contemporary black separatism, paying special attention to the period 1960–72. It focuses on separatist elements in five black social-movement organizations: The Nation of Islam, commonly known as the Black Muslims; the Congress of Racial Equality (CORE); the Student Non-Violent (later National) Coordinating Committee (SNCC); the Black Panther Party; and the Republic of New Africa (RNA). These organizations, among other things, have the common goals of liberating black people from white oppression and establishing black political, economic, and social autonomy. Their ideas, ideologies, leadership, membership, purposes, values, and goals are examined.

The movements discussed can be classified as territorial separatism (RNA); economic nationalism (CORE); revolutionary nationalism (the Black Panthers); religious nationalism (the Nation of Islam); and political nationalism (SNCC). I repeat that this work is concerned only with the separatist aspects and elements in these five organizations. Separatist social movements are usually treated theoretically in two ways. (1) Two groups in close competition with each other, having similar programs and resisting "two way-merger tendencies." (2) Separation (schismogenesis) within a parent body, producing splinter movements.[6] The contemporary black separatist movements have both of these characteristics, and they propose additionally to *separate from the general society to form autonomous societies,*[7] either within or outside of the United States as we now know it. Short of these two extremes, there are other separatist groups posing various kinds of semi- or quasi-autonomous societies.[8] Furthermore, these various dimensions of separation are expressed in signally yet subtly diverse ideologies.

Some organizations, like the Black Muslims, combine religion, politics, and economics in their ideology. Their movement is nationalistic, calling for a black nation, and revitalistic, glorifying the past history of peoples of African descent. It insists on closely cropped hair, coat and tie, and clean shaves for men; and, for women, usually long dresses, short hair, and the absence of cosmetics. Internally, it is a reform movement, calling on its members to abstain from alcohol and drugs and from sex without marriage. The Nation of Islam meets the definition of separatism not only in terms of its goals, which call for an absolute breakaway from the general (white) society, but also insofar as it purports to be a sect of Islam as a world religion.

The Congress of Racial Equality (CORE) calls for the separation of black communities from white within the United States urban centers. It proposes, furthermore, that black people should, in the broadest sense, control their own political destinies wherever they live. Since most blacks and most whites already live in separate communities in all areas of the United States, CORE insists that whites should not control the black communities. It also embraces Pan-Africanism.

The Republic of New Africa is a separatist movement organization that proposes to take over Mississippi, Alabama, Georgia, South Carolina, and Louisiana as the core of a black nation. This movement's ideology suggests that there is a natural territorial drive in human beings which makes them want to "have dominion over their own territory." The movement stresses that black people do not—and never can—control their destinies in the urban areas of the West and North. All black people, the movement preaches, should move back to these five states to form a clear majority and be a black nation.

The Black Panther Party began as a cultural (black) nationalist organization, later taking the position that black political independence must precede social and economic independence. Black political (separate) independence was their formula for achieving black self-determination. According to Henderson and Ledebur, *"the separatist thrust of the Black Panthers* is motivated by the continuing injustices which the American Negro has suffered throughout his history in this country, [citing a section] of the Declaration of Independence as justification for their separatist philosophy."[9] The Panthers do take the position, however, that in order to settle the question of black separation, a plebiscite should be undertaken in the black community. Nevertheless, though the Party's ideology does not specifically call for separation, it operates, in essence, not unlike an avowedly separatist movement organization.

The Party later moved from black nationalism to embrace Marxist-Leninism as its ideology; still later it expanded to include internationalism and intercommunalism. The organization's stated ideology then became raceless and classless. Despite the ideological pronouncements, however, the militance it encompassed and the anticapitalist ideology it came to espouse in fact caused most whites to equate it with black separatism. Moreover, it never allowed whites to become members of the Party, despite its claims of nonracial ideology and goals. The Party operated its organization *as if* it proposed to separate blacks and whites.

What was initially the Student Non-Violent Coordinating Committee later changed its name in July, 1969 to the Student National Coordinating Committee. It became a separatist organization, splintering from SCLC, and later promoted black and white national separation. SNCC, more than any other group, is responsible for the resurgence of the slogan "Black Power" and has contributed in no small way to the contemporary wave of black awareness. It more than any other embodied the philosophy of Malcolm X after he died. The prominence and publicity received by SNCC leaders Stokely Carmichael, H. "Rap" Brown, Julian Bond, John Lewis, Robert Moses, and others has had a profound influence on black attitudes, especially among young people. That influence today appears to have aided the proliferation of separate black groups within and in conjunction with established organizations. Examples include black studies in colleges and universities, unions and church organizations, the American Medical and American Dental associations, the American Sociological Association, and many other white-dominated groups. To say that SNCC was not wholly responsible for these developments is not to minimize the enormous effect it had.

Theoretical Considerations

A case could be made that black separatism should be viewed as a social problem and therefore explored in terms of theories of deviance. Though it is true that back separatism is regarded by most as deviant and aberrant, that device would, in my opinion, egregiously distort the social reality of black separatism. Black separatists *are*. And if their social reality is to be understood, the best and most applicable framework should be used to describe and analyze it. Separatism may be a problem for others, but others are crucial problems for separatists.

In describing the groups, I have used the term "movement organization," implying that the movement's organization is a product of a social movement. Theories of social movements in general may be used to analyze and explain black separatist movements and their organizations. I draw upon these theories with reservations. Social movements are usually conceptualized as a subcategory of collective behavior. In the past it was a possibly unfortunate tradition in the scholarly literature concerning collective behavior that organized collective action attempting to better the lot of a segment of the population—even when attempting changes within the system—was often viewed as the response of a mob composed of abnormal people bent on systematic destruction. That is, at first theorists approached the analysis of crowd behavior and related collective phenomena from the point of view that the individual had become subservient to the group, thus yielding his independent judgment to mindless, collective force.

Reasons for fear of certain kinds of crowd behavior are not entirely unfounded or incorrect, but many theorists as well as laymen still misplace their emphasis. They rush so quickly from movement to mob, from people to dynamics, that they fail to give sufficient account to real grievances and to the unavailability of satisfactory or conventionally approved mechanisms for redressing them. Fortunately, there are some newer conceptions in the field of collective behavior which suggest that it may be a part of the *normal* propensity for individuals to act collectively to solve problems. What is important is that before a group may be held to possess this sort of collective rationality, it must consist of people in interaction sensing that they constitute *a unit with a purpose*. Moreover, what may be called a "quasi-rational collectivity" depends more on informal understandings and shared symbols and may depart in some significant ways from the conventionally approved standards of the larger society.

What I am suggesting is that the study of collective behavior is tending in the direction of a model of social and cultural changes which examines the end-products of collective action rather than concentrating on the abnormal aspects of the phenomenon. Turner and Killian state more clearly—and most recently—the fallacy of attributing irrational or emotional connotations to collective behavior:

> When a person challenges the established dictates or is forced to act when cultural dictates are nonexistent, vague, or contradictory, his behavior becomes unpredictable to others about him, making him hard to deal with, and his fellows may find it difficult to understand his behavior. Hence to say he is acting emotionally or irrationally . . . is either fallacious or tautological.[10]

Nevertheless, in my opinion, if collective-behavior theory continues to be the framework in which social movements are examined (I hope it will not be), then treating non-normative collective behavior in the context of its relationship to conventional behavior and cultural and social norms seems more fruitful in the long run. I contend that there are other and more adequate frameworks for the analysis of social movements, especially because movements are rational sorts of instruments for mobilizing power against those who have all the more conventional bases of power at their disposal. Confusing social movements with unacceptable forms of collective behavior may be a deliberate tactic by constituted authority—despite academic objections—to undermine a movement's legitimacy. Constituted authority can easily confuse the issue, for it is apparent that many, including some scholars, confuse such elementary forms of collective behavior as riots, mobs, panics, and crazes with planned, rational, deliberate and long-term sustained social action characterized by social movements.

Skolnick, referring to "official" views of collective behavior, observes that most authorities

> define collective behavior as immoderate, and its underlying beliefs as exaggerated, strongly implies that "established" behavior may be conceived to the contrary. . . . Such an approach has important political implications, which ultimately renders much of collective behavior theory an ideological rather than analytical exercise. This inherently judgmental aspect of collective behavior theory is made all the more damaging by being unexpressed.[11]

The confusion can be avoided by analyzing social movements on their theoretical merits.[12] This is not, however, to suggest that the quality of social movement theory is better than that of collective behavior; it is to suggest that, whatever its shortcomings, social movement theory can avoid the almost automatic labeling of collective action as deviant behavior.

Social Movements, Organizations, and People

Social movements are characterized by and preoccupied with promoting or resisting change in the existing social arrangement of social systems. It is difficult to classify all social movements precisely because of their diversity: they range from secular to religious, from revolutionary to reactionary, from cooperative to schismatic; some are concerned with short-term change, others long-term; many aim at changing societal values and norms, still others are concerned with holding on to existing values and norms. Yet all social movements have characteristics in common, such as a shared value system, a sense of community, norms for action; and except for expressive movements, they all seek to influence society in various ways to accept their version of social arrangements based on their ideology. And each specific social movement is characterized by a distinctive organizational structure.

The specific social "movement organization" is, in short, where the action is. The term "movement organization" I use to identify a social movement's specific structural manifestation. The intent is to eliminate or minimize confusion when referring to a social movement, such as the civil rights movement (which comprises many organizations—the NAACP, SCLC, SNCC, etc.) on the one hand, and, for example, CORE's movement organization, referring specifically to CORE's organization as a part of the civil rights movement, on the other. The movement organization's structural components ensure a division of labor, and role differentiation, such as that of the leadership and that of the rank-and-file. In other words, in order to promote or resist change, a movement organization must have formal structure to cope with the many tasks inherent in tampering with the social change process.

Finally, social movements and their organizational manifestations are comprised of people—human beings interacting to promote or resist social arrangements that may profoundly affect the political economy of their individual and group lives. Approaching social movements from a sociopsychological perspective provides an opportunity to explore, intimate, speculate, and otherwise examine some of the psychodynamics of *individuals* comprising social movement organizations. While as a sociologist I am primarily concerned with *group interaction,* I also believe that to understand and explain the nature and character of group interaction, it is crucial to focus also at some point on the sociopsychological nature and character of the human components of movement organizations.

I believe I can characterize individual separatists by constructing five typologies of the hundreds of individuals I came to know in the five movement organizations. To do so, one must understand that black separatism is no more than the black struggle for justice, equality, and humanity against individual and institutional racism, injustice, and the historical and contemporary American denial of a fair chance for dignified black survival.

The behavior of black Americans regarding freedom suggests that most blacks—past as well as present—want only a fair chance to compete and get along in what is an obviously far from perfect society, to say the least. Why should it be so difficult to get so little? Why should there be so much physical and emotional pain and hardship to take hold of a promise long made but never more than partially and grudgingly met? Was the covenant that white America made with black America no more than the sign of God's covenant with Abraham, a pretty rainbow, a mere vision of life on vapor that could not be grasped or that disappeared when viewed from a different angle? Is there a white American who can say for certain and in good conscience that his own achievements would be the same if *his* great-grandparents had been slaves and his grandparents landless serfs, sharecroppers, or proletarians at the very bottom of the totem pole weighted down with disdain, inhumanity, hate, and oppressive indifference? Is there a black American—no matter how affluent, respected, and "accepted"—who does not feel torment and despair, frustration and anger, guilt and confusion, knowing that this allegedly most "open" of all societies (for whites) may never open for most black people? That is why many blacks are angry. It is also why many choose avenues not sanctioned by whites to pursue their own sociocultural realities. (A few individual blacks have always been successful despite systemic and institutional impediments against them. Nevertheless, separatists argue that most black people continue to be American political, social, and economic scapegoats.) Hence, logic be damned—things are not getting better and the logical way to "make it" takes too long, and even if a black person treads the long road to success, he is more often than not denied the benefits of his long-suffering pursuit. Even if he is successful, he knows that when millions of other blacks try to duplicate his efforts, their attempts, more often than not result in complete or partial denial of the fruits of their labor.

Though much of this work is academic, it is ultimately about people—individuals and groups seeking justice in American society. It is about people who are denied the fruits of their labor; it is also about people who are materially secure, but insecure about the denial of security to their brethren who had earned it but do not possess it. It is about people who at first unconsciously accepted the American Dream in all its utopian splendor, but later realized it was a nightmare; it is also about people who hold on to the dream while struggling to unmask the nightmare, hoping that it is a sheep in wolf's clothing. It is about people who seem to have given up struggling for dignified black existence in America; it is also about people who will contend for the opportunity to awaken from the nightmare. It is about people who have given up on America and its promise. They all ask the same question: how, without separation, can black people—individually and collectively—feel they control their own destiny or affect anything of consequence?

These movement people, these separatists, might be people you know or people like them whom you have known. At different places and in different times, perhaps, we have all been these people. Despite white stereotypes, the people in separatist movements are, after all, people. They are not all bad, though some might have done stupid or perhaps evil things. They are not all good, though some have been steadfastly noble and self-sacrificing. They are not all certain—though some have developed a dogged purpose and conviction that they are right; others use iron will and purpose and courage to block out and cover their fears and longings and ordinary human desires. Some want simply to be left alone.

The five types are as follows:

The Value-Suspended Ideologist

The value-suspended ideologist overtly rejects the values of the general society in favor of those promoted by a separatist movement organization; however, he *subconsciously* operates under the general society's value constraints. Thus he is in limbo between partially rejecting reformist values and ideology and accepting those of a separatist movement organization. He usually overcomes his dilemma by promoting the separatist movement's ideology, but not necessarily its values. For example, a separatist movement's ideology might have as one of its tenets the rejection of things material; the value-suspended ideologist may rhetorically support the movement's antimaterial stance. Subconsciously, however, because of his original socialization into the general society's materialistic mode (by being deprived of valued material things and admonished to strive to get them or having had them as a matter of course), he may not subscribe to the movement's non-materialistic values, but will promote its ideology. This member type is marginal; the strength of his separatist affiliation is unpredictable. He may remain a staunch movement supporter or he may defect from the movement; he could also abandon the separatist movement and return to the original group. In either case, choosing one or the other would mean that his values would no longer be suspended by ideological ambivalence.

The Transient Exchanger

A member who consistently rejects the values *and* ideology of the general society and accepts those of a separatist movement might be called a Transient Exchanger. The total rejection of the general society's socialization for the separatist movement points to the likelihood that he might—if a more attractive situation occurs—exchange his now held separatist ideology and values for another set. This type of member is easily swayed by nonsubstantive arguments, glittering generalities, and charismatic personalities. The real basis of his motivation is least known by himself but easily detected by those who would make use of him for their own purposes. He can easily become a "true believer" or even a fanatic. In general, he is prone to exchange ideological and value sets because he neglects to examine them in relationship to the social change process. He tends to regard only rapid or even radical change as important factors in altering power relations.

The Progress-Fixated Member

This type is so concerned with progress, accepting the movement organization's ideology, values, and goals as such, that it never dawns on him that the movement organization may be retrogressive. In reality, the movement organization's purpose and goals, and the logic of how to move from one to the other, are of little significance to this type because the idea of separatism per se as progressive dominates his *raison d'être* for joining a movement organization. In short, separatism as an ideology, not change, is what he seeks most.

The Vacillating Utopia Seeker

A fourth type, prior to his separatist affiliation, seems to espouse the virtues and values extant in the existing social arrangements and has achieved success under them. He is usually well off educationally and materially and enjoys a certain amount of prestige. His success comes as a result of a long period of hard work, and because his character, personality, and ability enable him to cope well in the existing social arrangement (his first utopia). It is after he achieves success that he becomes restless and generally dissatisfied with the oppression of his brethren.

His best change to redress the balance, as he perceives it, is to join a reform-oriented organization, the NAACP for example, using (legal) mechanisms of change sanctioned by the society. Joining such an organization gives him satisfaction in actually doing something to combat structures against his brethren; he is paying his dues, and thus relieving his feeling of guilt that his success may have been built upon the sacrifice and suffering of others (his second utopia).

After working long and patiently in a reform-oriented organization, finding that established, legal, and "acceptable" change mechanisms are too long and slow and compromised to make any difference in the end, he moves to the separatist-movement organization. In it he sees an opportunity to bring about change by short-circuiting institutional approaches to change. His continued membership in the separatist-movement organization usually depends on his position in it. His past experience and knowledge of the way change occurs in the general society set him aside from a rank-and-file member: he is impatient with the often irrelevant and petty preoccupations which concern the rank and file. He assumes that the other members of the organization are as aware of the necessary steps to a solution as he is.

He usually emerges as a leader of the separatist organization—its ideologue, or the major charismatic figure, or the intellectual, or the central organizing force, or some other post of major importance to the maintenance of the organization. Moreover, in times of financial stress and strain, he uses his own resources to sustain the organization. No separatist-movement organization can do without such an individual (this is his third utopia).

He is necessary to the movement organization, but he is risky, too. Once his staying power has been used up, he may well become cynical and bitter, feeling ineffective or unappreciated. Then, making the best of a bad bargain, he may well return to conventional society, unsatisfied but safe.

The Latent Revolutionary

A fifth kind of separatist may be called Latent Revolutionary because he is ambivalent about his relation to society in general and has only lukewarm enthusiasm for the separatist movement organization; he does not become excited about much of anything. He has usually wandered from organization to organization before settling on one more or less to his liking. Even his colleagues may dislike or distrust him.

He is, however, the one individual—whether the movement knows it or not—who can be counted upon to act out its extreme rhetoric. In most movements designed to bring about social change, there are two levels of goals: (1) the real or expected goals which are not articulated, and (2) goals articulated in extreme terms. In the second instance, leaders of the movements are aware that these goals are articulated to begin the negotiating process with the constituted authority. The intention (the first instance) was to reach a *rapprochement* somewhere in the middle—that is, a compromise between the separatist movement organization's extreme rhetorical demands as a goal and what the constituted authority is prepared to offer. If a movement publicly announces that "revolution comes through the barrel of a gun" but in reality means "if you don't make some concessions, there will be trouble," the latent revolutionary acts on the extreme rhetoric.

Consequently, the latent revolutionary may be responsible for further delegitimation of an already delegitimated (separatist) social movement. He may act out his repressed revolutionary impulses, his "thing," as it were, in acts of random aggression or suicidal forays directed against the constituted authority or its symbols. He acts in the name of the "struggle," the "revolution," "my people," "the movement," etc. His actions may influence others in the organization to do the same, but it is more likely that his actions will trigger coercive reaction from constituted authority, thus compromising what might be a functional safety-valve role played by the movement organization in preventing or limiting the spread of "revolutionary action" in the general society. In short, if his grievances, disaffection, and hostility cannot be directed or absorbed by the (separatist) movement organization, he is likely to do his (revolutionary) thing anywhere at any time. Movement organizations try to dissuade such known individuals from joining because they believe that their repertoire may not have the right psychological stock to play a role in their interaction with the society at large.

In summary, the types described above should be seen as persons seeking to cope with discrimination, racism, prejudice, poverty, and inequality in American society.[13] It is important to remember that these types will not be explicitly identified, but they are everywhere evident in the historical as well as the contemporary exploration of separation.

It is worth restating that black separatism in the United States is mostly regarded as nonrepresentative, "radical," or a militant fringe element in the black community. This view has been and continues to be perpetuated through continued recourse to outmoded constructs of collective behavior used as frameworks in analysis of social movements. In this work I will attempt to demonstrate that contemporary black separatism should be seen as an effort to redress the balance of power by creating methods and mechanisms whereby black people can control personal as well as significant collective aspects of their lives. In fact, black separatists may be conceptualized, and perhaps defined, as purposeful or unconscious agents for change which propose and attempt to implement political and sociocultural arrangements for black people that may differ from, and in some essential ways oppose, those of the larger society.

My investigations into contemporary separatism have led me

to realize it would be difficult to understand it if its historical roots were not explored. All of these movements are deeply rooted in the past efforts of black Americans to achieve freedom, and an historical perspective clearly demonstrates just how much continuity there is in the past and present black struggle for justice, dignity, and freedom in the United States. In the following five chapters I have provided a synoptic review of separatist tendencies from the 1770's through the 1950's.

1. BACKGROUND

2 THE ROOTS

From colonial times until the last decade of the nineteenth century, the dominant mode of black separatism may be characterized as emigrationism. The back-to-Africa tendency,[1] a specific variant, was Pan-Negroism, later called Pan-Africanism. Black separatism included also the nation-within-a-nation concept as well as separate black political parties. These attempts at self-determination began long before the 1960's, though many Americans, both black and white, find that hard to believe. It should be noted that black separatism, historically, can be seen as a consequence of whites excluding blacks from participation in the mainstream of American society. Blacks reacted then as now by posing alternatives that included compensating mechanisms.

From the very beginning, most Africans brought forcibly to America as slaves wanted to return to their homeland, and many, in fact, did so. Some even committed suicide on slave ships rather than leave Mother Africa and become slaves in the New World.[2] Once the Africans had been sold to a plantation owner, elaborate techniques were developed to prevent their escape. The myth of docile, fun-loving, timid, and agreeable slaves stood too long in the midst of evidence to the contrary.[3]

Though the vast majority of all Africans brought to the New World were slaves, many were indentured servants and did indeed, like white indentured servants, purchase their freedom. Others— few, to be sure—came as free immigrants from the West Indies; even fewer paid their way from Africa to the New World and were known as "free blacks."

To rationalize slavery, whites had to believe that Africans were inhuman savages. Not being able to sustain that thesis for long, however, they labeled Africans heathen. But Africans soon converted to Christianity, either to win their freedom or because they became true believers. Finally, between

> 1667 and 1682, the basis shifted to race. Virginia said it first, in her law of 1667: [Christianity] "doth not alter the condition of the person as to his bondage or freedom." After that [a] series of laws stripped the Negro slave of all rights and made color a badge of servitude. The Negro population . . . lunged forward. By 1710, the number had increased to 50,000. When the Declaration of Independence was signed, there were 500,000.[4]

Many of these free blacks themselves owned slaves and became affluent members of colonial American society. Like their white counterparts, they developed an abiding love for the country and placed faith in its promise of justice, liberty, and equality. These few had every reason to be hopeful and faithful, but the vast majority were never in a position to hope for the opportunity to be thankful, let alone keep the faith. Even when there was little reason for the majority of blacks to love their native land, however, many liked it enough to help defeat the colonial oppressor, England. Many others decided to take up the British offer of freedom provided that they would help to defeat the colonists. Despite the British defeat, some blacks were allowed to go to England and later, through British repatriation efforts, settled in Sierra Leone (established expressly for repatriated Africans).

The rebellious colonists, too, offered "free blacks" as well as slaves their freedom if they fought against the British oppressor. Britain, for the most part, though defeated, kept its promise of freedom and repatriation. The successful colonists, in the main, reneged on their promise. Slavery was not abolished in the Cotton Kingdom of the South; and the political compromise, a black being counted as three-fifths of a man, was a deal negotiated between northern and southern white men. Nevertheless, when Crispus Attucks, the black patriot who was the first to die in the Boston Massacre, lost his life defending the colonies against British oppression, he was acclaimed an American hero. When Salem Poor and Peter Salem, who among other blacks fought in the Revolutionary War, were commended for valor, they were also called heroes. But these same black heroes were banned from participation in decisions that would ultimately affect their freedom. It was one thing for blacks to fight and die for their country, something else again when it came to exercising that freedom. White Americans continued to use color as the measure of freedom and justice, and black people always came out on the short end of that yardstick. The net result of the stigma that white-dominated society placed on color was that black people, slave and free alike, found it difficult to feel at ease. American society has always *imposed* on blacks a sense of alienation and a desire for separateness, as shown by the formation of the first black Baptist Church of America, founded at Silver Bluff, South Carolina, in the 1770's. "But separatism did not become a serious movement until Negro mutual benefit societies and churches were formed during the period beginning with the adoption of the Constitution."[5]

In 1787 two events in Philadelphia deserve special note: (1) delegates met in the City of Brotherly Love to ratify the Constitution, including three clauses protecting slavery; and (2) Richard Allen and Absalom Jones, among others, were evicted from worshiping alongside white parishioners at St. George's Methodist Episcopal Church. In that same year, in the same city, the 27-year-old Allen, despite opposition from white Methodist elders, founded the Mother Bethel African Methodist Episcopal Church, and Jones founded the first black Episcopal church in America. Meanwhile, church separatism continued, and between 1787 and 1820 AME, Baptist, and other denominations witnessed black separation brought on by the increasingly discriminatory practices of white church people.

Shortly before their eviction from St. George's Church, Allen and Jones had formed the Free African Society, whose main purpose was to provide members with decent burials. The idea of the Philadelphia mutual aid society spread among other black communities in the North and became an important black voluntary association. Not only did the number of similar societies proliferate among blacks, but their purpose expanded to include financial shelter against illness or death, encourage thrift, etc. They also, later, provided financial backing for most of the early black businesses; some directed attention back to Africa by planning to send missionaries to "civilize" the natives. Soon many who desired to civilize also wanted to return to Africa as permanent residents—more precisely, resident citizens. Around the late 1700's and early 1800's, sentiment in favor of emigration was being expressed more frequently. In 1789 the Free African Society of Newport, Rhode Island, sent a proposal to the Free African Society of Philadelphia appealing for a return-to-Africa movement in order to escape an untenable position in the United

States.[6] It was not until 1815, however, that Paul Cuffee, a wealthy black New Bedford, Massachusetts, shipowner—at his own expense—repatriated thirty-eight free blacks to Sierra Leone.[7] Other nonreligious voluntary associations, such as the black masons in Boston, also separated from white parent bodies because of prejudice and discrimination.[8] There is no doubt that these separatist tendencies were in response to increasing oppression by white society.

In 1817, shortly before Cuffee's death, the American Colonization Society (ACS) was founded to accomplish with greater efficiency his repatriation plan.[9] With funds from the federal government, white philanthropists, and some state governments, the Society, in 1822, founded Liberia, a colony for black emigrants, located adjacent to Sierra Leone. By the outbreak of the Civil War the Society had transported 13,000 blacks to Liberia, most of whom were ex-slaves and whose masters freed them specifically on condition that they return to Africa, or simply leave the United States. Relatively few free blacks volunteered to join the colony, however, for most of them considered the United States their home. Many, in fact, refused to be repatriated.

At the same time that Southerners regarded the Society as a threat to slavery, their economic mainstay, others saw it as a way of ridding themselves of recalcitrant slaves. The Abolitionists frowned on ACS activities, considering them a device to rid the country of free blacks so that slavery could exist more securely.[10]

The 1820's found black people nearly silent about emigration to Africa, although a few denounced the Colonization Society. Except in Maryland, where the strongest white colonization society existed,[11] black people were less interested in returning to Africa than in removing the shackles of slavery, a goal then shared with the white abolitionists.

To this end, on March 16, 1827, *Freedom's Journal,* the first black newspaper, was published in New York City. The editors, John B. Russwurm and Samuel E. Cornish, used the weekly paper as a platform for their abolitionist appeals; they generally opposed the Colonization Society, although Russwurm, who later broke with his co-editor, embraced black emigration and the Colonization Society. *Freedom's Journal* then became an advocate of emigrationism. In the March 7, 1829, issue Russwurm, to make his position clear, wrote an editorial entitled "Our Rightful Place in Africa." He later went to Liberia himself as superintendent of schools, sponsored by the Society.[12]

With Russwurm's departure to Liberia, *Freedom's Journal*

became defunct, but Cornish continued his abolitionist appeal through its successor, a newspaper called *Rights of All,* which, like the original *Freedom's Journal,* was opposed to the Colonization Society and to black emigration to Africa. Also in 1829, David Walker, who owned a small clothing shop in Boston and was the Boston agent of *Freedom's Journal* before it changed its editorial policy, took issue with the Society. He published, at his own expense, a pamphlet entitled *Appeal in Four Articles.* His position was that colonization was a scheme to rid the country of blacks who had contributed immeasurably to its progress. He asked, "Will any of us leave our homes and go to Africa? I hope not." He believed that "America is more our country than it is the whites, we have enriched it with our *blood and tears.* The greatest riches in America have arisen from our blood and tears: and will they drive us from our property and homes, which we have earned with our blood?"[13]

Walker's advocacy of black people remaining in America was not unusual; indeed it was the usual response of most blacks and of the white abolitionist movement. What was unusual about his *Appeal* was its advocacy of armed rebellion by slaves to remove their oppression. Walker was specifically opposed by the leading white abolitionist, Benjamin Lundy, editor of the *Genius of Universal Emancipation,* as well as his associate editor, William Lloyd Garrison. Whites in the North and South, abolitionists as well as other liberals, including blacks, opposed the circulation of *Appeal* on the grounds that it was incendiary. Wiltse evaluates its impact: "The slaveholding South saw in it only incitement to servile rebellion, and went to fantastic lengths to suppress it. Even in the North, where slavery was generally opposed in principle, moderates insisted that the time for abolition had not yet come and agreed that the pamphlet was inappropriate and incendiary."[14]

The publication and subsequent circulation of the pamphlet in the South created fear, anger, and even more hatred. The short-term outcome was the imposition, of those caught circulating abolitionist materials, of severe penalties—in Georgia, for example, imprisonment and death. The long-term outcome was the growth of the abolition movement into a significant force that ultimately brought about the Emancipation Proclamation of 1863. According to Wiltse, "rumors came out of the South that a price of $1000 had been put upon Walker's head. Other rumors tripled the sum, and increased it tenfold if he were delivered alive."[15] It may be that someone did indeed collect a bounty, but it is unlikely that it included a tenfold sum because on June 28, 1830, David Walker was found dead near the doorway of his used clothing shop in Boston. Walker's death did not kill his *Appeal,* as we shall see.

The beginning of the 1830's witnessed black Americans turning inward for protection and mutual support, as evidenced by the rise of "Negro" conventions—that is, all-black sociopolitical movements. The all-black convention movement quickly lost its momentum, however, largely because of the impact of the abolitionist movement and the antiseparatist American Moral Reform Society, an all-black group but open to whites (who never joined). The Society's argument was that black people did not want to separate from whites; rather, blacks wanted the rest of the country to know that they were oppressed Americans. Samuel E. Cornish, co-founder of *Freedom's Journal* and the abolitionist, anticolonist publisher of *Rights of All,* denounced the Moral Reformers because he thought they demonstrated a lack of racial pride. He ultimately came to accept separatism, or, more precisely, "literal pluralism": "Oppressed Americans! *Who are they?* Nonsense, brethren! You are Colored Americans. The Indians are Red Americans, and the white people are White Americans and you are as good as they, and they are not better than you."[16] Cornish was instrumental in helping to lay the foundation for the convention movement's revival in 1843.

Despite the relative calm of the 1830's, there was a dramatic event that had a far-reaching effect on the institution of slavery. In 1831 Nathaniel Turner led a "liberation thrust," to some an insurrection, in which fifty-five whites were killed.[17] The Turner incident wasn't the first example of blacks openly expressing their dissatisfaction with their unbearable oppression. Earlier, in 1800, Gabriel Prosser planned an uprising against slavery in Henrico County, Virginia, but his plans did not materialize because of two slaves' complicity with whites. In 1822 Denmark Vesey's long-time plans of a revolt came to an end with his capture, after his co-conspirators also apparently informed whites of the planned action.[18] There was constant fear of slave revolts in the South, and there was incessant agitation in the North. Seething anger and frustration always lay beneath the surface, forcing Southern whites to keep the lid on tight lest they bubble to the top.

Blacks outside the slave states often fared no better than their slave brethren; though they were technically not slaves, they were victims of white prejudice and discrimination. In the 1840's and 50's (as in the 1960's) blacks outside the Cotton Curtain protested and agitated against disfranchisement, judicial discrimination, exclusion from public schools, and segregated public accommodations. Blacks in New York and Pennsylvania, for example, were unable to resist successfully their denial of voting rights, although in Rhode Island they defeated an effort that would have allowed voting rights to white men only. In Massachusetts blacks successfully protested segregated public transportation: in the early 1840's if blacks defied the segregation code, they were forcibly evicted from coaches designated "for whites only," but with the help of white abolitionists, in 1843 the railroads in Massachusetts stopped running separate coaches.[19]

These conditions and the state of affairs between black and white Americans in the decade of the 1840's led many blacks to see racial solidarity as the only solution, a kind of protective separatism, as it were. In 1843 the convention movement was revived, and there developed a serious debate among movement members as to whether violence and slave rebellions should be advocated. There were also proposals for organizing all blacks around economic concerns as well as a growing interest in the history of black achievements in Africa and the United States. Henry Highland Garnet, taking a position on the question of rebellion, called for slaves to rebel. In "An Address to the Slaves of the United States of America,"[20] later combined with David Walker's *Appeal,* he expressed the sense of identity which the "free" blacks felt with the slaves. He also called for the overthrow of the southern economic system, an effort that was to be based upon collective action on the part of the slaves themselves.[21] At the convention of 1843 this approach was very nearly adopted. Integrationists like Frederick Douglass and Charles L. Redmond argued that Garnet's "Address to the Slaves" would create further hardship for free blacks in the slave and border states, and a resolution endorsing Garnet's speech failed by only one vote. At the next convention, in 1847, the Garnet address came up again, and again it failed to pass. Toward the end of the 1840's, however, black people in the North were advocating resistance as the only means of destroying southern slavery.

During the 1850's Douglass led a victorious fight against the separate school system in Rochester, New York; and Benjamin Roberts, during one of the most notable desegregation campaigns, in Boston, in 1849, successfully sued the school board for excluding his daughter from a white school. It was not until 1855, however, that the Massachusetts Legislature outlawed school segregation.

Generally in the 1840's and 50's the theme of racial cooperation and solidarity continued to be dominant. Even Douglass, though an avowed integrationist, regarded black people as "my oppressed people," "a nation within a nation,"[22] and urged that a national league be organized.[23] The Colored National Convention of 1853, taking a more activist and race-oriented position than had previous conventions, sought to unite blacks by creating a national council to supervise a highly organized social policy of racial uplift.

Blacks even attempted to form a black political party: in 1855 a group in New York formed the New York State Suffrage Association. They intended to serve as the swing vote in close elections, because they were convinced that the major parties were not working for the best interests of black people. The Association did not run its own candidates, however, and reluctantly threw its support to the Republicans. (Note the date: years before the Civil War. The people were nominally free, yet they felt estranged from the mainstream of the American political system and found it necessary to form a separate, all-black party.)

The ACS had a resurgence after the passing of the Fugitive Slave Law as part of the Compromise of 1850. Some blacks embraced colonization because they felt it futile to struggle for equality in the United States. Among them were Alexander Crummell, Samuel Ringgold Ward, Henry Highland Garnet, and Martin R. Delany, all leaders in their own right. Bell has maintained that in the late 1850's the majority of prominent black men had become supporters of colonization.[24] Though there was a division among them as to where to settle—in Africa, Central America, the West Indies, or the far western frontier of the United States—they all agreed that it was best to establish separate communities for black people. Separatism here includes both migration and emigration. Blacks who accepted colonies as the solution held their own conventions in 1854, 1856, and 1858. Though there was some sentiment for the establishment of black colonies in other places, the most popular place was Africa, recalling Back-to-Africa separatist sentiments. Here the American Colonization Society played a prominent role. Even Alexander Crummell, who had received a degree from Cambridge University, became associated with the ACS and went to Liberia on its behalf. By this time many leading black individuals, as well as ordinary blacks, wanted to return to Africa because the situation in the United States had become for them untenable.[25]

The development of separatist leanings in the late 1840's and up to the Civil War should be understood in the context of developments against sentiments favoring racial equality and integration. In seeking to minimize intersectional strife, black people were mere pawns in the struggle to achieve national unity. The Compromise of 1850, the Kansas-Nebraska Act of 1854, the Dred Scott Decision of 1857—all left blacks with little hope of achieving the freedom and equality they so desperately sought. Therefore, blacks reasoned, separatism was the most feasible alternative.[26]

There were whites also who felt that the answer to the black dilemma was separation, and one of the most convincing was John Brown. He believed that people should not subjugate one another, but if subjugation did occur, drastic, even violent, countermeasures were in order. Though his raid on Harper's Ferry had an unfavorable ending, it pointed up the desperate situation blacks faced at that time.[27] It is noteworthy that during this period even Frederick Douglass became estranged from William Lloyd Garrison, the leading white abolitionist. The ultimate aims of the white abolitionists, in the final analysis, were different from those of the blacks. Black people wanted immediate and unconditional freedom and equality; whites at best urged gradual freedom based upon their liberal conceptions of decency and earned dignity. Douglass became so disillusioned that he made plans to emigrate to Haiti, but was persuaded to remain in the United States because of the hope he saw in the outbreak of the Civil War.

The War brought about a decline in the appeal of emigration because of the tangible support of northern whites for the immediate elimination of slavery. It gave blacks renewed hope of achieving equality in the United States, and their ideas and hopes again emphasized this end. Although the War also diverted major attention from the ACS, a significant personality continued to espouse the ACS's position of emigration of free blacks: Abraham Lincoln. In August 1862, in the midst of the War, Lincoln received a group of prominent black citizens of Washington, D.C., at the White House and laid out his argument for free blacks to go to the Caribbean or Latin America.

Lincoln's position was that it would be best for all concerned if free blacks emigrated, and that slavery, too, had had "its general evil effects on the white race." Moreover, were it not for the black presence, "there would not be war, although many men engaged on either side do not care for you one way or the other . . . *It is better for us both, therefore, to be separated."* He mentioned Liberia as a possible place to settle, but noted that many blacks, especially free blacks, would rather remain in the United States, or as close as possible to it. Thus the Central or Latin American alternatives.[28]

Lincoln's suggestion that free blacks settle "close to home" had more to do with the desire of northern business interests to colonize parts of the Isthmus of Panama and Haiti and to use free blacks there as laborers than his sympathy with nostalgic blacks who wanted to remain near by. Even before his meeting with the deputation of free blacks, Lincoln had at his disposal money to expedite the colonization scheme. Also, it had already been agreed that blacks held in detention in the District of Columbia and freed slaves under the auspices of the army would be the colony's first emigrants. The scheme had been initiated in October 1861 as the Chiriqui Project for Colonization.[29]

It turned out that Latin American governments, particularly Honduras, Nicaragua, and Costa Rica, as well as free blacks at home, rejected the idea of colonization in that area, and the first Lincoln Plan for separating blacks and whites was scrapped.

Because the country's attention was focused on the debilitating intersectional conflict, the ACS did not go out of business, but rather lowered its profile. Not for long, however, despite the issuance of Lincoln's Emancipation Proclamation in 1863. Between 1865 and 1870 it flourished again as unhappy freedmen sought viable freedom rather than peonage. For example, the "racial solidarity" doctrines of the 1840's and 1850's cropped up again: the Equal Rights League meeting in Philadelphia in 1865 declared that black unity was necessary to combat black oppression. To help stave off this feeling of alienation, the federal government gave blacks citizenship and voting rights. Emigration sentiments once again declined. Redkey observed that "as the freedmen found new privilege and power in the United States, [emigration] had less appeal."[30]

"New privilege and power" is an overoptimistic statement in terms of the results of the Emancipation Proclamation. In the first place, the Proclamation was an emergency effort to save the Union by bringing North-South hostilities to a quick end. Lincoln thought that "freeing the slaves in those states which are in rebellion against the United States" would result in the slaves joining the Union troops against the Confederacy. Many did, but as DuBois points out, "When northern armies entered the South they came as armies of emancipation. It was the last thing they planned to be. The North did not propose to attack property, nor did it propose to free slaves. This was to be a white man's war to preserve the Union, and the Union must be preserved."[31]

The upshot of the Civil War was that the Union won and black people made short-term gains. The "Radical Plan" of Reconstruction ensured that blacks would be able to vote and thus participate in the political system. The plan also minimized, for a time, the domination of southern ex-slave holders. Though many whites, North and South, feared that black participation would lead to control, it was far from the truth. Frazier makes the point: "The acts of Reconstruction governments have been popularly regarded as the work of incompetent, criminal, and savage Negroes who under the protection of federal bayonets imposed black domination upon the white south. This popular belief has been the result largely of a myth which had its origin in the editorials and reports in Southern newspapers." He cites as an example the *Fairfield Herald,* a South Carolina newspaper, which despaired of Reconstruction and was "against the hell-born policy which has trampled the fairest and noblest states of our great sisterhood beneath the unholy hoofs of African savages and shoulder-strapped brigands, the policy which has given up millions of our free-born, high-souled brethren and sisters, countrymen and country women of Washington, Rutledge, Marion, and Lee to the rule of gibbering, louse eaten, devil worshipping barbarians, from the jungles of Dahomey and peripatetic buccaneers from Cape Cod, Memphremagog, Hell, and Boston." This shrill extremism was representative of the general reaction by extremist whites to black political participation. Temporary black participation, not control, is the best term to describe the Reconstruction. Contrary to popular belief, blacks never at any time completely controlled a single legislature in the South.[32]

Despite this fact, whites in the South wanted total "redemption"—that is, no political participation at best, and minimal black participation at least—in order to restore complete white rule. This meant that the Radical Republicans and their northern supporters had to give way to the Democratic Party in the South. By 1870 Congress was in the mood to listen to the white South again, and in 1872 it removed the civil disabilities imposed upon the Confederate leaders by the Fourteenth Amendment. The removal of these restrictions enabled the old planter class to take over again the redemption campaign of the Democratic Party. With the aid of the Ku Klux Klan and the support of poor whites, the Democratic Party became synonymous with white supremacy. At the same time, the experienced leaders of the party found that they could make alliances with the rising commercial and industrial classes in the South as well as in the North.[33]

While the Democratic Party was re-tooling, the Republican-controlled federal government continued to wind down its protective role of safeguarding the rights of blacks and their allies. The Freedman's Bureau was discontinued in 1872. By 1876 the Democratic Party's rise to power in the South, combined with the desire to restore the Union and the merging of northern and southern political, commercial, and economic interests, set the stage for the withdrawal of all federal troops from the South. The election of 1876 and the Compromise of 1877 were clear triumphs for the commercial-industrial, Democratic-southern complex, for the South became fully redeemed after Rutherford B. Hayes withdrew the last federal troops from South Carolina and Louisiana in 1877.[34]

Southern redemption and preserving the union had meant, in essence, that blacks must be put in their place. Since they did not like that place, at the bottom of the socioeconomic and political ladder, emigration sentiments during this period re-emerged. Also, by 1850 cotton production had become unprofitable and many farmers could no longer make a living from it.[35] Ironically, the more cotton that was produced, the less money it yielded, and the blacks absorbed the bulk of the loss. Bracketed as they were by hope (the Civil War and Reconstruction) and despair (the Compromise of 1877 and a reinstitution of Jim Crow laws), it is not surprising that black men and women again counseled and worked for separation. "South Carolina is a case in point. Deprived of political and civil rights and denied economic opportunities, their insecurity heightened by the violent political campaign of 1876, Negroes looked longingly to Liberia for salvation."[36] The upshot of "Liberia fever" among these beleaguered black South Carolinians was the formation of the Liberian Exodus Joint Stock Steamship Company. With funds derived from sales of stock in the company, "a bark, the *Azor,*" was purchased in 1878 and about "two hundred and six" sailed for West Africa, arriving in Liberia during that summer. Despite this initial success, it was the one and only voyage the steamship company was to sponsor; about twenty-three passengers died during the trip for lack of proper medical care, and these shortcomings "somewhat tempered emigrationist zeal—only temporarily, however."[37]

How temporarily can be seen in the following example involving the dominant separatist modes of emigrationism or Back-to-Africanism. Benjamin "Pap" Singleton, who called himself the "Moses of the Colored Exodus," by the end of 1879 had led a contingent of about seventy-five hundred blacks from Alabama, Georgia, Mississippi, and Texas to Kansas in order to start anew. His success in persuading these poor souls to leave their homes stemmed from the fact that the states had refused to deliver on their promise to give blacks "forty acres and a mule." Though Singleton was largely successful in getting many people to "exodus" to Kansas, about 75 percent returned to the South.[38]

Kansas attracted not only blacks but white peons. Black and white peonage was not enough, however, to satisfy the white racists. As racism waxed in Kansas, Singleton turned first to Canada as a place for black settlement, then to Cyprus; but the lure of Africa eventually came to dominate him. In 1885 he founded the United Transatlantic Society to expedite black transportation to Africa. The society came to advocate more than mere transportation; it also passed "resolutions favoring 'Negro national existence'; and its records refer to a separate union as a *sine qua non* of Negro survival."[39] Though Singleton's Back-to-Africa Society did not realize its goals, its position on the need for a separate black nation became a dormant seed. Singleton himself died in 1892 still dreaming of a free and independent black nation in the United States—or Africa or anywhere.[40]

Although the South Carolina Back-to-Africa effort and Pap Singleton's "Kansas Exodus" and subsequent African emigration plan are cogent examples of black efforts to separate themselves from Southern peonage in general and white oppression in particular, much better known are the efforts of Martin Robinson Delany and Bishop Henry McNeil Turner. Delany, called by Theodore Draper the Father of Black Nationalism, began as a stay-at-homer (integrationist) and, in fact, coedited *The North Star,* Frederick Douglass' first abolitionist newspaper. Delany also attended medical school at Harvard. Though he loved his native land, in the early 1850's he became disenchanted by the passage of the Compromise of 1850 and the Fugitive Slave Law. The practical implication of the law was that it endangered the freedom of free blacks and escaped slaves alike. Who could say that a free black in New York might not be kidnapped and taken to a slave plantation? It often happened!

Journalism and medicine were only the seeds of Delany's outstanding career; he now became an emigrationist. In 1852 he wrote and privately published a book, *The Condition, Elevation, Emigration and Destiny of the Colored People of the United States.* Draper calls this book the *locus classicus* of black nationalism in America.[41] In the appendix Delany writes, "We are a nation within a nation; as the Poles in Russia, the Hungarians in Austria; the Welsh, Irish and Scotch in the British Dominions." He advocated the founding of a new black nation on the eastern rather than the western coast of Africa, because he disliked Liberia and the American Colonization Society, which he regarded as run by white racists.

Despite his black nationalist zeal, Delany displayed, as many black leaders did—and do—ambivalence toward leaving and founding a "new black nation" or staying to fight for political and economic rights in the United States. He was a consistent emigrationist for only about ten years, the decade of the 1850's. After 1861 and the outbreak of the Civil War, he separated himself from the cause of black emigrationism. Even at the height of his emigrationist sentiments, however, he never went far from the United States. He lived in Canada from 1856 to 1859, and he went to Africa in 1859 as an explorer, not as a settler. He returned to the United States and volunteered in the Union Army, holding the rank of Major of Infantry. "Then he more or less made peace with the country that he once said had bade him be gone and had driven him from her embraces." In the 1870's he finally settled in South Carolina and engaged in politics, becoming a judge in Charleston and, in the elections in 1876, threw his support to a moderate white, Wade Hampton, rather than "go all the way with the extreme black Reconstructionists, and, thus, indirectly helped to restore white rule in South Carolina."[42] Nevertheless, he continued to give lip service to African emigration, as exhibited by his endorsement of the Liberian Exodus Joint Stock Steamship Company. He came full circle, searching for a way out of the black dilemma.

Another leader and proponent of black separation through emigration was Bishop Henry M. Turner. He was, without a doubt, the most prominent and outspoken advocate of black emigration between the Civil War and the outbreak of World War I. Redkey writes that he possessed a "dominating personality, a biting tongue, and a pungent vocabulary which gained him high office and wide audiences, first in Georgia's Reconstruction politics and later in the African Methodist Episcopal (AME) Church." In his bitter disappointment with the American treatment of blacks, "the Bishop evolved an all-consuming nationalism which demanded emigration to Africa."[43] Born in South Carolina, where he encountered prejudice as a freeman, he felt ill at ease with racism all around him. His nationalism found its first outlet in New Orleans, where in 1858 he discovered a church governed solely by blacks, the African Methodist Episcopal (AME) church. He joined it, quickly rose to power, and even before he was elected to the episcopacy made his emigration ideas known. He urged blacks not to fight in the Union Army and to resist in the Confederacy.[44]

Turner believed that prejudice against black people was as strong in the North and West as in the South, and that black people could not escape their status by moving from the South to the North; in short, he was not a migrationist. He called for virtual separation of the races because "if the government that freed him cannot protect that freedom [black people should not] enlist in the armies of the government, or swear to defend the United States Constitution [which] is a dirty rag, a cheat, a libel and ought to be spit upon by every Negro in the land."[45] He believed that black people should either emigrate to Africa, the ancestral homeland, or prepare for extermination. In 1891, under the authorization of the AME Council of Bishops, Bishop Turner went to Africa. He was encouraged by what he found and returned to the United States in 1892 with renewed vigor to get blacks to move there. On his return he found a heightened interest among rural blacks, who would do almost anything to escape from the economic and political problems that beset them.

In 1892 the attention of the nation and a large part of the world was focused on the debate in the United States Congress on the Butler Bill, whether the federal government would give aid to Southern blacks who wanted to emigrate from the South to Africa. Closely associated with the introduction of the bill was the visit to America by Professor Edward W. Blyden of Liberia, whose purpose was to stir up interest among black Americans to emigrate to his country and to seek aid from the United States federal government for their repatriation. He came at the invitation of the American Colonization Society and with the blessing of Bishop Turner. The bill did not pass the Senate, but its discussion created a great deal of interest and argument about emigration per se. Nor did the failure of the bill deter hope among those who worked for emigration. Blyden was sure that nascent black nationalism would rise again. When he departed from New York for his return to Africa, Bishop Turner was there to see him off.[46]

Turner continued to push for African emigration, but a large-scale exodus never occurred. Nor did the Bishop favor massive emigration, for he, like Blyden (but for different reasons), believed that most black Americans were not fit to live in Africa. Though the Butler Bill failed to pass Congress and Blyden was able to stir up only lukewarm support for his emigration scheme, Turner continued to advocate it. The 1890's witnessed the emergence of forces and events that rivaled the Bishop's plans. Nevertheless, unlike Delany, he remained an ardent emigrationist until his death in 1915.

The separatist tendencies of migrationism and Back-to-Africa (emigrationism) received varying attention at various times, depending on the circumstances. In each case, heightened white racism pushed blacks to look for separate alternatives; once the alternatives were examined, the idea of freedom and black (separate) self-determination became dominant forces. Liberia is an example. Established in 1822 as a colony for black repatriation and emigration by the urging of American Colonization Society, in the minds of "free blacks" and slaves alike it represented a vision of freedom and dignity and an instance of black men controlling their own affairs through their own government. They seldom realized that Liberia was in reality completely dependent on the ACS and the United States government. Moreover, it was a pawn or "buffer zone" between British and French colonial interests in West Africa, and it represented both white humanitarian and white racist interests, assuming that some whites associated with the ACS were genuinely interested in removing the yoke of white oppression by sending blacks to Liberia.

In 1847 Liberia became self-governing, giving at least the appearance of bona fide black rule. Black American interest soared, though not to the extent that many of both races would have liked. Many then as now failed to ask why blacks born and reared in the United States should look to Liberia for freedom. The answers are both simple and complex: on the one hand, they should have looked there for freedom because they did not have it in the United States; on the other, they should continue to fight for freedom in the United States because it was their native land. The net result was often a combination of both factors, but it is clear that the black mass opted to remain in the United States. After all, to most black people, having been born and raised in the United States, Liberia was only a name.

The scene was set for an outpouring of sentiment and excitement over African emigration. Northern whites who had urged racial equality grew tired of the struggle, allowing southern whites who had urged a caste system (with blacks as peons rather than slaves) to be more confident of victory. For black people the results were political disfranchisement, economic subjugation, and loss of hope in finding a niche in American society. In general, the period from approximately the late 1820's through the Civil War was one of heightened black nationalist sentiment. The Civil War gave blacks renewed hope that, finally, the United States would live up to its promise. It was not to be. After Reconstruction ended, the black condition became steadily worse. By the 1890's blacks were again victims of disfranchisement, lynchings, Jim Crow laws, and disillusionment.

Delany, Bishop Turner, "Pap" Singleton, Blyden, and others should be seen in the context of the dire condition of Afro-Americans between 1850 and the rise of Marcus Garvey: these early leaders attempted to strengthen nascent black nationalism and its separatist strand principally among southern black peasants in order to better their lot, so that they could stay without suffering or, failing that, leave in a manner that would be least upsetting. The actual choices were far from ideal—to stay and suffer or to suffer by leaving the land of their birth.

3 SEPARATISTS IN DISGUISE

In general, from the end of the Reconstruction through the
"Progressive Era," the black condition grew progressively worse.
From the Compromise of 1877, black civil rights were eroded by
state laws, and by the mid 1890's Jim Crow was again virtually
intact throughout the nation. In 1892 the Populist Party lost the
election (it had also become racist); 1894 found the country in
an economic depression and, as always, blacks suffered the most
under adverse economic conditions; in 1895 the redoubtable
Frederick Douglass died; and in 1896 the Supreme Court of the
United States ruled against equality of education for blacks. As
a result, emigration came to be regarded by many as a more
favorable alternative than staying and suffering in the United
States.

In the midst of events that did not bode well for the black
condition, a new generation of black leaders emerged. Booker T.
Washington became a powerful voice after his Cotton States
Exposition Speech of 1895; W. E. B. DuBois received a doctorate
from Harvard University (1895), later becoming a leader in his
own right; William Monroe Trotter, receiving his B.A. in 1895
and advanced degree (1896) from Harvard, also later emerged as
an important leader. These men were the stars and supporting
actors for roles demanded by evolving circumstances and events.

The many schemes designed to transport black people to Africa—
even though most were strictly commercial enterprises—were
indications enough that deeply rooted discontent abounded
among the peasant element in most southern and some northern
communities. The failure of the sharecrop and crop-lien systems,
which depended primarily on cotton, beginning around 1890

was one of the underlying causes of the dire economic conditions. These conditions in turn prompted white as well as black southerners to make allowances in adjusting to them. Whites responded by increasingly mechanizing their farms, thus making black labor—sharecroppers as well as "crop-lieners"—redundant. Consequently, it is within the period 1890-1915 that the bulk of black peasants responded positively to "Back-to-Africa" efforts and schemes to ameliorate their plight.

Bishop Turner continued to agitate for African emigration, and the International Migration Society established in 1894, whipped up much excitement in its commercially oriented scheme to transport blacks to Africa and, in some instances, actually did carry through.[1] On March 19, 1895, the *Horsa,* a Danish ship chartered by the IMS, departed from Savannah, Georgia, for Liberia with 197 emigrants. It was a predictable fact that not all the emigrants would be happy with their new homeland, but only a few returned to the United States. The IMS, under its black president, Daniel J. Flummer and his white commercial-minded partners—helped by the cheerleading of Bishop Turner—had indeed struck a responsive chord in promoting African emigration.

Despite the shortcoming and hardships experienced by the previous emigrants to Liberia, by 1896 the IMS had signed up enough potential emigrants to make arrangements for chartering another ship for passage to Liberia. On March 2, 1896—the year of the *Plessy vs. Ferguson* or "Separate but Equal" Supreme Court decision—321 blacks boarded the IMS chartered *Laurada* and sailed from Savannah to Liberia. This proved to be the last IMS sponsored ship for African emigration. After the *Laurada* voyage, the IMS steadily deteriorated; many of the new settlers in Liberia returned to the states, or, barring that, settled in Sierra Leone or London (because there was not enough money to make the trip back to the States). Threats of war with Spain, an even further drop in cotton prices, and the inability of the Liberian government to aid the emigrants in case they needed it were contributing factors to the decline. President Flummer, however, attributed the decline of the IMS to its inability to send ships regularly to Liberia. The strongest reason was that blacks did not have enough money to make the necessary down payments for passage. Hard times, the war, apathy, and alienation all contributed. In some instances blacks became generally wary of emigration schemes because many were outright swindles. Samuel Chapman, of Muldron in the Oklahoma or Indian Territory, formed Liberian Emigration Clubs and promised to purchase a ship for African passage. In March, 1899, 104 blacks from Indian Territory went by train to New York and waited a week for Chapman to send them to Liberia. Neither Chapman nor the ship showed up, and the would-be emigrants, with the aid of local people, finally settled in New Jersey.

After the collapse of the International Migration Society in 1899, its former president, Flummer, established a new emigration scheme called the Liberian Colonization Society, with headquarters in Birmingham, Alabama. The total cost for transportation to Liberia was fifty dollars per passenger. In December 1900 Flummer promised that a ship with 200 blacks would sail for Liberia on January 30, 1901. Only about sixteen showed up at the Birmingham headquarters for the voyage. Flummer did manage to send the sixteen to Liberia, but this incident did not gain much publicity for Flummer and his new organization. He then went to Liberia for support.

Meanwhile, with the decline of Flummer's appeal, Bishop Turner's paper, *The Voice of the People,* among others, carried advertisements for a Nashville emigration organization, the International Migration and Steamship Company, founded in 1902. Its president, J. C. Bulis, offered Liberian transportation for fifty-two dollars. Apparently it received little or no response, for the advertisement, after running for some time, was stopped. Thinking that emigration was still on the minds of blacks, Bishop Turner replaced the Bulis ad with a summons for an African emigration convention, to be chaired by him and held in Nashville in October. The convention met with little fanfare and resolved to encourage and promote African emigration. One important outcome was the consolidation of many of the small, struggling emigration schemes, including the Nashville International Migration and Steamship Company, into the Colored National Emigration Association. The purpose of the newly consolidated association was to raise $100,000 to purchase a used steamship for emigration and commercial purposes. Shares were sold at five dollars, and members paid four dollars each for membership alone. Bishop Turner himself headed the organization and promised that he would obtain a ship or die in the attempt. Moreover, he declared, if a ship was not secured, he would refund money paid for its purchase. The convention ended with a call for another convention in Chattanooga the following May. At that meeting fewer than 125 delegates attended, but they asked Congress for 500 million dollars to aid in black emigration. The funds from Congress—foreseeably—were not forthcoming.

Fresh from his Liberian trip, Flummer appeared again, still promising Liberian emigration. While in Liberia he had secured the moral support (but no funds) of the Liberian President himself, G. W. Gibson. Nevertheless, he enlisted 250 blacks to pay passage to Liberia. He then contracted a steamship, *Donald,* to transport the emigrants to Liberia from Savannah. In spite of Flummer's promises and publicity, the *Donald* failed to sail, and this failure was for him the kiss of death: he lost the confidence of blacks in general and in particular Bishop Turner, who was an advantageous friend but a formidable foe.

Bishop Turner called for a massive effort to fire enthusiasm for emigration at a convention in Montgomery, Alabama, on June 24, 1903. In order to fan the spark, Turner attempted to get Senator John T. Morgan of Alabama—a supporter of the unsuccessful Butler Bill of 1892 and an advocate of racial separation—to address the convention. Morgan at first accepted, but later declined. To broaden the convention appeal, it was decided to emphasize the commercial prospects of the projected shipping undertaking rather than its emigration aspects. The convention was not successful, however, and Bishop Turner in 1906 did indeed return money to those who had invested (his death promise being forgotten). For the most part, this ended his active participation in campaigns to produce shipping schemes for Liberian emigration as the only solution to the race problem in the United States.

Redkey notes many minor emigration efforts to tap the unrest among many black peasants who wanted to leave the country: W. H. Ellis visited King Menelek of Abyssinia (Ethiopia) in 1903 in order to establish there a colony for black Americans; in 1904, the African Trading Company was formed to promote commerce and emigration; in the same year the New York and Liberia Steamship Company was established and the American and West African Steamship Company came into existence. The Liberian Trading and Emigration Association of the United States was formed in Newark, New Jersey; in 1906 the African Colonization Church opened a Liberian Temple in Washington, D.C.; also in 1906 there was another Ethiopian scheme, headed by a Captain Harry Deane of Chicago. Still other plans amounted to very little in terms of actually transporting blacks to Liberia.

In the final analysis, Liberia itself was not economically prepared to aid black Americans. It was in constant financial trouble. In 1908 it sent a delegation to the United States to seek aid. The implication of this event was clear; Liberia was not ready for black emigrants, and the economic condition of poor black peasants were not ready for Liberia. Hence, by 1910 Liberian emigration had become a moot issue, though emigration itself remained a dormant desire for many black people.

The mid 1890's was particularly eventful for Afro-Americans, considering that emigration efforts and sentiment were heightened along with the appearance of new alternatives to it. One of these alternatives would establish a new framework for black separation in the United States. The framework rested on hope that sprang from belief in a man and his program. The man was Booker T. Washington; the program, independent accommodation or "economic nationalism" or, some may call it, "servile separation." Some even call him a separatist in golden chains.

Washington was born a slave in Franklin County, Virginia, in 1858 or 1859. After passage of the Emancipation Proclamation in 1863, his family moved to West Virginia. Unable to attend school full time, he taught himself to read and he studied every chance he could find. Encouraged by his mother, to the chagrin of his step-father, Washington decided to attend Hampton Institute in Virginia.

He was admitted to Hampton and worked as a janitor to pay his way. After his second year, he returned home. While he was there his mother died. Without means and unable to get employment, he had no way of continuing his schooling. Fortunately, he was asked to return to Hampton two weeks early in order to help clean up before school opened, enabling him to earn enough money to go on.

He finished Hampton in 1875 as an honor student. According to him, his greatest benefits from Hampton were his contact with the principal, General S. C. Armstrong, and learning that education meant "independence and self-reliance" and "the ability to do something which the world wants done . . ." He returned home to teach in Malden, West Virginia after graduation.

In 1879 he went back to Hampton primarily to work with a group of Native Americans whom General Armstrong had brought from the western United States. In addition to directing the study of these students, Washington was asked by General Armstrong to head a night school for students who could not pay for day courses. He did, and the night school became "one of the permanent and most important features of the institution."

Even while in charge of the native American students and the night school, Washington pursued further studies. "In May 1881, near the close of my first year in teaching the night school, in a way that I had not dared expect, the opportunity opened for me to begin my life work." When the white citizens of Alabama, charged with the responsibility of selecting a person to head a school for blacks, approached the principal of Hampton Institute, he had no white person to recommend, but he could and did recommend Booker T. "Several days passed before anything more was heard about the matter. Some time afterward, one Sunday evening during the chapel exercises, a messenger came in and handed the General a telegram. At the end of the exercises he read the telegram to the school. In substance, these were his words: *Booker T. Washington will suit us. Send him at once.*"[2]

At first there was white opposition to having a black principal, but Washington eliminated most of it by assuring the whites that the education he was offering would not influence blacks from the rural areas to become "uppity" or make them disdainful of service in the white community. He therefore gained the support of the whites of Alabama, and he was also able to benefit from Northern philanthrophy. Tuskegee Institute, founded in 1881, grew rapidly. Several thousand acres of land were procured, many buildings were constructed, and students from all over the United States and several foreign countries came to the institution.

By the mid 1880's Washington's reputation and influence were known far beyond the Institute's immediate surroundings. Many people believed that his program of education and self-help for blacks and his policy of cooperation with whites in "all things essential to mutual progress" would lead to a solution of the race problem. Because of his prominence in the black community—and his acceptable leadership by the white power structure—he was invited to give a speech at the Cotton States Exposition held in Atlanta, Georgia, in 1895. The speech placated whites, North and South, firmly entrenching him as the "Compromiser" on racial matters between the North and South; it served also essentially to legitimize his leadership until his death in 1915. John Hope Franklin observed that

> in his celebrated address at the Cotton States Exposition in Atlanta in 1895, he placated white supremacists by renouncing social equality with the whites and [admonished blacks] to pursue careers in "agriculture, mechanics, in commerce, in domestic service, and in the professions" . . . . He called for the intelligent management of farms, ownership of land, habits of thrift, patience, and perseverance, and the cultivation of high morals and good manners.[3]

After his Atlanta Exposition speech, Washington became even

more influential as a black spokesman. He received large contributions from industrialists to carry on the work at Tuskegee and wielded more power within the black community than anyone else had ever done. Some of his authority over black people was derived from his political influence and from his popularity with the philanthropists. No black schools received contributions from Carnegie, Rockefeller, and others without Washington's support. He cultivated influential black leadership in the black communities, and it was virtually impossible to achieve a major position in the black churches if Washington or his position was attacked. He kept the black press in line by judicious advertisements and contributions. There were a few exceptions, but for the most part, the black press was not critical of his leadership.[4]

What were Washington's ideas on black self-determination and why did they create, on the one hand, hope and support and, on the other, apathy and opposition? What was his program and how was it to be implemented? Was his ultimate aim accommodation or was it a mechanism for achieving separation for black people? Emma Thornbrough quotes a white Washington contemporary speculating that "the Tuskegeean was silently preparing the way for assimilation and amalgamation of the races . . . or something equally dangerous—the building of a separate Negro nation within a nation."[5]

Separation to Washington was not something that had to be brought about—it already existed, designed and enforced by white people. As a matter of fact, it was institutionalized. He therefore stated in his Atlanta "Compromise" speech that "in all things that are purely social we can be as *separate* as the fingers, yet one as the hand in all things essential to mutual progress." In the same speech he observes: "the wisest among my race understands that the agitation of questions of social and political equality is the extremest of folly . . ." What he may have been saying is that the most important thing for black people to do is let whites rest with the fact that blacks do not want to socialize with them or to agitate for political equality. But blacks will work with and for them until economic self-sufficiency is achieved; separation is a reality—reconstruction is over, and the whites are afraid that blacks want to become political forces again. Since whites have institutionalized "jim crow" and taken the ballot, blacks should adhere to the gospel of wealth (money), and only later participate as equals.

The objectives of Washington's leadership included making ex-slaves and those not far from slavery free members of American society in general and their communities in particular. The basis of Washington's prescription for the development of rural black self-determination centered on vocational, industrial, and domestic training. Tuskegee Institute became the vehicle through which he manifested his predilection. He believed that if blacks made themselves useful where they lived, in time they could become self-sufficient citizens. In the meantime, he thought,

> the whole future of my race hinges on the question as to whether or not it can make itself of such indispensable value that the people in the town and the state where they reside will feel that our presence is necessary to the happiness and well-being of the community. No man who continues to add something to the material, intellectual, and moral well-being of the place in which he lives is long left without proper reward. This is a great human law which cannot be permanently nullified.[6]

The self-sufficiency aspect would follow, according to Washington, because blacks would have had the proper grounding through agriculture, mechanics, commerce, ownership of land, patience, thrift, and perseverance. Thus educational pursuits should initially follow these directions and prescriptions. Washington apparently took the position that before meaningful self-determination can be achieved, it must be preceded by self-sufficiency. Genovese speculated that he

> knew that slavery had ill-prepared his people for political leadership; he therefore retracted from political demands. He knew that slavery had rendered manual labor degrading; he therefore preached the gospel of hard work . . . He knew that slavery had undermined the family and elementary moral standards; he therefore preached self-reliance and self help.[7]

Clearly Washington spoke to the immediate means of separating illiterate ex-slaves from dependence upon the ex-slavemaster by advocating industrial and vocational training. Since he became the spokesman for all blacks, he had to broaden his platform to include northern blacks as well as the black bourgeoisie everywhere. What was his plan for bringing about or maintaining black bourgeoisie self-sufficiency and then self-determination? It must be answered that if Washington was clandestinely a separatist, he had a program for the ex-slaves on the lowest end of the socioeconomic scale—self-sufficiency or self-help—and for the bourgeoisie intellectuals a separatist program.

If Washington's prescription for lower-class blacks to gain self-determination was industrial and vocational training and then self-sufficiency, his prescription for the black bourgeoisie was economic independence through business enterprise. He believed that "Brains, property, and character for the Negro will settle the question of civil rights. . . . Good school teachers and plenty of money to pay them will be more potent in settling the race question than many civil rights bills and investigation committees."[8] Moreover, Washington exposed his plan to a full extent when he indicated that he would not forever relegate blacks to agriculture, mechanics, and domestic arts. They should, however, be stressed for the immediate future in addition to the training of ministers, doctors, lawyers, statesmen. In order for blacks as a group to prosper along economic lines, there must be a symbiotic relationship between blacks trained in vocational areas and the black professionals. In Washington's words, "if this generation will lay the material foundation, it will be the quickest and surest way for the succeeding generation to succeed in the cultivation of the fine arts, and to surround itself even with some of the luxuries of life, if desired."[9]

A fairly sound case can be made that Washington favored servile separation—blacks on the bottom and whites at the top, but a closer look at him may give a clearer indication of his intentions. Was he ultimately an accommodationist, or was he laying the foundation for viable black nationalism? Was he a covert black separatist?

Washington's public image was that of an accommodator, but as a private man he contradicted his public stance. He ostensibly denounced higher education for the masses because he knew that they, as a group, were hardly literate. His own children, however, received training in the trades through a grounding in liberal arts. Overtly he urged blacks to accept for a time the separate-but-equal doctrine, but he entered social circles at home and abroad which were open to few Southern whites.

Booker T. Washington was a very complex man. Outwardly he was simple and good-natured, naive, some have said, about many things, certainly about the "goodness" of Southern whites. But was he really? In public Washington spoke of the friendly relations between blacks and whites in the South, but he "clandestinely spent thousands of dollars financing the fruitless test cases taken to the Supreme Court against the Southern disfranchisement amendments (and even) on one occasion he hired a lobbyist to defeat legislation that, if passed, would have encouraged segregation on interstate trains in the North."[10] None other than DuBois himself was quoted as saying, "Actually Washington had no more faith in the white man than I do."[11] Washington was certainly not politically naive either. Rather he was a consummate politician, cunning and calculating. One example of his political acuity was that if he were laying the foundations for viable black separatism, he was placating Southern whites in the process ("viable black separatism" meaning the ability of black people to determine *their own* destiny wherever they lived, North or South).

Typically, the cunning Washington denied any interest in politics

> and urged Negroes to soft-pedal the desire for the franchise; behind the scenes, he was the most influential politician in the history of American Negroes, and surreptitiously fought the disfranchisement laws. He served as political adviser on Negro affairs to Presidents Roosevelt and Taft.[12]

As a matter of fact, all blacks who were appointed to office by Theodore Roosevelt and most by William Howard Taft were recommended by Washington. Some of them were Robert H. Terrell, who served as judge of the municipal court in Washington, 1901-21; Charles W. Anderson, collector of internal revenue in New York, 1905-15; and William H. Lewis, assistant attorney general, 1911-13. These were the highest black executive and judicial appointments made up to that time. Another example of Washington's cunning in achieving his ends in the midst of oppression was his "use" of the *New York Age* and its editor.

T. Thomas Fortune, the militant editor of this paper, founded the Afro-American League in 1890. At its initial convention Fortune established the tone by pointing out that whites believed that in relationship to them, all blacks were inferior in all respects. Fortune retaliated by pointing out that the Anglo-Saxon race was "the most consummate masters of hypocrisy, of roguery, of insolence, of arrogance, and of cowardice in the history of races." Arguing that he only wanted to highlight black bravery from these characteristics, he observed that Attucks, L'overture, Nat Turner, "and the two hundred thousand black soldiers of the (Civil War) were not cowards. And if (today) there comes violence, let those who oppose our just cause 'throw the first stone.' We have wealth, we have intelligence, we have courage; and we have a great deal of work to do."[13]

The relevance of Fortune to Washington is that *New York Age* was a "radical" platform where black Americans were able to voice their opinions. By 1895 the Afro-American League had become defunct and was revived in 1898 as the Afro-American Council. The council in many ways was a continuation of the earlier convention movement. It was captured in the early 1900's by Washington, and its resolutions became far less militant than before, although they continued to ask for full constitutional rights for black people. Overtly it seemed as if Washington was "silencing a militant," but a closer examination shows that he used the council secretly to attack the disfranchisement constitutions of the Southern states in 1903–04. Moreover, the council exemplified and explicitly articulated the view that only through united collective efforts, through race unity and self-help, could black men achieve their citizenship rights.[14]

Many of Washington's critics charge him with subsidizing publications like the *New York Age* in order to silence critics by buying them off. But Washington sold the *Age* and denied current interest in it; meanwhile, he continued to subsidize it. Why? "The argument centers around whether Washington maintained anonymous participation so as not to offend wealthy and white non-militant beneficiaries or in order to manage the volley from his black critics."[15] It is unlikely that he needed the *Age* to manage volleys in that he had several other news organs through which he could do the same.

A separatist/nationalist, if anything, is ultimately proud of his race and its achievements. What did Washington have to say about race pride and the race's achievements past, present, and future? Those who charge him with Uncle Tomism and telling darky stories to his white benefactors—the antithesis of race pride— must also account for the black version of his darky stories. His black version preached that educated blacks should be proud of and pay more attention to finding out the true history of the race. Moreover, more effort and money should be spent perpetuating in some durable form its achievements, so that from year to year, instead of looking back with regret, we can point to our children the rough path through which we grew strong and great.[16] If he truly believed in black assimilation and black subservience to whites, why would he speak of race pride and the importance of preserving black heritage for posterity? It seems hardly coincidental that in 1915, the same year of Washington's death, Carter G. Woodson, the black historian, established the Association for the Study of Negro Life and History and began the publication of the *Journal of Negro History* in 1916. In 1913 Washington had instituted "Negro Health Week" and, after the establishment of Woodson's Association, "Negro History Week," which became and continues to be an annual event. (The Association's name has been changed to fit the times—"Afro-American" Life instead of "Negro" Life; and "Negro History Week" is now "Black History Week.")

It was clear to Washington that lack of unity was one of the most important shortcomings in the black freedom struggle. Believing that to make gains, unity was necessary, he often used the Jewish people as the best model for blacks to follow. He observed that Jews, like blacks, have experienced much suffering, but they have clung together, perhaps, because of the long history of their trials and tribulations. Because of their unity and pride, he thought they would become more influential in the United States, despite not being universally loved even here, to say the least. He counseled that "unless the Negro learns more and more to imitate the Jew in these matters, to have faith in himself, he cannot expect to have any high degree of success."[17]

Washington predicted that eventually Jewish people would play an inclusive role in the American mainstream. Perhaps he could never envision black equality in white American society, and this may have been the significant factor in his Tuskegee-sponsored establishment of the all-black town of Mound Bayou, Mississippi, which exists to this day. Some have speculated that this was Washington's way of institutionalizing "ideologies of self-help, economic development, and racial solidarity."[18] The present-day all-black towns, as well as the "black central city," are not unrelated to this early attempt by Washington to create black separatism; only the setting has changed.

To maintain that Washington ultimately believed in black separation and worked toward its implementation is not to say that he was fully successful. Franklin correctly observes that, "during his lifetime, lynchings decreased only slightly, the Negro was effectively disfranchised, and the black workers were systematically excluded from the major labor organizations; but Washington's influence, sometimes for better and sometimes for worse, was so great that there is considerable justification in calling the period 'The Age of Booker T. Washington.'"[19]

Washington's leadership went a long way toward dominating the period 1895-1915, but as we have seen, it did not completely eliminate sentiment for Back-to-Africa emigration. Neither was he immune from criticism and bitter rivalries from other leaders in the black community. His most strident and persistent criticism came from DuBois, who wrote: "The question then comes: Is it possible, and probable, that nine millions of men, can make effective progress in economic lines if they are deprived of political rights . . ?"[20] His answer was no. DuBois took the position in 1903 that business and vocational pursuits alone were not the way to black viability without political equality. It is confusing to note that DuBois was largely responsible for the position that Washington took: DuBois proposed, at an Atlanta University Conference in 1899, "The organization in every town and hamlet where colored people dwell, of Negro Business Men's Leagues, and the gradual federation from these of state and national organizations."[21] One year later Washington established the National Negro Business League.[22] Apparently DuBois changed his mind about the efficiency of Washington's methods of achieving economic self-sufficiency, for he later felt that the philosophy of the NAACP was on the right path—namely that political and social agitation would enhance economic equality.

DuBois also objected to Washington's stress on vocational and industrial training. It is true that Washington emphasized these areas, but it is also true that he did not object to purely academic education. Washington argued that he thought it somewhat strange and the height of absurdity for a child to spend valuable time learning French grammar "amid the weeds and dirt of a neglected home." But Washington also said he favored any kind of training, whether in the languages or mathematics, that gives strength and culture to the mind.

Education had different meanings to Washington and DuBois. To Washington, education meant that although the Negro should not be deprived by unfair means of his franchise, political agitation alone would not save him; that back of the ballot he must have property, industry, skill, economy, intelligence, and character; and that no race without these elements could permanently succeed.[23] DuBois, on the other hand, called for the education of the "talented tenth" of the black population, arguing that every race possessed a number of talented individuals and that his "tenth" should be recognized and embraced to "uphold the race." Both objectives seem to have merit, and the two philosophies, despite their differences, are complementary. Washington felt that before political involvement could develop, there must exist a base of education and skill; DuBois felt that blacks must have the franchise irrespective of their educational background.

The upshot of the controversy was the temporary polarization of the two philosophies. Washington institutionalized his position through the Negro Business League, his string of newspapers,

Tuskegee Institute, and his many disciples who became established, educated individuals in the various communities. DuBois' position was institutionalized through the "Niagara Movement" and its outcome, the NAACP. The controversy continues today in various guises. In retrospect, it seems that during Washington's and DuBois' time it would have been the height of folly to expect blacks—only a generation away from legal slavery—to be sophisticated enough, as a mass, to compete politically with the white majority in the North and South. It was a fact that blacks were disfranchised, and practically unsound to say the least. To assert that blacks *should* have the ballot and that they *should* participate in political life was right, but it was also right that Washington should advocate a route by which the masses of black people could find ways to become an integral part of American society. Not all blacks were of the "talented tenth" and not all wanted to become agricultural workers, blacksmiths, domestic servants, mechanics, or skilled laborers. What was needed at the time was the approach of both Washington and DuBois, for they reflected the diversity of black people seeking a solution in a situation they did not control. (Finally accepting Washington's original position, DuBois came to the conclusion in 1940 that the education of blacks could not best be served in the white schools because "they would not in most cases receive decent treatment nor real education . . . it is not theory but fact that faces the Negro in education. He has education in large proportion and he must organize and plan these segregated schools so that they become efficient, well-housed, well-equipped, with the best teachers . . . properly paid teachers for educating their children."[24]) Washington had already stated his belief that "brains, property, good schools and well paid teachers will do more . . ."

Washington was influential among those economically destitute blacks living in the intimidating atmosphere of the Klan-controlled, post-Reconstruction South. His advocacy of vocational training—which to the black separatist and most nationalists is a means of retaining the educated black in a servile position—often represented a way of achieving a livelihood where no alternative means of advancement was possible. It is of utmost importance to note that Washington's program was acceptable to his followers by virtue of the fact that it suited their past experiences. He addressed himself to ex-slaves, not to Northern, "militant," highly trained intellectuals. He urged ex-slaves to escape from the bottom—extreme bottom—of the socioeconomic hierarchy, a position to which many of them were bitterly reconciled, since they had no hope of ever extricating themselves. What is obvious to some, and what others deliberately ignore, is that once Washington's prescriptions were followed, the doors opened vistas that were never before dreamed of. The foundation he laid was done in the face of apprehensive ex-slavemasters who were unable to foresee the consequences of vocational training for the masses and liberal arts training for the "talented tenth."

In this connection it must be observed that those who controlled the power in the South did accept Washington's leadership but did not or could not toally manipulate it. That is, the ex-slavemasters in the South did not want their ex-slaves to have any education.[25] But Washington gained their confidence and did educate many black people in their presence. Those who worked their way through the shops and classrooms of Tuskegee did so to improve their conditions. "If they had gained the tacit approval of persons interested in not having them progress too far, this fact does not convert them into dupes, nor does it qualify the reality of their ambitions."[26]

Washington's era tended to absorb much of the black extremism, but it did not absorb all of it as the emigration schemes described above have shown. To be sure, many of the emigrationists were militants and opposed Washington's philosophy and politics; but, in general, the emigration tendency was "out-directed" and not much concerned with the attainment of rights in the United States. Hence, many conflictive situations were avoided.

W. E. B. DuBois was Washington's most strident and persistent critic. Perhaps less well-known is the role played by William Monroe Trotter in Washington's leadership period. As noted, Trotter was graduated from Harvard (Phi Beta Kappa) in 1895, the same year that DuBois became the first black to receive a Harvard doctorate, and began his career in a quiet fashion. He dabbled in real estate and other commercially oriented enterprises, and in his bachelor period was a handsome, debonair gentleman. He was one of the lions of Boston's black middle class: educated at Harvard and talented, he had also inherited about $20,000. Trotter's bachelor days came to an end on June 27, 1899, when he married Geraldine Louise Pindell. She, like Trotter, came from a black family with a tradition of adamantly demanding their rights. Happily settled in Dorchester on a hilltop, they enjoyed their marriage.[27]

Despite his relative affluence and education, and being middle class, Trotter was aware of racism, though he kept his hatred of it to himself. (At Harvard, though he later admitted that his Harvard days were the most positive in terms of racial acceptance, he slowly began to gravitate to the Boston middle class, which had a long tradition of racial militancy.) By 1901 Trotter could no longer stomach the leadership of the "Sage of Tuskegee" and launched the *Boston Guardian.* The *Guardian* opposed in every fashion Washington's apparent compromise of black political and social rights.

As a result of the dominance of Washington's leadership, the two Harvard men, DuBois and Trotter, joined together in their opposition to Washington. Though they disagreed on many occasions over means as well as ends, the two men played a significant role in the formulation in 1905 of the Niagara Movement, an all-black organization whose purpose was to foster organized opposition to the "Tuskegee Machine." Probably the most outstanding achievement of this organization was that upon it was founded, in 1909, the National Association for the Advancement of Colored People. DuBois became the editor of the NAACP's news organ, *The Crisis.* DuBois and Trotter parted company and became bitter enemies. The schism between DuBois and Trotter focused on DuBois' acceptance of interracial financing and leadership while Trotter insisted on a black-led, black-financed organization which would, without restriction, speak to the needs and desires of black people. The outcome of their differences resulted in Trotter founding the Negro Equal Rights League (NERL).

The rise of the NAACP and its staunch advocacy of racial justice through legalistic jabs here and thrusts there engendered more black support than Trotter's "leftist" *Guardian* and his Negro Equal Rights League. Booker T. Washington, though still the dominant leadership figure, was being seriously challenged by the NAACP. With the election of Woodrow Wilson, a southerner and a racist, to the Presidency, another era of racial oppression was ushered in. Though Wilson had the support of a significant block of the black vote, including DuBois and Trotter, he nevertheless reneged on campaign promises by allowing his southern cabinet officers to turn back the clock in racial matters—though not without constant reminders from Trotter that the Wilson Administration had a responsibility of justice for all.

In sum, the Progressive Era may have meant advancement and progress for the nation as a whole, but it was, as Rayford Logan calls it, the nadir for black people. Like the end of Reconstruction, the Progressive Era again ushered in Jim Crow and complete white control in the political arena: the last black congressman,

George H. White of North Carolina, made his farewell speech in 1901. Once again, black people and their sympathizers had to work for political advantages from the outside. Complete black exclusion from the political process may have been progressive but only for whites.

In assessing the era dominated by Washington's leadership, including his opposition, we can see that the general thrust was toward integration. DuBois, Trotter, and other militants, such as Archibald Grimke, Clement Morgan, Kelly Miller (sometimes), Ida Wells-Barnett, and William Sinclair, adamantly demanded that black Americans not be racially barred from equal participation in American democracy.

Between 1895 and 1915, though individuals like Washington, DuBois, and Trotter dominated ideas and programs for bettering the black condition in the United States and the temperature of emigraton fever was significantly lower by 1910 than around the turn of the century, leaders of Back-to-Africa efforts continued to crop up. One of these was Chief Alfred C. Sam from the Gold Coast (Ghana) in West Africa. He appeared in Oklahoma in the summer of 1913 selling stock in his Akim Trading Company, Ltd., promising to take blacks to the Gold Coast, where he owned land. He collected money; purchased a steamship, the *Liberia;* and to the surprise of his critics sailed from Galveston, Texas, with sixty emigrants. Political, economic, and diplomatic complications caused Sam to lose his ship, and some of the sixty emigrants eventually returned to the States.[28] The scheme could hardly be called a success but it did demonstrate that the desire of many black people to go to Africa was still present. The point was not lost on either DuBois or the Sage of Tuskegee.

DuBois was aware of the desire of many blacks to emigrate to Africa, but he nevertheless opposed it. In a paper written in 1897 entitled "The Conservation of Races," DuBois argued that black Americans were the vanguard of Pan-Negroism, that blacks wherever they lived should feel a commitment to one another and an emotional tie to Africa. To this end he was instrumental in organizing the first Pan-Negro Congress held in London in 1900. Subsequently between 1919 and 1927, he organized several Pan-African Conferences to promote Pan-African brotherhood as well as to end capitalist exploitation of blacks everywhere.

Washington was very much aware that Martin R. Delany, Edward W. Blyden, and Bishop Henry McNeil Turner—among a few of the ardent emigrationists—had long proposed African emigration as the only solution to the white problem in America. Washington's response to both emigration and Pan-Africanism was, typically, economic. Recognizing the salience of the emigrationist arguments, he organized a conference on Africa at Tuskegee in 1912 and followed it with the organization of the African Union Company. The purpose of the company was to promote trade between black Americans and the Gold Coast in West Africa; he also contacted the German government about setting up trade relations on the East Coast of Africa, since the Germans were in control of German East Africa at that time.

He inspired many africans with his self-help ideology, and the African Union Company, among other things, would have served to foster black American and African solidarity by exporting black American technological skill to aid in African development. This arrangement would also serve the dual purpose of satisfying emigration sentiments and fostering a kind of Pan-Africanism which may have been then, as well as now, the most feasible form for black people of the diaspora to communicate with one another. Washington's scheme never came to fruition because of the outbreak of World War I and his own death in 1915.

In the final analysis, Washington did encourage Pan-Africanism and even some militant African liberation efforts: "He encouraged the efforts of a Moussa Mangoumbel, a Senegalese living in France, to promote world-wide Negro brotherhood. He also took an interest in similar Pan-African efforts of West Indian and African expatriates in London, most notably those of Duse Mohammad, editor of the *African Times and Orient Review.*"[29]

Toward the end of his life, Washington became less concerned with tact and more open in decrying racial oppression. In 1911 at the National Colored Teachers Association, he registered his opposition to lynching and "any practice in any state that results in not enforcing the law with a certainty and justice, regardless of race and color." In 1912 he wrote an article in *Century* magazine entitled, "Is the Negro Having a Fair Chance?" His answer was *no.* On another occasion he had a speaking engagement in Tampa, Florida. When he took the stage, there was a sheet down the middle of the audience separating whites and blacks. Without any introductory remarks he indicated that he traveled throughout the United States and abroad, but he had never seen the races separated in such a manner. In a very stern manner he stated: "Now, before I begin my remarks, I want that thing taken down from there." The sheets came down. In one of his last pieces of advice to black people, Washington again called for race unity admonishing black people to lay aside personal differences and petty jealousies. The race needed individuals "who are willing to lay their lives upon the altar of our race's welfare as a sacrifice." Now he was less concerned, as he always had been, with abstract protest. He knew and counseled that "all black organizations had to work together to solve the Negro's complex problem."[30]

Washington died on November 14, 1915. His last plea for unity reflected the shift in the black population from the rural South to the urban industrial North. What would he have prescribed for this significant segment of recent peasants now turned proletarians? What would have been his program for urban viable black separatism? We can only speculate that the answer lies in the next act of the drama, which was to emerge in the urban North—the "Urban Black Blues."

Before relinquishing the stage to Marcus Garvey, the star, however, another word should be said relative to black separatism and continuity. In attempting to understand black separatism in America, the spill-over effects of one period to another should be observed. The idea of emigrationism, for an example, has persisted for as long as there have been black people in America—high at some times, low at others, and differing in type and emphasis as well. Paul Cuffee's motives for black emigration were different from those of Edward W. Blyden's. Moreover, the migrationists' motives ostensibly differed from those of the Back-to-Africa school. But despite the different types and approaches, they all had one common element: they sought the separatist alternative at times when white America clearly and blatantly tightened the noose—sometimes literally—of racism and oppression. The 1820's, 30's, 40's, 50's, 70's, and 90's and the Progressive Era saw black oppression in extreme forms, and in these periods black separatist alternatives through emigration were sought in earnest.

The colonization schemes found their greatest response in these periods of extreme oppression. After the "Populist Revolt" had become anti-black and Congress had voted down the emigration bill that would have ensured governmental aid to blacks who wanted to emigrate, blacks knew they were in desperate straits. Those who desired emigration found that they had no means of financing their passage. Then came Washington with his self-help program, admonishing black peasants to "let their buckets down where they were" because there was no other help in sight. There was nothing else that oppressed people not quite a generation away from slavery could do. The Robber Barons monopolized big industry, and the educated white elite, North and South, monopolized the political system. Since blacks could not, even if they so desired, compete equally with those realities, he chose to opt not for utopian solutions but for ideological ones.

Ideology, as Mannheim notes, is composed of ideas that depict the world in such a manner as to render the inequalities of the existing order acceptable and right, and defined this way is always conservative. Ideas that stir people to break away from the existing order, to bring about new conditions that seemed unrealizable and fantastic at the time, are utopian.[32] Washington cannot be accused of promoting utopian ideas. He viewed the harsh reality of the recent ex-slave in an ideological sense and refused to allow southern peasant blacks to disillusion themselves with utopian fantasies.

The refusal to romanticize, to paint utopian pictures of the past or future, lost Washington a prominent place in the contemporary mood of black America. His ideology was firmly planted in the temper and reality of the times. It just might be that he consciously gave up becoming a saint in future black nationalist lore in order to point up that the oppressed condition of black people merited the maximum realization of their oppression wherever they might be.

In his last years Washington may have felt that with the black population changing from rural to urban, and considering the response that the International Migration Society and others like it received, an urban program was needed. After all, black peasants who had responded to the emigration efforts but were not able to emigrate were the same people who migrated from the South to nonsouthern large cities. Hence we return to the question of what to do if the new proletariat retains emigration sentiments.

One answer takes us to Marcus Garvey. Harold Cruse argues that, in reality, Garvey's philosophy and program was not unlike those of Booker T. Washington's in that initially Garvey attempted to link his movement with Tuskegee Institute. He notes that Garvey's first wife, Mrs. Amy Jacques Garvey, wrote in her book *Garvey and Garveyism* that she and her husband "went to Tuskegee Normal and Industrial Institute primarily to pay homage to the late Booker T. Washington [because] since his death there was no one with a positive program for the masses—North or South." Cruse then observes that young nationalist militants usually deny Garvey's admiration of Washington, and correctly observes that they will invariably "uphold Garvey, put down Washington, and be confused about DuBois."[32]

4 MILITANT BLACK NATIONALISM

Marcus Garvey was born in Jamaica on August 17, 1887.[1] He attended elementary school and possibly a secondary school in St. Ann's Bay.[2] At the age of 14, because of family financial difficulties, his education was interrupted and he was sent as an apprentice to his godfather, a printer in St. Ann's Bay. Garvey found the printing trade there limiting and moved to Kingston, the capital, where he made quick gains but soon became involved in a strike that cost him his job. He later found another at the Government Printing Office in Kingston and began editing his first periodical, *The Watchman*. This venture failed, but Garvey continued his political activities in an organization known as the National Club, which had a bimonthly publication called *Our Own*.

Between 1909 and 1912 Garvey traveled to Nicaragua, Honduras, Colombia, and Venezuela attempting to organize black workers in Central America but was not very successful, although the black people kept coming to hear him. He returned to Jamaica convinced that blacks must unite to do something about their oppressed condition.

In 1912 Garvey traveled to England, where he observed and experienced racial discrimination. He talked with dock workers and argued methods for black liberation with Indian and African students, who were at that time also colonial subjects. For a time he was employed by the *African Times and Orient Review*, a militant monthly magazine published in London by Duse Mohammad Ali. "He became closely associated with Ali, a scholar of Egyptian extraction whose main preoccupation was home-rule for Egypt" and at this time Garvey developed an intense interest in African history.³ After reading Washington's *Up from Slavery,* he was inspired personally to do something about the oppressed condition of black peoples. He asked himself, where were black peoples' strong governments, military, and leaders of international repute. Not finding them, he declared that he would help make "a new world of black men, not peons, serfs, dogs and slaves, but a nation of sturdy men making their impression upon civilization and causing a new light to dawn upon the human race."⁴ He knew his vision of black power could not be fulfilled in London and therefore returned to Jamaica on July 14, 1914.

Within five days of his landing he had founded the Universal Negro Improvement Association, whose purpose was to "unite all the Negro peoples of the world into one great body to establish a country and government absolutely their own."⁵ The motto of the Association was "One God! One Aim! One Destiny!" Garvey was designated President and Traveling Companion, and his future wife, Amy Ashwood, held the position of Associate Secretary.

One of the plans was the immediate uplift of blacks in Jamaica. The Association proposed to establish an institution modeled on Washington's Tuskegee Institute. Garvey had been corresponding with Washington regarding the establishment of the college for Jamaican Negroes, and Washington had invited him to America to discuss the idea, but before Garvey was able to leave Jamaica, Washington died. This was a great blow to Garvey who had been *relying on Washington for his moral and financial support.*⁶ In spite of the setback, however, he still planned to vistit America, and on March 23, 1916, exactly four months and nine days after the death of Washington, he arrived in the United States.⁷ He immediately started on his program of visiting black leaders and lecturing on the goals of the UNIA:

> The ferment in race relations and rising tide of black nationalism among Negroes during and after World War I were [some] of the conditions which gave Garvey his greatest chances for success in America, for in a sense black America was waiting for him.⁸

Garvey's first public appearance was in the role of soapbox orator in Harlem. Late in 1916, after visiting thirty-eight states and everywhere finding the same conditions, he set up a branch of the UNIA in Harlem, and in a few months enrolled about a thousand members. The bulk of initial UNIA members were originally from the West Indies.

Garvey's first two attempts to establish the UNIA in Harlem

were thwarted because some members were determined to advance their own ends, not those of the UNIA, which they successfully disrupted. Finally Garvey himself took sole charge and had the organization incorporated. He then provided a meeting place and secretarial help and began anew to recruit.[9]

Garvey tells us he recruited two thousand new members in three weeks, and from that point onward the organization grew at a tremendous pace. He then founded *Negro World,* the Association's newspaper. He asserts that he edited the newspaper, worked for the Association, and at the same time traveled throughout the United States, establishing thirty branches in various cities—all free of charge to the Association until November 1920. By his count, his efforts through writings, speeches, etc., resulted in two million members by June 1919.[10]

Although Garvey's claims of the phenomenal rise of the UNIA differ somewhat from those of his contemporaries, by 1919 the *Negro World* had become the most widely read black newspaper in America. The paper carried news of interest to black peoples throughout the world and included a Spanish-language section for the black people of South and Central America. The paper's motto was "Up You Mighty Race," and it is not surprising that several European nations banned it in their colonies. The editorials recalled the past glories of the black race and reminded their readers of the brilliance of blacks, the heroism and daring of the leaders of slave rebellions, and the grandeur that was once Africa's before the white man colonized it. The paper even refused to accept white advertisements for such items as skin-bleaching and hair-straightening compounds.[11] The readers were constantly reminded that in order for them to return to this grandeur, Africa had to be freed from colonial domination.

By 1919 Garvey had gained worldwide attention by attacking (verbally) whites and mulattoes and extolling Pan-Africanism, Pan-Blackism, and black-is-beautiful ideals. He emphasized the need for blacks to return to Mother Africa to restore her splendor and glory. His preachings struck a responsive chord among black people because what they needed at that time most of all was something or someone who could buoy their sense of worthiness. For his pains, Garvey received an overwhelming response from blacks and managed to swell the UNIA's coffers.[12] He contributed to his own charismatic appeal. The response was, in essence, "Let's get the show on the African road."

As a result of this support from the black masses, Garvey had to offer more than plans, editorials, and speeches. In June 1919 he announced that the UNIA would soon establish a merchant marine to engage in trade among blacks all over the world. This was the famous Black Star Line. "Drawn from Booker T. Washington's philosophy that Negroes must become independent of white capital and operate their own business activities, the Black Star Line was a supremely audacious move that aroused the greatest excitement in the colored world."[13]

Cronon speculates that the enterprise made blacks feel as if they could participate in a venture all their own, working for the betterment of the race and at the same time making money in a manner resembling, say, the financial wizard J. P. Morgan. Whether poor black peasants in the South or downtrodden black prole-tarians had ever heard of Morgan is questionable, but it is certain that if they did know of him, he was not about to help them out of their miserable plight. Garvey said to those who were reluctant to invest in the Line that it presented to black people the oppor-tunity to progress industrially and commercially by taking out shares in the Line, whether one invested a large or small amount. Since the Line had world rights of trade, it would "turn over large profits and dividends to stockholders, and operate to their best interest even whilst they will be asleep."[14] Garvey incorporated this new venture on June 27, 1919. The first announced capitaliza-tion was $500,000, which was later raised. One hundred thousand shares of stock were to be sold at five dollars a share. Sale of Black Star stock was limited to blacks, and no individual could purchase over 200 shares. It is important to note that the Black Star Line was first and foremost a commercial venture, with im-mediate African emigration of secondary importance.[15]

Many of Garvey's critics denounced his plans for the Line as a scheme to defraud the ignorant black masses, as others in the recent past had done. Others maintained that blacks by them-selves could not sustain a fleet of ships. Despite these criticisms, Garvey announced that the UNIA had acquired its first ship, the *S.S. Yarmouth,* a thirty-two-year-old coasting vessel bought for $168,500 and renamed the *S.S. Frederick Douglass* (ironically, Douglass was an unswerving integrationist who married a white). The move greatly enhanced the respectability of the UNIA as an organization and Garvey as a sincere leader. "The *Frederick Douglass* was given a new coat of paint, repaired, and staffed with an all-black crew from Captain to messmen."[16] The UNIA mem-bership, in fact, reached proportions never before reached by a black organization. No one knows for sure how large it was, but estimates range from 100,000 to 6,000,000.

As a result of the UNIA's success, the possibility of establishing an African Empire seemed more real. Hence in 1920 Garvey issued a call for a convention of blacks from all parts of the world to meet in New York City from the first to the thirty-first of August. The UNIA bought three apartment houses for offices and purchased the foundation of a church, which was covered and used for a meeting center.[17]

The *Negro World* proclaimed that the convention would be one of the largest meetings of its kind in the history of black people. The convention would seek to learn about the conditions of black people throughout the world. Garvey indicated that one of the most important matters would be the drawing up of a Negro Declaration of Rights, which would be presented to the governments of the world. And so the black world focused its attention on Liberty Hall, the convention center. Black delegates from around the black world—Africa, the West Indies, Central and South America—and from each of the United States descended upon the center.[18] Garvey chose the first of August as the opening day of the convention, ostensibly because it was on that day that the slaves in the West Indies had been "freed."[19] The convention opened and the "Harlem streets rang with stirring martial airs and the measured tramp of smartly uniformed marching bands."[20]

The convention adopted a "Declaration of Rights of the Negro Peoples of the World," containing 66 articles; a universal anthem ("Ethiopia, the Land of Our Fathers"); and an African tricolor of red, black, and green.[21] Logically, an all-black state called for a black God, and the convention established the African Orthodox Church.[22] The convention also established the African Legion, the Black Cross Nurses, the Universal Africa Motor Corps, and the Black Eagle Flying Corps. It created titles and distinctions such as Knight of the Nile, Earl of the Congo, Viscount of the Niger, and Baron of the Zambesi.

Toward the end of the convention Garvey and the delegates staged the largest parade ever to be held in Harlem up to that time. Ottley writes:

> His Excellency, Marcus Garvey, Provisional President of Africa, led the demonstration bedecked in a dazzling uniform of purple, green, and black, with gold braid, and a thrilling hat with white plumes . . . He rode in a big high-mounted black Packard automobile and graciously, but with restraint becoming a sovereign, acknowledged the ovations of the crowds that lined the sidewalks.[23]

The highest point of the convention was the speech given by Garvey at Madison Square Garden. It was an enormous success and touched off thunderous applause when he declared that the real barrier to returning to Africa was white colonial domination. But, warned Garvey, black people from all over the world are going to return to Africa "four hundred million strong and we mean to retake every square inch of the twelve million square miles of African territory belonging to us by right divine."[24]

Despite Garvey's call for action, he was aware that many blacks were neither interested in nor fit for the Africa return but would respond positively to liberation efforts in the United States. They should "cast their buckets" down where they lived. One analyst of the Garvey movement observes that Garvey was working on the principle of domestic economic independence from whites. The UNIA had built an extensive system of business enterprises, a scheme often equated by some (and therefore damned) with the program of Booker T. Washington, who was the leading advocate of black capitalism in the years prior to the founding of the UNIA. But unlike Washington, Garvey received no support from black businessmen. They stood aloof as he launched his Black Star Line and his Negro Factories Corporation.[25]

Whereas Washington's urban program of economic independence would in the main benefit the bourgeoisie, Garvey's plan was aimed at the average man on the street. The result of his commercial scheme was that it temporarily stimulated Black is Beautiful commerce: the first large-scale production and sale of black baby dolls in the country; many people smoked Marcus Garvey Brand cigars; millinery shops owned by Garveyites offered black-made and black-designed products; and Columbia Records put out a record entitled "Black Star Line." Garvey was more than the talk of the town, for his reputation had reached most black peoples of the world and stirred the interest of many white businessmen.

But Garvey also had his problems along with his success. He became embroiled in legal skirmishes. Before the Black Star Line was incorporated, the Assistant District Attorney for New York had warned Garvey of the illegality of selling unincorporated stock. He was also sued for libel by Cyril Briggs, editor of the *Crusader,* an anti-Garvey, socialist magazine. And Garvey had to initiate a libel suit against the Chicago *Defender,* an anti-Garvey black newspaper oriented toward the rising black middle classes.

In 1921 Garvey left the country on a tour of the West Indies to drum up sales for the Black Star Line. He incurred the wrath of the American embassies and consulates and was for a time prevented from reentering the United States. Eventually he was allowed to return in time to prepare for the 1921 UNIA Convention.

The second convention was not as successful as the one the year before, primarily because throughout the meeting rumors were flying that there was mismanagement of the Black Star Line. Besides the *S.S. Frederick Douglass,* the UNIA had acquired the *S.S. Shadyside* in April 1920 for $35,000. This vessel was used as an excursion boat on the Hudson River, but sank in the winter of 1921, and no salvage was attempted. The UNIA also purchased the *S.S. Kanawha.* Its market value was about $10,000, yet the Line paid $60,000, and after two or three disastrous attempts at trips, the ship was abandoned for junk in a Cuban port. The *S.S. General Goethals* was purchased for $100,000 in 1924 and refitted at a cost of $60,000. This ship was obviously better than the others, but it met the same tragic fate. It never returned to New York from its maiden voyage.[26]

If Garvey received rumblings of dissatisfaction from his own membership, they were only a prelude to the treatment he received from his black adversaries and the federal government. His critics, who included several prominent black leaders, called for a complete investigation of the Black Star Line. On January 12, 1922, Garvey and three other officials of the UNIA were arrested and indicted. After a fourteen-month delay, the case against Garvey began in May 1923. The charges were the use of the mails to defraud and conspiracy to use the mails to defraud. Garvey's associates were acquitted on both counts, and Garvey was tried on only one. He acted as his own lawyer and was convicted and fined $1,000 and given five years in the Atlanta penitentiary. Freed under heavy bail, he continued to act as the Provisional President of Africa.[27] His trial was regarded as persecution, and there was world-wide sentiment in his favor—by black peoples, of course.

In 1920 Garvey, to further his colonization scheme, had corresponded with the government of Liberia, and from the response he received had good reasons to be optimistic about repatriating blacks to that country. As a matter of fact, the Mayor of Monrovia was given a high post in the UNIA at a salary of $12,000 a year. From 1920 to about 1924, the Liberian government treated the UNIA as a sovereign power, then abruptly it informed the Associated Press (but not the UNIA) that all existing agreements between the Liberian government and the UNIA had been canceled. Brisbane sums up the situation this way:

Garvey was not taken completely by surprise because he was aware that the Liberian government was under pressure from various sources to renege on its agreement with the UNIA regarding a certain tract of land to which it had been given rights. The Firestone Rubber Company was very much interested in the same tract. Because Liberia was a poor, indebted, corrupt, and somewhat backward country needing all the money it could beg, borrow, or get by chicanery, it played both ends against the middle: the UNIA was used as cannon fodder in Liberia's drawn-out negotiations with the United States government and the Firestone Rubber Company. By August 1924 Garvey and the UNIA could no longer be of use to Liberian officials, who had by then come to an agreement with both the United States government and Firestone that one million acres would be leased to Firestone for ninety-nine years at a rate of six cents per acre yearly, to be paid in gold coin. It included the same land earlier promised to the UNIA! Shortly after this transaction, and with Firestone help, the Liberian government received a five-million dollar loan from a New York City bank.[28] The Liberians must have concluded, and rightly so, that they could not have got a similar deal from Garvey and his UNIA.

The years 1923 and 1924 were significant for Garvey because by the end of 1924 his career was beginning to plummet. Notwithstanding the 1924 Liberian fiasco, in 1923 his mail fraud conviction was only the tip of the iceberg: a barrage of lawsuits against him and the UNIA were initiated, and in August 1924 he was indicted by a federal grand jury on the charge of income tax evasion. DuBois, Garvey's persistent critic, wrote scathingly in the May 1924 issue of *Crisis* (page 30) that Garvey was the black man's most dangerous enemy because he was either a lunatic or traitor; that those who defended him were unworthy and did not deserve the respect of decent Americans, and that Garvey—an open Ku Klux Klan ally—should be "locked up or sent home." Indeed, it was not long before he *was* locked up. Late in 1924 some of Garvey's enemies signed a petition and sent it to the Department of Justice demanding his immediate imprisonment or deportation. On February 25, 1925, Garvey's appeal of his 1923 conviction was denied. He again decided to act as his own lawyer. He lost, and in the same month was incarcerated in the Atlanta Penitentiary for five years.

Despite his imprisonment, Garvey continued to send frequent messages of encouragement from his prison cell, and his second wife, Amy Jacques Garvey, carried on the work of the UNIA.

There were attempts to revive the Spirit of 1920 (the first convention), but the absence of the Provisional President of Africa made all the difference. The UNIA was no longer able to arouse enthusiasm among the black masses. The organization itself was by now facing internal turmoil. Though Garvey was still regarded as its leader, his lieutenants displayed voracious appetites for money, and their hunger eventually rendered the organization inoperable. Garvey himself was pardoned by President Coolidge in November 1927 and was deported to his native Jamaica. For ten years or so he unsuccessfully attempted to revive the UNIA. Apparently without spirit and destitute, he passed away in London in 1940 without ever setting foot on the soil of Mother Africa.

Marcus Garvey was the UNIA's sole architect. The movement's values, in essence, reflected only slight differences from those of mainstream America. Lewis makes the point, however, that Garvey's ideological creation is paradoxical. Garvey's militant call for black nationalism might be too quickly called extremely radical, but its content and emphasis, its depiction of political, social, and economic reality, all reflected "the conventional American world view." That is, in exhorting blacks to be proud of their blackness and black historical achievements, "Garvey was merely turning the white American's racial chauvinism on its head." His ideas of justice and world order were based on the nation-state concept, which most Americans would embrace. His economic philosophy, like Washington's and most Americans', was bourgeois. Finally, "except for its emphasis on the return to Africa, the only 'radicalism' in Garvey's thought (was) his basic assumption that black men could and would manage their affairs in the same manner as did white men." [29]

What, in fact, *was* the Garvey movement's ideology? The "Declaration of the Rights of the Negro Peoples of the World" was its framework. Note that the bulk of Garvey's appeal emphasized racial solidarity and African nationalism. If there was a right time to emphasize these two elements, it was from the time of the first World War through the period known as the Harlem Renaissance. The African continent was experiencing the shock waves of the World War—especially in East Africa. It was immediately after the uprising in Malawi, where John Chilembwe, an American-trained minister, had engaged the colonialist oppressors in armed rebellion in 1915.[30] Black African troops were being used in the war in Europe, and colonial governments were struggling with each other to control African territories, while at the same time white settlers were carving out specific parts of Africa for themselves—the Kenya Highlands, Zimbabwe (Southern Rhodesia), and, of course, the traditional land of the Xhosa-speaking peoples (the Republic of South Africa). It was a time of readjustment for Africans, and the period in which the basis of African nationalism was laid. It was the 1920's, when proto-nationalists Harry Thuku and Jomo Kenyatta, to name only two, were agitating and organizing for African rights in Kenya, thus laying the foundation for African nationalist aspirations.

Black soldiers from the United States had fought in the war in Europe to make the world safe for democracy, yet their rights in the citadel of democracy were violated with impunity. The need for manpower in Northern industries—added to the mechanization of Southern agriculture—had lured blacks by the thousands away from the South.[31] These recent migrants to the cities were crowded into already existing slum areas—and areas soon to become slums. After the war was over, demobilization of the soldiers, black and white, caused severe economic pressures. There were frequent race riots before, during, and after the war.[32] The depraved conditions of black people in their new surroundings made them uneasy, restless, and constantly in search of a way out of their urban dilemma.

The tactics used by Booker T. Washington were no longer appropriate for the urban masses of black people, though his analysis and strategy were sound. At his death in 1915, Washington's views elicited response from only a small segment of the urban mass black population, although they did continue to appeal to the black bourgeoisie. For the most part, he addressed his mass appeal to Southern blacks. One could see how unconvincing his tactics would appear to the same mass of poor southern blacks after they had become poor urban dwellers. Immediately prior to the Garvey movement, they had had no national spokesman; their plight was not alleviated by the Urban League, created in 1911 to assist largely middle-class urban dwellers, or the NAACP, which was a middle-class, integration-oriented, legal-minded, white-led organization. Neither did Trotter's Negro Equal Rights League speak to the needs of *poor* urban blacks.

The black underclass plight was at its lowest ebb when Garvey came on the scene with a call for black people to glory in all things black, take pride in the black man's racial identity, and emphasize racial purity. He told them to reject black powerlessness in white society and at the same time to work for the attainment of power in their ancestral home, Africa. The best way to prepare for the return to Africa was to develop economic self-reliance and power in America.

Garvey was adamant about the need for blacks to return to Africa because he believed they could never receive justice in the New World: "if the Negro were to live in the Western Hemisphere for another 500 years he would still be outnumbered by other races who are prejudiced against him . . . The future of the Negro outside of Africa, spells ruin and disaster."[33] He believed in the purity of race, and its preservation. Hence it was easy for him to be friendly with the Ku Klux Klan. He said, "I believe in a pure black race just as all self-respecting whites believe in a pure white race, as far as that can be."[34] Garvey told the Klan in June 1922 that because the UNIA was a separatist organization seeking a home in Africa, it opposed miscegenation or any social contact between the races. This, of course, did not put him in good standing with many black leaders and white liberals. Nevertheless, Garvey pointed out that he regarded the Klan, the Anglo-Saxon Clubs, and the White American societies as better friends to blacks than all other liberal "hypocritical whites put together." The Klan was at least honest and open in its attitudes and actions toward blacks. In reality, asserted Garvey, underneath the liberalism and tolerance, when it comes to economic, social, and political competition, every white man is a potential Klansman.

Though some argue that Garvey's reasoning was sound, his comments favorable to racist white organizations incurred the wrath of anti-Garvey forces as well as some members of his own movement. Garvey even allowed Klansmen to address the UNIA on several occasions. Some found it too much to accept white racist support to promote the UNIA. As a result, Carter G. Woodson refused to continue contributing historical articles to the *Negro World;* DuBois lamented Garvey's action time after time in the *Crisis;* A. Philip Randolph and others planned to hold "Garvey Must Go" meetings in New York; and the white liberal-black coalition generally derided Garvey for his favorable Klan attitude. Even though he later altered his remarks by recanting his position that blacks should do nothing about the Klan, he continued to believe in racial purity.

Garvey even applied his racial-purity theme to blacks of mixed blood. He had no place in his movement for mulattoes. His insistence on racial purity touched off a debate between himself and DuBois, among others. He believed that the black and white races were at a point where both were crying out for racial purity. He accused DuBois and the NAACP of attempting to create a new colored race of people through miscegenation by eliminating both black and white. He did, however, see DuBois' plan succeeding in most of the West Indies and some of the South American countries, though not in the United States and Africa.[35]

To be sure, Garvey recognized that to excite members and followers emotionally is an important element of any ideology. He accomplished this by recalling Mother Africa's past glories in the fashion of a true cultural nationalist. He related the ways in which whites had tried to rob blacks of their culture and discredit their history. One of his examples was that whites try to make blacks believe that Egyptians, in all their past glory, were not black people. Moreover, every impartial student of history knows that blacks ruled the world around 1350 B.C.: when whites were savages and barbarians living in caves, thousands of black professors were teaching in the universities of Alexandria, then a citadel of learning. Glorious Greece and splendorous Rome inherited their civilization from Egypt and in fact robbed her of her arts and letters without giving her credit. It is predictable that whites would endeavor to keep blacks ignorant of black history and past achievements; white pride and ego would find it impossible to admit that three thousand years ago black people were founders and teachers of art, science, and literature. Garvey admits that black power in the world no longer existed, but it was about to reemerge in the twentieth century through the rebuilding of Africa; from oppressed blacks "a new African civilization, a new culture shall spring up . . . and the Nile shall once more flow through the land of science, of art, of literature, wherein will live black men of the highest learning and . . . accomplishment."[36]

The allusions to Africa's past greatness was an attempt to give the downtrodden black masses a utopian vision. "Up You Mighty Race" was at the back of Garvey's mind; he wanted to arouse latent pride to "flow like a mighty stream" in order to "awaken black people to their true destiny."

Marcus Garvey was a charismatic leader. His dynamic personality, his oratorical ability, his crowd-pleasing antics, his superb use of the dramatic moment—all played an important part in maintaining his image. One of his unfriendly contemporaries has described him as physically ugly: protruding jaws, fat and sleek, bulldog-like face, squat, with piglike eyes. He describes Garvey's personality as boastful, egotistic, tyrannical, intolerant, cunning, shifty, smooth, suave, avaricious, gifted at self-advertisement, and without shame in self-laudation.[37] Whether that is an accurate portrait is a matter of perspective; what is more important is that he possessed an uncanny ability to appeal to the unsatisfied psychic needs of the black masses.

Separatist movements are likely to depend upon a charismatic leader for strength and morale, but no leader, no matter how charismatic, can risk putting all the movement's eggs in one basket. A close analysis of the UNIA indicates that Garvey, after the organization became a viable force, depended upon other functionaries to carry out his strategy. Ironically, Garvey himself possessed administrative skill, but seldom took the time to exhibit it. There is evidence that Garvey himself knew that the establishment of the Black Star Line was premature, but he was persuaded by his inner council to undertake the venture. He knew that in order for the UNIA to maintain its level of interest and membership, he needed to make a dramatic gesture.

Garvey, after all, began his movement as an agitator. He made his first appearance in Harlem as a soap-box orator. He also had some pretty stiff competition from other black separatist nationalists. But it was his agitating that received the warmest response from the black masses. He stated the movement's objective in absolute terms and often through slogans: One Aim! One Destiny! Up You Mighty Race! Africa for the Africans! He proposed bold tactics: "We are marshaling the 400,000,000 Negroes of the world to fight for the emancipation of the race and the redemption of the country of our fathers."[38] He was a symbol of courage and of willingness to become a martyr rather than compromise (which would have eventually detracted from his charisma). On balance, then, considering the time and place, Garvey was a very successful ideologue and propagandist, but his organizational efforts were less than successful, thanks to his weak administration. The fall of the Black Star Line was the outcome.

His African colonization scheme met with disaster because he seemingly did not understand—or refused to recognize—the forces of international politics. Africa was dominated by European powers who were unlikely to stand idly by while 400,000,000 blacks marched "from Cape to Cairo" to reclaim their homeland. Moreover, there was no universal agreement that all blacks wanted to return to Africa. Garvey himself, like Bishop Turner, Blyden, and other Pan-Africanists, did not believe that all blacks *should* return. He underestimated the impact of foreign interest in the independent African states of that day—Liberia and Ethiopia. Garvey was somewhat naive about the internal politics of Liberia;

he should have taken more pains to assess the internal as well as the external political ramifications of his Liberian scheme. And at that time Ethiopians did not consider themselves black; it took Mussolini and an apathetic white Western community in the mid-1930's to make them realize that they too were African—at least in a political sense.

Another shortcoming of Garvey's leadership and organization was that he managed to divide the forces he was attempting to unite. When he lashed out against mulattoes and "mixed-blood Negroes," he was in fact attacking a significant number of black Americans and the source of most black leadership.

Garvey entrusted the business end of the UNIA to others and those he trusted were most responsible for the mismanagement of funds. Some stole outright. He must take the blame, however, for he created the organization.

Garvey's organizational failure should be seen in relationship to outside forces. There is a close relationship between the success of an organization's goals and the reaction by established authority. Because Garvey was regarded as promoting a separatist nationalist ideology that was not acceptable to those in power, he was at odds with constituted authority. Perhaps realizing this, and knowing that the bulk of the black masses would not and could not return to Africa, he promised to alter power relations between blacks and whites in America. To this end, he founded the Negro Factories Corporation, run solely by blacks, its main purpose being to build and operate factories in large industrial centers in the United States. Beginning with the idea that they would "manufacture every marketable commodity," black people were called upon to support this enterprise, and the Corporation developed a chain of cooperative grocery stores, a restaurant, a steam laundry, a tailor and dress-making shop, a millinery store, and a publishing house.[39]

Clearly, Garvey proposed to bring to fruition Washington's goal of "economic separatism" in urban America. Washington had been concerned about economic separatism—or black independence—in the rural South, and Garvey applied his philosophy to urban America, with the Back-to-Africa label as an added incentive. He knew that black people had already had large doses of economic self-determination from Washington and of Back-to-Africa from Bishop Turner, Blyden, and others; he therefore had to combine the two with dynamic variables. Perhaps he saw that it was necessary to augment economic independence and Back-to-Africa with race chauvinism, pride in one's racial heritage, glorification of the African past, confidence in oneself, and other ego-bolstering tactics. (Ideologically, at this point, he had already reconstructed DuBois and Washington.) All of these factors were necessary and proper because they provided escape mechanisms for the poor black masses who lived in the cities.

Garvey apparently felt that the newly arrived urban blacks could not gain independence by using Washington's philosophy of self-help because they were solely dependent upon whites for unskilled work. Hence, ostensibly, he had to divorce himself from Washington's position. Garvey himself observed that "If Washington had lived he would have had to change his program. No leader can successfully lead this race of ours without giving an interpretation of the awakened spirit of the New Negro, who does not seek industrial opportunity alone, but a political voice . . . The new deal includes the program of Booker T. Washington and has gone much further."[40] But many felt that Garvey must completely denounce Washington as a leader in order to make his program more attractive. In 1921 he accommodated them by asserting: "We have been misrepresented by our leadership. We have been taught to beg rather than to make demands. Booker T. Washington was not a leader of the Negro race. We do not look to Tuskegee."[41] Yet in 1924 he renamed the *Yarmouth* the *Booker T. Washington!*

Many movement leaders find themselves having to say many things that they ordinarily would not. Garvey is a case in point. Cruse observes that

> Negro nationalism in America could not have arisen under the leadership of Marcus Garvey *without an economic philosophy having been laid down by Booker T. Washington.* And Marcus Garvey could not have been inspired to put Washington's philosophy into practice without the added ingredient of African nationalism . . .[42]

Interestingly, Washington's personal secretary at Tuskegee, Emmett J. Scott, became one of Garvey's close working colleagues.[43] With these factors in mind, it can be seen that the foundation for the response Garvey received from black people in urban America was laid by Washington and other nationalistic forces. Add to Washington's foundation the World War (which influenced the black move from the South to work in Northern factories), black urban concentration,[44] prejudice and discrimination, Back-to-Africa sentiments, hopelessness, and despair, and it becomes easier to see how Garvey achieved his large black following.

Constituted authority is always suspicious of any large movement and especially a movement that proposes to affect existing power relations. Garvey organized a movement that had a tremendous potential for changing power relations between blacks and whites in America. In analyzing the methods utilized by the authority in channeling or managing Garvey's potential, the first step was to attempt to divide and conquer. Garvey was himself helpful in this regard by transferring the West Indian caste mentality to America, where it existed to be sure but was not so strong. The divide and conquer tactic was used by pitting other black organizations against Garvey—the NAACP, the Socialist Party, the African Blood Brotherhood, and the Communist Party. These organizations were represented by strong leaders who were influential among black people—DuBois, Randolph, Briggs, and others. The communications arms of their organizations castigated Garvey.

Garvey made an error in attempting to compete in a capitalistic system with little knowledge of the system. His schemes were not adequately managed or capitalized to compete with American white industrial capitalism. Many of his contemporaries, in retrospect, charge him with having been an unabashed capitalist, which would have been a mistake, given his overall black-liberation scheme. His Marxist supporters argue, however, that the capitalist system itself was and is largely responsible for the exploitative nature of black-white relations in the first place. Garvey himself maintained that, contrary to Marxist theorists, the real problem is not class per se, but race. He asked, "What racial difference is there between a white communist, republican or democrat?" Beyond these arguments, others claim that capitalism does not conform to the nature of black peoples, and therefore Garvey's pro-capitalist stance had pernicious ramifications for the black liberation struggle at that time.

Garvey, to his credit, was aware of the wider implications of capitalism in his African scheme. He did suggest that he would limit individual as well as corporation wealth—one million and five million respectively—once blacks had returned to Africa. Hence criticism of his antisocialist position is somewhat unjustified. The establishment of the Negro Factories Corporation represented his awareness that America is a capitalist country and that the promotion of equality and liberation must necessarily take a capitalist form, fighting fire with fire. He therefore spoke to the environmental experience of the black masses, urging them to engage in industry, and commerce, and perhaps emulate the Rockefellers, Firestones, and Morgans. The name of the game was big business and ultimately green power. That is, the masses were aware of all these capitalist elements, but had never experienced them at first hand. Garvey's problem was that his schemes never had enough capital to get a running start. Under-capitalization, in addition to having to conform to the rules of the white-run system, made Garvey's organization and movement constantly vulnerable to the channeling tendency of those who control societal power. This tendency soon gave way to obvious chicanery, for Garvey's conviction for "defrauding through the mails" was based on flimsy evidence. The real intent was shown when the judge called the jury in after they had been unable to come to a decision and counseled them on the danger of "letting the tiger loose." Shortly thereafter, Garvey was sentenced to the Atlanta penitentiary.

Garvey's movement centered on his charisma, and its impact can best be gauged by the spin-off effects it produced. Some believe that Garvey did influence African, West Indian, and, to be sure, black American nationalists to continue struggling for freedom, "by any means necessary." That Garvey had millions of followers proves that he *offered what the black masses wanted,* and this fact was not lost on those who controlled power; for white Americans, the myth that blacks could not organize and have visions of freedom in America, as well as elsewhere, could never be the same. For many black Americans in search of a way out of the oppressive restraints of white power, Garvey and Garveyism served as a model for ideological and utopian black liberation.

5 SUBDUED SEPARATISM

The Communist Party, like a number of organizations, admired Marcus Garvey's mass appeal and eventually adopted a form of separatism in order to tap the latent forces responsible for his success. Garvey himself rejected American Communism, preferring capitalism because he thought that the white capitalist was the black worker's only convenient friend; the capitalist was willing to use the black worker wherever and whenever possible, at least as long as black pay was well below the wage scale of white union workers. Garvey reasoned that although black workers were paid less than white, they were earning enough to live on and apparently were able to invest a portion of their earnings in such liberation enterprises as the Black Star Lines and the Negro Factories Corporation. Garvey's rejection of trade unionism did not endear him to union leaders, either black or white. Socialists Cyril Briggs, Otto Huiswood, Chandler Owen, and A. Philip Randolph, for example, were only a few of Garvey's black opponents.

Garvey's attitude toward Communism is important because it provides a background for the Party's position soon after Garvey was exiled and Garveyism began to wane. In general, from 1928 to around 1934 the Communist Party adopted a program geared to black workers, called "Self Determination in the Black Belt." Because Garvey had been successful in relating to the black masses (workers), the Party appealed to them in a similar fashion by addressing itself to the "national" (separatist/nationalist) question.

The Communist Party in the United States grew out of a split in 1919 between factions in the Socialist Party over whether to support the Russian communists. Eventually the Communist

International (Comintern) ordered the left-wing factions, which had split from the Socialist Party, to form the United Communist Party, which had initially been an underground organization. In late 1921, however, the Comintern urged the United Communist Party to become the Workers' Party, although it still maintained its underground position. The Workers' Party later became, once more at the behest of the Comintern, the Communist Party of the United States (CP, or CPUS).[1]

Unlike the Socialist Party, which indicated that it had nothing special to offer the black worker and could not make a special appeal on the basis of race, the CP immediately addressed itself to black people by pointing out that black oppression resulted from white economic bondage and white oppression. These factors, according to the Party, complicated the prospects of black-white worker solidarity but did not alter the fundamental proletarian character of Communism. Initially Communists viewed racial oppression merely as an expression of economic bondage, for which a solution could be found in black and white worker solidarity. But this was the same position held by the Socialists, and they had not been successful in appealing to the black masses. Hence, it became clear to the CP that it had to offer the black masses more than worker class-consciousness and solidarity. In 1928 the CP abandoned that position after much discussion and alteration of policy, but what happened prior to that change is of great importance.

From about 1920 to 1928, the CP's position was not to oppose organizations working for racial betterment but to ally with them and take over organizational directions (toward Communism, of course) by "boring from within." Initially the CP had not opposed the Garvey movement but was very impressed by the UNIA's lower-class appeal. The National Urban League (NUL) and the NAACP, for example, were organizations geared toward aggrandizing the black bourgeoisie, while Garvey appealed to the lumpen proletariat, particularly religious leaders. He deftly injected religious appeal with his specific political demands, appealing to the black masses in a way that had formerly been found only in black churches. But Garvey's Back-to-Africa and race-pride appeals were elements, according to the Communists, that smacked of Black Zionism and race chauvinism and did not contribute to black and white worker solidarity. Despite these elements, however, the CP continued to support the UNIA.[2]

Although the communists tolerated the development of race pride and consciousness among blacks and were disappointed with the Back-to-Africa emphasis, before 1928 they did not want either development to find expression in the separate-nation idea in either the United States or Africa. Ironically, because of outside developments, the Party itself would soon come to advocate the separate-state position. These developments—fostered by the Comintern in Moscow—included the following operating guidelines: establishment of a Negro Commission to address itself to the black question throughout the world; support for every black movement that tended to undermine or weaken capitalism and imperialism or their further penetration; formation of a united front between black and white workers; and use of black Party members to influence black workers.[3]

The outcome of these policy proposals was that, despite all the recruitment drives and other CP activity to gain black members, at the Sixth Congress of the Comintern held in Moscow in 1928 the CPUS had fewer than two hundred black members. The boring-from-within tactic had failed to alter bourgeois organizational directions significantly toward the Communist position, and, failing to influence the UNIA, it had also failed to influence the black masses.[4]

The 1928 Comintern Congress, to compensate for its failure to capture the support of the black masses, adopted the policy of Self-Determination in the Black Belt. Thus the Communists fell back on the black national question by way of a policy of self-determination.

The theory behind the policy had been addressed in 1913 by Joseph Stalin, who then defined a nation as "an historically evolved, stable community of language, territory, economic life, and psychological make-up manifested in a community of culture." A group of people who qualifies can arrange their own life, with the right to enter into federal relations with other nations as well as the right to secede. The definition was formulated in order to persuade Russian minorities to join the Bolsheviks against Czarist rule, but the Comintern and the CPUS attempted to adapt the Russian problem to the realities of the black situation in America.

The Comintern was advised by the "Negro Commission," particularly by Otto Huiswood, a West Indian, that when people reach a "special psychological stage," their reaction to oppression assumes a posture of self-determination. According to him blacks in America were at such a stage. But the Comintern was also advised against adopting the self-determination policy, because black Americans had been conditioned to want to become a part of the American nation, not to separate from it. Therefore, the most appropriate slogan would be one calling for social equality. This advice was ignored, however, in favor of the "black nation" concept.

The self-determination resolution passed, but it was unclear how the CPUS should proceed in actually implementing it. It was clear that in the North there should be increased pressure on trade unions to admit and minister to black workers on the basis of equality. The "Southern strategy" was, however, unclear and ambiguous, indicating merely that a "struggle for self-determination" should be waged. This ambiguity was a blessing in disguise for the CPUS, whose support of the policy had been less than lukewarm in the first place.[5] For two years the CPUS discussed and deliberated over the policy without doing anything concrete.

Ambiguity and confusion notwithstanding, there was method in the Comintern's madness: by calling for self-determination, it hoped to satisfy the nationalist aspirations of blacks who were still attracted to "black chauvinism" and "Black Zionism," and to turn them away from Garveyism to Communism. In the American South, according to Stalinism, blacks met all the requirements of a nation, since they represented an historically evolved, stable entity defined by language and territory and manifesting a community culture.[6] Because of these characteristics the American CP should generally advocate a national revolutionary movement for the right of blacks, looking toward self-determination in the Southern states where they formed a majority. The Black Belt, according to the Comintern, consisted of eastern Virginia, North Carolina, South Carolina, central Georgia, Alabama, the Delta regions of Mississippi and Louisiana, and the coastal regions of Texas. Simultaneously, the struggle for full social and political equality for blacks in other parts of the United States should be intensified.

In 1930 the Comintern attempted to be more explicit in its guidelines for dealing with the self-determination question: advancement of self-determination among Southern blacks; exposure of black bourgeois groups and individuals who were siphoning off "revolutionary aspirations of the Negro masses into reformist channels"; and engendering trust between the black and white working class. It also wanted to wage war against white chauvinism (racism).[7] The new guidelines, in essence, put teeth into the 1928 guidelines by explicitly outlining a four-year program and by setting aside funds for organizing black farmers and sharecroppers and the unemployed industrial workers who were victims of the developing depression.

To realize the new organizational guidelines, the CP did not establish a direct link between itself and the masses but formed satellite groups to deal with the specific problems faced by blacks. Wilson Record lists four types of organizations formed for this purpose: (1) "branches of the Party itself," composed of selected farmers and workers; (2) "revolutionary" trade unions (steel, coal, textiles); (3) sharecropper and tenant farmer leagues; and (4) unemployment councils in some large southern urban centers.[8] These groups did little to impress the black masses and were ineffective in bringing about tangible changes. In fact, to the chagrin of the CP, most blacks, particularly the black bourgeoisie, rejected the self-determination program. Consequently, in 1930 the League of Struggle for Negro Rights (LSNR) was reformulated from the American Negro Labor Congress (ANLC) and attempted to promote a broad-based program to include every segment of the black community, North and South, bourgeoisie and proletarians. Nonetheless, the NAACP and other bourgeois organizations called the self-determination policy "a plan of plain segregation." These black groups opposed not only the Black Nation policy, but also many black Communists. For most black Americans the proposal for a separate nation in America sounded like Jim Crow dressed in clothing made in Moscow.

The "Self-Determination in the Black Belt" policy created more problems than it solved. Among them was the important question of the role and status of the white working class in the proposed Black Belt. The Party responded to this question by pointing out the reality of black cultural, economic, and territorial unity, based on its majority status in the Belt. Another problem was the Party's misreading of the role of the black church and other bourgeois organizations, like the NAACP and the NUL, in the everyday lives of the black masses. It is true that Garveyism had siphoned off a small portion, but in the 1930's the bulk of black people still clung to these nonrevolutionary groups.

The Party persevered in its attempt to influence the masses. It had long encouraged black party participation nationally and internationally, and it had made some headway by encouraging blacks to become not only rank-and-file members, but also leaders in the Party itself. Some Party officials took the position that oppressed black people should be equal not in the limited sense but economically, socially, and politically.[9] Among its black leadership cadre were Benjamin Davis, Jr., James W. Ford, Doxey A. Wilkerson, and Harry Haywood. After the Harlem or Negro Renaissance waned in the late 1920's, the Party attracted and embraced a significant number of the stars and supporting cast, among whom were Langston Hughes, Richard Wright, and Claude McKay.

In pursuing its policy of self-determination, the Party had found it expedient to reject out of hand almost all elements of the black bourgeoisie, including artists and intellectuals. Traditionally, the Party asserted, black artists and intellectuals were unaware of black revolutionary traditions and thus failed to incorporate in their works protest and revolution. What they did, according to the Party, was cater to the white critics and demean the black lumpen. But the Party finally changed its position toward black artists and intellectuals, urging them to aid in creating a "nationalist consciousness."[10]

The olive branch notwithstanding, the Party did not immediately find a large cadre of black artists and intellectuals flocking to the cause. A few did come, however, and among them, as indicated, was Langston Hughes of Negro Renaissance fame. Hughes claimed that he was "propelled by the backwash of the 'Harlem Renaissance,'" living off his "poems which seemed to please the fancy of kindhearted New York ladies with money to help young writers."[11] But by the end of the 1920's both the Harlem Renaissance and the moneyed, kind-hearted ladies became victims of the developing depression. Hughes graduated from Lincoln University in 1929 while enjoying the success of his first novel, *Not without Laughter*. Then came the crash and the end of patrons, scholarships, fellowships, and literary prizes. But the fact remained that Hughes's only vocation was writing, and from it he somehow had to make his living.

Hughes was perceptive and sensitive and was very much aware of race and color. He did not "want to write for the pulps, or turn out fake 'true' stories to sell under anonymous names," nor did he want to "bat out slick, non-Negro short stories" for magazines like the *Saturday Evening Post*. What he wanted was to write as seriously as he "knew how about the Negro people, and make that kind of writing earn [him] a living."[12] Hughes and the Party found they had mutual interests: the artist wanted to write about the oppressed black condition, and the party wanted black artists as members who would do exactly that. In 1930 Hughes became president of the LSNR, ostensibly a coalition of many black organizations, but in reality a Party front.

The fact remains, however, that most black Renaissance artistic and intellectual leaders did not become Party members; they remained associated with bourgeois organizations and other leftist but noncommunist protest organizations. Langston Hughes is one example of a Harlem Renaissance black artist who was attracted to the Party. Another was Claude McKay who had formerly served as foreign correspondent for Garvey's *Negro World*. In 1922 he published *Harlem Shadows,* in which his famous poem "If We Must Die" appeared. The lines in that poem, "If we must die, let us not die like dogs," may be taken as an indication of his position regarding black oppression. Richard Wright also embraced Communism, becoming a Party member after the 1928-34 "self-determination" period. It is important to note that when he joined the Party, he expressed black nationalism in his writings, a position the Party had at that time (1937) abandoned.

Not only did the Party seek to attract black artists and intellectuals in its attempt to gain the loyalty of the black masses, but it also attempted to receive extensive national and international press coverage from its legal defense of selected black causes. The Party was able to launch and finance legal defense through the International Labor Defense (ILD)—among other similar organizations—formed by the Comintern in 1925. The Party recognized the propaganda value of displaying special interest in black victims of injustice, and in the United States there was never a lack of opportunity to do so. The problem was to be selective. Realizing the propaganda potential of the ILD, William L. Patterson, an able black administrator, lawyer, and writer, was made its executive secretary.

Being an organ of the Comintern, the ILD adhered closely to the Comintern's position on the black question: following the Sixth World Congress in 1928, it adopted the self-determination policy. Though the ILD became one of the Comintern's most effective legal instruments in the period 1928-34, it was not widely known until its involvement with the Scottsboro Case in 1931—despite its part in the Sacco-Vanzetti case.[13]

In late March 1931 nine black youths were charged with allegedly raping two white women while on a freight train near Scottsboro, Alabama. Within weeks the youths were sentenced to death in the electric chair. The "Scottsboro Boys" denied the rape charges, and the women—with evidently questionable characters—later "confessed" that they had not been raped. Initially the NAACP took upon itself to coordinate all the matters involving the case and retained Clarence Darrow and Garfield Hayes to defend the young blacks. The CP and ILD then swung into action, eventually undermining the efforts of Darrow and Hayes, arguing that the case involved more than legal questions.

American justice to black people was the main issue and public opinion—at home and abroad—had to be brought to bear if justice was to prevail. Public opinion through marches and rallies, mock trials, pamphlets, leaflets, etc. was aroused, and the higher courts reversed the lower court decisions, eventually exonerating all the defendants. (The procedure, however, took several years and it was many years later before the last defendant was freed.) Meanwhile the CP reaped enormous publicity gains from the deliberations. Some have intimated that the CP reaped more gain than publicity; in drumming up financial support, the Party and the ILD in the name of Scottsboro may have legitimately used money "for pamphlets advocating self-determination for Negroes in the Black Belt for the payment of lawyers' fees."[14]

It is difficult to conclude that had the Party concentrated on the case itself, it would have been successful in obtaining the victims' release. Moreover, though the Party reaped windfall publicity from the case, who can say that mass pressure was unnecessary when, at that time in the Deep South (and even Up South), black people were not allowed to serve on juries. Who could expect black men to obtain justice from an all-white jury when the charge was that they had allegedly raped a white woman? The Party pointed out the injustice of the southern jury system in this connection and thus prompted the inclusion of blacks on juries.

The Angelo Herndon case is another example of how the Party through the ILD involved itself in another publicity campaign. In 1933 Herndon, already a party member, led a relief march of about a thousand black and white families on the Georgia capitol building in Atlanta. He was arrested for violating an 1886 law designed to curb agitation among newly freed slaves. The ILD appealed the case, it went to the Supreme Court, and Herndon was eventually acquitted. Although the Party launched "Free Angelo Herndon" demonstrations, they, unlike those of the Scottsboro campaign, did not catch on, and the Party shortly thereafter abandoned efforts to provide either large-scale demonstrations or legal aid for blacks who suffered from injustice, contenting itself with releasing trenchant news releases decrying exploitation and injustice. Herndon later quite the Party and denounced it, contending that it was only interested in "publicity and not systemic injustice meted out to black people."[15] The switch from mounting large demonstrations and other publicity-oriented activities was indicative of a change in Party tactics— but not strategy—for attracting a large black following.

Beginning around 1933, the Party realized that its self-determination policy was less than successful, to say the least, and it was time to explore other means of attracting the black masses. In short, the policy of self-determination in the Black Belt was beginning to fade around 1933, and there is evidence to suggest that the change began even earlier. To be sure, by 1934 the Party launched its "united front" campaign, but it was essentially the same boring-from-within tactic pursued prior to the Comintern's Sixth World Congress in 1928. The Party had come full circle.

It would be misleading to leave this synopsis of the CP's self-determination policy between 1928 and 1934 standing alone. Many things happened that had profound effects upon black people generally and the Party in particular. Among them was the incipient move by blacks to vote Democratic instead of automatically voting Republican. In 1928, for example, Al Smith received a significant portion of the black vote, and in 1932, despite James Ford's candidacy for vice president on the Communist ticket, blacks overwhelmingly supported Franklin D. Roosevelt. In fact, "A presidential candidate poll published by *Opportunity* magazine in May, 1932 showed that out of 3,973 Negroes polled, only 51 planned to support the Communist nominee."[16] Considering that *Opportunity* magazine was a publication of the NUL, which opposed the Communists, and that voting here refers to the non-South, where integration, not self-determination, was the Communist policy, it is difficult to say how blacks in the Black Belt would have voted had they been allowed to do so; but by 1932, among blacks who voted, there had emerged a Democratic trend that by 1934 had become almost completely Democratic.

The trend to vote Democratic must be seen as a result of the Republican's assumption that because theirs was the party of Lincoln, the black vote was already in its hip pocket. It was, until 1928: in the presidential election of 1924 blacks overwhelmingly supported the Republican nominee. But one can conjecture that the "New Negro"—fostered by the Harlem Renaissance, Garvey and Garveyism, and even the militant call for equality by the Communists—came to realize that it would be most expedient to play the role of a broker, available to the highest bidder. By 1928 the highest bidders among the contingency were still the Republicans and the "Lincoln legacy." But loyalty to dead heroes fades quickly in the face of new realities fostered by social change. Herbert Hoover, the Republican winner of the

1928 presidential election, did not endear himself to blacks: in
1930 he nominated John J. Parker, an avowed Southern racist,
to sit on the bench of the Supreme Court. Parker, to be sure,
was not confirmed by the Senate, after massive lobbying by the
NUL, NAACP, and other black organizations and interests had
made it clear that numerous lynchings had occurred in North
Carolina during his gubernatorial administration without a word
of discouragement from him.

Besides paying little attention to the plight of black people,
Hoover did not pay enough attention to the nation's economy.
The year 1932 found 15 million Americans unemployed and
innumerable businesses and fortunes in ruins. Blacks, who suffer
economically even in times of prosperity, suffered disproportion-
ately more than whites. It was evident that Hoover's sole plan for
dealing with the ailing economy was faith that the capitalist
system would correct itself through natural competition. Even
if this plan had worked, and there is no evidence that it would
have, those on the bottom of the economic heap would have
continued to suffer the most. Those forgotten people needed a
new deal.

Franklin Roosevelt and the New Deal programs did in fact
offer Americans new programs for dealing with the depression.
Though these programs did not constitute a long-term panacea
for workers, many of these agricultural, conservation, and industrial programs were designed to affect the immediate needs
of workers, black and white alike. Because, among other things,
the New Deal did more than anything else to aid black people,
including Communist promises and grandiose rhetoric, blacks
hitched their hopes and votes to the Democratic New Deal star.
By 1934 there was a Democratic voting trend among blacks, and
by 1936 Roosevelt and the Democrats had clearly won the black
vote. Hence, the period 1928–34 found the contending forces of
separation and integration manifesting themselves in the Communists' "Self-Determination in the Black Belt" policy and the
American system's New Deal policy. But one should look generally at what can be said about other factors and forces contributing to America's "winning" and Communism's "losing" the
allegiance of black people in this period.

Garvey's most significant appeal had centered on making black
people viable citizens in the mainstream of American culture.
Garvey indicated that black people could never live in freedom
and equality among white Americans, but he nevertheless worked
harder at doing just that than preparing them for the return to

Africa. American Communists, black and white, realized that black people, even if they wanted a separate black state, were in no position to achieve it because in the Black Belt region *blacks could not even vote,* let alone establish a political state! But this reality was naively ignored by the Comintern, despite admonishments to the contrary.

There were other reasons why the self-determination policy lost, among them the fact that in the United States red and black mixed only on the black nationalist flag. The Comintern and the American Communists felt it necessary for black and white Communists to demonstrate, agitate, and socialize for their common cause. Again, the reality of race relations in the United States was at odds with this desired end; white Communists exhibited racist attitudes and behavior toward blacks just as did most other white Americans.

It would be unfair to suggest that the Communist Party did not have any effect upon the black struggle at that time. Often it captured the imagination of black people when black and white Communists unhesitatingly attacked injustice where they found it, fought to better the lot of black workers, put black artists, intellectuals, and political leaders in responsible positions, and called attention to the exploitative nature of capitalism. The Party's failure to capture the black masses was primarily because its tactics were foreign and often insincere, and its strategy was designed for a "world proletarian revolution" that American workers, then and now, black and white, were not prepared to undertake.

Black separatism is an elusive and subtle phenomenon. At times blacks embrace some form of it because they are denied access to what most other Americans take for granted; at other times they aggressively pursue separatism as an end in itself; and at still others they endorse separatist ideology as a mechanism for fostering integration. There is still another aspect: at times black separatism seems to become anything that articulate leaders of small groups say it is. Beyond all these manifestations is an overriding reality: black separatism is a vehicle used by black people to adjust to, or alter, the reality of personal, group, and systemic oppression in America. Realizing the adaptations that blacks utilized in coping with oppression, the Comintern formulated the self-determination policy.

But in a crunch, and the depression did present a dire threat to the system, more often than not people will choose to keep even a system that oppresses rather than try an unfamiliar alternative. Hence, the New Deal held sway over the black masses; and even among white workers there is no evidence that the CPUS made significant gains.

The fall of Marcus Garvey and the decline of Garveyism's mass appeal, the Communists' self-determination policy, and the palliative New Deal constituted only a part of the ebb tide of black separatism from the late 1920's to the mid-1930's. Though the depression had a nullifying impact on lingering mass support for Garveyism, Garveyites joined other nationalist/separatist organizations and continued their nationalist efforts. Garvey organizations still exist today![17] The sects led by Daddy Grace and Father Divine also absorbed some ex-Garveyites.[18]

During this same period organizations and groups representing various combinations of nationalism/separatism waxed and waned. The Ethiopian Peace Movement was founded in Chicago in 1932. This group (as opposed to a movement in the sociological sense) supported African repatriation. It later supported Theodore Bilbo's Negro Repatriation Bill in 1939 by circulating a petition urging support for the Bilbo Bill, and planned a "march on Washington," with a surprisingly large number of signatures on the petition. Also in Chicago, in 1934, the National Movement for the Establishment of a Forty-Ninth State was founded by Oscar C. Brown, a lawyer and businessman. Although it did not call for separation from the Union, it wanted Commonwealth status for the new state, the principal inhabitants of which were to be black. Never catching on big outside Chicago, the organization remained active until around the mid-1940's, where it died from a lack of support and interest from the black masses.

During the early depression years there evolved a Don't-Buy-Where-You-Can't-Work campaign. "Starting in Chicago in 1929, the idea of boycotting and picketing discriminatory ghetto stores spread spontaneously across the country." These first boycotts were initiated by Suli Abdul Hamid, known in Chicago "as Bishop Conshankin, a former religious mystic." He would walk through the black ghetto community with a stepladder and, upon finding a discriminatory store, would mount the ladder admonishing blacks to spend their money where they were able to work, and urging jobs for blacks. Hamid eventually moved to New York, where in Harlem he became known as the "Harlem Hitler" because of his pejorative references to white shop owners; hence, many of these campaigns were termed anti-Semitic. Vincent indicates that the initial "jobs campaigns" were led by blacks "close to the grass roots" but the black middle class later joined them.[19] These campaigns may be seen as a form of "economic separatism," because they eventually took the character of "racial solidarity" efforts.

W. E. B. DuBois became disenchanted with the NAACP over, among other things, its lack of emphasis on the economics of the black struggle. He concluded that if black people could not "live in decent sections of a city . . . or educate their children in decent schools or enter industry at a living wage or . . . receive promotion and advancement according to his desserts, [they] must organize [their] own economic life so that just as far as possible these discriminations would not reduce [them] to abject exploitation." Distinguishing between integration and segregation, DuBois rejected the idea that integration was the only solution to the race problem; he observed that sometimes segregation would be "necessary to our survival and a step toward the ultimate breaking down of barriers, to increase by voluntary action our separation from our fellow men."[20] DuBois subsequently turned to socialism and later, in his book *Dusk of Dawn,* published in 1940, elaborated upon the necessity of separatism, especially in things economic and educational.

In this period the Nation of Islam emerged, with far-reaching implications for the future. Today it remains a significant black separatist organization. The Black Muslims had their beginnings in the Back-to-Islam movement founded by Timothy Drew, a native of North Carolina, who changed his name to Noble Drew Ali. About 1913, at the age of twenty-seven, he is reputed to have established a Moorish-American Science Temple in Newark, New Jersey. In the next fifteen years temples were opened in Pittsburgh, Detroit, and Chicago, among other places.[21]

Drew based his organization on the idea that black Americans could achieve dignity and self-determination by making themselves into Asiatics, specifically Moors, or Moorish-Americans whose ancestors had come from Morocco. He composed a 64-page *Holy Koran,* which became the organization's bible. The book proclaimed that Noble Ali Drew was a prophet ordained by Allah. He taught that white Europeans had subjugated the Moorish-Americans by calling them "Negroes," "colored," "black," or Ethiopian. By casting off these names in favor of Moorish-American ones, black freedom and identity could be regained.[22]

Drew taught that one must have a nationality before he can

have a god. He admired Marcus Garvey but never advocated leaving the United States or founding an independent state. Chicago became his main center of operation. In 1929 his leadership was challenged by Sheik Claude Greene. In the struggle between the Drew and Greene factions, Greene was killed in March 1929. Drew was arrested for the murder and released on bond; a few weeks later he died mysteriously. "His followers soon split among themsevles, each strong man with his own temple."[23]

In mid 1930 an esoteric peddler who was thought to be an Arab appeared in the black community of Detroit. He sold silks and other "foreign" things to the blacks, which he claimed were like those the black people wore in their homeland across the sea. He counseled against eating certain foods, and more importantly he first taught blacks their "true" religion from the Christian Bible. Later they were introduced to the Holy Qur'an and told that the Christian Bible was not the proper book for the Black Nation.

He became known as the "prophet," and his preachings and teachings became increasingly antiwhite. He dramatically deprecated the Christian Bible. The outcome was that his followers grew too numerous for house-to-house meetings, and a hall was rented and named the Temple of Islam. The "movement known as the Black Muslims was born." The founder of the first temple was known as "Mr. Farrad Mohammad or Mr. F. Mohammad Ali. He was also known as Professor Ford, Mr. Wali Farrad and W. D. Fard."[24] "One story had him born in Mecca . . . another . . . gave him a British education in preparation for a career in the diplomatic service of the Kingdom of Hejaz."[25] His true origin is still unknown.

Nevertheless, his success in Detroit caused the authorities to take notice: he established a University of Islam, a Moslem Girls' Training (MGT) and General Civilization Class, and the Fruit of Islam (FOI). The police received rumors that Fard was conducting blood sacrifices in his rituals, and jailed him in 1932. He was ordered out of Detroit in 1933 and moved to Chicago, where he was immediately arrested. Fard gradually withdrew from public view (perhaps because of the fear of arrest) but at the same time indicated that he was the "Ruler of the Universe" or "God Allah"[26] (no doubt to enhance the legitimation of his charismatic authority).

Fard's doctrine was nationalistic in that his message was to "the Nation of Islam." His followers were told to think not as Americans but as citizens of the Holy City of Mecca. Their flag was the Moslem flag. They were not to accept the American

Constitution or to serve in the armed forces. One splinter group, however, refusing to go along with Fard's anti-Americanism, created a serious faction in his movement.

"In late 1933 or some time in 1934 Fard disappeared as suddenly and mysteriously as he had appeared. His followers apparently divided into two camps—those who recognized his divinity as Allah, the true God, and those who did not. The former, known as the 'Temple People,' accepted as their leaders one of Fard's chief lieutenants, Elijah Poole."[27]

Poole and his family had migrated from rural Georgia to Detroit in the 1920's. He had been given by Fard the Islamic surname Muhammad and had devoted himself to Fard and the movement. Because the organization grew too large for one man to operate, Elijah Muhammad was named by Fard the chief Minister of Islam. "Elijah Muhammad was almost singlehandedly responsible for the deification of Fard and for the perpetuation of his teachings in the early years after Fard disappeared."[28]

After Fard's disappearance, the Muslims lost their aggressiveness, and the organization and membership began to decline in size and power. Elijah Muhammad thought it best to establish headquarters at Temple No. 2 in Chicago. There in his new headquarters in 1934 he began to reshape the movement under his own leadership. He assumed the title of prophet and prior to his death was called the "Messenger of Allah"—that is, Fard's messenger.[29]

After Elijah Muhammad took over the Nation, it neither grew dramatically nor declined drastically. According to Essien-Udom, it did not come again to the public's attention until it was involved in a courtroom incident in March 1935, and not until 1942 was it seriously involved with control agencies. In May of that year Elijah Muhammed was arrested for resisting the draft—even though he was 44 years old, well past the legal draft age. The real motive lay in the Nation's refusal to bear arms or engage in violence without the consent of Allah. Muhammad taught that the Japanese had not harmed black people and therefore blacks should not fight the white man's war. He was also charged with sedition, but that charge was dropped and he was "sentenced to serve five years in the Federal Correction Institution at Milan, Michigan. He was released in 1946."[30]

Not only was Muhammed arrested but many of his followers with him, for "failing to register for the draft." The FBI kept close watch on the organization and, along with the local police, raided the Chicago headquarters, arresting about eighty people.

The organization continued to exist, however, and much of the leadership came from Muhammad while imprisoned. Elijah's wife, Clara, is said by some to have been the group's mainstay during Muhammad's incarceration. She kept up the correspondence, conveyed messages to Muhammad on her visits, and generally provided the morale needed to keep the organization alive.

After his release from prison, Muhammad immediately began revitalizing the Nation. A Temple headquarters was bought and later, needing more space because of expanded membership and programs, the present Temple was purchased; he indicates that between 1940 and 1960, satellite temples were organized in twenty-eight cities of fifteen states and the District of Columbia; and by early 1960, fifty Temples were reported in twenty-two states. It should be cautioned that the dramatic increase in Muslim size and membership should not be attributed solely to the charisma of Muhammad. Important among the reasons for the increase is the significant black migration of rural blacks to cities from 1940 to 1960. War production and the subsequent settlement of demobilized black soldiers from World War II and the "Korean conflict" increased the urban black population. The lack of jobs, disillusionment with the "urban promise," and racial oppression in another form no doubt contributed to the Nation's appeal. But foremost among the reasons for the large increase in Muslim membership was the conversion of Malcolm Little to the Nation.

Little was born in Omaha, Nebraska, in 1925. One of eleven children, his father was a Baptist minister and, more importantly, a Garveyite; Earl Little believed in the dignity of black people and was supported in this belief by his wife, who was a native of Grenada, West Indies. When Malcolm was six years old, white racists set fire to the Littles' home. The fire was practically ignored by the fire department. The Littles then moved to Lansing, Michigan, where Earl Little continued to teach and preach black dignity. For his pains, Earl was killed, and without sufficient support the Little family broke up, the children going in different directions. Malcolm was sent to a boys' institution and eventually dropped out, moving to Boston, becoming a hustler, pimp, gambler, and whatever it takes for black men to survive in the oppressed black ghetto. He was eventually caught and sentenced to Concord, Massachusetts, Reformatory for ten years. While he was there, he never forgot his father's murder, for it was a "unique experience." At this time he discovered, through his brother

Reginald, the Nation of Islam. In 1947, one year after Muhammad's release from the Milan, Michigan, prison, Little was converted to Elijah Muhammad's teachings by a fellow inmate who belonged to the Detroit Temple. After serving seven and one-half years, he was paroled, and upon his release he became a "true believer" and, subsequently, "Malcolm X," a minister of the Nation of Islam and Elijah Muhammad's righthand man. (See also below, pages 104–108.)

In 1935 among black people, at least among middle-class blacks, the idea evolved of pooling their energies and resources in order to come to grips better with black oppression. Sponsored by the Division of Social Sciences at Howard University and chaired by Ralph Bunche, a meeting of the Sponsoring Committee (of the incipient National Negro Congress) was held in Washington in 1935. From February 14 through February 16, 1936, the organizing committee met in Chicago, where 817 delegates represented 585 organizations. The National Negro Congress (NNC) was born and its purpose was to be an umbrella organization, giving direction and unity for all black unions and religious and fraternal groups. A. Philip Randolph became chairman of the Congress.

From 1936 to its last meeting in 1940 (it did not meet in 1938–39), the Communists attempted to take over the NNC. They finally succeeded in 1940. The organization failed to continue after this takeover because it was obvious that it was Communist-controlled, and blacks had had enough of Communist self-serving involvement. Randolph, still a Socialist, stepped down, or was forced out, in favor of a Party member but reminded the Congress that it should be watchful of organizations that used the NNC to further their own against the Congress' best interest.

Randolph then organized the March on Washington Movement (MOWM), having as its goal fair employment in industries producing war materials. By that time he was the leading black spokesman in America. The March on Washington never came off, largely because of President Roosevelt's issuance of Executive Order 8802 establishing the first Fair Employment Practices Commission (FEPC). Neither Roosevelt nor his Commission did much to promote fair employment for blacks, but they did prevent the planned march. The MOWM and Randolph's leadership of it are important because of the separatist potential. Killian points out that "Randolph recognized the importance of black consciousness to the development of a movement which would involve the Negro masses. In trying to make MOWM an all-black movement . . . only a few years earlier Randolph, as president of the National Negro Congress, had been bitterly disillusioned by the ease with which white communists had taken over the organization. He did not want the same thing to happen to the MOWM."[31] Many blacks then understood that Communists (as liberals) would dull the movement's effectiveness, and in the 1960's many blacks came to take the ideological position that whites (liberals) should be eliminated from all leadership positions and eventually from black organizations.

The early 1940's found the Nation of Islam, the MOWM, and a few other organizations pursuing separatist-oriented alternatives to ameliorate the black plight, while interracial organizations like the Urban League and the NAACP were working for the same ends. In this same period another interracial organization was established by the Fellowship of Reconciliation (FOR), a Quaker pacifist organization itself founded during World War I. In the spring of 1942 the Chicago Congress of Racial Equality was organized; one year later it was federated, becoming the Congress of Racial Equality (CORE).

FOR was a predominately white organization, having several blacks among its officials, including Bayard Rustin and James Farmer. It was concerned with the cause of pacifism as well as race relations, and even at that time had black officials in the South. CORE's purpose was to promote social action in the United States through the utilization of nonviolent direct-action tactics which Mohandas Ghandi had successfully used in India against British colonial oppression. Initially CORE attempted to win over opponents through negotiation; failing that, it intended to use agitation as a means of bringing public attention to, for example, a segregated establishment. If public opinion did not succeed in prompting the establishment to remove its color ban, then CORE would engage in direct action—pickets, boycotts, and sit-ins.

In 1946 CORE moved its headquarters from Chicago to New York, where it remains today. Its membership did not grow rapidly until the mid-1950's when it began to recruit students and became more active in the South. Under the leadership of James Farmer, CORE became a trainer of sit-iners, and by the late 1950's it had substantially increased its membership. In the early 1960's it promoted the Freedom Rides, which produced the initial confrontation between CORE and southern racists. These confrontations and the subsequent escalation of activity in the South resulted in CORE, along with the Student Non-Violent Coordinating Committee eventually embracing separatism.

In summary, one may conclude that the Harlem or Negro Renaissance served as the cultural wing of aroused black consciousness, while Garvey and Garveyism attempted to place an umbrella over all aspects of black life—cultural, economic, and political. The late 1920's and 1930's found the Communist Party, through various means, groping to sustain and capture the Garvey mystique in winning over the black masses. "Boring from within," "self-determination in the Black Belt," and the "United Front" were some of the Communist tactics. None was successful because the masses remained indifferent; but some leading individuals did become Party members.

During the depression, though much separatist activity continued, the New Deal—not separatism—captured the minds and stomachs of the black masses.[32] The Nation of Islam and the Forty-Ninth State, among others, nevertheless evolved and persisted. Some of the Don't-Buy-Where-You-Can't-Work campaigns, which utilized the boycott to get jobs in enterprises owned by whites, could be construed as having separatist overtones—or undertones. In 1934 DuBois, rejecting integration as it then stood, suggested that separation (segregation), assuming continued black exclusion by whites, may be the best and only alternative to continued segregation. By 1940 he had rejected integration as feasible, proposing instead a separate economy and educational system.

In 1941 A. Philip Randolph, who had long championed the interests of the black working class, temporarily took a separatist turn in the March on Washington Movement, which he led. The MOWM consciously drew on the power and support of the black masses. In 1942 CORE, which later became a separatist organization, was founded, using nonviolence and direct action as tactics to combat black exclusion. Around the mid-1940's the Communist Party again unsuccessfully attempted to win over the black masses to its position by advocating self-determination.

After World War II and through the early 1960's, the black struggle centered on the theme of integration. However, the Nation of Islam, the small groups that succeeded Garvey, and other local separatist-oriented groups and organizations persisted in separatist ideologies and activities. Beneath the serenity of the 1950's lurked latent forces that would soon develop and nurture the integration or civil rights movement: the 1954 *Brown vs.*

Topeka Supreme Court decision, the Montgomery Bus Boycott, and the rise of Dr. Martin Luther King, Jr. But there also lurked the ever-present separatist potential.

In the later 1950's Malcolm X, the incisive and fiery minister of the Nation of Islam, and Robert Williams came to national attention by criticizing the integration movement and advocating armed self-defense. The intensity of the integration movement and its eventual failure unleashed forces responsible for the uniting of the radical civil-rights or integration groups—such as CORE and SNCC—with such older nationalist-separatist organizations as the Nation of Islam or Black Muslims, and the Garveyites. The convergence of these forces eventually manifested itself in contemporary black separatist movements and movement organizations. The next chapter is concerned with them.

II.◆THE CONTEMPORARY PERIOD

6 SEPARATIST IDEOLOGIES, I

In the late 1950's and early 1960's the civil rights movement, though not yet fully equipped, was gearing to become more militant in its pursuit of integration, at that time the dominant ideological tendency among black Americans. Despite the fact that integration was emphasized, however, separatism remained, as it always has, a subdominant theme. The Nation of Islam through Malcolm X and the many local separatist groups and organizations continued to embrace it; Robert F. Williams, by advocating armed self-defense, came to advocate Revolutionary Black Nationalism, eventually becoming the honorary President of the Republic of New Africa. Because CORE and SNCC were originally founded as interracial, integration-oriented movement organizations, it is necessary to explore their past also, in order to understand their evolution from integration to separatism.

The Nation of Islam or Black Muslims

The Nation of Islam, the oldest of the contemporary black separatist movements treated in this work, profoundly admires Marcus Garvey. The late Elijah Muhammad himself denied that the Nation originated in Drew's Temple, but he had high regard for Garvey.[1] According to Vincent, Elijah Poole (Muhammad) was "a corporal in the Chicago division [of the UNIA] and was one of many Garveyites attracted to Prophet Wallace Fard and his 'Nation of Islam.'"[2]

Drew and Garvey, according to Muhammad, failed to liberate

black people because their ideologies lacked the proper ingredients. Drew's movement was mostly religious-separatist, while Garvey's focused on the political economy of separatism. Though the Nation's ideology had a religious orientation, it proposed to "correct" Garvey's and Drew's historical mistakes by combining religion with economic, political, social, and cultural ingredients to achieve black liberation.

According to Elijah Muhammad, the maker and owner of the universe is Allah, who made black people the original inhabitants of the earth. From them came all other races, yellow, brown, and white. Whites have only inhabited the earth for about 6,000 years and were created by a black scientist from "a small life germ." The universe of the black nation was designed over 66 trillion years ago by twenty-four scientists, with one acting as God. The black nation gave birth to another God named Yakub 6,600 years ago (the twenty-three scientists predicted over 15,000 years ago that the year 8400 would see the birth of Yakub). He would be born near Mecca at a time when satisfaction and dissatisfaction would be 70 and 30 percent respectively. Mr. Yakub would then "accidentally" make the white race, which would rule the black race for 5,000 years. Later one would also be born who would destroy Yakub's accident.

When Yakub was about six years old, one day, while playing with two pieces of steel, he noticed their magnetic attraction for each other. He informed his uncle (that is, black people) that he (Yakub) would later make a people who would rule him. In steel, with its magnetic drawing capacity, Yakub had found the principle upon which to base his later teaching. Because he was a brilliant student, he learned early and fast, and after graduating from all the institutions of learning, he began preaching and proselytizing in Mecca and attracted many followers.

Yakub's ministry in Mecca was apparently successful, for he made many converts, causing great concern among the authorities. A large number of his followers were arrested, but as fast as this happened, many more took their places. Eventually Yakub himself was arrested, and the King of Mecca was notified. The king immediately understood that Yakub was no ordinary fellow and, at Yakub's request, agreed to give him whatever he requested. Yakub wanted the king to give him and his followers enough money and "other necessities" to last for twenty years, at which time they would leave Mecca.

After twenty years all of Yakub's followers were rounded up and placed on ships; "they numbered 59,999," with Yakub bringing the total to 60,000. After making sure that all were healthy and fit to travel with him, Yakub and his followers "sailed out to an Isle in the Aegean Sea called 'Pelan' (Bible 'Patmos'). Once there, Yakub had his followers officially name him their king." He then revealed to his chosen doctors, nurses, ministers, and cremators his plan to make "a new people."

The plan was as follows. All who wanted to marry would be required to see the doctor, and if "two real black ones" wanted to marry, the doctor would take some blood from them and, pretending to have examined it, inform them that because their blood did not mix, they should "find another mate." The doctor would give them a certificate to take to their minister, in case they wanted to marry anyway. The minister, however, would refuse to marry them. But if two brown people followed the same procedure, they would be allowed to marry. The nurses were ordered to take the black babies and by lying to their mothers find some way to get rid of them. The cremators would burn them. The brown babies were saved "so as to graft the white out of it." Because the white babies were created by lying and murder, these characteristics were "born into the very nature of the white baby," and they naturally wanted to murder black people.

Yakub told his (white) creation that they should return to Mecca, the black nation, and create havoc among the black people, causing them to kill each other. He also told them that they must manipulate themselves into the position of being allowed to "help [blacks] settle their disputes, and restore peace among themselves. Once they consented, he could then rule them. And rule he did.

After just six months in the black nation, the white devils had fomented chaos and confusion, and the black people were fighting among themselves. The blacks eventually resorted to taking the matter to the king, who informed them that there would be no peace until the black nation drove the white devils out of their midst.

The black nation then rounded up all the devils, stripping them of their clothes and the literature which the white devils had copied from the black people, and "let them go into the hills of West Asia, the place they now call Europe." To ensure that those who were able to negotiate the Arabian Desert—many did not—and get to Europe would not return to the Paradise of the black nation, they were confined in Europe by "roping it off" from the rest of "East and West Asia" by armed border patrols. For two thousand years the white devils remained isolated, living in caves, going naked, eating raw meat, without literature—un-human, illiterate.

Without a civilization for two thousand years, the devils became savages. Some tried to graft themselves back into the black nation, but only got as far as the gorilla; the entire "monkey family are from this 2,000 year history of the white race in Europe." They walked on all fours, climbed trees, and used dogs for protection. Some dogs were tamed to live in the caves with them and became much prized pets—their best friends, as it were.

After two thousand years, however, Allah through Musa (Moses) brought the white race back into civilization and they took their places—as Yakub had intended—as rulers. Musa had, in essence, to recivilize them: he taught them to wear clothes, to cook meat and season it with salt, to eat fish on Friday. But they were so savage that Musa had to sleep in a ring of fire for his own protec-tion. They were very much afraid of fire. The white devils finally became so evil that Musa took the worst of the lot (about 300) and killed them with dynamite. Musa was scolded for this deed, but he believed they should all be killed. This, however, was not permitted by Allah.

They were destined to rule the black nation—including brown, red and yellow people—and it has come to pass. It had to, because, according to the Bible, God said, "Let us make man in our image [the white devils], after our likeness: Let them have dominion over the fish of the sea; and over the fowl of the air; and over the cattle, and over all the earth; and over every creeping thing that creepeth upon the earth. Be fruitful and multiply; and replenish the earth, and subdue it" (Genesis 1:26, 28). Rule they did.

The description could only refer to the Caucasian race, accord-ing to Muhammad, because they are the only people who have in the last 400 years used their knowledge to subdue all the black peoples; they have even used black people against other blacks to further the white devils' rule. They try to replenish the earth with their own people and try to kill peoples of the black nation by birth control and other devices to maintain their rule.

But they are also destined to lose their control because they cannot live peacefully—even among themselves. Their blue eyes and their "pale white skin" do not have the natural ingredients to foster love, friendship, and true harmony. Black people, on the other hand, are mutually kind and loving and should under-stand that the white devil is by nature evil—blue-eyed, naturally evil imitations of true black humanity.

Allah, being the (black) Creator of the universe, recognizes the inherent evilness of the white devils and will allow them to rule only two thousand years. Allah will then send his representative (Fard) to inform the black people of the white devil's true nature. But Fard's Messenger (Elijah Muhammad) would be the one to end the white devil's two-thousand-year rule. The two thousand years are now up and to end the white devil's rule, blacks must be taught the truth. The one overriding, ineluctable truth is that whites are naturally evil and blacks are naturally good; unlikes repel and likes attract. Blacks must separate themselves from the white devils if blacks are to regain their true identity.[3]

This synopsis of Muslim eschatology is not complete, but it does provide a broad enough framework to understand how the Muslim ideology evolves around the origin of the white devil. Here are some explanations:

—Black people are the original people, made in God's image.
—Black people are basically good, and whites are by nature evil; it is not the whites' fault, it is just their nature.
—Whites went back to Asia and established rule over nine tenths of that continent when Columbus came to the Western Hemisphere. They have been in the United States 400 years and have committed the unpardonable sin of enslaving so-called American Negroes.
—So-called Negro labor has helped build up this land, and when Negroes ask for freedom and pay for their labors, the white devils refuse to share the wealth.
—The white devil will use any means to keep the so-called Negro from knowing his true identity, including feigned acceptance and equality and even intermarriage.
—The devil's worst enemy is unity of the so-called American Negroes. The devil divides them by urging them to accept Christianity, whereas the black man's true religion is Islam.
—So-called American Negroes are really Asiatic people from the tribe of Shabazz.
—The so-called American Negro's only salvation is to separate from the white devil.

The Muslim ideological appeal is based on complete racial separation and is designed to absorb the man in the street; it is designed, like Garvey's Universal Negro Improvement Association, to awaken the great mass of "so-called Negroes" to the truth of their heritage and destiny. The first truth is, according to them, that because Islam is the black man's true religion, all blacks should join the Nation. The second truth is that black people are the Original People, and it is just a matter of time before the white devils will lose their power and control. From these stem subsidiary truths: (1) blacks can never know their true Asian and Islamic names. Therefore, Muslims change their last names to "X" or take on Islamic or Arabic names, for example, Muhammad Shabazz. (2) The Muslims built their organization on a strictly nonwhite basis—again like the UNIA.[4] (3) Blacks and whites must be separated, and therefore (4) blacks must have land for themselves, either in the United States or in Africa or Asia.

The land question is a crucial element in the Muslim ideology because it will ultimately comprise the vehicle for black and white separation. Muhammad makes the point that the Constitution does not have guarantees for blacks, only whites. In any case, it is silly to want to integrate with the four-hundred-year-old enemy. Moreover, nationhood is built on land ownership, and the black nation of Shabazz must have land of its own because no people can live freely without owning its own land.[5]

The Muslim appeal to the mass is calculated to exclude the black bourgeoisie because they are "too far gone" to understand the "truth" of Muhammad's teachings. The black middle class, to its detriment according to the Muslims, has isolated itself from the black mass while deriving its well being from them. But it has only managed to insulate itself minimally from the white devil's machinations, and often acts as the devil's instrument in oppressing the black mass.

It then follows that the Muslims recruit from prisons and street corners and places where the black man is likely to feel most acutely the brunt of white racism. For black prisoners, Muslim membership seems not only to confer higher status and a sense of individuality, but to provide an institutionalized outlet for hostility against white oppression and/or imprisonment. Moreover, for the streetcorner hustler, pimp, prostitute, dope addict, or derelict, the asceticism of the Muslims is an education of sorts about how to get along in the world of white oppression and about the direct and indirect means whereby whites limit black freedom. One indirect means, according to Muhammad, is the teachings of Christianity itself, especially the parts where heaven is somewhere in the sky and God is somewhere up there, too. Muhammad taught that

\There is no such thing as seeing God or the devil after you die. . . . All of that is fantasy, false stories made up by your slave masters to further enslave you. God is a man [Fard] ; the devil is a man [the white man] ; Heaven and Hell are two conditions, and both are right here on this earth. You have already suffered the worst kind of hell [slavery] in the hands of the only real devil.[6] /

This philosophy obviously attracts blacks who have been left out and at the same time questions the efficacy of deferred gratification for the materially deprived black mass.

Whites, then, will eventually be destroyed, and during this destruction blacks will enjoy a sort of Passover (though only if they embrace the Nation of Islam). This Muslim view of "afterlife" coupled with the doctrine of separation is a bridge between black religious indoctrination and political reality—that is, disciplinary doctrines. This means that blacks are barred by whites from even attempting the same achievements as whites. In order to avoid circumvention by whites, blacks must completely separate from whites into their own black communities. The remedies prescribed by Muhammad for curing the ills he finds among blacks go hand in hand with his choice of a predestinarian world view.

Apart from the conditions of white oppression, Muhammad saw the gravest shortcoming of black people as a lack of self-control accompanied by a pervasive, debilitating disunity. Separation was thus designed to enhance black community control and to lessen the psychological impact of white domination. That is, no matter how much blacks are told they are superior to whites, the reality of white presence is always there—economically, politically, and socially. Muhammad, in a speech in Atlanta in 1959, made the point that blacks in the United States have not been allowed the freedom to pursue their talents to their fullest extent. But it is a fact that blacks possess a vast reservoir of talent: black farmers grow food, and many blacks have the knowledge and skill to establish manufacturing concerns and other kinds of businesses and commercial enterprises. In order to utilize this reservoir, however, blacks must rid themselves of the self-hate and inferiority complexes fostered by whites and seek unity and self-determination.[7]

The rigorous Muslim prohibitions against dancing, smoking, adultery, and so on that are sanctioned by and, in turn, become the badge of "chosenness" of the Muslim believer may be seen as an attempt to foster self-help through *individual* rehabilitation. Muhammad attributed black lower-class status and blocked mobility to white oppression, but he did not believe that the solution to the problem lay in appealing to whites. Blacks must sever their ties with whites and purge their communities of undesirable black elements—not by expelling them, but by rehabilitating them (the prisons being a good example). The most expedient mechanism for rehabilitation, both in prison and in black communities, was exoneration of blacks for having succumbed to such vices. As a corollary, blacks must throw off the white man's religion, because it is the religion of the devil and because it has not been of service in making better black communities. Christianity, to Muhammad, was not only the slave master's religion, but also another form of escapism that turned efforts away from communal rehabilitation ("the poor shall be with us always").

The dogma of the Muslims offers both religious and secular alternatives to the plight of black people in America. From their perspective, the white man as devil has a literal meaning, since the oppression of blacks by whites is a documented reality. That blacks must free themselves physically (community control) and psychologically (self-help and rehabilitation) presupposes the elimination of whites from positions of control over the lives of black people.

Other aspects of the Nation's ideology touch on quasi-political isolationism, individual self-improvement, psychological and physical migrationism and emigrationism, and cultural and "economic" nationalism. In short, the Black Muslims believe that the Nation of Islam is a nation within a nation.

It has been noted that the late Malcolm X played a significant role in the Nation of Islam. In fact, he spent most of his active political life in the Muslim movement, and he therefore deserves special mention.

Malcolm X or El-Hajj Malik El-Shabazz

One could safely conclude that in the late 1950's and the first three or four years of the 60's, Malcolm X was largely responsible for the increased publicity, interest, and membership in the Muslim organization. He was at once the most popular figure in the Muslim organization (even more well known than Elijah Muhammad, and most certainly a better speaker) and a leading figure in the development of black pride and awareness. He led black people to reexamine the positions and the outlook on life designed for them by whites. He therefore also deserves a special place in the neoseparatist surge that followed after the mid-60's, especially by younger black people.

As a Muslim, Malcolm X became Elijah Muhammad's right-hand man, a spokesman for the Muslims, and one of the organization's leading ideologues, finally becoming a minister. His sharp mind and eloquent speech often served to elaborate Muhammad's often cryptic and halting exhortations about the black man's plight. An example can be seen in Muhammad's rejection of "Negro":

> I say "so-called" because you are *not* a *"Negro."* There is no such thing as a race of *"Negroes."* . . . You are members of the Asiatic nation, from the tribe of *Shabazz.* "Negro" is a false label forced upon you by your slave master![8]

Malcolm later elaborated on the argument:

> The black man's history [goes] way back, but when you refer to him as a Negro, you can only go as far back as the Negro goes. [Going] beyond the shores of America looking for the history of the black man, and you're looking for him under the term Negro, you won't find him. He doesn't exist. So you end up thinking you didn't play any role in history.[9]

Malcolm X originally accepted the Muslim position that the white race was inherently evil, and therefore black people must separate from them. He led blacks to understand their position in the world. To accept the status of a minority group in the United States was wrong in view of the fact that Third World peoples constituted 70 percent of the world's population. The truth was that white people were the real minority; in the United States, black people were victims of "internal colonialism," and the black communities in the United States were no different from those in European-held Third World colonies.

Malcolm X rejected the charge that he and the Muslims were black racists, the other side of the Ku Klux Klan coin. He pointed out that the Muslims had never lynched anyone and—to draw the analogy with the Klan—would have much bloodshed to catch up with. The Muslims never initiated violence but were often its victims. Though the Fruit of Islam (FOI) seemed to be the organization's paramilitary arm, Malcolm and other Muslim officials insisted that it is only a protective mechanism—mostly to protect the Nation's leaders and other officials. (Perhaps the violence perpetrated by "official" societal control agencies, such as the police, was designed to influence the FOI to engage in battle, and so decimate it, eliminating the "threat.") But Malcolm rejected nonviolence as a tactic, claiming that Dr. Martin Luther

King and other apostles of nonviolence were misguided if they thought the white devil would suddenly feel guilty while beating black demonstrators. He counseled blacks to defend themselves when attacked, though he never advocated initiating violence.

Intermarriage and integration (integrate into what?) were rejected by Malcolm because he saw the former as a ploy to destroy blacks through biological assimilation and the latter as folly. Why, he asked, would the white slave masters' grandchildren and great-grandchildren want to integrate with the descendants of their ancestors' slaves? Moreover, why would the slaves' grandchildren want to integrate with inherently evil devils? Even during slavery, according to Malcolm, there were *Blacks* (field niggers) who rejected their positions and revolted, like Gabriel Prosser, Denmark Vesey, and "Nat" Turner. *Negroes* (house niggers), on the other hand, accepted their plight and even empathized with an ill master (oh Lawdy, Masta, we is sick!). Real *blacks* would help the master out of his misery!

Malcolm's belief in the Muslim self-help doctrine sent him fishing for converts on the streets, in pool halls, and anywhere down-and-out blacks might be found. Because of his own experience and what he saw around him, he came to regard drug addiction as one of the most dangerous elements "keeping the black man down." In fact, he regarded heroin, cocaine, and other addictive drugs as deliberate instruments used by whites to keep the black ghetto politically and economically impotent. Hence, he waged war against pushers and peddlers, whom he regarded as pawns in the employ of larger forces. He wondered how it was that they could openly exhibit their wares even in the presence of policemen and not be apprehended, while a child taking an apple from a supermarket would be pursued, caught, and put away in a place for juvenile delinquents. He concluded that the source of the drug supply—and its middlemen—had to be attacked.

The prominence and publicity soon made Malcolm X a celebrity, especially among many young blacks, and a menace to white control agencies. He became a much sought-after speaker on the white college circuit, and he began to travel abroad. Although the broadened travel and contact had an impact on his thinking, he remained a staunch Muslim, ideologically and politically. But in November 1963 John F. Kennedy was assassinated, and Malcolm, adhering to Muslim ideology, commented that the assassination was "the chickens coming home to roost." He likewise evaluated a plane crash, killing a large number of whites, in essence, as, "Allah taking care of business." These statements were too much for Elijah Muhammad. Among other reasons, public sentiment—black and white—against the Muslims was greatly aggravated by Malcolm's statements. By suspending him Muhammad exhibited his and the organization's sympathy for the slain President and the white air crash victims while at the same time cooling a potential hot rival for the organization's leadership. Malcolm and the Nation of Islam never recovered from his suspension.

Many factors were responsible for Malcolm X's transformation, chief among them his belief that Elijah Muhammad wanted him dead[10] and his changing beliefs about the political role blacks should play. In short, he differed with Elijah Muhammad on the issue of the Nation of Islam's political involvement in the civil rights movement and in the general political nature of the black struggle. The Muslims at that time believed that black people should not become involved in the white man's politics and that blacks should spend all their time on self-improvement.[11] In effect, Malcolm criticized the Nation's predestination dogma— the white "devils" would be destroyed by Allah—as another means of nonpolitical involvement. He observes:

> Muhammad was with Allah . . . the rest of us have not seen Allah; we don't have this divine patience, and we are not so willing to wait on God. The younger Black Muslims want to see some action.[12]

Malcolm began his Muslim career accepting the Muslim's concept of complete territorial separation. Careful reading of his last speeches and public statements suggests that he eventually rejected complete black territorial separatism as undesirable and unattainable, but he nevertheless continued to espouse other forms of black nationalism. He still believed that the Black Muslim program—minus territorial separation—was best for black American liberation. He believed that white people per se were not inherently evil, but rather the American political, economic, and social systems made white Americans racist and evil.[13] While visiting the Middle East and Africa, he was amazed that peoples of all colors lived under Islam peacefully together with color mattering not at all. Malcolm was impressed by an African diplomat who indicated to him that "as long as he was on the African continent, he never thought in terms of race, that he dealt with human beings, never noticing their color. He said he was more aware of language differences than of color differences.

He said that only when he returned to America would he become aware of color differences."[14]

After visiting the Middle East and Africa, Malcolm X, who now adopted the Arabic name El-Hajj Malik El-Shabazz, indicated that black liberation required political organization and involvement. Early in 1965, therefore, he founded the Organization of Afro-American Unity (OAAU) in Harlem as an umbrella or United Front organization designed to encompass all the disparate black liberation groups and organizations, nationalist, separatist, and integrationist, but no white groups.

Malcolm X was killed in February 1965. Beyond his original statements about the OAAU, his ultimate organizational goals will never be known, but it is certain that although he remained committed to the Nation, he differed with Elijah Muhammad's style of Islam. What is of paramount importance is Malcolm's political conception of the black struggle, which gives a clue to the ideology and philosophy of contemporary black separatist thought. The OAAU was based on the idea that black-white solidarity must exist, but it can be brought about only after blacks organize themselves.[15]

Though Malcolm X will never return to electrify audiences with his fiery rhetoric, put down white racists with his agile mind, embarrass middle-class blacks who oppose his program, or bring his sharp insight to bear on complex problem-solving, he is alive in the minds and souls of many black and white Americans, even if for different reasons. It is safe to say that among many young black people today, Malcolm X achieved fame. More importantly, his legacy and teachings were passed on to other separatist/nationalist movement organizations.

The Student Non-Violent Coordinating Committee (SNCC)

A discussion of separatist movement ideology necessarily pays some attention to the civil rights movement because two of separatism's principal actors—CORE and SNCC—grew out of it. To understand separatism it is necessary to explain some of the integration-oriented forces responsible for its emergence. It is ironic that separatism emerged from the intense integration-oriented movement. The following is a brief overview of SNCC's emergence as an organization and how it came to accept separatism.

The sit-in movement in the South in the late 1950's was responsible for SNCC's emergence as an organization. At first the sit-ins consisted mostly of young southern blacks, but they later attracted nationwide attention and participation from many groups: Catholics, Protestants, Jews—young and old blacks and whites.

The sit-ins, which had been used earlier in the North by CORE, caught by surprise Southern segregationists and conservative, traditional black organizations. The NAACP and CORE, for example, had no plans for large-scale, direct-action sit-ins in the South. The Southern Christian Leadership Conference (SCLC), which grew out of the Rosa Parks-inspired Montgomery Bus Boycott led by Fred Shuttlesworth and Martin Luther King, Jr., among others, had an office in Atlanta but no plans for the mass action characterized by the sit-ins. In many instances some old-guard Negro organizations attempted to stem the sit-in tide; some publicly supported them while simultaneously continuing to undermine their continuation, but to no avail, because these young blacks were adamant and refused to relent. "We are not going to allow anyone to turn us around—our eyes are on the sparrow."

Despite the persistence and spread of the sit-ins, they had no true organization or direction; they just happened in community after community, often as an end in themselves because they were usually emotional and individual acts. Seeing the need to provide purpose and direction, however, Ella Baker, a graduate of Shaw University in Raleigh, North Carolina, and a long-time civil rights activist who, in 1957, had come South to organize mass rallies for SCLC, decided to act. She had established the SCLC office in Atlanta, and from there, in late February 1960, she asked for and received $800 from SCLC leadership to finance a meeting in late February 1960 of sit-in leaders at Shaw University in Raleigh. It was not until Easter weekend that the meeting took place, mainly because of the spread of demonstrations and the ensuing difficulty of gathering people together. Nevertheless, the meeting was attended by about 200 delegates, 126 of them "student delegates from fifty-eight different southern communities in twelve states."

Though the gathering was sponsored by SCLC, the group decided to become operationally independent. A temporary committee, with Ed King as administrative secretary, was established, meeting monthly to coordinate the various student movements throughout the South. In May 1960 the entire group met again at Atlanta University and established the Temporary Student Non-Violent Coordinating Committee (TSNCC). Marion Barry, a graduate student at Fisk University, was elected chairman.

TSNCC adopted nonviolence as its philosophy and set up its office in one corner of the Atlanta SCLC office. By October 1960, it had become a viable organization and had dropped the T. It now consisted of one delegate from each of the sixteen southern states and the District of Columbia. Delegates from other organizations, such as the NAACP, SCLC, National Student Association, Southern Education Fund., etc., also had voting privileges.

Significantly, SNCC became an organization that deliberately paid little attention to proper bureaucratic procedure and behavior. From the outset it operated on the principle of getting maximum mileage out of particular events and utilizing individual capabilities: it initially focused on sit-ins, then on the "Jail – No Bail" aspect of the movement; its newsletter, *The Student Voice,* focused on the SNCC'ers who were "doing something." One SNCC newsletter, for example, carried a poem by Julian Bond, one of SNCC's founders, affirming that he, too, heard America singing; and from his perspective, "Fats" Domino, "Little Richard," Ray Charles, Charlie Parker, and Horace Silver, among others, gave him the strength to "keep on keeping on."[16]

SNCC continued to branch out, encompassing more activities, tactics, and personnel. Michel's "Iron Law of Oligarchy" (the centalizing tendency) never caught up with it. Seven convenient stages to 1966 can be identified: (1) in 1961 SNCC joined CORE in the Freedom Rides, where both groups experienced extreme white-racist violence, making the violence associated with the sit-ins tame by comparison. This white violence merely set the stage for questioning the efficacy of nonviolence. (Do these people have any morality to which we can appeal?)

(2) Among the victims of white mob violence were James Forman, John Lewis, Robert Moses, Stokely Carmichael from SNCC, and James Farmer, CORE's national director. (Can we honestly continue our philosophy of nonviolence in light of this inhuman violence?)

(3) In 1961–62 the Freedom Rides exposed another myth and taught SNCC and CORE a lesson about the nature of justice regarding black people. The truth, as opposed to the myth, was that although racism was not confined to the South, only there was it allowed to exhibit itself openly and violently. The Freedom Riders demonstrated that official justice at the highest levels (the Department of Justice) refused to come to their aid even when there was irrefutable evidence that it should do so.

(4) The August 1963 March on Washington found about a quarter of a million people gathered in the nation's capital to

protest injustice. The demonstrators were interrracial, interfaith, and intergenerational. Despite all the eloquence that followed, all the hopes that were aroused, all the good will that was generated, and all the peace that prevailed, one statement was not made. John Lewis, one of the victims of white mob violence and then SNCC's chairman, had prepared a speech for the Washington occasion, but Archbishop Patrick O'Boyle felt that part of it was too strong. The omitted material pointed out that the federal government had the legal and constitutional powers to circumvent white violence in the South, but declined to use it. Lewis asked—but not in his speech that day—"Whose side is the government on?" ("Could it be that the government is on the side of the oppressor?")

(5) In 1964 the bombing of black churches (at one killing three little black girls while attending Sunday School); the murder of civil rights workers Michael Schwerner, Andrew Goodman, and James Chaney, among others; the daily beatings and continued humiliation—all convinced some SNCC and CORE members that other methods of fighting oppression should be pursued. Voter registration—under the Council of Federated Organizations (COFO), comprised of CORE, SNCC, NAACP, and SCLC, which had been organized in 1962—again became an important mechanism. Since most blacks in the Deep South did not vote because of white-imposed literacy tests ("Can you read a Chinese newspaper? or interpret the Constitution?"), the poll tax, and other locally contrived exclusionary devices, COFO at first did not concentrate on voting.

SNCC hit upon the idea of holding a black election. Blacks first attempted to vote in "official" elections and were turned away. From these disenfranchised voters in Mississippi, SNCC drew up a slate of candidates (both black and white) and held its own election. There was an 80 percent voter turnout (proving that blacks *wanted* to vote, but were illegally barred from doing so). The Mississippi Freedom Democratic Party (MFDP) was then sent to the 1964 National Democratic Convention to challenge the regular, all-white, nonrepresentative delegation. There, seating of the MFDP delegation as a group was denied by the leadership of the Democratic Party in favor of the racist delegation! ("How can black people gain political autonomy over their lives in the face of pervasive white political domination?")

(6) Still reeling from the shock of their rejection at the "Democratic" convention, SNCC began to question whether it should become an all-black organization, and at the same time it began to

wonder whether black political action alone was the best solution to black oppression.

(7) In 1965 SNCC answered those questions by organizing the Lowndes County Freedom Organization, taking the position that blacks must lead their own organizations, thus eliminating white leaders. By 1966 SNCC had moved to eliminate whites from the organization. This painful action cost SNCC dearly in terms of support—both moral and financial—but these young black people felt they were right. SNCC elected Stokely Carmichael chairman, and when on the Meredith Mississippi Freedom March he cried, "Black Power!" the spread of black separatism was ensured.

The Student National Coordination Committee (SNCC)

In 1966 SNCC became an all-black organization. To most of the white public, "Black Power" sounded anti-integrationist and emotionally dreadful.[17] But SNCC felt that in order for black people to speak from a position of strength, they should and must organize themselves without white help; in order to control their political, social, and economic lives, they must control their own communities through Black Power. The phrase has been defined many times by leaders black and white. The most authoritative definition could be expected from the person who used the term first, but because it had many implications, and because white people found it threatening, black men and women have had to define it again and again.[18]

Initially, SNCC was an interracial organization primarily concerned with nonviolent change in the South. Because educated white Northerners held many of the leadership positions and made many of the organizational decisions, the black members felt that this was simply another case of white paternalism. Some black members felt that what black people needed were black models of leadership and black decision-makers. Hence, SNCC's separatism was based on its belief in black people determining their own destinies—in other words, black power independent of white power. The immediate outcome was expulsion of whites from leadership positions (and eventually from the organization), but SNCC was basing its conception of independent black power on two prior experiences, one in the immediate past, the other more remote. SNCC was responsible for the establishment of the Mississippi Freedom Democratic Party (MFDP), which challenged the "regular" delegation in 1964 at the Democratic National Convention when the MFDP was compromised in favor of the traditional, racist delegation. SNCC was then convinced that whites could not be trusted and that blacks must determine their own destiny by any means necessary. This experience led SNCC to believe that blacks should no longer enter into political coalitions with whites. That was the most recent example. For an earlier one, they cited the Reconstruction period as a time when whites used blacks for their own purposes until they were no longer necessary.

To negate the possibility of whites ever again using blacks for their own aggrandizement, SNCC called for totally independent political action outside the established political parties. The Lowndes County Freedom Party established in Lowndes County, Alabama, is an example: One year after the 1964 Democratic Convention, SNCC laid the foundation for the building of the Lowndes County Freedom Organization in Alabama. "Democratic" was dropped for obvious reasons. The party's symbol became the Black Panther (which later took on an even greater significance when Huey Newton and Bobby Seale organized the Black Panther Party).

Community control of black institutions and black destinies was an outgrowth of SNCC's experience in the Deep South. Julius Lester, a former SNCC field secretary, felt that the idea of letting the people lead themselves developed out of SNCC's experience in Mississippi:

> SNCC field workers provided the impetus to a community, but let the community choose its leaders from its own ranks. To symbolize their new feeling, they [the SNCC field workers] began wearing denim work overalls, saying that they, too, were one of the community, that community of the poor. They rejected the idea of the "talented tenth" [DuBois' alternative to Washington's emphasis on vocational training] who would come out of the colleges to lead. There would be no "talented tenth." Only the Community.[19]

Many times SNCC field workers organized a voter registration drive only to have people march down to the place of registration to be physically and psychologically victimized. The net result was that the Southern black community began to favor organization in order to exhibit black power at the polls and help to ensure that their votes would be counted in state elections. This action by SNCC was an important factor in the passage of the Voting Rights Bill.

SNCC expanded its ideology from black political control of black communities in the rural South to cultural and political nationalism and separatism in the North. Even in the South, SNCC rejected the "talented tenth" concept and did the same as it stretched its ever broadening ideological wings to the urban North. SNCC's Chicago office, for example, pointed out that "the black brother in the ghetto will lead the black power movement and make the changes that are necessary for its success." SNCC equates the poor rural Southern black with the poor Northern "ghetto brother." Both, according to SNCC, had been given the short end of the stick by the black bourgeoisie acting on behalf of the white power structure. Bourgeois blacks could not be a part of the Black Power Movement because they lived between the white world and the true black society, essentially marginal people with divided loyalties. These black caricatures of white capitalists, despite their superior education and expertise, cannot be trusted under any circumstances unless they are cured of the disease of white values. Meanwhile, the "ghetto brothers," the street brothers and blacks not afflicted with white values, must lead the Black Power Movement.

The leadership of the ghetto brothers is desired because these people already live outside the white-imposed value system; they already operate from the perspective of a black value system. These brothers already believe that black is better than white because, among other reasons, blacks—unlike whites—do not suffer the guilt of having enslaved and exploited, dehumanized, and murdered millions of blacks and other non-whites for their own selfish ends. Thus the result of white atrocities makes it easier for the street brothers to "hate all things white."

SNCC's Chicago contingent believed that the implication was clear: black people had to regain their own lost customs, values, and life styles. Specifically, black people must cease worshiping a white Jesus and white Christianity; blacks must "regain respect for the lost religion of our fathers, the spirits of the black earth of Africa." Besides religion, black people must regain or create their own language to ensure that whites cannot understand black conversation. In addition, the masses must also be educated to the truth of other elements of blackness. As examples, blacks who wear diamonds are actually contributing to black exploitation and dehumanization of black brothers and sisters in South Africa, where one of every three black babies die before the age of one; black men must not go to other countries to exterminate other non-white people. In order to create a sane black society, blacks "must disrupt the white man's system"; blacks must publish their own newspapers and obtain their own radio stations. In short, "black unity is strength—let's use it now to give Black Power."[20]

Other significant outgrowths of SNCC's ideology were the concepts of internal colonialism and the Third World and a reemphasis on Pan-Africanism (since Pan-Negroism or Pan-Africanism has long been an ideology in the black world). SNCC indicated that black people in America are in a perpetual state of slavery and are exploited and oppressed like black people all over the world. This pointed up the connections between universal non-white colonization, exploitation, and white oppression in general. Black Americans are not alone in the struggle for self-determination, but are a part of a worldwide network of liberation efforts. Black Americans must unite and be ready to help blacks and other oppressed peoples everywhere. Because blacks in America live inside the most powerful of the enemy camps, they are duty bound to other oppressed peoples to revolt against, and thus weaken, the bulwark of Third World oppression. Oppressed whites were conspicuously omitted from the Third World, based on SNCC's operational definitions of colonization and exploitation.

Stokely Carmichael differentiated colonization and exploitation in relationship to the oppressed poor whites. He observed that there should be a united front composed of Asian, native, and Chicano Americans, Puerto Ricans, and all non-white people, but not the poor whites. The reason was that poor whites are exploited and the blacks are colonized: "Exploitation is when you exploit somebody of your own race. Colonization is when you exploit somebody of a different race. We [the blacks] are colonized. They are exploited [the poor whites]."[21] Carmichael and Charles V. Hamilton observe: "To put it another way . . . black people in this country form a colony, and it is not in the interest of the colonial power to liberate them. Black people are legal citizens of the United States with . . . the same *legal* rights as other citizens. Yet they stand as colonial subjects in relation to white society. Thus institutional racism has another name: Colonialism."[22] They contend that the colonial status of black people—but not whites—operates in three areas: political, economic, and social. Politically, internal colonialism operates because the colonial subjects have their political decisions made for them through "indirect rule"—that is, the decisions are made by the white power structure. The ghetto is economically exploited from the outside, which leaves it dependent upon the larger society. Equating the paternalistic attitudes of poverty agencies with the paternalism of African missionaries, Carmichael and Hamilton conclude that the historical, political, and economic results of colonialism are the same—they relegate blacks to an inferior position.[23]

"Internal colonialism" is related to Pan-Africanism and the Third World in that all non-white peoples are exploited by whites, and Carmichael wanted blacks to join the Third World, believing it to be the only way to save black humanity and bring about black salvation, which the West has failed to do. The struggle must be waged from the Third World if it is to be successful.[24]

The land question was another important factor in SNCC's ideology. SNCC mostly dealt with that question by calling for political control of the land in the rural South and in the Northern ghetto, "community control," as it were. But some SNCC members insisted that territorial separatism was necessary. Carmichael proposed to solve the land question by joining a land base in Africa and/or conceivably acquiring land in the United States.

In sum SNCC maintained that black power means the political and economic power and cultural independence of black people to determine their destiny individually and collectively, in and out of their own communities. SNCC asserted that blacks in America constitute a colony and that the situation of black people is no different from that of oppressed, colonized peoples throughout the world. This was later linked to the oppressed condition of the Third World. SNCC also maintained that black people all over the world are of African descent and that all blacks should return to Africa.

The outstanding spokesmen for SNCC were Stokely Carmichael, H. "Rap" Brown, James Forman, and John Lewis. SNCC was the vanguard organization—following and emulating Malcolm X, the individual—for the development of black power in the black community. Evidently SNCC's ideological development never transcended Malcolm's philosophy. It is fair to say, however, that the young souls in SNCC were profoundly affected by Malcolm's philosophy while he lived, and probably even more after he died.

The Congress of Racial Equality (CORE)

CORE originated in 1942 as a nonviolent direct-action protest movement. "It articulated the philosophy and applied the tactics of non-violent direct action for nearly two decades before the 'civil rights revolution' burst upon the national scene in 1960."[25] From 1960 to the present, CORE has shifted its ideology, goals, and tactics to fit changing needs, desires, and perceptions of what is necessary to effect black liberation in America.

Between CORE's beginnings and its present status are the specific and general developments responsible for the organization's shift from integration to separation. In general, the two decades from 1940 to 1960 may be characterized as periods when blacks—as well as their white allies—struggled for liberation by fighting for racial equality—integration. The 1960's introduced nuances in sentiments, tactics, ideologies, and goals which influenced many individual blacks as well as black civil rights organizations geared to alleviate black oppression—CORE among them—to question integration as the main thrust of the black struggle for liberation. By 1963-64 the outcome of the questioning resulted in a shift from interracial, integration-oriented activities and programs to ones specifically aimed at the black poor in the rural Deep South (mostly SNCC) and in black ghettoes in the North (mostly CORE).

Ironically, the most extreme changes undertaken by CORE were blueprinted by James Farmer, once its charismatic national director, who led the organization through the militant integration period from the sit-ins of the early 1960's to the formal abandonment of integration as an organizational goal in 1966. Farmer's proposals in his book *Freedom—When?* may be taken, in fact, as the basis of CORE's black power position in the Northern ghettoes.[26] The irony is that Farmer chose not to remain CORE's national director after its adoption of black power as its formal ideological posture. Having some reservations about CORE's use of the slogan, he stepped down in favor of Floyd McKissick, who had no reservations at all about it.

Black Power caused a great deal of confusion among members of CORE. To some it meant black capitalism, to others it meant black cultural nationalism, and to still others it meant black nationalism *and* being anti-white. These attitudes culminated in a change in CORE's leadership and ideological direction. Here is how it happened.

James Farmer charted the new direction for CORE in the light of the "new" insights he had gained from Malcolm X and the realization of the importance of the economic problems facing the black masses. These new insights, combined with the black nationalist tradition in Northern ghettoes, prompted him to propose solutions in the form of programs that would appeal to all segments of the urban ghettoes, including the nationalists. (a) Farmer, though not personally convinced, implemented CORE's decision to enter politics as a result of tremendous pressure by the membership; CORE, like the Muslims, had been a nonpartisan organization. (b) He prompted the organization to develop cooperatives, especially in the South, conceived and operated by black people. (c) He opposed, again because of membership pressure, the election of a white person as national director of CORE. (d) Finally, he proposed community development as a means of prompting self-help among black ghetto dwellers.

Farmer may be called the architect of CORE's new position, but for two reasons he was not the engineer: (1) CORE membership and (2) Farmer's own background and ideological orientation. In the first place, it had been suggested that the membership, not the leadership, was responsible for the organization's shift from integration to separation. Even by 1963 the black membership in CORE had become concerned about the black ghetto, with CORE's traditional goal of integration becoming less important. Always sensitive to desires of the membership, Farmer began to make it clear that the black ghettoes could no longer be ignored. Hence, he was prompted by the black members of CORE to devise a program to speak to the ghetto constituency—aided and abetted by the temper of the times. (It may be more accurate to say that CORE's new direction was charted by a number of people, among them Rudy Lombard, Roy Innis, and the late Dr. George Wiley, but Farmer was the chief spokesman.) Thus in 1964, at CORE's national convention in Durham, North Carolina, the theme was the "Black Ghetto: An Awakening Giant."

In the second place, Farmer's background of passivity and belief in nonviolence may have inhibited him from actually implementing the new position of black power. After having joined the Quaker Friends of Reconciliation (FOR) in the early 1940's and being instrumental in organizing CORE in 1942, his belief in nonviolence was probably too deep to abandon in its entirety. In addition, Farmer at one time believed that integration was not just one more way to deal with the problems of segregation, inequality, and injustice; he also saw it as the essence of freedom. He writes, "The only way Negro separation would not mean segregation is if the Negro *chooses* to live separately, and this will happen only when total freedom of choice is a reality in America."[27]

Among CORE members there emerged another force which may have contributed to Farmer's decision to step down as national director. Some CORE members—being mostly middle class—believed that black people must first tackle the economic question, because without a solid economic base all other questions are academic. Hence, black capitalism became a major factor, along with the shift to black power. The idea that black capitalism offered black people the same opportunity as other Americans had, of course, been proposed by many as *the* solution to the question of black oppression.

Though Farmer did not oppose black capitalism as one of the important factors in aiding the black cause, it was Black Power and its separatist implication that bothered him.[28] They did not bother Floyd B. McKissick, CORE's next national director. Farmer, having concluded that the CORE membership would adopt Black Power and its separatist implication as its new slogan, acknowledged the winds of change and stepped down as national director in March 1965. He was replaced by McKissick, who guided the organization into the Baltimore National Convention, which endorsed Black Power. "At the 1966 CORE convention in Baltimore, all the radicalizing trends of the past several years converged and exploded, precipitating a clear break with CORE's nonviolent, integrationist past."[29] McKissick, not Farmer, represented CORE's new direction. Farmer did remain an active member, but he continued to endorse only those basic principles for which he had worked so long and hard: nonviolence, desegregation, and individual freedom.

McKissick, a graduate of Morehouse College in Atlanta and the Law School of the University of North Carolina, was militant and articulate; many CORE members felt that he was the right man in the right place. Among other things, McKissick proposed in 1967—as SNCC had done earlier—that blacks consolidate their voting strength, and called for an independent political party; he by no means rejected capitalism per se, but opposed it as a solution to black oppression, largely because blacks could not get into the system. Because of the pent-up hostility in the black ghetto, McKissick urged that CORE act as an intermediary between angry, militant ghetto dwellers and corporate and governmental interests. Predicting eventual confrontation between the power structure and the ghettoes, he suggested that CORE could help avert a confrontation and thus alter America's self-destructive course if CORE's economic programs were adequately funded and put into action.[30]

During McKissick's tenure, there was a steadily growing militant shift, among young blacks especially, and most established organizations showed a militant tendency. CORE, despite the militant and articulate McKissick, found it difficult to focus only on its programs for ghetto dwellers. Its membership was also composed of people who felt that militant rhetoric about the black plight ought to be matched with ideological conviction; that conviction turned out to be not only abandoning integration as a goal (as the membership had advocated at the Baltimore convention in 1966), but embracing black nationalism and separatism as CORE's overt ideology. McKissick was perhaps not totally opposed to all aspects of black nationalism, but he felt that the economic and ideological questions should not be confused. Seemingly a Washington-Garvey hybrid, believing that the key to power in the United States was economic power, he chose to continue emphasizing the black capitalist direction, thus losing popularity and support.

In 1968 at the Cincinnati convention, Roy Innis replaced McKissick as CORE's national director. Innis styled himself a black nationalist and defined black power as the "methodology for the implementation of the goals of black nationalism" and black nationalism as the "philosophy of self-determination of an oppressed people." According to Innis, the only acceptable solution to the problems of black people in America was the nationalist solution. That is, the existing institutional and geographic separation of blacks and whites in urban centers can be defined as "natural sociological units." But they must also be defined in political terms, because these units are unequal as they now exist. They must be equalized through "parallel institutional systems" because, as the result of years of institutional racism, blacks are exploited and oppressed. Whites will eventually allow this arrangement, according to Innis, because "blacks have the ability to withdraw a sacred commodity from America: peace and tranquility." Moreoever, Innis contended—somewhat like McKissick—that genocide was the only alternative to the CORE program. "He told the CORE delegates [in 1968] that for the white power structure the choice of options will be based on anticipated costs. He thinks genocide is much more expensive, both in terms of money and in terms of white lives."[31]

Under Innis' leadership CORE proposed that Harlem should be governed not by the New York City Board of Education, but rather by a black board of education, elected by Harlem residents. Moreover, if Harlem became a separate school system, the legis-

SEPARATIST IDEOLOGIES, I 121

lature of the State of New York should allocate funds directly to the Harlem (black) school board. This means that the New York City School Board would be bypassed and the children of Harlem would receive an education geared to black values and goals. CORE accepted the neighborhood school concept and opposed busing to achieve racial balance. Underlying Innis' and CORE's position on education and politics was the concept of community control.

CORE's programs and proposals for the elimination of black oppression under McKissick centered on black capitalism through self-help, governmental aid, and private business involvement. However, Roy Innis had broadened his nationalist involvement by paying some attention to Pan-Africanism. He had, in fact, visited Uganda in an effort to promote the relationship of Africans and black Americans. He was seeking to persuade both black Americans and Africans of the benefit of trained black American personnel going to Africa to aid in economic development. These efforts on the part of Innis were in the tradition of Washington and Garvey. Some have said that CORE, like Washington, promoted "bourgeois nationalism" and was the contemporary exemplification of these historical movements.

CORE, in its early age of Black Power, closely identified with SNCC; their basic beliefs and ideologies were not significantly different. However, some CORE individuals advocated working within the system—even though the organization opposed it—and forming alliances with other white groups. The CORE leaders were favorably disposed toward cooperatives but more inclined toward job-training and developing a black economic base centered in the ghetto.

In summary, at the outset CORE was an interracial movement organization specifically oriented toward promoting racial equality; it is currently a black separatist organization, having excluded white membership entirely by 1968. In its beginning, CORE promoted Ghandian nonviolence; currently the organization endorses armed self-defense, though it has never directly utilized it. As it developed, by the mid-1960's it had numerous chapters stretching from the East Coast to the West; today CORE consists of a national headquarters with considerably fewer chapters. At the beginning it was rooted in the American pacifist movement of the 1930's, specifically the Christian Pacifist Fellowship of Reconciliation (FOR); today it is based on black separatism/ nationalism geared to eliminate black oppression. It began under the charismatic guidance and direction of James Farmer, born in Marshall, Texas; its present director is Roy Innis, a native of St. Croix, Virgin Islands.

The ideological evolution of SNCC and CORE from integration to separatism has been seen as the need of the organizations to accommodate situations and circumstances militating against integration as a practical goal. The Nation of Islam's separatist posture—aided by Malcolm X's cogent and incisive rhetoric and ideas—eventually became less objectionable as an ideology. SNCC and CORE then adopted a separatist ideology which varied from that of the Nation of Islam as well as between the two organizations themselves. Chapter 7 will consider the Black Panther Party and the Republic of New Africa.

7 SEPARATIST IDEOLOGIES, II

The Black Panther Party and the Republic of New Africa (RNA) must have concluded that the Nation of Islam, CORE, and SNCC did not have the correct ideological or strategic approach to black liberation, for although they organized late, the Panthers in 1966 and the RNA in 1968, they considered themselves a vanguard, utilizing openly antitraditional approaches and tactics. The Panthers called themselves "Revolutionary Black Nationalists," and the RNA proposed to establish a black nation in the "Wilderness of North America." Though much of their rhetoric is not unlike that of the other three organizations, their ideological content and modes of operation are different enough from them to merit separate discussion.

The Black Panther Party

The Black Panthers were formed in Oakland, California, in October 1966 by Huey P. Newton and Bobby Seale.[1] It was the martyred Malcolm X's emphasis on self-defense and his effort to lead the struggle for freedom "by any means necessary" that most impressed Newton and Seale, and they frequently quoted his famous statement: "We should be peaceful, law-abiding, but the time has come to fight back in self-defense whenever and wherever the black man is being unjustly and unlawfully attacked. If the government thinks I am wrong for saying this, then let the government do its job." The government did not do its job, and Huey Newton and Bobby Seale broke away from the Soul Students

Advisory Council of Merritt College and formed the Black Panther Party for Self-Defense. (The Panther symbol came from the Lowndes County Freedom Organization that SNCC had launched in Alabama six months earlier. The Panther, according to Newton, symbolizes an animal that will not attack but will tenaciously defend itself.) The name was later shortened to Black Panther Party because the aim of the organization grew to include more than self-defense. In October 1966 the new party launched a ten-point platform and program.[2]

At the outset the Panthers seemed to be little more than just another local group of black nationalists basing their ideology on the practical problems of the urban ghetto. They were unique, however, in that they had armed patrols which drove through the streets of Oakland and kept watch on the police who had wrought havoc in the black community by using unnecessary force. Newton, the Party's chief ideologist, had attended San Francisco Law School for a year. He knew the law governing the bearing of arms, and he made sure that the armed Panther patrols stuck to the letter of the law. For example, the Panthers—with gun and law book in hand—would follow police cars through the black community in Oakland to put a stop to police brutality. They would make sure that blacks stopped by the police did not have their rights violated. Predictably, the police took a dim view of this action, but the black community was greatly impressed. They were even more impressed when Newton, Seale, and others faced down a group of policemen outside Panther Headquarters. The black community had every good reason to see the Panthers in a different light because police brutality ceased, or at least became minimal. The Panthers became the talk of the town, and it was clear that black talk differed significantly from white talk.[3]

The Panthers indeed engaged in more than self-defense (though this endeavor could have taken full time). They were deeply involved in protesting rent eviction, informing welfare recipients of their legal rights, teaching classes in Black History, and demanding and winning school traffic lights. (The traffic lights were important because on one corner where there should have been a light, the authorities refused to supply one, despite the fact that several black children had been killed coming home from school. The black community was enraged because of the authorities' indifference. Newton told the Oakland authorities that if a light was not installed, the Panthers would come down with guns and block traffic to ensure the safe crossing of the students. The traffic light was installed.)

The party's initial successes with arms spread far and wide. They became more than the talk of the town, they became the talk of the country. Another publicity factor was that Eldridge Cleaver, author of *Soul on Ice,* became a member of the party. He tells how much impressed he was when an armed guard of Black Panthers escorted Mrs. Betty Shabazz (widow of Malcolm X) on her appearance at Black House, San Francisco:

> The most beautiful sight I had ever seen. Four black men wearing black berets, powder-blue shirts, black leather jackets, black trousers, shiny black shoes—and each with a gun! In front was Huey P. Newton. Beside him was Bobby Hutton [who was later murdered by the police]. Where was my mind? Blown![4]

Cleaver joined the party and became Minister of Information and the central figure in the Party's ideological formulation.

Huey Newton wrote in *Ebony* that the Black Panthers were revolutionary nationalists as opposed to cultural nationalists and that they did not believe it was necessary to return to the culture of eleventh-century Africa (the Ghana-Mali-Songhai era). The reality of the present made it necessary for the Panthers not to retreat to the past; the African heritage must be respected and the useful aspects would be kept, but the outdated—though unique—elements would not form the basis of Panther behavior.[5]

The almost complete rejection of African heritage stemmed from Newton's definition of revolutionary and reactionary nationalism. Revolutionary nationalism had as its goal putting the people in power—"Power to the People."[6] Reactionary or cultural nationalism resulted in the oppression of the people. He pointed out that cultural nationalism connotes returning to the African heritage as a way of regaining political freedom and dignity, and is often more reactionary than responsive to political oppression. He used Haiti as an example of cultural nationalism: the late "Papa Doc" Duvalier displaced the colonial oppressors, replacing them with himself as the new oppressor. Newton asserted that "many of the nationalists in this country seem to desire the same ends." The African heritage, then, would not liberate black people.

A good example of revolutionary nationalism, according to Newton, was the revolution in Algeria engineered by Ahmed Ben Bella. The leaders of that revolution, he continued, were not motivated by the profit motive, which exploited and thus kept the people in a state of slavery. Instead they nationalized the industries and plowed the would-be profits back into the community. Hence, the wealth was controlled by the people, the essence of socialism.

Thus the Panthers' revolutionary nationalism was built around what it saw as a contradiction between what it desired (power to the people—socialism) and American capitalism. The wealth of the United States was based on slavery, and slavery was capitalism in the extreme. The Panthers therefore declared war on both racism and capitalism.[7]

Eldridge Cleaver believed that in order to solve the racial question, it was necessary to destroy the present system: "The answer is not black capitalism, or black athletes, or black actors, or blacks in cigarette ads; that is just a way of incorporating black people in a device. The answer is to do away with the device."[8] Inasmuch as the Panthers regarded themselves as "field niggers" in contrast to "house niggers," they saw themselves as the vanguard organization to accomplish that end.[9]

The Panthers were also concerned with the land question, "internal colonialism," and black liberation. Cleaver had this to say about the relationship:

> It is a reality when people say that there is a "black colony" and a "white mother country." Only if this distinction is borne clearly in mind is it possible to understand that there are two different sets of political dynamics now functioning in America.[10]

He said that black America must begin functioning as a nation and must demand that its sovereignty be recognized by other nations of the world. Marcus Garvey had wanted black people to have land but failed to reach that goal, for reasons beyond his control. One of the reasons for Garvey's failure centered on his refusal to solicit black mass opinion on the land question. The Black Panther Party, however, called for a United Nations' supervised plebiscite in black communities throughout the nation. The result would settle the question whether black people considered themselves a "nation within a nation," because a plebiscite would avoid the past mistakes of black nationalists by allowing the people to vote on what they wanted. It would avoid, according to Cleaver, "calling for a response from the black masses that they were unable to give, and offering a solution that could not be delivered."[11]

Huey Newton believed that the black colony in America had a unique and universal mission: "The Black people in America are the only people who can free the world, loosen the yoke of colonialism, and destroy the war machine." Since he believed the main problem was oppression, he called for all oppressed people to help destroy the existing capitalist system; the system—whether of state, classical, or monopoly capital—existed for the sole benefit of the owners of production. All people of the working class should seize the means of production. But blacks had first to free themselves psychologically in order to "be capable of meaningful self-determination. Only in socialism can men practice the self-determination necessary to provide for their freedom." Therefore, race was only one factor in black oppression, just one in a complex range of systemic oppressive forces. The Black Panther Party's ultimate objective, then, was to provide for the people to participate in the decisions that affected their lives, thus making them free.[12]

The Party maintained that SNCC and other cultural black nationalist organizations were black racists and were therefore blinded to the real culprit of oppression—capitalism and imperialism. Cleaver claimed that "Black Power" was necessary at the time it was initially articulated by SNCC and other groups. But later it

> . . . provided the power structure with its new weapon against our people . . . [which] seized upon it and turned it into the rationale for Black Capitalism. . . . The Nixon Administration preside[d] over the implementation of Black Capitalism under the slogan Black Power; what value does that slogan now have to our people's struggle for liberation?[13]

Black nationalism was not the best answer to the problem of black oppression because more than blacks were victims of oppression. Marxist-Leninism became the new Panther ideology.

The Panthers began to encourage alliances with other white radical/revolutionary groups. To this end, in July 1969, they sponsored in Oakland, California, a National Conference for a United Front Against Fascism, out of which came local National Committees to Combat Fascism. About 90 percent of those attending the conference were white.[14] These National Committees were designed to take in whites, especially those who asked why they could not join the Black Panther Party. Chairman Bobby's answer was that, "We see the National Committee as the political organizing bureaus of the Black Panther Party."[15]

Yet whites were not allowed to become members of the Party. The Panthers formed an alliance with the Students for a Democratic Society (SDS), though it did not work out well.[16] They did, however, get along very well with the Communist Party.[17] The Panthers also recognized the Young Lords Organization, a Chicago-based Puerto Rican radical group[18] who endorsed the Panthers' "mother country" concept.[19] Indeed, around 1970 a White Panther Party was formed, allying itself closely with the Marxist-Leninism of the Black Panthers.[20]

To further broaden its ideology the Party shifted its emphasis to internationalism, still soft-pedaling its black nationalist ideology after having formed alliances with Communists, "white radicals," and "New Left radicals." This caused many black nationalists in the Party to wince, and some even to leave.

The most difficult problem for the Panthers, from an ideological point of view, was to rationalize in one ideological construct the land question, black nationalism, internationalism, and Marxist-Leninism. They attempted to do so in the following way. Their black nationalism was stressed by calling for black unity, and their Marxist-Leninism by emphasizing the need for both blacks and whites to attack the "oppressive, fascist, racist system"— even though whites were barred from becoming members of the Black Panther Party. Continuing the "strain toward consistency," Newton, the Panther's chief ideologue, at first indicated that only blacks were colonized, later that all of the "American people have been colonized, if you view exploitation as a colonized effect, now they're exploited." Thus exploitation and colonization were equated.[21] Newton, finally rejecting the RNA's separate state idea, argued that even five or six black states would not survive if the rest of the United States remained capitalistic. These "explanations" still left the ideological pieces strewn untidily.

It was to shore up these ideological loose ends that the Panthers moved from a purely black nationalist group to Marxist-Leninism to internationalism and finally to "inter-communalism," which holds that the world is made up of various communities and that every world community should control its own destiny so that "we can all develop a culture that is essentially human, a culture that will provide the best in all homo sapiens, and we have to live together, because technology has thrown us together whether we like it or not."[22] No community should have control over any other community. In essence, the individuals of the various communities were "citizens of the world." The freedom of the people is, however, limited by imperialist/colonialists—the United

States being the biggest threat to freedom. Intercommunalism advocated one centralized government with no nation-state because strong nations tended to dominate weaker nations.

This display of ideological dexterity netted the Panthers considerable praise and prestige from the American Left but cost them dearly in maintaining the interest and thus membership of blacks they needed. They should have learned from the Communist Party's courting of blacks that ideological hat tricks did not increase black membership. The Panthers were, in fact, good learners: by 1970-71 they were again emphasizing black nationalism (separatism).

Combining black power, nationalism, separatism, and Pan-Africanism, Cleaver indicated that the Zionists founded a virtual government-in-exile for a people in exile.

> They would build their organization, their government, and then later on they would get some land and set the government and the people down on the land, like placing one's hat on top of one's head. The Jews did it. It worked. So now Afro-Americans must do the same thing.[23]

The Panthers finally came back to what it was blacks were concerned with—food, clothing, housing, justice—here on the ground in America.

The Republic of New Africa (RNA)

The RNA was formally organized in March 1968 in Detroit, delcaring itself the provisional government for all black Americans. A revolutionary nationalist organization, RNA concentrated on territorial separation, stipulating complete separation between blacks and whites. To achieve separation, it called for the establishment of a black nation comprised of South Carolina, Georgia, Alabama, Mississippi, and Louisiana. The self-chosen government was initially comprised of Robert F. Williams, president, who was driven into exile for his self-defense activities in Monroe, North Carolina, and Milton R. Henry, first vice president, whose younger brother, Richard B. Henry, was minister of information.

The organization had a military arm, the Black Legion (styled after Marcus Garvey's African Legion and the Nation of Islam's Fruit of Islam), whose members wore black uniforms with leopard skin epaulettes, black berets, black combat boots with white lace, and white pistol belts—without weapons.[24] The uniform was much the same as that of the Black Panthers initially, although it did not attract the same widespread attention.

According to Milton Henry, there were RNA consulates in most of the larger cities, including New York, Baltimore, Pittsburgh, Philadelphia, Washington, Chicago, Cleveland, San Francisco, and Los Angeles. He maintained that each consulate had a consul, vice-consul, and two secretaries. These consulates did not issue passports, because the United States government might have used that as an excuse to attack the offices.[25]

The ideological roots of the RNA were deep—going back to the 1940's. Milton and Richard Henry were born in Philadelphia and attended Central High, the white school located across town from where they lived. Though Benjamin Franklin High was in their neighborhood, their parents insisted that they attend Central. Both were good students and excelled in their academic work, exhibiting a strong need to achieve. Both went to college.

Milton dropped out of Lincoln University to enlist in the army on the eve of the Second World War. He became a lieutenant in the segregated 99th Pursuit Squadron (after the NAACP pressured the army to allow blacks to become pilots). He was sent to Maxwell Field in Alabama, where he encountered Southern racism: a white bus driver wanted him to sit in the back. Refusing to do so, Milton (not realizing that white bus drivers then had police powers vis-à-vis black people) was labeled a troublemaker for not knowing his "place" and sent to Selfridge, Michigan, where he protested the segregated Officers and NCO Clubs. He was court-martialed and given a dishonorable discharge for "conduct not becoming an officer."

Milton returned to Lincoln University and completed his degree, then attended Yale University School of Law. While he was a student at Yale, A. Philip Randolph and Bayard Rustin established an organization called the League for Nonviolent Civil Disobedience to a Segregated Army, enlisting Milton and Richard to organize the Philadelphia chapter. The Henrys urged blacks not to serve in a segregated army, and thereby became targets of the FBI. Nothing came of the investigations, however, because in that year President Truman banned segregation in the armed forces.

In 1950 Milton Henry was graduated from Yale Law School with honors. He took the Pennsylvania Bar examination and failed. The failure was no surprise—it represented a long-established pattern among blacks of South Philadelphia: only a select few passed. Dunbar points out that the Philadelphia post office had many black law school graduates who had "failed" the Pennsylvania bar.[26] "The exam included essay questions and an oral section that called upon the examiner to make personal judgments about the applicants. It also required an applicant's photograph and biographical data. . . . Thus year after disappointing year, outstanding black graduates of some of the nation's best law schools were screened out." After Milton took the bar exam, his grades were not posted, and he subsequently had to go for an interview. At the interview he was asked if he would promise not to fight civil rights cases. He refused. Many failed because, like Milton, they refused to sell out, but others did promise not to fight, and passed. The outcome of these pass-and-fail manipulations was bad for civil rights but good for the Philadelphia post office.

Milton then moved to Pontiac, Michigan, where he passed the Michigan bar and established his practice. He soon became politically involved in the black community, later filing a suit on behalf of his daughter to integrate the Pontiac school system. He ran for a seat on the city council and won, but became disenchanted over the corruption in politics and resigned.

Meanwhile, in 1952, Richard, at Milton's urging, moved to Detroit. Richard had studied journalism at Temple and the University of Ottawa. Using his journalistic training, he worked as a reporter for a black weekly, the *Michigan Chronicle,* and later became the managing editor of another weekly, partially financed by Milton.

Always very close, the brothers complemented each other in several ways: Milton was an excellent speaker, Richard was not; Richard was a good organizer, Milton was not; Milton could lead after the groundwork had been laid, Richard could lay the groundwork; Richard was the plodder, the convincer, Milton was flamboyant, dashing—"Yale grad, former pilot, brilliant criminal lawyer." Both, however, had always been concerned about black freedom. Richard, for example, in 1958 while traveling as a civilian writer for the United States Air Force Information Office, was ordered out of a white waiting room at the Municipal Airport in Greenville, South Carolina. He brought suit and a district judge ruled against him.

The Henry brothers have been very active in forming civil rights organizations in the Detroit black community. In 1961 they founded one called the Group on Advanced Leadership (GOAL), whose objective was to initiate consumer boycotts to improve the position of black employees in chain stores located in black communities—reminiscent of the Don't-Buy-Where-You-Can't-Work campaigns of the 1930's. GOAL also attempted to persuade banks to hire blacks, and initiated suits against police brutality. It was more successful in the former than the latter.

In 1963 Richard withdrew his son from school, protesting the use of a history text in the eighth grade which did not include an account of African history. Agreeing that the book "lacked balance," school officials kept the book but added two supplementary chapters. In 1966 Richard withdrew his daughter from the ninth grade, protesting textbook "omissions." Again school officials added a supplementary text.

Eventually the Henrys became disenchanted with fighting for civil rights case by case. They realized that racial oppression in America was so pervasive and institutionalized that it had to be attacked on a broader scale. The realization was fostered by Milton's association in the early 1960's with the redoubtable Malcolm X. Milton and Malcolm became close friends and traveled together to Africa. Milton said that these travels brought home to him Malcolm's point that separation is the ground for independence.

In Africa he was struck by the fact that in Ghana, for example, people who attended Lincoln with him were in postions of power and making decisions affecting the lives of their countrymen. He then realized that he had never made decisions about anything of consequence and that, like him, blacks in America would never do so until self-determination was achieved. He then began to view black people in America as a "nation within a nation" and part of a world-wide struggle between whites and peoples of color everywhere.

By 1964 the Henrys had rejected integration as a goal for the black freedom struggle. Yet they were neither prepared to accept Malcolm X's position that blacks should demand a separate state nor prepared to join the Nation of Islam. They were, however, profoundly shocked by Malcolm X's murder. They did not accept the official version, which holds that the Muslims were responsible, but believed that his murder involved a conspiracy much broader than the Nation of Islam.

Having become disenchanted with GOAL because its aims were too reformist, in 1967 the Henrys helped found the Malcolm X Society, which emphasized self-defense (against police brutality); internationalizing the black struggle—that is, linking up with the "Third World"; and demanding that some land in the United States be turned over to black people, the Black Nation as it were.

The Malcolm X Society operated on the assumpton that the cost of integration in the United States was too high a price for black people to pay.

From around the latter part of 1967 to the first part of 1968, the Henrys moved to strengthen the society. Richard quit his job as a writer of technical manuals at the United States Army's tank-automobile center at Warren, Michigan, to devote all his time to the society. Milton continued his law practice. They also took African names: Milton became Brother Gaidi Obadele and Richard, Brother Imari Abubakari Obadele. Brother Imari wrote a booklet, *War in America: The Malcolm X Doctrine,* demanding five southern states for the black nation as part of the reparations whites owed blacks for over three hundred years of slavery and inhumane treatment. The five states chosen were those with the highest proportions of blacks in their populations and where blacks already owned a large portion of land.

In March 1968 the Henrys, along with others, met in Detroit and formed the Republic of New Africa (RNA). Robert F. Williams, as noted, was designated the new organization's provisional president. Williams was once president of the Monroe, North Carolina, chapter of the NAACP. In 1959 he asserted that blacks should defend themselves against racist violence. In Monroe—as in the South in general—whites often amused themselves by driving through the black community shooting shotgun blasts. Williams decided that blacks should retaliate against this dangerous nonsense. He therefore formed the male NAACP members into a militia-type organization, and the next fun-seeking group had their fire returned in kind. The NAACP subsequently suspended Williams for his pains. Though suspended, Williams continued to advocate and organize self-defense groups.

In 1961 an incident occurred which forced him to move. For reasons not entirely clear, a white couple "wandered" into the black sector and became "lost" (though they were Monroe residents). Somehow Williams was charged with "detaining" the couple and was given the choice of either leaving Monroe or going to jail. He chose exile.

Williams went to Cuba, where he wrote and made radio broadcasts exhorting blacks to engage in revolutionary action to rid themselves of oppression. Moreover, he called for freedom fighters to wage guerrilla war against the "imperialist mother country" by using Molotov cocktails, lye and acid bombs, gasoline firebombs, and other easily made weapons. According to him, however, he was not advocating the overthrow of the government but, rather

self-defense for brutalized Afro-Americans. If in the process
of executing our Constitutional and God-given right of self-
defense, the racist U.S. Government, which refuses to protect
our people, is destroyed, the end result stems from certain
historical factors of social relativity. . . . America is a house on
on fire, FREEDOM NOW!, or let it burn, let it burn. Praise the
Lord and pass the ammunition.[27]

Such statements left no doubt as to his position on the liberation
struggle. Neither did the RNA's choice of Williams for President
obscure their position.

Robert S. Browne, a former professor at Fairleigh Dickinson
University and currently director of the Black Economic Research
Center in New York City, whose ideology the RNA thought had
promise, has written extensively on the desirability of black and
white communities separating because of what he believes to be
distinct cultural differences.[28] His writings have, in fact, formed
the base of the RNA's ideology. Browne called for the partitioning
of the United States into two separate and independent nations.
He argued that there is ambivalence as to whether blacks constitute a cultural group significantly distinct from the majority
culture in ways that are ethnically rather than socioeconomically
based. He contended that there is a cultural difference that has
heretofore been simplified into integration versus separation, and,
further, that the concept of Black Power may not be the most
expedient slogan to describe the change from "Negro" to *Black*
because the slogan "Black Power," to guilty whites, "conjures up
violence, anarchy, and revenge." But to many blacks, "Black
Power" symbolized "unity and a newly found pride in the blackness with which the Creator endowed us and which we realize
must always be our mark of identification." He asked if this
newly found black consciousness was irreconcilable with the
larger American society, and he seemed to answer affirmatively.

He wondered whether integration was painless genocide for
black people, in that black communities were too often losing
their better trained people to newly available positions in white
establishments. Nevertheless, Browne thought that black Americans were becoming increasingly more distrustful of white America for a number of reasons, among them: (1) American culture
approved and seemed to enjoy violence; (2) it spent almost half
its national budget on military expenditures; (3) the American
war machine pursued with zeal, to the astonishment of the civil-
ized world, the destruction of poor and illiterate Vietnam peasants.

Browne wondered if black Americans should or could be comfortable in a white society that seemed to enjoy violence, is openly jingoistic, and intentionally or inadvertently practicing genocide. He mentioned that the Germans herded the Jews into concentration camps and ovens, which was a solemn warning to minority peoples everywhere. Black people had no homeland they could honestly call home, and thus were unique. He argued that Africa was not the answer, because only a handful of blacks were able to travel to the newly independent African countries to experience black brotherhood and dignity, and even for many of those who did go, the gratification of brotherhood was not enough to make up for the ensuing cultural estrangement. They had been away too long to experience the "at home" sensation they were eagerly seeking. Africa could, however, serve as a symbolic homeland.

A just solution for the land dilemma of black Americans, according to Browne, would recognize that black Americans were left with the United States as a homeland because it is here, not Africa, where black labor played a major role in the development of the United States. As a result, blacks are well within their rights to demand an opportunity to enjoy this land, as other immigrant groups have done. But in order to do so, white Americans demanded that black Americans must integrate, give up their cultural identity in order to enjoy citizenship. This is painful but tolerable to the middle-class black but was becoming intolerable to the masses.

On the one hand, the black who refuses to identify with white models is more often than not labeled by whites a deviant. From there it is a short distance to challenging constituted authority and ending up incarcerated. That is why blacks, who are around ten percent of the population, constitute 50 percent of the prison population. On the other hand, blacks who choose integration as a solution to the black dilemma have only a snowball's chance in hell of being completely accepted. One way out of the tragic situation is to partition the United States formally "into two totally separate and independent nations, one white and one black." Black separatism, as exemplified in the movement organizations of the Black Panthers, Black Muslims, SNCC, and CORE, among others, illustrates that blacks are in fact groping for a separatist solution to their problems. Ghetto improvement efforts, though most are not separatist in that they operate within the system, are doomed to failure because they are predicated upon white-imposed separatism that already existed and are not designed to eliminate inequality, but rather perpetuate it. But, "to a black who sees salvation for the black man only in a complete divorce of the two races, these efforts at ghetto improvements appear futile, perhaps even harmful." The most feasible solution was separation of blacks and whites into two independent nations.

In May 1968 Brother Gaidi mailed to President Nixon and handed two State Department officials a note demanding $400 billion in reparations, the designated five states, and the beginning of negotiations between the United States of America and the Republic of New Africa. The note was never acknowledged by the President and ignored by the State Department—at least in terms of a formal or informal reply.

The RNA, Henry maintained, had already begun the shift from government-in-exile to government-in-fact, for one hundred acres of land had been bought in Mississippi, and that would be enough for a base headquarters. The RNA would organize along the lines of cooperative and collective farms. The collective farm would not only feed the people but also provide a center where people could protect themselves and work out the politics of their existence. Considering the population of Mississippi—less than three million, with blacks comprising more than 40 percent—it would not take many black people to equal the number of whites in some counties, or to outnumber them. However, the numbers were significant only when the voters could be protected with arms.

The strategy of taking control, according to Henry, could be peaceful or violent. In a large black population in a state such as Mississippi, for example, if blacks moved from urban ghettoes to selected counties, they would outnumber whites and consequently could outvote them. Blacks would then select their own sheriff, who traditionally wielded tremendous power. The black sheriff could deputize other blacks, resulting in a potent, legitimate force. Blacks could replicate the feat in several counties and eventually control the states. This is the peaceful method of winning control. The trouble, Henry believed, was that whites would not allow it to happen unless blacks could ensure that their votes would be counted. Hence the need for a Black Legion, to protect and oversee the voting procedure.

Land was the key to the problem. Henry used the analogy of Jews purchasing land in Palestine as an example of the RNA's need for land in Mississippi: "[Land in Palestine] gave [Jews] a base from which they could legitimately say, 'We have land and we want to change the sovereignty.' That's the way we are operating already."

Henry observed that the racial problems of the North were not going to be settled, and eventually the United States government would come around to talk to the RNA about separation. That is, of course, after large-scale guerrilla activities had been initiated by blacks in the northern cities.

He further indicated that if the United States Army interfered, the RNA could cope with the situation by obtaining aid from allies like China—though only after China was sure that the RNA was capable of a separate and independent existence. That could be shown by controlling a land mass and having a majority of the people there not subject to United States jurisdiction. Then China would back the Republic with missiles. Still the best way to do it was not to engage in warfare; neutralization of the United States Army was the most desirable approach. Castro survived by neutralizing the United States, and the RNA could do it too.

But until China saw fit to help, the RNA had retaliatory firepower, the second-strike capability of RNA guerrillas in many metropolitan areas. That is, if the RNA decided to take over Mississippi and the United States government sent troops to prevent it, the RNA's urban guerrillas would strike to prevent the army—not local forces—from interfering. The local forces would be handled by the Black Legion. Once the land was secured, the RNA could be recognized as a sovereign nation and could then receive military aid from other countries.

One may ask why the United States government would allow the RNA to secede when it would not allow the Confederacy to do so. Henry maintained that the RNA was in a different situation. In the first place, the Civil War was fought in the South alone, but today blacks all over the country want self-determination, separation, and land. The mass of blacks would not be discouraged by having many killed. If the killing of many colonists in the Revolutionary War had discouraged the majority, the colonists could not have been successful against British power. The guerrilla warfare and sabotage, successful in Vietnam, could take place in the United States today. Once it had commenced, all blacks would be forced to join the RNA, because whites would not take the time to distinguish between "good" and "bad" blacks.

Once the black nation was secure, the RNA would expropriate the existing industries in the South. The United States government could give the companies tax credits for their losses—a kind of reparation for black separation. The government of the RNA would operate the plants under "Ujamaa," an African conception of the organization of society which was broader than socialism. If there were not enough black technicians, outside technicians would be given resident visas. Whites who felt they could live in that kind of society could stay. The whites who did not like blacks would not come anyway, or if they did, would not stay long.[29]

In sum, the RNA—rejecting the idea of returning to Africa—proposed to establish the Black Nation in five Southern states. It declared itself the government of all black Americans and urged them to return to the five states and be a black nation. It believes that eventually whites will allow this alternative because of the increasingly difficult relations between the races.

The Black Panther Party and the RNA may be seen as "expressive vanguard" organizations in that they attempted through ideological appeal to convince a few blacks that to gain black freedom extraordinary and even extreme steps must be taken. The realization must be initially individual and not necessarily directed at objects of immediate social change. This is the expressive aspect. The vanguard part was their willingness to serve as the generators of ideas and protectors of those who partook of them; they knew that, based on past experience and patterns of participation, a large number of blacks would not initially join them, but hoped that their ideological potency would eventually net a groundswell of support.

8 ECONOMIC PROGRAMS

If a social movement is to serve as a catalyst for change, its ideology must encompass a broad spectrum of social and political views and be capable of adapting to various internal and external pressures. Hence, ideology tends to receive a greal deal of attention from members of the movement and from its analysts. Undoubtedly, ideology is a crucial element, but it must be seen in proper perspective with other variables, one of which is the economic program or strategy. A well-organized, theoretically sound ideology without a corresponding economic program is like a beautiful and well-made fishing tackle without bait. This chapter will explore some aspects of the economic programs of the black separatist organizations and how they propose to incorporate separatist economics in the black liberation process.

The Nation of Islam

Land or territory is central to the Nation's economic philosophy, because, according to them, neither a nation nor a sense of nationhood can develop without it. As noted earlier, the Messenger believed in the separation of the races, but had not specified where the black nation should be established—in the United States or in Africa. Muhammad claimed that blacks already constituted a "nation within a nation" without the benefits of freedom, justice, and equal opportunity enjoyed by white Americans. Hence, black separation was the only feasible way in which black people could achieve justice and freedom: physical separation would occur in stages, social separation would come about when blacks avoided all unnecessary social contacts with whites, and economic separation was in progress through the creation over time of black businesses and farms. Finally, political separation would be achieved when blacks ceased relating to white institutions and culture. What were the specifics of the Muslim economic program?

Muhammad's book *Message to the Black Man in America* provided for the theoretical basis. Other specific aspects can be found in almost all editions of the Muslim newspaper, *Muhammad Speaks.* All of the most important economic proposals center on black separation and black unity. Specific proposals include the following:

(1) Spend money only among blacks (preferably Muslims) in business.

(2) Build black enterprises through the Nation and reinvest the profits for further business expansion.

(3) Emulate whites in business techniques and economic behavior: be thrifty, save money, and work hard.

(4) Muslim economic organization was described as "communalism," where members were expected to contribute 10 percent of their earnings to the Nation to be used for the establishment of Muslim businesses. Hence, the businesses were owned not privately but by the central organization. The profits from operations were shared with the Muslim temples, and temple officers decided how to spend the money. Most of the profits were utilized to support temple expenses and provide for the sick, unemployed, and aged. About 25 percent is now used to operate the University of Islam.[1]

(5) Muhammad claimed that black people had thousands of dollars in white banks and that this money should be put to use by blacks for economic development. They could buy land, and produce cotton, grains, and livestock: the cattle and sheep could be used for food, leather products, and wool; cotton could be the basic fiber. Muslims, according to Muhammad, should first go to the soil to promote independence from white food and clothing enterprises. Blacks could then build warehouses to store food and other necessities for blacks, thus creating an autonomous black economy.[2]

(6) Muhammad emphasized the necessity for careful economic planning through schemes such as a Three Year Economic Savings Program. In order to accumulate enough capital for Muslims to purchase land, he indicated that blacks must stop buying lavish automobiles, clothes, and other unnecessary consumer items and instead put money into the Muslim economic program.

(7) No one knows exactly what the Muslim income really

was, but in 1962 Essien-Udom estimated it at between $300,000 and $500,000.[3] Since that time, however, the Nation has received a loan or loans from the United Arab Republic and has asked the United States Government for a $6 million dollar loan. Muslim economic fortunes have risen, and some estimate the organization's total worth to be in the area of several millions.

In summary, the Muslim economic program concentrated on membership contributions, which were plowed into business investments. These business establishments—restaurants, clothing stores, gas stations, barber shops, apartment houses—were small, service-oriented enterprises that eventually expanded into industrial establishments. The Muslims, unlike Garvey, whom they admire, because they are urban-situated, are basing their staged program of economic self-sufficiency on an industrial and an agricultural base. Like Washington, the Muslims see the first step in economic self-sufficiency as having the ability to feed oneself. They therefore combined the Washington and Garvey program. Washington would have applauded their back-to-the-soil emphasis, but would have frowned on their militant rhetorical denunciation of whites, for as a practical man of affairs, he knew that whites still held almost all the power in American society. Power frowns on militant powerlessness.

Garvey, on the other hand, would have applauded Muslim militance but be confused over their emphasis on an agricultural base. Garvey felt that black people must get right on with commercial and industrial enterprises. He would applaud Muslim emulation of white business techniques to establish these enterprises, but would wonder about their emphasis on religion.

Both Garvey and Washington would have been confused about Muslim emphasis on "communalism," because both were basically capitalists. Perhaps both would have been soothed by Muhammad's rationale for using communalism as a technique (or means) rather than an end: (1) it served to promote savings habits and a responsible approach to economic self-development; (2) it served as an outlet for individual investment in Muslim enterprise owned by the temple; and (3) it served to create a sense of mutual and reciprocal responsibility among Muslims.

In sum, Washington and Garvey would have applauded many aspects of Muslim economic undertakings, although they might not have been enamored with many of its philosophical, religious, and secular constructs (such as calling for the freedom of all black prisoners). It is certain, however, that future black organizations will not agree with the present Muslim economic philosophy, and just as the Muslims have added to and abandoned specific aspects of Washington and Garvey programs, so they will be abandoned.

Congress of Racial Equality

CORE's rhetoric on "black power," "black capitalism," and the black masses in urban ghettoes in the mid-1960's was a prelude to its emergence in 1968 as a separatist organization. In fact, its attention to these areas did not prevent it from deriving most or all of its resources from membership dues and donations from well-to-do individuals and corporations, though its techniques and rationale for soliciting funds for integration were somewhat different from those for a separatist program. When Innis became CORE's national director in 1968, he moved to align the organization's separatist ideology with an economic plan.

Innis labeled his plan "separatist economics" and called for a new social contract between white and black America, because white American institutions did not permit blacks to participate on an equal basis. Innis demanded that blacks in urban centers must become political subdivisions of the state rather than remain "sub-colonial appendages to the cities"; they must control all important institutions in their communities. He then differentiated between revolution and liberation, suggesting that only "boy militants" and "romantics" talk of revolution at this stage of black development. The emphasis should be *liberation,* "a more pragmatic and necessary step." Liberation can be achieved by separation—controlling the institutions and flow of goods and services in black communities. Hence, the oppressed black condition can be changed by placing these instruments in black hands, thus eliminating the present condition of segregation. The proposed change in power arrangements was meant to bring about *separation* (where black people can voluntarily live together), not *segregation* (where blacks are forced to live together). Under segregation, blacks live together but do not control their own communities. Under separation, blacks would voluntarily live together and control their lives.

Innis identified three phases. Phase I (short range) would enable blacks to control the economy in their communities through the establishment of community-development corporations (CDC's); Phase II (middle range) would combine community control with the ideological indoctrination of community control and self-determination; Phase III would involve the drafting of a new United States constitution based on the theory that the social contract did not apply to blacks; blacks had no hand in its formulation. A new constitution must be made dealing with white and black people as two distinct groups occupying the same land at the same time. The new constitution proposed by CORE would make it possible for blacks to maximize their political interests so that they would at least receive a per capita share of the political power. This share, as CORE envisions it, would mean that black people could stop relating to the larger nation as a dependent colonized people and begin to assert power through community control. The black "colony" would then be a "nation within a nation."[4]

The pragmatic consequences of such control are illustrated by Innis: one must consider the massive expenditures of community institutions to buy goods and services. Harlem schools, for example, buy close to $100 million yearly in goods and services. Most are contracted outside Harlem. But suppose Harlemites themselves formed a $100 million dollar corporation to supply books to Harlem and act as middlemen who buy and sell books to other schools at a profit? The profits would then come to the black community instead of going outside it. More than simply supplying books, consider the Harlem budget for sanitation, health, and hospital services, among others. These could be guaranteed markets representing massive sums of money—if people were selling to their own institutions. If people control their own institutions, they can determine who gets contracts and who does not.

To this end CORE moved to create a Harlem School System that would bypass the city and report directly to the state. Bills to this effect have frequently been introduced in the New York State Legislature, but they have never passed. CORE, however, did persuade the state to allow Harlem to run its own hospitals.[5]

Innis felt that too often blacks bought "Mickey Mouse" (trivial) programs that relied almost entirely on emotional appeal, purported to grapple with black economic development, but made little or no change in the economic condition of black people. What blacks need, according to Innis, is the intellectual rigor that will generate programs to improve blacks' chances of survival and their chances to develop in America as a people.

CORE's fullest and most intellectually rigorous philosophical and detailed statement of its economic program and rationale may be found in its fund appeal presented to potential funding sources in Cleveland, Ohio, in 1968. CORE had a number of chapters, strong as well as weak, and its Cleveland chapter, a particularly strong one, devised this proposal, with Innis' approval and aid.[6]

The Cleveland Economic Proposal—"Open Application for Funding Grants to CORE Development Corporation and Invitation to Cooperate with CORE Development Corporation in Projects to Raise the Economic Productiveness of Ghetto Residents and Other Poor"—was based on the idea that the present stage of capitalism is capable of allowing every human to realize economic freedom. The reason: labor has become less important as a source of productive power, while capital equipment has become more important. People should therefore share in the income derived from capital, and if they did so, they would be made economically free. In other words, the Protestant ethic, which emphasizes man's physical contribution in the productive process is no longer necessary because ownership of capital production through cybernation and automation are the main sources of income. To continue to insist that income be legitimated "through symbolic toil" is to disregard man's scientific, technological, and managerial achievements in "shifting the burden of economic production from man to the forces of nature harnessed in non-human labor." The work ethic is not completely shunned, however: "the CORE program . . . conserves the puritan ethic as a moral principle, but adapts it to the industrial age."

How should income be derived? One way is to break the link between productive contribution and income and base distribution on individual need. The welfare system and the negative income tax promote only dependency. CORE porposed an alternative system: income should be derived from (1) individual labor power and (2) the productivity of capital equipment to which the individual holds title. But would this not result in a continuation of the present pattern of income inequality, since some hold more stock than others? Without structural changes, the answer is yes. Structural or institutional changes must therefore occur in order for low-income blacks to increase their productive capacity, thereby enabling them to receive legitimately enough income to meet their needs and reasonable desires. Low-income productive capacity can be raised, according to CORE, not necessarily by changing dominant institutional structures, but by the establishment of a series of economic institutions that would enable blacks to acquire capital. This series would not be antagonistic to capitalist structures but would be compatible with the capitalistic system; it would, in fact, protect the institution of private property.

The outcome of the establishment of these economic institutions should (1) create or raise the ability of low-income or no income individuals to become the owners of productive capital; (2) enable proverty-stricken black individuals and families who live in ghetto areas to acquire ownership of moderate and diversified productive capital instruments; and (3) allow the productive expansion of goods and services in the economy in line with a citizen's abilities to consume at stable prices. The system of distributing income produced by capital on the basis of labor and welfare must be avoided.

CORE believed that economic viability in America required the ownership of property; hence, black freedom depended on the ability to control productive property. To achieve this goal, CORE proposed that existing corporations, in partnership with CORE, establish plants and industries in ghettos where the corporation would "contribute" initial partnership capital in a given time period. The partnership—CORE and the corporation—would then determine where in ghettos particular industries would purchase or construct the property's physical facilities. The facilities would be rented on a long-term basis to the corporation or another non-partner firm; the rental income would be used to repay the corporate partners their capital contribution plus interest at a prime rate. Upon full repayment of the corporate partner's contribution plus interest, the corporate partner's interest would terminate. This arrangement should be attractive, according to CORE, because in the early stages the corporation could deduct losses from its income tax returns.

After the initial stage of forming a partnership with a corporation or corporations, selecting and purchasing property, and constructing physical facilities, CORE would establish a community development corporation (CDC), which would, in essence, represent CORE's interest in the partnership arrangement (or at the initial stage of the partnership, CORE would represent the community development corporation). Since CDC ownership is to be determined through stock and shares, CORE would determine individual specifications on a broad base of black participation, which would be limited to ghetto residents whose income was below a specific minimum. Ultimately, when the rental payments began to exceed the amount owed the corporate partner, the profits would be distributed to ghetto shareholders as well as equity ownership of land, buildings, and capital equipment. Thus the ghetto resident would become a property owner, sharing in capital rather than labor production.

CORE further suggested that the firm operating in the ghetto set aside a portion of its stock for an equity-sharing plan for ghetto residence employees. That is, the firm would dispense part of its wages through an equity-sharing or bonus program; the. outcome would place a large share of the firm's ownership in the hands of ghetto residents. Again, the tax break would accrue to the corporation.

In order for ghetto residents and firms to acquire the capital for initial investment, as well as the establishment of CORE's CDC, CORE proposed a Special Guarantee Fund, whereby wealthy individuals, foundations, charities, corporations—and eventually CORE's own economic fund source—would provide the initial capital. To this end, indicating that the federal government through the Homestead and Federal Housing Acts made it possible for poor whites to own property, CORE, aided by the late Senator Robert F. Kennedy in early 1968, introduced in the House of Representatives two bills: the Community Self-Development Act and the Rural Development Incentive Act.

The Community Self-Development Act was designed to enhance total control of poor communities by its residents. The bill provided for the United States government to establish a National Community Corporation Certification Board under the President of the United States free from all other agencies and departments. The certification board would encourage the development of local community corporations, monitor their organization procedures, and issue charters. It would also coordinate the activities of other federal agencies involved in the community and would act as a funding source to local CDC's. The CDC's would be organized in communities with no fewer than 5,000 residents of sixteen years and over and a maximum of 300,000. A "development index" would determine community eligibility as follows: (1) the ratio of (a) the percentage of the national unemployed labor force (or within a specific standard metropolitan statistical area), whichever is lower, to (b) the percentage of the unemployed labor force in a particular community. (2) The ratio of (a) median family income in a particular community to (b) the national median family income, or that within the Standard Metropolitan statistical area, whichever is the largest. The lesser of these two ratios so computed would be the "development index" for that community.

Outstanding shares would represent the ownership of CDC;

shares would be in one class (common) at a par value of five dollars. This stock would be purchased by members of the CDC in cash or labor performed for the CDC.

Funds for the establishment of the national development corporations would be derived from the federal government starting at $50 million in 1971 and rising to $125 million in the fiscal year 1972. Ostensibly, a United States Community Development Bank, with branches located in CDC areas, would be established to expedite capital funding. Moreover, a proposed United States Community Development Bank would serve to create credit in local communities, extending credit to stockholders and other eligible individuals in the CDC area.

The Rural Development Incentive Act, on the other hand, was designed to create incentives for the establishment of job-producing industrial and commercial firms in rural areas. CORE proposed this act in recognition of the fact that too often poor people moved from rural areas to the ghettos, thus further contributing to depressed conditions in the inner city. The establishment of job-producing commerce and industry in rural areas would slow or stop rural to inner city migration, which was a major contributor to inner city economic disparity in the first place.

In summary, CORE asserted that the lack of control over institutions—both social and economic—was one of the most outstanding weaknesses in black communities. Not only did white institutions teach false values, but they also controlled the flow of goods and services in black communities. Hence the call for a new social contract. A new constitution between blacks and whites in the United States would enable money earned by blacks and the tax dollars they pay to be used to provide guaranteed markets for black-owned and controlled enterprises. The Community Self-Determination and Rural Development Incentive Act provided the legal framework for Innis' and CORE's economic thrust. Unfortunately for CORE, nothing ever came of the bills, despite substantial initial support.

Nevertheless, CORE continued to press for black economic self-sufficiency in the ghetto and continued to develop farm cooperatives. In Opelousas, Louisiana, for example, CORE organized over 300 black farmers into a cooperative called Grand Marie. CORE's militant rhetoric—and the fear it produced in private and public institutions in America—reduced its chance to bring to fruition its proposed economic program. It is fair to say that CORE's proposals are no different from the accepted capitalistic tenets of economic development, and if lasting peace is ever to come to the black urban ghettos, eventually CORE's program, or one similar to it, must be seriously considered.

The Student National Coordinating Committee

It has been asserted that the ideological basis of black separatism in the 1960's was laid by Malcolm X. SNCC and its spokesmen—Carmichael, James Forman, H. "Rap" Brown, Cleveland Sellers, Courtland Cox, John Lewis—were Malcolm's disciples, and could therefore argue that SNCC's failure to develop an organizational economic program stems from Malcolm X's failure to develop one. Malcolm's philosophy of black liberation changed a great deal from the time he broke with the Nation of Islam to his establishment of the Organization of Afro-American Unity (OAAU). He still believed that separation in the final analysis would be the most realistic solution to the problem, but, like Garvey, he came to realize that in the meantime black people needed short-run programs to cope with the oppression at hand. Hence he called his program for separatism "black nationalism." "Our political philosophy will be black nationalism. Our economic and social philosophy will be black nationalism. Our cultural emphasis will be black nationalism."[7]

Malcolm pointed out that black people wanted freedom, justice, and equality and that integration as well as separation was a way to achieve these goals. In the final analysis, according to Malcolm, since we are all human beings, "we are fighting for the right to live as free humans *in this society*."[8] He went on to assert that blacks should maintain their identification with Africa as Jews do with Israel. That is, they could "emigrate" to Africa culturally, philosophically, and psychologically even while remaining in the United States.

Though Malcolm X changed ideological positions on some important issues, he never wavered from his belief that capitalism was at the root of the black problem. He believed that capitalism was exploitative and dehumanizing and that it would eventually collapse. A capitalist, according to him, was parasitic: "he cannot be anything but a bloodsucker if he's going to be a capitalist. He's got to get it from somewhere other than himself, and that's where he gets it—from somewhere or someone other than himself."[9] He believed that socialism for black people was the economic wave of the future because Africa was tending in that direction. Within the context of the American capitalist structure, however, Malcolm advocated the Muslim (Washington-Garvey) position that blacks must pool their resources and initially establish small businesses.

Malcolm X counseled blacks that the economic philosophy of black nationalism meant the control of the economy in black communities and, in order to control, "we have to learn how to operate the businesses of our community . . . because we haven't learned the importance of owning and operating businesses [which are] controlled by outsiders, the stores are controlled by people who don't even live in our community."[10] Thus Malcolm X's OAAU under section four, "Economic Security," proposed the development of a pool of Technician Banks to aid in the economic development of the black ghettos and African nations. The Technician Bank would, in essence, provide a clearing house for black skills in the United States, and at the same time supply Africa with specifically needed skills.[11]

In sum, Malcolm X spoke to the need to liberate black people from the shackles of oppression psychologically, culturally, and economically. He called for black control of black organizations, black business, and black communities. He saw the capitalist system, rather than white people, as the primary cause of black oppression. Both the Democratic and the Republican parties were oppressive in their treatment of black people. As a result, he called for independent black political action in order to offset the inaction of the parties in fostering black liberation. Finally, he analyzed the black condition in the United States as analogous to African colonies and other territories under European domination, in that blacks in the United States were victims of "Internal Colonialism." Oppressed and colonial peoples, in the final analysis, had to come together in some kind of internationalism to combat colonial domination.

SNCC attempted to actualize Malcolm's ideas into a workable ideological framework. Because SNCC members were, for the most part, characterized as political nationalists, their "economic program" had more to do with politics than economics. To be sure, SNCC's political program would have had profound residual economic ramifications, but the *organization itself* was not focusing primarily on change in economic relationships. However, individual SNCC members, some of them leaders, had many theoretical things to say about economics and black liberation.

In 1967 Stokely Carmichael, a former SNCC chairman, charged, as did Malcolm, that capitalism was the arch enemy in the struggle for black liberation. Contrary to CORE's position, SNCC asserted that black capitalism was not the answer to the black economic question: black capitalists would only replace white capitalists. Black people needed money to "go into the communal pocket . . . for capitalism by its very nature cannot create structures free from exploitation. We are fighting for the redistribution of wealth in the United States." [12] By 1968, however, Carmichael, though fired by SNCC, was saying that Marxism, advocated by the Panthers, because it dealt only with economic questions, was not the central question in the black struggle—white racism was. He linked racism, capitalism, and imperialism: "The government of the United States of America is racist and imperialist. Therefore, we are fighting the government of the United States." [13] He suggested that neither Communism nor Socialism was relevant to the black struggle and that blacks, in order to end exploitation and racism, would have to move beyond both. His ostensible ambivalence perhaps had to do with his disenchantment with his organizational associations: first with SNCC and later the Panthers.

The most accurate indicator of Carmichael's belief in an economic program for black people is to be found in *Black Power*, co-authored with the respected black political scientist Charles V. Hamilton. Believing that blacks in America constitute an internal colony, Carmichael and Hamilton, in the chapter entitled "The Search for New Forms," advocated an economic plan similar to that of CORE. They observed that almost all of the money earned by white merchants in black communities is taken out without benefit to those communities. To stem this outflow of black money, blacks should establish a community rebate plan according to which they would not spend their money with merchants until an agreement was reached whereby the merchant would reinvest "forty to fifty percent of his net profit in the indigenous [black] community." In the end,

> Such a community rebate plan will require careful organization and tight discipline on the part of the black people.
> But it is possible, and has in fact already been put into effect by some ethnic communities. White America realizes the market in the black community; black America must begin to realize the potential of that market. [14]

Seemingly, Carmichael and Hamilton were calling for reform in the economic system in order for black people to improve their economic positions; but because *Black Power* and SNCC focused on political change, it followed that their most important proposals involved political relationships between black communities and power structures. Their call for black political parties—that is, independent black political action—underscored their general plan for political action.[15] The Mississippi Freedom Democratic Party (MFDP) and the Lowndes County Freedom Organization were examples cited by Carmichael and Hamilton.

Still pursuing SNCC's economic policy through individual action, after Carmichael, James Forman, a former SNCC Executive Secretary, eventually called on white churches for $500 million in reparations in payment for slavery imposed on blacks by white America. Of course, like the many Germans who denied responsibility, even knowledge, of the Jewish Holocaust, white Americans denied responsibility for enslaving blacks. Forman had earlier petitioned the United Nations to speak to the question of American imperialism abroad and internal colonialism at home. For the most part, these were political acts designed to encourage whites to speak out for justice and blacks to engage in political action for their own liberation.

In summary, SNCC, as a political nationalist organization, did not have an economic blueprint for black liberation but believed that independent black political action would lead to ultimate black freedom and equality. Eloquent rhetoric, militant speeches and statements, and conferences did not, however, substitute for an economic program. Booker T. Washington might have added that it did not matter what kind of political rhetoric one articulated as long as it was backed by an economic program.

The Black Panther Party

The initial Party economic program was a reflection of the Panthers' original ideological position: the Black Panther Party, according to its spokesmen, was a vanguard party because it bridged the long-standing ideological chasm between Marxism, which emphasized class oppression, and Black Nationalism, which placed emphasis on racial oppression. Hence their ideology permitted them to speak to class and racial oppression at the same time.

According to the Panthers, capitalism was an economic system designed for black exploitation. The capitalistic system, they continued, was dominated by a few hundred white, monopolistic corporations which controlled the entire economic structure of North America and almost the entire world economy. Economic domination formed the base for the world-wide suppression of dark-skinned peoples.

The Panthers believed that monopoly capital had eliminated free enterprise. Nevertheless, their economic goals evolved to include decent housing, educational programs for black people, and full employment (these goals were printed in each issue of the *Black Panther.*) The Panthers asserted that the federal government was responsible for providing full employment or a guaranteed annual income; if the government did not provide for full employment, the business community should do so. If the business community failed to provide full employment, the means of production should be taken from businessmen and placed in the community. Members of the community would then make certain that business ensured everyone a position and a decent standard of living.

In that white landlords usually did not provide decent housing, property should be expropriated and established on a cooperative basis, augmented by governmental assistance. The Panthers also asked for a cash indemnity for the genocide of fifty million blacks (based on estimates of black deaths resulting from transportation from Africa, and, once in the New World, slavery itself) and the unfulfilled promise (debt) of forty acres and two mules promised to blacks as reparations (or retribution) for slavery. Though the Panthers later denounced Black Power, largely because of their rift with Carmichael, at one point they embraced it because they viewed it as "a projection of sovereignty . . . that black people can focus on and through which they can make a distinction between . . . the white mother country of America and the black colony dispersed throughout the continent on absentee owned land, making Afro-America a decentralized colony. Black power says to black people that it is possible for them to build a national organization on someone else's land."[16] We should remember that the above statement was made by Eldridge Cleaver, who was later ousted from the Party and who later denounced both Carmichael and black power in favor of a Marxist or class analysis of the race question.

Despite the Panthers' emphasis on Marxism-Leninism as their ideology, and the need to change the racist governmental leadership, they had to contend with the reality of their environment. Compromising between economic reality and their ultimate goal of Marxism-Leninism, "the economic system that would be supported by the Panthers would be one of cooperative black business. This form of organization would ensure that profits generated by businesses would benefit the entire black community and would not fall into the hands of a few to be utilized for their private benefit."[17] To this end, black business was seen as a means toward "survival and national liberation" not an end in itself, because "there is no way to achieve liberation inside the framework of CHUCK's [the white man's] economic system; we can achieve a certain degree of autonomy in the economic sphere but in the final analysis black political independence must precede black economic independence! Black Power!"[18]

Panther survival programs, such as free clothing and breakfast programs, were, in many instances, financed—not always voluntarily—by black business on the rationale that the black bourgeoisie must aid in the liberation process. In the Party's early stages of development, the black middle class (especially businessmen) were viewed by Panthers as part of the exploitive class; blacks could and would exploit the poor black proletariat just as did the white bourgeoisie. By 1972, however, the Panthers had developed a sophisticated economic scheme for black economic advancement and had systematically linked politics and economics in the liberation process. As previously noted, the Panthers had also changed their tactics in relation to the black community, including the black bourgeoisie and the constituted authority (since coercive control methods had dampened the Panthers' original revolutionary zeal). The black bourgeoisie had consequently become victims rather than oppressors under the monopoly capitalist system, and electoral rather than revolutionary black nationalist politics had become the vehicle on which Panther economic goals would be carried. The change—in tactics at least—according to Seale involved the following economic realities:

The Panthers' new economic thrust centered on their version of a community organization program. The program's initial testing involved the Oakland community and the mayoral candidacy of Bobby Seale. The first step was to register black voters and with the new voting strength vote out existing gerrymandered systems, after voting in a slate of black officials. Unlike the Republic of New Africa, the Panthers did not believe that it was possible to take a number of states for a black nation, but rather that the goal must be achieved, if at all, by taking over "city by city and county by county where black people have the potential to build that broad revolutionary framework . . ." In this way, according the Seale, the Panthers were not working in the system, but "working against corruption and getting those racists out of the system, to expropriate." In Oakland, according to Seale, Panther workers were sent out to organize potential blacks by precincts. At the same time, Panthers solicited small contributions—nickels, dimes, quarters—from these predominately black precincts, possibly netting as much as $6,000 weekly.

The survival programs envisioned nonprofit corporations, controlled by the community and represented by trustees—ministers and others who had worked with Panther survival programs. At the same time, the precinct workers were organized for Seale's mayoral bid; "they [could] raise two or three hundred or four hundred thousand dollars in a matter of a couple of months." Since many white businessmen had indicated they would leave if Seale were elected, their exit would allow blacks the opportunity, with collected survival funds, to purchase and run these businesses. The black community cooperatives could then buy goods at wholesale and sell them to blacks at a 20 to 25 percent discount.

In order to build community cooperatives that community people control, "you have to have . . . control of the city government and the city agencies to protect that institution of the people." The role of black businessmen would be to use part of their profits to establish a United Black Fund, which would aid survival and other community programs.[19]

The Black Panther Party, like all the other organizations (CORE, SNCC, and the Nation of Islam) eventually focused their economic development program on black community cooperatives. Unlike the rest, however, the Panthers attempted to elect their own people to political office, to aid in the implementation or smooth operation of these community-based cooperatives. They also decided to expand their plan nationwide in a kind of grassroots campaign to elect blacks to replace racist whites. It is fair to say that neither their proposed election of Panthers to political office nor their comprehensive ghetto development program got off the ground. The failure may have been because, among other things, their initial plan of action was too far removed from the immediate needs of the man in the street.

The Republic of New Africa (RNA)

The RNA's economic program may be classified as socialistic. Brother Imari criticized black capitalism as a means of ameliorating the economic conditions of blacks because "it is either political/economic idiocy or old time fraud to suggest that, by promoting black enterprise within the U.S. system, we can in any forseeable future end either the tragedy of the black poor . . . or the frustration of the black middle class." He also disparaged a minimum wage, a guaranteed income, or increased welfare as answers to the black economic problem—though he agreed that they may be temporarily expedient. Further, according to Imari, before blacks plan any economic strategies for sharing in the American economy, they should consider continuing budget deficits, the solidification of the European Common Market, past and present threats to the dollar, and runaway inflation. In order to promote black economic viability without black capitalism, welfare, or some sort of guaranteed income, Imari combined economics and politics: "We blacks have never been able to get anything from America in the past unless whites somehow thought it benefited them. I believe that whites in the North—who attribute all kinds of things to blacks, from the high cost of welfare to busing to the 'loss' of cities like New York—can be shown that the peaceful granting of sovereignty to a black nation in Mississippi, *even* a black nation whose economics are cooperative, is the simplest, cheapest, most logical way to 'save America' *for them* (something they care about) and end the black depression for us (something they do not really care about)."[20]

Imari recognized that the new nation must have an initial economic base from which to take off. The initial financing should come from the United States government in the form of reparations. Imari pointed out that "the principle of reparations for national wrongs, as for personal wrongs, was well established in international law. The West German government, for instance, has paid $850 million in equipment and credits in reparations to Israel for wrongs committed by the Nazis against Jews in Europe."[21] Not only should the government supply economic reparations, but, according to Imari, it should also supply machinery, factories, laboratories, and land. On land demanded by the RNA, blacks comprised a significant portion of the population: Mississippi (40 percent), Louisiana (32 percent), Alabama (30 percent), Georgia (29 percent), and South Carolina (35 percent).

Milton Henry (Brother Gaidi) pointed out that the thrust for land was central to the building of a black nation, because black people already had one of the basic resources which, in the final analysis, made a great nation: skilled men. He states:

When men combined with skill are applied to land, you have some measure of national size and greatness. Based on this formula, we are a nation of forty million of the most trained

blacks on earth. When put in touch with a mass of land which
has agricultural potential, timber and mineral resources and
which has access to the sea, we can become potentially the
greatest nation on earth. Japan, with ninety to a hundred million people, pressed into a land mass one-half the size of the
United States, lacking iron, bauxite, copper, gold, silver, zinc,
tin, lead and cotton, has, through the application of its people's intellectual and technical skills to their available and im-
portable resources, made itself the third greatest industrial
power on earth. Black men with forty million trained people
dedicated to making a new life for themselves, operating on a
land mass one-sixth the size of the United States, could become the greatest industrial nation on earth. Only our lack of
faith in what we are and what we possess could prevent us
from seeking that goal.

If the Japanese, by dividing their skilled persons into Zaibat-
su or families such as Matsui, devoted to banking and trading
and mining, or Mitsubishi, devoted to industries, chemicals
and electronics or Sumitomo and Matsuda, devoted to their
various economic pursuits, could make their nation whole and
viable, black people in America put in touch with resourceful
land could transcend the Japanese achievements. Young black
men graduating from universities could enter the service of
their black nation and help it develop its potential. What is to
prevent us from running our own sea ports, traversing our own
shipping lanes, undertaking our own economic course and as-
sisting our beleaguered brothers in Africa and other parts of
the black diaspora? [22]

Henry pointed out that the five states, in addition to their
natural resources, provide access to the sea which, once the black
nation was formed, would allow trade with other parts of the
world, especially South America, Mexico, and Cuba. "Therefore,
our getting land and the gulf port, access to the sea, is essential
to black liberation. A viable black nation cannot be developed
using white-controlled ports."

In summary, the RNA's economic program envisions initial
reparations from the United States government. It would utilize
the funds for development projects in the five states. In the final
analysis the RNA is a political nationalist organization, proposing
to gain control of five states in an "acceptable" political fashion—
by voting out the incumbent whites and replacing them with black
(nationalist) politicians. The emphasis on political control left the

RNA little opportunity to develop a detailed economic program. And by placing emphasis on traditionally skilled blacks as the core of RNA economic development, the organization assumed that the proposed nation's economic system would operate like that of the United States. Though at times it alludes to "Ujamaa" or African Socialism as its system, no detailed description of how it would operate has ever been given.

Economic Programs: The Conceptual Basis

The differences as well as similarities of organizational economic programs present a complex array of ideas and approaches to separatist economic philosophy. Except for the Nation of Islam's and CORE's proposed economic programs, the rest paid little attention to economic infrastructure and long-range contingencies. All the movement organizations depended heavily on their membership for financial support. The Nation had other sources of income, from its various small businesses, to support its program; but nevertheless it, too, depended on its members for survival.

The organizational economic programs all seem to aver a socialistic-economic organization. That is, in that they all ostensibly rejected capitalism as a model of economic organization, they all differed as to the model system. Though some of the details as to why they rejected capitalism differed, they all ended by accepting the colonial analogy—black communities in the United States are victims of the Mother Country–colony relationship in the same way that Europe and her dominated and exploited colonies are or were in the Third World. Internal colonialism rendered black communities impotent to cope with the reality of a capitalistic economic system, and therefore blacks had to develop or adopt—or some combination of the two—some form of socialism.

Most of the forty to fifty billion dollars circulated in black communities tended to end outside them, and the little that remained was controlled by those who lived outside the communities. Blacks who lived in black communities and owned capital and businesses exercised tight-fisted control over the few dollars they had, thus defying the basic economic principle of money circulating through several hands and enterprises before leaving the community. Hence the combination of outsiders (exploiters) controlling ghetto enterprises and taking out resources, and the few blacks (elites, bourgeoisie) who had businesses and other capital resources circumventing the circulation process, nearly negated any possibility of economic development based on capitalistic principles.

These viewpoints led the organizations to reject capitalism as an economic system. Accepting the analogy of internal colonialism, they thought that some form of socialism was most desirable for amelioration of the black condition. In that the general economy was around a trillion dollars and blacks had a slippery handle on forty to fifty billion, 3 percent of the total, it was readily evident that economic development, or even survival, depended on pooling the scarce resources of black communities. And if pooling modest resources for economic development is a form of socialism, pooling large amounts is capitalism!

Each organization also favored some form of reparations in payment for slavery and other forms of economic exclusion after slavery legally ended. The reasoning behind the demands for reparations was straightforward: blacks were held in bondage without pay for about 250 years (if one begins with Virginia's first slave law in 1662; however, blacks were in reality slaves long before this date) and, therefore they should be compensated for their labor at a fair market price. The organizations derived different figures for reparations. Some, like the Panthers, RNA, and Nation of Islam, demanded direct monetary compensation as well as land.

Though many argue that the black demand for reparations is not unprecedented in history, the complexity and impracticality of such an arrangement makes it difficult if not impossible to implement.[23] Also, many reject out of hand any suggestion that blacks should receive reparations for, they say, there are too many historically wronged people who would also qualify for reparations. These reservations and rejections notwithstanding, the black separatist organizations and some whites continue to advance the claim.

(Insofar as the reality of blacks receiving reparations is concerned, considering all the arguments on both sides, the major issue is not whether black people deserve some sort of compensation for slavery—most agree that they do. The major issue is whether the slaveowners' descendants will take responsibility for their forebears' misdeeds. To do so is to admit that their present enjoyment of affluence and luxury is at the expense of the slaves and their descendants. Will people in positions of dominance indict themselves or share their ill-gotten power with the exploited powerless?)

Clearly the organizations' separatist economic proposals and

Table 1. Separatist Economic Programs

Organization	Operational Economic System[a]	Proposed Economic System[b]	Demand Reparations[c]
Nation of Islam	Member-business[d]	Cooperative Capitalism[e]	Yes
CORE	Member-chapter[f] "Black Capitalism"	Cooperative Socialism[g]	Yes
SNCC	Member-chapter-public[h]	Capitalistic Socialism[i]	Yes
Panthers	Membership[j]	Socialism	Yes
RNA	Membership-public	Cooperative Socialism	Yes

[a] The source from which each movement derives its financial base. This implies that the general American economic system is the framework in which all the organizations presently operate.

[b] The kind of economic system advocated by the respective organizations. Evidently most organizations indicated that they rejected pure capitalism as the best economic system for black people.

[c] All the organizations favor some form of compensation—usually as reparations payment to blacks for slavery.

[d] The organization derived its financial base from its membership as well as from the business it operates.

[e] From all indications the organization proposes to use capitalism as the system of making money, but would use cooperatives as a means of distributing it.

[f] CORE received its financial base from membership contributions as well as from foundations, governmental, and other private sources.

[g] Meaning that a socialistic economic system was proposed, and cooperatives would be used as a distribution mechanism.

[h] SNCC, for the most part, received its financial base from its parent organization (SCLC), then from individual and organization contributions (public), and finally from each chapter maintaining itself until the movement organization's demise.

[i] Meaning that the organization called for some sort of socialism, but suggested that it be achieved through capitalism. Carmichael and Hamilton's "Black Power" is a good example.

[j] Meaning that for all practical purposes the organization's membership supplied the financial base. It then followed that the way in which the members obtained the money they contributed may be significant (but not for our purposes here).

their demands for reparations present a dilemma for all concerned. In the first place, despite their cogent analysis of the black economic plight, capitalism in the United States is a pervasive reality. Though it is not laissez-faire capitalism, it is far from socialism. After all, the regulated still theoretically control the regulators.

Why else should it take so long for regulatory agencies to ban effectively from the market products that have been proven dangerous to consumers (for whom the regulators regulate)? The outcome of separatist economics usually resulted in, not socialistic-economic principles as articulated by the organizations, but socialistic rhetoric operating in a capitalistic mode. In other words, creating and operating a microeconomic system on socialistic principles in a long-established macroeconomic system (capitalism) based on a constituency (blacks) that has never been allowed economic and political equality, is next to impossible without a full-scale revolution in the political sense or a revolution in economic behavior against the dominant economic system. Blacks on a large scale did neither. Neither did a significant proportion of whites.

In a sense, the dominance of capitalist centripetal force over the centrifugal socialistic tendency resulted in the organizations having simultaneously to denounce the oppressor and utilize his system. Except for not selling shares to the public, the Nation of Islam operated not unlike any other capitalistic corporation: its chain of command, its table of organization, and its vast array of existing and proposed enterprises reflected in its corporate structure what they call a blueprint for a "nation within a nation." The Muslims argued that their economic program is geared specifically to what the black masses need: food, clothing, shelter, technology, and good health.

Its assets and activities also are suggestive of corporate figures: over eighty temples across the country; thousands of tithes and pledges generating several million dollars in nontaxable income; income from *Muhammed Speaks*; the $3 million loan from Libya. Other corporations borrow from the Arabs and negotiate loans from the United States government. (If the aircraft [Lockheed] and transportation [Penn Central] industries did it, why not the Nation? After all, the aircraft and transportation systems are vital to the nation's economy and security. Is not the Nation the nation's largest black ghetto industry, which siphons off hustlers, pimps, drunks, junkies, prostitutes, and others who cost the taxpayers money? Are the streets not safer without them?)

In addition to its corporate-like financial operations, it has come to understand the political relationship between money and politics. An editorial in *Muhammed Speaks* regarding the Nation and politics observed:

For the uninitiated, the Nation of Islam—by that definition is

already a potent force on the American political frontier. In
the city of Chicago alone, in 1974 the Nation of Islam paid
more than $1 million in local taxes . . . [and] more than $1.3
million was paid in wages last year in Chicago. These wages, to
more than 1,000 full-time, part-time, permanent and temporary employees, were also taxed.[25]

The editorial stressed that the Nation indirectly saved taxpayers
money by giving hope to people who at one time lived solely off
taxpayers. Their newly found Muslim-inspired hope has now made
them taxpayers and also contributors to the well-being of the
general American community.

The Muslim efforts did not go unrecognized by the power structures in many cities where they operated: Newark, East Orange,
New York, Dallas, Fort Worth, and Chicago, among others. The
Muslims were praised for their splendid efforts and accomplishments in aiding the black poor to become good and proven citizens.[26] Brashler, writing in a semicynical vein for *New York
Magazine*, made the point that things have changed when the
governor of Illinois and Mayor Daley of Chicago, two of the
most powerful politicians in the United States, laud the establishment of and accomplishments of the Nation in Chicago's
black ghetto. To show their sincerity and appreciation, both of
these men would proclaim a day in March 1974 as

> the Honorable Elijah Muhammad Day. And there would be
> a $50-a-plate dinner at the Conrad Hilton, a testimonial from
> the heavyweights—PUSH's Jesse Jackson, Lieutenant Governor
> of Illinois Neil Hartigan, [ex-President] Nixon's Stanley Scott,
> [ex-CORE National Director] Floyd McKissick—and they
> would all eat bad food just to sing the praises of the little fez
> . . . who finally crashed into the sphere of respectability by
> making a little cash."[27]

One can conclude that the Nation and the power structure mixed
money and politics, ultimately the only game in town.

Though players may use different size bats, and gloves with brand
names of their choice, and even multicolored uniforms, all must adhere to the basic rules. The Nation's "blue-eyed devil" rhetoric and
its rigid membership requirements had to be altered to fit the rules.
To this end, the late Elijah Muhammad urged his followers to thank
whites for the opportunity the Nation had received to expand its
multimillion-dollar movement. He urged his followers to stop blam-
ing the slave owners for their shortcomings and blame themselves.

After Muhammad's death in early 1975, his son and successor, Wallace, announced that the Nation no longer barred whites from becoming members! What this meant was that the Nation had become the largest ghetto entrepreneur and consequently had come to grips with the topics of finance—common and preferred stock; long and short-term investments; municipal bonds; commercial, marketing, and savings banks; mortgages; borrowing policies; licensing regulations; and all the red tape and politics thereof. For their bank they had to cope with local, state, and federal guidelines, agencies, and politics. The same with their other businesses. In short, when the Nation became a multi-million-dollar operation, including real estate holdings, farms, department stores, bakeries, restaurants, schools, hospitals and a bank, among other businesses, the political game had to be played in boardrooms and smoke-filled political haunts, with robot-like technicians, inflexible and dull-witted bureaucrats, and business people who only understood profit—all with blue eyes who do not live in the ghetto. The Nation could not beat them, so it asked them to join, knowing they would not. But in this instance the importance lay in what the Nation said, not what whites did.

Though all the organizations proposed socialistic-economic alternatives, capitalism remained the dominant, overriding reality. CORE's well-thought-out economic program eventually came to nought because it required too much initial capital investment from the white business community, a risk they were not willing to take. It was risky because (1) CORE, with its separatist ideology, proposed to act as the middle man between white capital and the black communities or masses, and (2) the lack of skills in the black communities made profit, or even recouping initial investment, questionable. A third reason was probably the most important: if black communities did become viable economic units, where would capitalists dump their surplus goods and where would they obtain the necesaary cheap labor? In short, what would happen if the internal colony became independent? The best solution was to negate the possibility.

Meanwhile, CORE continued to propose separatist economics while playing the capitalist game. The bulk of its revenues still came from corporate donations through direct grants and advertisements in the organization's magazine *CORE* and from federal and municipal grants. Reasons for these grants were easy to see: CORE launched a campaign against drug abuse as an "enemy of the people"; it formed the Committee to Help Aid Prisoners

(CHAP) to provide transportation for families and friends of inmates to visit on a regular basis; from the fall of 1971 to the summer of 1972, financial support from New York School District 16 enabled CORE to "redirect the energies" of New York City street gangs; and it established in Baltimore "the CORE Target City Youth Program . . . making employables out of unemployables," funded by the U.S. Department of Labor and the Department of Health, Education and Welfare. Specifically, CORE trained "young people to be secretaries, clerks, printers, and repairmen. We're taking them off relief rolls and putting them on payrolls. Last year [1972] CORE placed 83 young people in training-related jobs, 6 graduates of the program returned to school or entered college, and 7 people who dropped out of the program (due to personal financial difficulties) were placed in jobs unrelated to their Target City training."[28] These undertakings hardly sound like separatist economics, and the corporate community agreed.

CORE, like most nonprofit voluntary associations, continued to rely on membership fees and other contributions for survival. Its magazine became an important source of revenue by soliciting advertisements from the business community; in its 1973/74 Annual Report, for example, the magazine grossed from ads $380,343.40 while membership fees and nonbusiness contributions brought in $133,515.75; magazine sales netted $41,000. Its largest source of revenue came from the federal government for the Baltimore Training Project ($433,000.00).[29]

Like CORE, the Panthers became involved with the local needs of black people and began to establish projects that qualified for Office of Economic Opportunity grants. Pursuing those grants may have contributed to the organization's schism and eventual decline (aided by coercive social control) as a potent movement. One hint on how the Panthers handled funds was seen in Rule 22, dictating that "all chapters, branches and components of the . . . Party must submit a monthly financial report to the Ministry of Finance, and also the Central Committee." Rule 24 states that "no chapter or branch shall accept grants, poverty funds, money or any other aid from any government agency without contacting the Central Headquarters [in Oakland]." In that all funds were centrally controlled, some members of the Central Committee were accused of high living and neglecting the needs of the people. Eventually the organization declined in influence (or publicity) and began working with "grants, poverty funds, and other aid" from various sources. It, too, finally buckled under the weight of the operational economic system.

The RNA never enjoyed the kind of economic viability the other organizations had. It was always a membership-financed organization, because its ideology and how it proposed to make black separatism a reality never tempted corporations and government—despite, or because of, its demand for reparations—to contribute. to its operation. Its financial base, therefore, was almost wholly dependent on contributions from the black public and its small membership. Unfortunately, no black separatist organization ever long survived with support from the black public alone. Blacks who could comfortably contribute were middle-class and they tended to support other kinds of national voluntary associations, such as the NAACP and the Urban League, and local associations, like fraternities and sororities. The black poor (the majority) were in no position to support any voluntary association because it was a constant struggle to support themselves—if they could indeed do so without welfare or some other form of public assistance. Therefore, the RNA and like organizations, such as the Black Liberation Army, were left to struggle for survival and to base their appeal on ideology and sentiment. But these elements without a concommitantly strong economic base or program almost assured that the RNA would for the foreseeable future remain a fringe movement crying in the wilderness. Since people often kill prophets of bad news, economic starvation was just as good a way to go as any other.

Separatist economic programs, then, generally proposed socialist solutions but were constrained to operate within the existing capitalist framework. Though their proposals were not realized, together they touched on the fact that economic development initially required some form of centralized organizational structure to direct capital outlays and investment in the most beneficial way, not for individuals, but for the group as a whole. That is, in black urban America where there was a concentration of population, low income, low savings, low investment, large family units, little capital inflow and a large outflow, little entrepreneurial and managerial experience, and a low level of technical skill, a centralized development-bank approach was necessary.[30] The free-market concept was negated by the foregoing factors. One could argue that the centralized approach was initially used by today's leading capitalist nations, and most certainly (through X-year plans) by socialist and communist countries. England, the United States, Japan, and Germany have all used at one time or another development banks, credit banks, and other credit corporations for the purpose of shifting capital from abundant and productive areas to those where it can promote balanced development.

Hence, the separatist economic programs were not wrong in their general approach, but lacked the material and human resources to effect long-term programs. The major difficulty, however, had to do with accepting the "internal colony" argument. Unlike Africa or Asia, when ghettos expelled or otherwise encouraged the "colonial oppressor" to leave, he did not return to Europe and leave the people free to forge their own destinies. Rather, he returned to the suburbs and further contributed to economic, social, and political complications for the inner city. The skilled and experienced capitalist can play the game from near or far, the ghetto or the suburbs. Separatist economics were not only barred from having good seats, they were relegated to viewing the action from outside the arena.

9 INTERRELATIONS AND COMPARISONS

All the separatist movements share one fundamental goal: black liberation from white oppression. Beneath the surface, and just as important, is the fostering of a positive feeling of worth, a feeling the late Dr. Martin Luther King, Jr., called "somebodyness." But the reason there are movements instead of one movement, and organizations instead of a single separatist movement organization, is that they all have different approaches, methods, tactics, and strategies for eliminating white oppression and achieving black liberation.

That separatist movement organizations operate independently of one another does not mean that they have to compete with one another. Ideally, it would be more desirable for the organizations to cooperate, dividing their labor and focusing their efforts, for although the movements do sometimes ally, they sometimes develop bitter enmity, resulting from their differing approaches to the question of black liberation. The basic reason for these approaches stems from one fundamental fact: they have all sought to influence large numbers of people to join their respective organizations. In order to enhance large memberships, each organization attempted to make its ideology more appealing than that of the others by combining the "right" ingredients, realizing that the more people in the organization, the better chance it has to promote change.

Though all the organizations could identify the tree of white oppression, they could not agree on whether to attack the trunk or the branches. Some chose to leave it alone entirely, thinking the tree would eventually die a natural death. They seemed not to consider a third option: to attack the roots. The result of these different emphases among the organizations which followed one of the technical forms of separation was competition. Competition among the organizations affords an opportunity to examine more closely the ideological ingredients as well as how the organizations viewed and related to one another. Some of the issues on which the organizations agreed and disagreed, accepted and rejected, damned and blessed include the following: (1) the location of the Black Nation and how that location would be decided, that is, whether (a) in the United States or Africa, (b) by plebiscite or by organizational decision; (2) Pan-Africanism; (3) political direction; (4) cultural nationalism; (5) black capitalism; (6) through or outside the system.

SNCC and CORE

The Congress of Racial Equality was one of the organizations represented at the meeting at Atlanta University in May 1960 when the Temporary Student Non-Violent Coordinating Committee was formed. Len Holt, a CORE lawyer from Norfolk, Virginia, represented CORE at that meeting. Evidently CORE was one of the initial influences on SNCC's emergence as a direct action organization. (CORE had engaged in direct action since the 1940's and was among the first organizations to use the sit-in as a direct-action tactic.)

Traditionally, CORE was a northern-based organization with only a few staff people in the South. Once the sit-ins began, CORE acted as an educational and organizing agent in the tactics of nonviolence. Both SNCC and CORE were initially composed of both black and white members. (This arrangement continued up to about 1965–66; then the active membership of both organizations became almost all black.) In 1961 and 1962 both organizations engaged in sit-in demonstrations, apparently supporting each other reciprocally.

SNCC-CORE cooperation was extensive and significant for a period of five or six years. One of the most significant factors was the Freedom Rides of 1961. CORE had been a forerunner in an earlier and less well known Freedom Ride. In 1947 Bayard Rustin and a group representing CORE and the Fellowship of Reconciliation (FOR) engaged in a "Journey of Reconciliation" to test a recent Supreme Court decision outlawing racial discrimination in interstate travel. Riding two buses through the upper South, their experience was that during interstate travel neither white passengers nor diners would strenuously object to blacks sitting any place they chose.[1] Fourteen years later (1961) the Supreme Court, in the Boynton Case, extended desegregation from carriers themselves to terminal facilities. Tom Gaither and Gordon Carey, two CORE members, talked of a new Freedom Ride through the Deep South to test the new ruling; it was agreed to by the National Director of CORE, James Farmer. Farmer and James Peck (who had undertaken the ride with Bayard Rustin and others in 1947) were the first to volunteer for the new rides.

On May 1, 1961, seven blacks and six whites met in Washington, D.C. to receive nonviolence training. On May 4 the group, in two separate buses, one a Greyhound and the other a Trailways, started on a trip from Washington to New Orleans, Louisiana. The rides provoked whites to resort to blind and brutal savagery. Zinn recounts a description by one of the Freedom Riders describing a white mob at the Birmingham bus terminal: The mob attacked everyone black in sight, causing mass flight. The mob caught all the male Freedom Riders and beat them at will. One brutally beaten rider was John Lewis, who was left lying on the ground, blood streaming from his head.[2] Lewis later became SNCC's chairman.

Another SNCC leader, Stokely Carmichael, received part of his rite of passage of white brutality when his group was put in the Parchman Mississippi Penitentiary. One of the most unforgettable characters there was Sheriff Tyson, who seemed always to wear boots that were too large and who would for no apparent reason, out of the blue, blurt out, "You goddam smart uppity nigger, why you always trying to be so uppity for? I'm going to see to it that you don't ever get out of this place." Tyson warned them to stop singing, and when they refused, he took their mattresses. Still not intimidated by Tyson or the hard cell floor, they continued to sing. Tyson then ordered that one of the inmates, Freddy Leonard, be put into the wrist-breakers, which causes one to writhe and twist. Carmichael in no uncertain terms told Tyson how wrong and unjust he was. Tyson retorted, "I don't want to hear all that shit nigger," and started to put the wrist-breakers on Carmichael.[3]

Instances of physical and psychological brutality can be multiplied by the thousands. At the August 1963 March on Washington, John Lewis gave the most bitter speech, but still had to tone it down. All of the other speakers talked of the dream of brotherhood and brotherly love. It seemed as if all America, white and black, wanted to share in that dream, but American reality was that CORE Freedom Riders and others working to register black people to vote were victims of hate and brutality, of bitter resentment and mob violence. White lawlessness against these youngsters who were fighting for human dignity received only token responses. The federal government did not respond effectively. Its agencies rationalized, "We're only an investigative body, not an enforcement body; this is a local problem and we can act only when we receive a request for help from the local authorities." Zinn points out that the Department of Justice prosecuted nine civil rights workers in Albany, Georgia, in 1963 for picketing a white grocer's store. John Lewis in his 1963 speech asserted that the federal government, not southern racists, had indicted the civil rights workers for peacefully protesting against discrimination. He then asked what the federal government did when a deputy sheriff in Albany almost beat Attorney C. B. King to death? What did the federal government do when the pregnant wife of Slater King was assaulted by Albany policemen, causing her to lose her baby?[4] The answer: nothing of consequence. Lewis asked, "Whose side is the federal government on?" The question was omitted from Lewis' prepared speech because Catholic Archbishop Patrick O'Boyle objected to it. The omission allowed those who wanted to hear only a melodious tune to hear it; many knew that the melody was off key—John Lewis,, Stokely Carmichael, James Farmer, Malcolm X, Robert Williams, Elijah Muhammad, SNCC, CORE, the Revolutionary Action Movement (RAM). Others knew it too: the white people who continue to deny black humanity.

The Freedom Rides planted the idea, not prominent until several years later in SNCC and CORE, that nonviolence might not be the most effective available technique for securing change. Why lie supine in the face of enormous force applied without scruple? Zinn pointed out that the use of nonviolent direct action in southern "outlaw communities" was met in the same way that totalitarian states met opposition, "by open brutality or overwhelming force." He cites as an example the city of Jackson, Mississippi, using its own creation, a Thompson Tank—an armored car with machine guns to carry a dozen armed policemen—to deal with demonstrations. This, continues Zinn, prompted talk among blacks of self-defense, making Malcolm X's exhortation to blacks to arm themselves difficult to refute. The murder of Medgar Evers, the bombing of a black church in Birmingham killing three little black girls attending Sunday School, and endless police brutality made arguments against it sound absurd. Any other group of people who took up arms "against the tyranny of their government would be hailed as 'Freedom Fighters,' But Negroes were expected to adhere to nonviolence."[5]

SNCC and CORE lost faith in the willingness of white America and its federal government to come to the aid of black people in the crunch. In 1964 SNCC promoted an integrated Mississippi Freedom Democratic Party, which challenged the regular all-white racist delegation. (The state is 40 percent black.) CORE supported SNCC in its unsuccessful attempt. In May 1964 CORE also changed its traditional stance on nonpartisan political involvement. It opposed Mayor Robert Wagner of New York City and Presidential candidate Barry Goldwater. By 1966 both organizations had shifted from their 1964 positions of integration to gain a share of power for black people without white allies, and thus without financial support.

By 1966 also SNCC and CORE were emphasizing black economic, social, and political involvement. SNCC's new "radicalism," Zinn rightly argues, was the direct result of white racist violence experienced by young blacks in southern cotton fields, jail and prison cells and not from Communists or "outside agitators."[6] Emphasizing that black people had to help themselves, SNCC concluded that whites can only help blacks by organizing in the white community where the power really lies, where oppression of blacks festers and grows. CORE, in turn, looked to the ghetto. The theme of its 1964 convention in Durham, North Carolina, was "The Black Ghetto: An Awakening Giant."

In 1966, when SNCC's Stokely Carmichael called for Black Power, CORE was supporting the slogan and the idea in intent and spirit. Though both organizations had arrived at the concept of black power at about the same time, CORE's activities were for the most part Northern urban; SNCC's, Southern rural.

It was a good division of labor. The younger SNCC viewed CORE as a partner in the struggle for black liberation, and as somewhat of a father. What CORE later got from SNCC was the impetus to turn from direct action to community organization. Their relationship did not suddenly stop in 1966, but the later developments between them did not end as well as they began.

The common experience of CORE and SNCC with southern white brutality led both organizations to conclude that black people had to solve their own problems without the white liberals, who had become an irritation and a drag. Yet the two organizations did not stay on a common path for long; their proposed solutions ultimately turned out to be quite different, because of differences in their respective locations, leaders, and membership.

In November of 1963 the Council of Federated Organizations (COFO) was formed to bring to bear the different resources of SNCC, CORE, NAACP, SCLC, and small, local groups working for civil rights.[7] Dr. Aaron Henry of Mississippi was elected President, SNCC's Robert Moses became Program Director, and Dave Dennis, a CORE Field Secretary, was elected Assistant Program Director.

CORE insisted, despite the unity theme, that it be given some special area of Mississippi so that it could get some news coverage to aid in its fund-raising efforts in the North. Before long, in fact, all of the distinct organizations made claims to being COFO's most important component. An example was this point made on SNCC's behalf: "SNCC supplies the personnel in four of the five Congressional districts of the state, 95 percent of the staff in the state headquarters in Jackson, and 90 to 95 percent of the money for operating the civil rights program and facilities throughout the entire state. . . . Civil Rights in Mississippi is COFO. SNCC for all practical purposes is COFO."[8]

But CORE was urban-based and received a large portion of its financial backing from white Northerners. It had to justify its expenditures in the South. Zinn again accurately observes that rivalry, conflict, petty jealousy, and differences over tactics and strategy was a way of life in COFO. But their basic raison d'être always seemed to bring them together in a good working relationship during times of crisis.[9]

One of the specific issues that produced friction between CORE and SNCC was the Mississippi Freedom Democratic Party's bid to be recognized at the 1964 Democratic National Convention held in Atlantic City, New Jersey. COFO, in the long hot summer of 63, had sponsored a Freedom Registration. Later came the mock election—"mock" in a dual sense: Since it was not recognized by the constituted authority in Mississippi, it mocked the state's claim to democracy. The fall of 1963 saw Aaron Henry and Edwin King running for governor and lieutenant governor on the Freedom ticket. They polled 80,000 votes, outside the official polling booths. In 1963 any Mississippi black who tried to register or vote officially was likely to find himself the victim of intimidation or attack. Stories of prospective black voters being fired on or evicted or attacked are legion, not just among the field workers who were there, but in reports of the United States Commission on Civil Rights.[10] Yet the Henry/King campaign left no doubt that blacks wanted to vote.

Still later, a state convention was held and a chairman elected. It was decided that the MFDP would go to Atlantic City to challenge the "regular" racist delegation at the 1964 Democratic Convention. The outcome of the challenge was that the MFDP was hardly recognized. SNCC and CORE concluded that other measures were necessary.

The challenge also partially split CORE from SNCC. SNCC totally rejected the "compromises" offered by the National Democratic Party (later establishing the Lowndes County organization to promote independent, separate black political action), while some of CORE's leaders were willing to accept them.

In 1964 also CORE began to shift from direct action to black community organization. CORE saw the realism in SNCC's program of promoting participation among those who had not been able to influence the system that oppresses them.[11] The MFDP and SNCC's Lowndes County organizational efforts were designed for oppressed people who needed to participate in attempts to eliminate their oppression. Said CORE's James Farmer, "We know as clearly as ever that freedom cannot be won solely by engineers, although a considerable amount of engineering will be necessary."[12] Farmer was ready to apply the SNCC approach to major cities after the explosions that had rocked Birmingham (1963), Rochester and Harlem (1964), Watts (1965), and Chicago and Cleveland (1966).

The 1964 CORE theme of "The Black Ghetto: An Awakening Giant" emphasized even more strongly CORE's 1965 and 1966 national conventions. CORE's new direction, away from integration-oriented direct action, led to a change in its leadership. In 1965 Floyd McKissick became the new national director, about a year after CORE chose not to remain nonpartisan. Whether that policy decision prompted Farmer to step down is not clear. In any case, blacks had developed a more assertive political consciousness, and a new question arose in both black and white minds: Was white America ready to accommodate this new black assertiveness, or would blacks have to disrupt the system before the power structure would begin to take them seriously? CORE and SNCC, represented by McKissick and Carmichael on Meet the Press in August 1966, shared the view that nonviolence was no longer a strategy that could attain equality in America. McKissick felt that in the early 60's blacks who participated in demonstrations were intimidated by white violence, but by the mid-60's its preponderance prompted blacks to rethink the efficacy of nonviolence. Blacks would continue to participate in

demonstrations, but they would not agree to be hit and not return blow for blow.[13] CORE's position was that nonviolence
and self-defense were not mutually exclusive. SNCC's Carmichael
opted more clearly for self-defense, stating that black Americans
must protect themselves against their protection. "We have to
protect ourselves against state troopers, against police in Mississippi, against Jim Clark, against . . . Rizzo [then Chief of Police,
later Mayor] in Philadelphia [and] if we do not protect ourselves,
since the police forces and the federal government [do not], then
who is going to protect us?"[14]

Despite the disagreement between the two organizations at the
1964 National Democratic Convention, CORE continued to view
SNCC as a partner from that time and during the height of the
Black Power period. CORE changed leadership again in 1968,
with Roy Innis becoming the National Director. CORE continued,
but more strongly, in the direction of community control of the
black ghetto. This direction ultimately led to the parting of CORE
and SNCC, with SNCC concentrating on rural Southern politics
and CORE on autonomous black organization in the great urban
ghettos. CORE's rhetoric, however, stayed diffuse enough to satisfy many different ideological positions. For example Roy Innis
observed, in a statement that gains no stature after textual analysis: "There is a compelling need to emphasize the socio-psychological aspect of Black Power. We can cry 'Black Power' until doomsday
[but] until black people accept values meaningful to themselves,
there can be no completely effective organizing for the development of Black Power."[15]

Yet CORE had a program, and in the end came to view SNCC
as an organization without one. CORE, for the most part, took on
black capitalism as its major orientation. In contrast, when SNCC
leader Ivanhoe Donaldson responded to a Bayard Rustin question
about what program SNCC had, he answered, "I'm not sure we
have to justify ourselves with a program in this country. We have
a program because we have a base." In response to Donaldson's
statement, Cruse observes that SNCC's strength lay not in structure and organization, but in the rhetoric of its leading spokesmen.[16]

When SNCC began to assert that blacks and other nonwhites
must take up arms against American imperialism, Innis called
them "boy militants" and proposed that blacks should work for
control of their communities. With the decline and disappearance
of SNCC as an active organization, CORE probably considered
itself in the mainstream of black thought. It seemed evident in

any event, with SNCC defunct and the SCLC nearly reduced to silence and inactivity, that there was no longer any strong Southern black voice or style of thought.

Oddly enough it was in the South where SNCC and CORE and others achieved their one genuine partnership, not with the New Left, as suggested by Inge Powell Bell. She believes that CORE's slide to its new position of political participation and community involvement was prompted by the "New Left." She argues that groups most prominently identified with the emergence of the New Left included the SDS, "an organization devoted to a broad range of domestic and foreign policy concerns, organized in 1960," and SNCC, emerging from the sit-in activity, "and the Free Speech Movement, which developed at the University of California at Berkeley in 1964-1965."[17] Bell makes the point that the New Left saw the liberal establishment holding the dominant power base; thus the responsibility for poverty, racism, segregation, and a reactionary foreign policy lay with the Democrats, the liberals, and organized labor. It seems rather strange that the new left underestimated the Dixiecrats and reactionaries, to say nothing of what later came to be called "middle America."

Let us grant that the New Left did have an impact on CORE. But its ideas were not new to black people. American oppression, the need for "participatory democracy," materialism, over-bureaucratization, etc. were themes which black people live with year after year. The New Left contributed to and sympathized with the CORE and SNCC position on black power, but was hardly responsible for it. Indeed, the black experience and black ideology was a critical part of the entire New Left pitch. Moreover, the New Left never seemed to grasp how absurd it was to tell a Delta sharecropper or a poor ghetto slum dweller that materialism is corrupting. Nor did he have to be told that the government was racist, that he should participate in the political process; and that the bureaucracy ostensibly designed to administer his welfare or unemployment check, assuming he was lucky enough to get one, functioned for the benefit of the bureaucrat. The New Left articulated with fanatic zeal a reality that black people have experienced for centuries.

Typical of this faulty notion of the influence of the New Left on black people in general and CORE in particular is the following: "The new left's condemnation of American society as unreformable and its decisive break with liberal Democrats, the administration, organized labor, the 'liberal establishment,' played directly into the growing trend toward Negro nationalism in the direct action movement."[18] Because of the chronology of events, along with the zealous and gallant efforts of black people over a long period of time to come to grips with their oppression, a more correct assessment of the New Left may be that much of the force of its rhetoric depended on the ready example of blacks still oppressed, and that its hopes and techniques for "liberating" America had earlier been articulated by blacks struggling against their oppression. The proposition holds even to slogans and symbols.

The raised fist (which is not an original black gesture but was popularized by them during the 1960's), "Right on," long hair (the natural or Afro), and other black originals were appropriated by many so-called liberation movements, and by Madison Avenue as well. Yet we need to recognize how ironically revealing it was that only when white groups shouted the reality of oppression did it become believable. It is understandable how a mostly white New Left became the spokesman for black activism and civil rights in the minds of a large portion of white America, including many academics like Professor Bell.[19]

Since the Black Panthers proposed to be a Marxist-Leninist Party, and in fact formed alliances with New Left groups, how did CORE and the Panthers relate to one another?

CORE and the Panthers

CORE viewed the Black Panthers as a group completely out of touch with the black community. Though CORE evaluated urban unrest (passive and active) as the natural outcome of oppressed conditions, its advocacy of violence as a reaction to violence inflicted by the oppressor sometimes seems lukewarm. Thus, although the Panther position of self-defense was not very different in principle, it has been far more emphatically and openly applied.

CORE understood that the Black Panther Party came into being in self-defense to protect blacks from police brutality and intimidation. But according to CORE, the Panthers were not equipped to deal with programmatic solutions to the problems of the black communities. What did they suggest after agitation and defense? Where were their positive plans?

CORE dismissed the Panthers as mere ideological revolutionaries who sought solutions outside the traditional American frameworks of avenues to problem solving. CORE has never actually espoused black revolution, as the Panthers have. In fact, the closest they came was at the 1968 National CORE Convention in Columbus, Ohio, when a delegate advocated that CORE initiate a campaign against genocide, including the creation of a black community police force to protect black people and the arming of the black community. He went on to call for total separation of whites and blacks ("self-determination is impossible in close proximity to whites") and the establishment of a national homeland in the southeastern part of the United States or in South Africa. But his resolution was tabled and never came up again.[20]

CORE was more cautious, perhaps more prudent, and considered the Panther position of carrying arms for self-defense and overtly advocating the arming of the black community as irrational and an invitation to open attack by law enforcement agencies. Moreoever, Panther truculence was held to jeopardize the safety of the very masses the Panthers proposed to protect. CORE also reasoned that those same masses were not prepared to do more than listen to Panther talk of revolution, so that the gap between word and deed was far greater for the Panther audience than for its speakers.

In general, CORE considered the Panthers more expressive than instrumental, appealing to young ghetto dwellers who were more concerned with the emotional appeal of uniforms, rhetoric, and guns than with tangible programs to deal with the political and economic poverty of the ghetto. CORE did assume a posture of black power, trying to establish mass appeal, but still it felt that the leadership had to come not from the bottom, but from the black middle class. According to CORE, Panther leadership and followers simply were not well enough trained or highly enough skilled to carry out sustained specific attacks on the practical problems of the black masses.

The Panthers viewed CORE, on the other hand, as a "cultural nationalist" organization composed of bourgeois blacks. The Panthers believed that Black Power, SNCC-style, was adopted by CORE and translated by CORE to mean black capitalism. Cleaver, in a *Playboy* interview in October 1968, answered a question about the efficacy of "militant" black organizations, such as CORE, working for black capitalism by replying that it was an attempt on the part of the power structure to get black people into the capitalist economic system. He did not feel it would work, because their efforts would not go far and deep enough to give black people community control of all their institutions. Cleaver pointed out that of all the many militant black organizations, CORE rushed in most enthusiastically to embrace that delusion; in some cities they formed a large part of the staff. But they didn't have the decisive control, and that is all important. They can call these new devices "community" corporations, but private firms from the outside can always pull out and Congress can always cut down on the federal funds, as happened in the war on poverty.[21] He believed that CORE's strategy for black economic development would ultimately benefit individuals but not blacks as a group. For example, James Farmer, CORE's former National Director, took an appointment in the Nixon Administrator as Assistant Secretary of Health, Education and Welfare to implement Nixon's, and perhaps CORE's, ideas on black capitalism. But although Farmer benefited from the appointment, blacks did not. The same kind of individual gain accrued to Floyd McKissick, who replaced Farmer as CORE's National Director, when he founded a business, Floyd McKissick, Inc.[22] The Panthers took the position that black people should be represented by leaders chosen by them who would go into the political arena and set forth their desires and needs.

The Panthers regarded CORE's militant stance as a valuable but outmoded tactic. It was not designed to deal with police brutality in the black communities. (The Panthers called for armed self-defense in those communities.)

In short, the Panthers regard CORE as an organization that profits from the black power era, is not revolutionary, and thus is of no value to the revolution that the Panthers have envisioned.

CORE and the Nation of Islam

At the 1966 National Convention, when CORE ostensibly abandoned integration as an organization aim, instead adopting "black power through racial coexistence," the black power resolution noted that in the distant and recent past, using the Garvey movement and the Nation of Islam as examples, only the concept of black nationalism had been able to mobilize a large number of black people.

The same point was highlighted much earlier in a debate held at Cornell University in March 1962 between James Farmer, then National Director of CORE, and Malcolm X, then representing the Nation of Islam. At that time, CORE's policy was integration through interracial direct action, while the Muslim position was then racial separation. Malcolm X made the point that according to the teachings of the honorable Elijah Muhammad, the so-called Negroes would never achieve integration in America. He cited a column by James Reston on the editorial page of the *New York Times* of December 15, 1961. Writing from London, Reston pointed out that European statesmen were concerned with "the time when Russia, Europe and America will have to unite together to ward off the threat of China and the non-white world." In short, since Russia was a white country, the real problem was race, not communism.

Malcolm X conceded that if CORE could achieve black freedom, justice, and equality through integration, the Muslims would go along with the integrationists. But integration had shown that it was not going to bring human dignity to dark mankind; hence, integration was not the best solution to the problem. Malcolm X concluded that since blacks could not achieve human dignity as long as whites dominated all of the institutions in American society, the most feasible alternative for black people, and whites, too, for that matter, was to leave the United States because "the American government has proven its inability to bring about integration or give us freedom, justice and equality mixed up with white people." Malcolm argued that the failure or inability of the federal government to promote black equality, justice, and dignity pointed up the efficacy of Elijah Muhammad's proposed solution: Since the government is neither prepared to send blacks to Africa nor bring about integration, the best solution is black and white national separation in the United States, where blacks can work toward solving their own problems; black people merit their own land (territory) because they have for four hundred years contributed their labor, slave and free, to make the nation what it is.

Farmer insisted that CORE's objectives were best met through integration, because "the disease and the evils that we have pointed to in our American culture have grown out of segregation and its partner, prejudice. We are for integration, which is the repudiation of the evil of segregation. . . . Our objective is to have each individual accepted on the basis of his individual merit and not on the basis of his color."[23]

Though Farmer never became the kind of separatist Malcolm X advocated in 1962, he did change his mind relative to the tactics of interracial direct action and the *methods* in which black people were to achieve dignity, justice, and equality in American society.

In his book *Freedom—When?* Farmer discusses his changed perception of Malcolm X's personal role and that of the Muslims as a group leading him to display a sensitive understanding of the dynamics involved in the Muslims' black nationalist/separatist appeal. His new sensitivity led him to reflect on his long experience in interracial civil rights activity, where most whites were often surprised and disappointed with blacks who displayed any affinity for black nationalism, especially that proposed by the Nation of Islam. Whites regard black nationalism and separation as reverse racism, a cult of violence, or simply un-American. On the surface, most blacks would not generally disagree with these sentiments; but beyond and beneath them, the long black experience with structured social inequality enables them to see and feel in the separatist appeal what whites can only empathize with and imagine. That is, when the nationalist-separatists extoll blackness, telling black people that they can be liberated only when they accept their blackness, that it was white civilization that taught blacks to hate themselves, and that blacks must free their minds and bodies from this white lore, black nationalism-separatism becomes more appealing. It essentially takes on a psychological role in that it repairs and perhaps bolsters damaged black egos, a necessary stage prior to engaging in economic and social corrective action. This psychological function is simultaneously what whites misunderstand and why even many sophisticated blacks accept the functional aspects of black separatism while looking askance at the more exotic myths.

The Muslims merit respect not only because of their insight into the black psyche, according to Farmer, but also because of their success. They have had astounding success in eliminating or reducing drug addiction, prostitution, juvenile delinquency, and other social ills among their members, and have had a profound impact on nonmembers. The group set and adhered to almost puritanical standards regarding sexual and personal morality and emphasized the Puritan ethic of hard work, frugality, and character building. The Nation and other black nationalist groups exhorted blacks to help themselves by cleaning up their own minds, bodies, and streets, by emphasizing education, and by starting businesses, patronizing and hiring other blacks. This, of course, says Farmer, is simply a black version "of the Protestant ethic which appeals to the basic American middle-class values held by most Negroes."

Continuing to comprehend and explain Malcolm X's impact on his thinking, Farmer thought it unfair for Malcolm X to be branded a black racist, and the Muslims racists-in-reverse, a black Ku Klux Klan. Reflecting on Malcolm's statement that the Nation had not, unlike the Klan, lynched anyone, but the Klan had many years and a lot of blood on the Nation, Farmer felt that in the United States it was still an unwritten law that black people had no rights that must be respected by whites. He thus regarded whites who equated the Nation of Islam with the Ku Klux Klan as having a "monstrous deficiency of moral sense." Farmer noted that as a result of this false equation, Malcolm X's idea of self-defense was sensible and there is in fact something grotesquely wrong when a victim of brutality is taught not to defend himself. Moreover, where black people are the constant victims of brutality and the government has refused or is unwilling to protect them, according to Farmer, rifle clubs, a perfectly legal undertaking, should be formed for protection of lives and property. He came to share this view with Malcolm X as the result of an experience of having almost been the victim of a white mob in Louisiana, when the Deacons for Defense and Justice, a black rifle club that had been formed in Jonesboro and Bogalusa, Louisiana, came to his rescue. Farmer thus had a personal reason for concluding that Malcolm X was correct when he stated that black freedom could be won by ballots or bullets, and in many instances it was true that "the law *is* a mask for white oppression."

Malcolm X's life was too short, but it was long enough for Farmer to see the two of them moving closer, perhaps crossing the same path. Malcolm X predicted that Farmer would become a nationalist, while Farmer predicted that Malcolm X would become an integrationist. They were both right: Malcolm X died attempting to enter a civil rights (he called it "human rights") movement through the OAAU he had previously derided as foolish, while Farmer eventually comprehended the political impact of Malcolm X's emphasis on nationalism. Although they never fully accepted each other's philosophy and ideology regarding black liberation, they did respect each other in the process of gaining a better understanding of the complex dynamics of the black freedom struggle.

Under Farmer's leadership and subsequent leaders, CORE learned from Malcolm X and the Muslims that black leadership and a sensitive understanding of the psychology of the black masses necessitate frequenting slum-ghetto establishments, tenements, street corners, pool halls, etc., where the people are. As a consequence, CORE initiated a variety of self-help programs aimed at creating jobs, training people to develop skills, encouraging small business, starting remedial education programs, etc.

CORE realized the potential impact it could have on the black community if it could politicize the Muslim program. At that time the Muslims spurned political involvement (one reason Malcolm X quit the Nation was that he understood the necessity of politicizing the black masses). In addition to involving the ghetto dwellers in their own liberation, CORE saw the wisdom of the Muslim position that pride must be instilled or reinstilled in the black masses. Farmer makes the point that like the black nationalists, CORE must endeavor to come to grips with the black sense of inferiority by making black people feel they are a legitimate part of American life. Thus, in addition to emphasizing programs aimed at improving the skill level of slum-ghetto dwellers, CORE also dealt with the psychology of inferiority by stressing cultural elements of the black experience. But unlike the nationalists it accused of offering only doctrine and no program, CORE's position was that black pride and self-assertive black people could sustain a feeling of being partners in American society only as long as it was grounded in programmatic community efforts.

The direction CORE took from the mid-1960's to the present seemingly is based on Farmer's outline. Farmer, who became a keen observer of the nationalist scene, was able to extract from Malcolm X and the Muslims specific aspects of black nationalism and adapt them to CORE's potential. In sum, during the mid-1960's CORE viewed the Muslims as a positive force in the black ghettos of urban America.[24]

When CORE endorsed Black Power at the Baltimore convention in 1966, Lonnie X, a Black Muslim, spoke on the problem of black identity. By this time James Farmer had relinquished his position to Floyd McKissick, who had apparently read Farmer's book closely. In a convention position paper McKissick indicated that Black Power "does not mean black separatism or the Black Muslims' approach. It means an honest recognition of the beauty of blackness and negritude."[25] Though the resolution did not endorse the Muslims' approach, the circumstances indicated that there was no enmity between the two organizations.

As CORE evolved over time, with changes in leadership and direction, the Muslim or nationalist influence remained. Seemingly the greatest differences between the two organizations involved the methods of coping with the problems of the black masses. CORE was concerned with developing black viability in an integrated society, while the Muslims were concentrating on developing an insulated black society. Moreover, CORE was not sold on the idea of a separate black nation for black Americans in the United States or elsewhere. Therefore, CORE's program was mainly concerned with making black power felt along the lines that other ethnic groups have used in an American nation of many different ethnic and racial groups.

From the beginning of CORE's existence to the point where it began to identify with the masses, the Muslims viewed it as just another integration-oriented organization. The Muslims were particularly critical of the early CORE position on nonviolence. Muslims advocated self-defense and built the Fruit of Islam (FOI) as a crack self-defense corps to serve in case of enemy attack. In short, the Muslims viewed CORE and other nonviolent black organizations as unrealistic and untenable in a violent society.

Moreover, the Muslims saw CORE as an organization that did not speak to the material and psychological needs of lower-class blacks. Between 1963 and 1965, when CORE began to place emphasis on the black ghetto, it soft-pedaled its philosophical and ideological conflicts with the Muslims, especially those relating to the northern ghettos. CORE no longer overtly opposed black chauvinism, and it played down social integration as the end-product of its efforts. Militance, as opposed to nonviolence, became its instrument in struggles with the white power structure.

With CORE's new emphasis on the masses and the ghetto dweller, the Muslims felt that they could now have a meaningful dialogue. CORE, likewise, felt a close kinship with the Muslims and admired their ability to appeal to lower-class blacks as well as their adeptness at countering asinine white racist myths with some of their own.

Despite the new understanding between the two organizations, some basic differences remained. The Muslims always thought of CORE as middle class, at first interracially, then, after the black power declaration, black, but still middle class. Moreover, CORE leaders' reformist approaches led the Muslims to view CORE as being primarily concerned with using self-determination as a means of bringing about integration. This view was strengthened by the examples of Floyd McKissick and James Farmer, both former National Directors of CORE, under whose leadership CORE's ghetto involvement and separation were initiated. McKissick became a "black capitalist" and established Floyd McKissick Enterprises, and in 1969 James Farmer became an official in the Nixon Administration (generally viewed as hostile to blacks, though not, perhaps to black capitalists). However, Farmer later left the administration because he felt that the policies of the administration were not helpful to blacks, that they were, perhaps, purposefully injurious.

The Muslims viewed CORE's attempt to establish cooperatives in the South as a positive step toward self-determination. In order to become functionally separate, as the Muslims' organ *Muhammad Speaks* constantly reminds the reader, black people must learn technical skills and be able to support (feed) themselves. The Muslims condemned CORE's attempt to foster training programs in the ghetto, but Muslims have their own schools to train their own people, and CORE does not. Although Muslims also encouraged their members to obtain technical and other forms of education in the white man's schools, they held that the training programs stressed by CORE were ultimately of more use to "integration" than to separation. CORE did admonish its members to bring their skills back to the ghetto, but the Muslims sanctioned work only if it was for and in the Nation. This position, of course, was modified to include working outside the Muslim community for practical reasons.

Another example of their differences concerns education. In its quest for community control in New York, CORE supports a black board of education in a black school district. In fact, it has urged the state legislature to treat Harlem as a separate school entity, asking that the legislature allocate funds directly to the black school district without channeling the funds through the New York City Board of Education. Although the Muslims applaud this undertaking, they think it futile until blacks can be taught the truth about themselves, that Islam is the original religion of black people.

In the end, the Muslims view CORE's efforts more or less sympathetically but of doubtful value, because they are not aimed at territorial separation of blacks and whites in the United States.

CORE and the RNA

The Republic of New Africa founded in 1968 was a relatively new organization with a limited national impact. About the only issue to which CORE and the RNA should have related was the effort of the latter organization to establish a land base in the South. Some few members of CORE also believed that blacks should constitute a separate black nation in the United States. These dissidents were not satisfied with the CORE position of self-determination (community control?) in the urban ghettos. In an effort to satisfy this element in the organization, as well as those with genuine interest in cooperative production in the South, CORE made a piecemeal effort to establish cooperatives in Louisiana, one of the states the RNA proposes to include in its black nation.

CORE viewed the RNA as misreading the black masses when it advocated a separate nation in the South. Population data did not support the RNA's contention that black people should move back to the South to become a majority voting bloc in order to control the five states, county by county. CORE made the decision to cope with the problems of black people where they were and viewed the RNA proposal as unworkable and naive.

SNCC and the Nation of Islam

SNCC was ambivalent about the Black Muslims largely because of the treatment Malcolm X had received from the Nation. SNCC viewed Malcolm X's position as essentially correct, and much of SNCC's rhetoric was, in essence, a paraphrasing of Malcolm X.

Before SNCC's articulation of Black Power—that is, before it became an all-black organization—it maintained that the Nation had isolated itself from the mainstream of black America. At the outset SNCC was a direct-action movement, guided by the belief that the problems of black oppression had to be attacked head on. It obviously did not view an organization such as the Nation of Islam as such a movement. SNCC at first did not believe that "all whites were devils," but preached that blacks and whites could live together in harmony. Since SNCC was then integrationist, when Malcolm X indicated that black people should take up arms to defend themselves, it disagreed, holding (though not unanimously) that nonviolence would eventually win.

In the process of abandoning integration and nonviolence, SNCC slowly took the position that black people in America had to gain political power—in the system, as exemplified by the establishment of the Mississippi Freedom Democratic Party, or partly outside it, by the establishment of an independent black political party (as in the case of the Lowndes County Freedom Party in Alabama). Their position contrasted with that of the Muslims, who felt that it was the height of folly to play any kind of politics in the white man's system. Eventually, according to the Muslims, Allah would take care of the white man, and black people would then be free of oppression from the devil.

After SNCC became an all-black (separatist) organization, the ideological gap between it and the Nation narrowed. SNCC accepted the idea of the separate nation. It is difficult, however, to determine whether this ideological position was accepted by the total membership or by only a few in the organization. Whatever the case, SNCC's position relative to the separate state encompassed more than just the separate state in America or in Africa: it spoke to the *colonial* nature of black oppression in America and offered Pan-Africanism as a means of throwing off the yoke of oppression. (The Muslims are not quite sure whether the separate nation should inhabit the United States or Africa.)

Both organizations agreed that black people must determine their own destinies. SNCC eventually rejected coalitions with whites, while the Muslims never entertained the thought of working *with* the devil (many work *for* him but only until Allah corrects the situation).

Despite the closing of the ideological gap, SNCC never had a close relationship with the Nation. Both organizations remained cool toward each other. Apparently the Nation's theology did not appeal to the SNCC membership. Moreover, SNCC's membership was relatively young (college students) and the stringent or restrained life styles of the Nation were another possible hindrance to a positive outlook by SNCC's membership. Finally, SNCC became disenchanted with the Muslims, largely because even during the heat of the civil rights demonstrations in the South, the Muslims refused to become involved.[26]

The Nation of Islam, at the beginning of SNCC's organizational life, regarded it as integrationist-oriented. We have seen how, before Malcolm X quit the Muslims, he had questioned the integrationist orientation of the civil rights movement. SNCC, however, admired Malcolm X's position on most issues.

By 1966 the Muslims were aware of the need to have at least a degree of peace between themselves and other civil rights groups, for they were in trouble enough because of the violent reaction of the constituted authority toward them. It was therefore to their advantage not to criticize specific organizations. However, it was part of their basic doctrine to criticize the integration thrust of the civil rights movement in general. When even this general criticism needed toning down, the Muslims began to preach unity. This was apparent in a statement made by Abkan

Muhammad, the youngest son of Elijah Muhammad and the recipient of an orthodox Islamic education at Al-Azhar University in Egypt: "It is time for all of us, CORE, the NAACP, Dr. Martin Luther King, and the Black Muslims, to sit down together behind closed doors and unite."[27] His statement was intended to reduce tension between the Muslims and integration-oriented groups, especially those under the aegis of King.

The Muslims viewed themselves as having had a profound impact on the development of SNCC's black nationalist thought. SNCC's call for Black Power was, according to the Muslims, only a public articulation of a philosophy the Muslims had had all along. The development of SNCC's position on self-defense came as a result of Malcolm X's position that blacks should defend themselves against violence. The Muslims' call for land and separation became one of the most debated issues in SNCC. Many felt that the call for separate land in the United States was unrealistic, while others felt that Africa would be the most realistic solution. The Muslims' call for compensation for 300 years of free labor found some SNCC members receptive; James Forman is the most outstanding example of a SNCC person who took the idea of reparations seriously.[28]

The Muslims' success in instilling a pride of blackness was taken up by SNCC. "Black is Beautiful," "Black Pride," "Soul Brother," etc. are slogans utilized by SNCC as a result of the Muslim influence in general and of Malcolm X in particular. Perhaps the Muslims saw in SNCC a group of young blacks who might spread their philosophy without the eschatological ramifications dictated by the Muslim doctrine. There is no evidence, however, that the Muslims infiltrated SNCC; SNCC's political stance negated possible Muslim participation. Moreover, SNCC, in its early stages, was interracial.

By 1966 SNCC's Black Power position had laid the foundation for acceptance of some of the Muslim ideology. The Muslims spurned political participation, however, largely because they could not accept SNCC's desire to gain Black Power in the land of the devil. As SNCC became more vocal in condemning United States foreign policy, exposing neocolonialism and generally extolling black nationalism, the Nation became more confident that SNCC members would become Muslims, and many have done so.

The Muslims were especially proud of SNCC's position on Zionism and the Arab-Israeli conflict. Since the Muslims are an accepted Islamic sect, their position on any Jew/Arab conflict is pro-Arab. SNCC saw the Arab/Israeli problem as a case of Israelis working for American imperialism. Most white Americans, of course, condemned SNCC for its position, and thereafter the Muslims viewed it as a brother organization, persecuted as the Muslims were by the white devils.

In sum, the Muslims viewed SNCC as an organization that evolved, maturing as it embraced black nationalism as a means of coping with black oppression. Important differences remained, of course. The Muslims couched their attempt to cope with black oppression in religious and nationalistic terms while SNCC saw the problem as strictly political. The Muslims' approach was encapsulated and disciplined in tight organizational form, while SNCC's political appeal reflected the state of near anarchy in which the organization began. SNCC remained a vague political form, changing and transient.

SNCC and the Panthers

In May 1966 Stokely Carmichael's call for Black Power scared whites, stirred blacks to action, and put the constituted authority on twenty-four hour alert duty. In August 1966 up-tight whites, aroused blacks, and alert-duty worn constituted authorities were in for another jolt. The Black Panther Party came into being in Oakland and soon spread its chapters across the nation. Why the Panthers when SNCC already had the nation up in arms? How did the two militant organizations relate to one another?

The Panthers rejected the concept of black power because it would not give "power to all the people" but only to those blacks manipulated by the power structure so as to make black capitalism attractive to the poor masses. The Panthers wanted all capitalism destroyed in order to eliminate racism, oppression, and exploitation. SNCC and Carmichael, in the end, did not fit the Panther mold, and the Panthers branded them as reactionary forces militating against the ultimate power being held by the people.

Moreover, the Panthers viewed SNCC as an organization with "paranoia about white control." The Panthers distinguished between the white liberal and the white revolutionary, whereas SNCC in the end did not. To SNCC, according to Huey Newton, because the white liberal and white revolutionary are both white, they both must be rejected out of hand. But to the Panthers white revolutionaries can act to give support to the revolution in the mother country. As noted previously, the Panthers did form alliances with radical white groups, and because of their socialist orientation, they believed in the solidarity of the oppressed black, brown, red, yellow, and white. SNCC, the Panthers held, "denies the humanity of other people and such a view is doomed to failure." According to Cleaver, SNCC also laid the foundation upon which the power structure "coopted" black radical groups. Finally, because of this foundation, the Panthers viewed SNCC as enemies of the people, Uncle Tom lackeys, and yellow running dogs. SNCC viewed the Panthers in the same pejorative light as the Panthers viewed SNCC. SNCC concluded that the Black Panther Party was too dogmatic and violence-prone, and derided the Panthers for having discovered a "new ideology" that was in fact no more than another variation of Marxism. What is important in terms of ideological conflict is that SNCC, unlike the Panthers, came to reject completely sociopolitical coalitions with whites.

The above description of the relationship of the two organizations omits important and revealing details. They were not always in conflict; they began their relationship in revolutionary harmony. Around the mid-sixties both organizations declared that they were the only black revolutionary groups around, and it would be valuable to the liberation movement if the two organizations could work together. To this end, SNCC's Stokely Carmichael, H. "Rap" Brown, and James Forman were made "honorary Ministers" in the Black Panther Party. It is difficult to imagine SNCC and the Black Panthers arm in arm marching together toward black liberation, but they did.

At the beginning of the relationship between SNCC and the Panthers, it was to the benefit of the Panthers (since they were a relatively new group) to utilize SNCC's prominence. In July 1967 the Panthers and SNCC announced an informal working alliance. Forman became the Black Panthers' Minister of Foreign Affairs, Brown became Minister of Justice, and Carmichael became Prime Minister. One month later SNCC announced that it had expelled Carmichael and dissolved the alliance. SNCC indicated that the arrangement had been made by individuals in the group and *not the total membership*. Forman and Brown resigned from the Panthers. Carmichael, expelled, at this point remained in the Panther camp.

The Panthers apparently regarded their relationship with SNCC not as a working alliance but as a merger. SNCC, however, never considered the relationship to be of lasting value. According to a

SNCC field secretary, "The actuality is that no functional merger ever existed, and the possibility of there being one was remote from the beginning."[29] SNCC was a "member-thrust" organization, meaning that the membership rather than the leaders made policy decisions.

Lester indicated that SNCC's membership was cool to the merger because it did not know much about the Panthers. The Panthers drafted Carmichael, Lester feels, because at that time (early 1967) SNCC, with Carmichael as its leading representative, could do more for the Panthers than vice versa. Many in SNCC felt that this was a tactical error on the part of Carmichael, but SNCC did nothing because it lacked the ability to discipline its members.

Eldridge Cleaver, at that time Panther Information Minister, spoke at a Peace and Freedom Party forum on February 11, 1967. He did little to improve SNCC-Panther relations by observing that the Panthers had worked out a "merger," not an alliance as SNCC had thought. Moreover, he asserted that SNCC was composed mostly of black hippies and black college students who had dropped out of the black middle class, and implied that SNCC's ideology had been derived from the Panthers. No wonder SNCC's membership balked at a merger, for if Cleaver's remarks were accurate, SNCC would have been smothered rather than merged.

SNCC's disenchantment with the Panthers went further than the alliance-merger question. In June 1968 SNCC reaffirmed its independence from the Panthers by voting not to adopt their ten-point program. It was the opinion of SNCC that the Panther program was more reformist than revolutionary.

SNCC was critical of Newton's comments that it had been controlled by white radicals, whereas, according to Lester, one of SNCC's unique features was that it had been controlled by blacks since its beginning in 1960 and that whites were eventually excluded not because they had too much power but because they were ineffective workers in the black community. From that position came Carmichael's view that whites would be more important in the black movement if they worked in the white community, and blacks should organize the black community (the same position taken by Malcolm X when he organized the Organization of Afro-American Unity).

How did Stokely Carmichael fare in the Black Panther Party? After Carmichael was expelled from SNCC, he did not resign from the Panthers. In August 1968 he went to the Bay area to help the Panthers organize the black community and to help establish the Black United Front (an umbrella organization for all black organizations). The Panthers did not fully agree with Carmichael's objectives in establishing the Front. Carmichael was of the opinion that all black people must come together in order to fight oppression ("Every Negro is a potential black man"); but in 1968 the Panthers saw members of the black middle class as bootlickers, lackeys, Uncle Toms, and house niggers (the Panthers were "Field Niggers").

The Panthers viewed Carmichael's stance as irrational cultural nationalism and racist. Moreover, according to Cleaver, Carmichael himself was a seeker of individual glory and a rhetorician without the fortitude to act.

The Panthers' disenchantment with Carmichael reached its zenith when Carmichael rejected Marxism-Leninism. When Cleaver took refuge in Algeria and headed the International Section of the Black Panther Party, he and Carmichael had a final meeting to try to resolve their differences. At the Pan-African Cultural Festival held in Algiers in July 1969, Carmichael said he believed that those "who talk about 'Marxist-Leninism' so hard . . . are people groping for an answer." Thus Marxism-Leninism becomes a religion, and Marx becomes Jesus Christ. Admitting he did not understand all of Marxism-Leninism, Carmichael indicated that for him to say he was a Marxist-Leninist would make him "intellectually dishonest and, in fact, a damn liar."[30]

In addition to ideological heresy, the Panthers charged Carmichael with being a government informer. Carmichael and his wife, the famed South African singer Miriam Makeba, returned to the United States in March 1970 after having lived in Conakry, Guinea, for a little over a year. Carmichael was subpoenaed by the Senate Subcommittee on Internal Security. His appearance was not publicized (the *Congressional Record,* which routinely lists all committees and subcommittee meetings, did not mention this meeting). A prominent member of the Subcommittee refused to answer questions relative to the meeting, but Carmichael indicated that he had himself invoked the Fifth Amendment.[31]

The founder and Chairman of the Black Panther Party, Huey P. Newton, to remove any lingering doubts about the Panthers' sentiment toward Carmichael held a press conference on August 26, 1970, to repudiate the charge that the Panthers had a delegation of members in Jordan led by Carmichael. The point was that Newton and the Panthers wanted to make it clear that Carmichael was no longer associated with the Party. Moreover, as a result of the Subcommittee meeting and the subsequent silence,

Newton charged Carmichael with being an agent of the Central Intelligence Agency.

Finally, at the same press conference, Newton left no doubt that he was cutting all ties with Carmichael. He reiterated that the Black Panther Party did not subscribe to Black Power as defined by Carmichael and seemingly accepted by President Nixon. Both Carmichael and Nixon seem to agree upon the stipulated definition, which is no more than black capitalism, which is reactionary and certainly not a philosophy that would meet the interest of the people. By reading Carmichael out of the Party, SNCC and the Panthers effectively severed all formal ties for all time.

SNCC and the Republic of New Africa

The RNA styles itself a revolutionary nationalist organization, and SNCC thought favorably of it. The RNA proclaimed Malcolm X, Marcus Garvey, W. E. B. DuBois, and Robert Williams as patron saints of the organization. All of these personalities were in good standing with SNCC, and once can therefore assume that the organizations had mutual respect for each other.

In 1970 Stokely Carmichael indicated that the RNA was one of the organizations he would not attack.[31] SNCC was already essentially defunct by the time the RNA was formally organized in March 1968 in Detroit. Actually, it is hard to know if SNCC had any formal position on the matter, but Carmichael's sentiment for the RNA, as a former SNCC leader, may have represented a large portion of what the SNCC membership may have thought of the RNA. The RNA stood for the same goals as SNCC: separation from whites, internationalization of the black struggle (Pan-Africanism), etc. The two organizations could well have been compatible partners in the struggle for black liberation had SNCC only continued to exist. However, many members of SNCC ultimately thought that blacks had to return to Africa to gain freedom, while the RNA continued to maintain that blacks should gain control of five southern states and become a new black nation.

The Panthers and the Nation of Islam

The Panthers view the Black Muslims as an organization that has outlived its relevance. Because of the Nation's outstanding work in the rehabilitation of prison inmates, it was seen as a postive force, laying the groundwork for black liberation. Cleaver observes that in prisons it was a common sight to "see several Muslims walking around the yard, each with a potential convert to whom he would be explaining the *Message to the Black Man* as taught by Elijah Muhammad."[32]

According to Cleaver all that has changed; the Muslims are no longer importantly regarded by prison inmates, officials, or themselves. The reasons for the decline in esteem are many, but the most obvious is that because Allah has failed to do what the Muslims claim, the Muslims are no longer taken seriously regarding their predictions of doom for white devils.

According to Cleaver, a second major reason for the decline was the split that developed over the Muslims' ouster, and according to him, the callous murder of Malcolm X, whom prisoners generally held in high esteem. Cleaver believes that Malcolm's ouster was engineered from above in the Muslim hierarchy and that it was the height of ingratitude for the Nation to treat Malcolm the way they did after he was almost singlehandedly responsible for their success. The outcome of Malcolm's treatment, at least as far as prisoners are concerned, is that Malcolm's ghost will haunt the Nation. In Cleaver's words, "In prisons he sits in judgment of every Muslim and his martyrdom is a chicken that has come home to roost wherever Black Muslims congregate."[33] Cleaver is of the opinion that, in addition to the Nation's treatment of Malcolm X, another important reason for the decline of the Muslims in prisons is the inexplicable failure of the outside Muslim officials to render any legal assistance to those behind the walls. Muslims in California, for example, who wanted to take the California Department of Correction into court in order to win their constitutional right to practice their religion while in prison were placed in the ideologically humiliating position of asking the "white devils" of the American Civil Liberties Union to represent them in court.

The most distinct difference between the Black Panthers and the Nation of Islam centers on their conception of liberation. The Panthers think of the Muslims as "black racists" because they see everything in terms of color (the devil is white), whereas the Panthers view liberation in terms of "the system" (we must destroy capitalism).[34]

The land question is another area in which Panthers and Muslims differ. Muhammad said that the Muslims must have some land in order for black people to develop an economic base. Cleaver, too, believes that there is in fact a yearning for land among black Americans. But he also believed that there is something amiss in the Muslim Program for gaining land in the United States. The Muslim slogan "We must have some land!" in practice impeded rather than enhanced the movement. Although the slogan seems to protest the lack of black self-determination, it is not revolutionary because it merely asks the oppressor to "give" black people some land. "The oppressor is not about to give niggers a damn thing." More than that, the racist oppressors are doing all they can to cut off welfare payments, refuse medical care to the sick, deprive blacks of educational opportunities, and leave black babies to die from a lack of adequate nutrition, among other reasons. Therefore, "no black person in his right mind" should wait "for those same pigs to give up some of this land, say five or six states."[35]

Cleaver's position seems to be the same as that proposed by Malcolm X and echoed by Ameer Baraka: that black people in America should begin *functioning* as a nation; black people are already separate in the ghettoes of America. They should claim the land where they live and be a nation. Cleaver concludes that the Panther proposal, point 10 in their program, to hold a plebiscite in black communities across the nation is an important step in confronting the land question.

In a speech at Syracuse University in the spring of 1971, Huey Newton said in essence that he had written off the Black Muslims because they had proved to be counterrevolutionary by asking the United States government for a six-million-dollar loan. Newton points out that revolutionaries use other methods of obtaining money, certainly not by asking the oppressor for a loan.[36]

In conclusion, the Panthers became disenchanted with the Muslims over all major issues. They recognized, however, that the Muslims, too, were seeking an answer to the black dilemma in white racist America. In general, the Muslim view of the Panthers is a reaction to Panther ideological attacks against the Nation. A large part of the Panther ideological perspective was derived from Malcolm X (Cleaver's, Newton's, and Seale's); when Malcolm X was expelled from the Nation, many Muslims, drawn to the movement by him, became disenchanted with how the Messenger treated him. Moreover, many people still think that Malcolm X was murdered by Muslims. In his autobiography, for example, Malcolm made it clear that the Muslims were out to get him.[37] The item is significant, for *The Autobiography of Mal-*

colm X is "must" reading on the Muslim and Panther recruiting grounds, the prisons and the ghetto neighborhoods of the young black lower class. Malcolm's anti-Muslim heresy became part of today's Panther orthodoxy. Clearly, the Muslims needed to fight back.

The Muslims leveled their heavy ideological guns at Marxism-Leninism, calling it inapplicable to American black-white relations. The central problem in America is *racism,* they say, not *capitalism.* Moreover, Muslims reject the idea that capitalism is responsible for exploitation and racism. Whites are held to be inherently evil, incapable of accepting blacks under *any* system. Elijah argued that the white race was hostile to him and oppressed blacks "because we are of the Original Black Race whom they were created to hate from the very beginning of their existence, 6000 years ago."[38] Therefore, any attempt to live with the devil, under any system, is folly.

The Muslims view the Panthers' attempt to deal with police brutality by carrying guns as impractical and suicidal. According to Muhammad, the Muslims have stripped themselves of arms, indicating to whites that there is no intention of attacking them, because to attack would mean that the Muslims have the ability to manufacture weapons, whereas the truth is that guns must be obtained from whites themselves. Therefore, the Panther posture of meeting violence with violence is foolish.[39]

Finally, Muslims, who have taken the position that black people must have a homeland in the United States or in Africa (whichever is more expedient), find it ridiculous that Panthers do not believe in separate homelands for blacks and whites. Panthers maintain, however, that the issue is not entirely settled, so continue to advocate a plebiscite to make a final determination of the desires of black people.

The Black Panthers and the Republic of New Africa

In replying to an inquiry by the RNA as to the position the Panthers take on black separation, Huey Newton, in September 1969, made the following points: (1) the Black Panther Party has demanded a plebiscite to be supervised by the United Nations so that black people themselves can determine their position on the question of separation. (2) The Black Panther Party will be subject to the will of the majority of the people, but also feel that the RNA is justified in demanding land in the United States and the right of black people to secede from the Union. He felt that this did not constitute a contradiction between the Panther and RNA positions.

The Panthers feel that it is a matter of timing and that certain conditions must exist before that choice is made. Blacks, even if they had five or six states, according to Newton, could not "function in freedom side by side with a capitalistic imperialistic country." He cites Africa as being victimized by imperialism: "it would [not] be any different if we were to have a separate country here in North America." The Panthers are bent on destroying capitalism first by forming coalitions and alliances with "people that are equally dissatisfied with the system." The RNA should "struggle with us, but . . . at this time the Black Panther Party feels that we don't want to be in an enclave type situation where we would be more isolated than we already are now."[40] Again Newton called for a united struggle against the system.[41]

Eldridge Cleaver, upon being asked about any other black organizations which he considered to be in the vanguard and which might participate in a coalition, indicated that the Republic of New Africa might fit. He said, "I'm very interested in and I have a lot of respect for a group called the Republic of New Africa."[42] In an interview in *Playboy* in October 1968 before he went into exile, Cleaver was questioned about the plan envisioned by the Republic of New Africa, and at that time he said that he was not sympathetic with their approach, and black people should be polled on the issue. This is the same stand that Newton took. The Panthers maintain that the enemy is not white, but systemic.

The Panthers and the RNA admired each other for boldness and made a valiant attempt to downplay their difference. They were largely successful in their endeavor, but it is evident in a not too careful reading of their respective ideological positions that there were basic ideological inconsistencies which kept them apart.

Conclusions

Comparison of the differing goals of the organizations points up the complexity of racial oppression in America by illustrating how blacks themselves view it, and the many approaches to solving their problem. At the same time, how the organizations relate to one another points up the impracticality, or at least the workability, of some of the proposed solutions.

Interorganizational relations almost always ended as conflictive competition rather than competitive cooperation. These movements relate to one another because of many factors, but the overriding one is that they all operate to cope with black freedom in a racist society. Hence, they must cope with the general society's elements of social control, compete for members, and at the same time continually monitor black and white public opinion. All of these factors together enable movements to dance to their own music while listening to the public piper.

III. IN PERSPECTIVE

10 CHANGE AND THE MOVEMENT ORGANIZATIONS

Social movement organizations usually modify and adjust their ideologies, strategies, and goals to facilitate adaptation to social change in the society at large as well as within the organization. Change and adjustment are caused by such internal factors as conflict between or among organizations (as we saw in the preceding chapter), membership stability, and the use and quality of social control; external factors, generally speaking, center on the relative willingness of the society to accept or accommodate the movement organization's activities and goals and the extent and degree to which it will use social control.[1] The five black movement organizations should be viewed within this framework as they cause and adjust to social change in the United States.

Between 1960 and the mid-1970's the movement for black liberation changed. Ideas were modified, leaders came and went, and, most important, the climate in which the movements originated was itself altered. Did the changes occur primarily because of external conditions that could not be controlled, or because of tendencies toward scatter and weakness that might have been better managed? Were the intra- and inter-movement factions and frictions merely responses to external forces which made the movement necessary in the first place?

The Setting

President Kennedy, pressured by the civil rights forces, specifically the massive March on Washington in August 1963, had proposed a broad slate of legislation to ameliorate the condition of black people in America. Ironically, his death may have been the prime factor in having the proposed legislation passed by Congress, for it enabled the political savvy of Lyndon Johnson to be brought into play. Johnson played on public sentiment in the name of the assassinated President in order to get the legislation passed. His landslide victory in 1964 was seen by many as the repudiation of a reactionary Republican in favor of the more moderate leadership of the successor of John F. Kennedy. At the same time, the landslide seemed to be a mandate to continue the progressive path in the area of civil rights.

Congress, as a result, passed the most pervasive and far-reaching civil rights legislation since Reconstruction. The 1964 Civil Rights Bill and subsequent legislation provided for educational opportunities, voting rights, fair housing, equal employment opportunities, and an Office of Economic Opportunity to wage the War on Poverty. These measures were meant to provide for the equality of opportunity in all phases of American life for black Americans, and President Johnson himself indicated that he would overcome poverty, ignorance, and racism by giving all Americans an equal opportunity to fulfill their maximum potential. Moreover, it was, he felt, the moral duty of government to provide these opportunities.

Despite the 1964 legislative landmarks, black America exploded in the ghettos all over the country. The uprisings of the mid and later 1960's resembled the earlier sit-in movement in intensity, spread, and confrontation. Rebellions in Harlem, Rochester, and Philadelphia were poignant proofs that the racial crisis in America had not subsided. In 1965 the anger in the Watts riots shocked white and black America. And Lewis Killian, a keen observer and rigorous analyst of the racial scene in the United States, indicated that between the summer of 1966 and 1967 there were 49 riots.[2]

By 1968 there was pervasive discontent over the manner in which Johnson had handled both the Vietnam War and the race question. To many he had pandered to the whims of black militants and allowed the black masses to get out of hand. Moreover, except for the Nation of Islam (always a separatist organization) between 1964 and 1968 SNCC and CORE changed their goals from integration to separation, the Black Panther Party came into being as a revolutionary nationalist organization, and the RNA was in the gestation period.

By the middle of the Johnson Administration, white Americans were disenchanted with the black revolution, and by 1968 law and order was the dominant political theme. The rise of Stokely

Carmichael and H. "Rap" Brown as black power leaders of SNCC; Floyd McKissick of CORE, who supported black power; the Black Panther Party's Huey P. Newton, Bobby Seale, and Eldridge Cleaver; and the Malcolm X Society's Milton and Richard Henry constituted too much black militance for white America to tolerate. The murder of Martin Luther King, Jr., on April 4, 1968, seemed to many white Americans the end of moderate black leadership. The elementary forms of collective behavior exhibited by blacks in retaliation for King's death added racist credence to white America's assertion of the need for law and order. Killian observed that whites felt threatened and overpowered by blacks demanding rapid social change and consequently began to regard the black movement "as dangerous and truly revolutionary." To blacks, however, "a lessening of protest would mean the end of progress. Thus the cycle that leads a social movement into increasing reliance upon aggressive displays of power is set in motion."[3]

These factors seemingly should receive equal attention with the war in assessing the 1968 election outcome. Whites had become tired of black protests, riots, demonstrations, and general militance. They began to feel that the battle arena should be changed to one where law and order would prevail. Whites, according to Killian, believed that black public protest was another form of coercion and should be curtailed, or it would become "more widely imitated and become an even greater rival to the process of peaceful change through democratic government."[4] This attitude among whites became an important domestic factor in the 1968 pre-election period.

One way whites rationalized the need for law and order in relation to the black quest for justice and equality was to disprove the strategy used by blacks to achieve their goals. The correct strategy for blacks, whites counseled, would center on the idea that social change in a democracy is effected through "public debate and legislative deliberation" and not "direct action and emergency legislation." In the final analysis, "the success of such emergency tactics poses a threat to the normal processes of majority rule."[5]

In short, the emergency measures of the federal government, the black protests and demonstrations, cries of black power, the increasing separatist tendencies and organizations, and the nationalizing of the quest for black justice and equality signaled an end to the white exhibition of good will to blacks conditioned by distance. In the midst of these development, Silberman early observed the waning of liberal white northern sentiment regarding black civil rights activity. He writes that they were discovering that in the deep recesses of their souls, northern whites were not that different from southern whites. "For a brief period following the demonstrations in Birmingham in the spring of 1963, a brief period, it appeared that the American conscience had been touched; a wave of sympathy for the Negro and of revulsion over white brutality seemed to course through the nation. But then the counter-action set in, revealing a degree of anti-Negro prejudice and hatred that surprised even the most sophisticated observer."[6] The changed conditions in 1968 called for changes in tactics to deal with black efforts to redress their grievances. The election of an administration that would deal with blacks as honest brokers on the promise to return the country to law and order and bring us together was the option chosen by white Americans, but the decision of the "silent majority" to utilize democratic legislative techniques to restore peace and tranquility has resulted in (as they knew it would) the restoration of physical and psychological manfestations of white rule. There were no black leaders in the top echelons of government, and even though Thurgood Marshall, not appointed in the law and order administration of Richard Nixon, to be sure, was an Associate Justice of the Supreme Court of the United States, his one vote was neutralized by the appointment of at least two Justices who are of the opposite ideological persuasion.

The presidential election of 1972, in retrospect, serves to illustrate that people will tolerate almost any extreme of democratic violation in order to ensure domestic tranquility, including the suppression and oppression of black people's search for equality of opportunity. The path that the Nixon Administration took in eliminating possibilities for the black masses to advance may be likened to the age-old tactic of putting blacks in their places. In 1972 there was a close resemblance to the place black people occupied, politically, after the presidential election of 1876.

The Transformation of SNCC

SNCC no longer exists as a movement. Its demise stems from several factors, including financial starvation and a lack of coordinated organizational leadership. Initially supported by SCLC, NAACP, CORE, churches, colleges, the Northern Student Movement, and various other sources, by 1965 it had an operating budget of about $80,000, about 200 low-paid field "secretaries," and 250 full-time volunteers in rural southern communities. In 1966 it concluded that whites should no longer be official SNCC members and embraced black self-determination (Black Power) as its ideology. At least one of the unanticipated outcomes was the drying up of white financial sources. Whites were not about to support an organization they could not join.

SNCC became more militant and decided to expand its activity to northern ghettoes. It originated in, and became effective in, southern political affairs: voter registration, political education campaigns, etc. But northern politics and social circumstances were something else again. In every northern city there were already militant and even separatist organizations geared to deal with black problems, whether they were effective or not. The incursion of yet another group created strain, and more energy was exerted in internal ideological combat than against the common target. SNCC therefore felt that it had to be more militant than the other separatist organizations.

Another factor was the presence of War on Poverty programs in northern ghettoes, aimed at those at the lowest end of the socio-economic scale, the same group the existing militant groups spoke for and the same one SNCC allegedly represented. Oberschall observed that "the anti-poverty programs became an important source of employment for black activists, local community leaders . . . and [they] paid very well."[7] Because these programs served to increase competition among groups speaking for the black poor, instead of consolidating their efforts in alleviating problems of the black poor, each organization inflexibly held that its program was the best and only solution. Instead of hanging together, they were hanged separately. If some had strong necks, SNCC was not among them.

For one thing, SNCC never had the support of the black masses outside the South. At the outset, SNCC was primarily composed of students who empathized with the black masses and, in many cases, were sons and daughters. These youngsters attempted to ameliorate the black mass condition by any means necessary, not ruling out separatism. Ironically, for their pains they, not their mothers and fathers, reaped the benefits of their labor, through War on Poverty programs, newly created openings in industry, government, and universities, based on their education and training; but not much happened for the brother on the street or the unskilled, uneducated parents. These SNCC youngsters were catalytic agents, pressing for the implementation of the American Dream:

jobs, decent housing, dignity, and a fair chance to "make it." Society found it expedient to include many who participated in SNCC, because of their educational achievements, skills, and various other accomplishments. Hence their attachment to the movement declined in the face of society's decision to include (if not embrace) some of SNCC's goals.

Most former SNCC members settled into societal roles, believing that change could be effected only through systemic channels; a few remained true believers in the necessity of radical change outside the existing framework. A look at what happened to the leaders may be instructive.

After Stokely Carmichael was expelled from SNCC and quit the Black Panther Party, he later married a famous singer of Xhosa origin, Miriam Makeba. [8] Their official residence is Conakry, Guinea, where they have become citizens. (According to some accounts, Carmichael lives in Washington, D.C., also has a residence in New York City, and frequently visits Guinea.) Even though SNCC as an organization no longer exists, Carmichael maintains his SNCC-derived conviction that no less than a revolution is necessary to change American society for the betterment of the black condition. He now believes that black people must unite all their organizational and ideological factions, to close ranks in order to confront the white power structure. As head of the African People's Revolutionary Party, headquartered in Conakry, he plans to organize all black organizations into a National Black United Front. He still rejects coalition with white groups. His new organization proposes to establish ground rules among black leaders on how to settle disputes and differences among themselves and their organizations, developing lines of communication among leaders of the black masses that presently do not exist, and coalescing the United Front.

Carmichael remains an ardent advocate of Pan-Africanism as a result of living and studying with the late Kwame Nkrumah, the deposed former President of Ghana. Nkrumah taught that Africa could be free only if she embraced Pan-Africanism in order to struggle against neo-colonialism or neo-imperialism. [9] Carmichael, elaborating upon Malcolm X's idea, broadened "Pan-Africanism" to include all black peoples of African descent. Black Americans, black West Indians, and blacks everywhere are Africans; hence, Pan-Africanism calls for all black peoples of the African Diaspora to look to mother Africa for their salvation. Particularly in America, Carmichael sees the first step as the closing of ranks in the black community.

Carmichael may be thought of as the most prominent ex-SNCC leader because, under his chairmanship, SNCC publicly eliminated whites from leadership positions and eventually from the organization and shocked the nation by calling for Black Power. But there are many other SNCC leaders and spokesmen who are continuing the struggle with the same zeal. James Forman is grappling with the black liberation question in many ways. At the National Black Economic Development Conference in Detroit on April 26, 1969, he proposed a *Manifesto to the White Christian Churches and the Jewish Synagogues in the United States of America and All Other Racist Institutions*. The Conference was sponsored by the Inter-religious Foundation for Community Organizations (IFCO), an interfaith coalition of major Protestant and Jewish groups formed in 1967 to fund militant community action.

Forman demanded five hundred million dollars from the IFCO organizations as partial reparation for past social discrimination and slave labor. The money would be used in the black community for black liberation without any control from the donors. Some think of Forman as a militant black nationalist and a revolutionary Marxist; others call him a crazy radical. No one label adequately describes the man. His book, *The Making of Black Revolutionaries*, is a good source to show what motivates him.

Julian Bond took a different path. He was never a SNCC chairman, but he was one of the vanguard members and gained national prominence as a politician when he was elected to the Georgia legislature. Because of his antiwar statements while still a member of SNCC, however, he was refused his seat. The courts ruled in his favor and he subsequently took his place among Georgia state legislators. At the 1968 Democratic National Convention held in Chicago, Bond was nominated for Vice President. He was too young, among other things, to accept the nomination and said so. He is one of the most popular young political spokesmen in America today and is often spoken of as a future presidential possibility.

To find a solution to the problem of black people, Bond has cast his lot with politics. He thinks that black people should now play a new kind of politics. They should "have no permanent friends, no permanent enemies, only important interests." He is not optimistic about the "new" southern politics. To him they look like the old: "the South of black oppression, the South of cheap labor, the South of cheap politics and the South of cheap prices placed on black men's lives. A great many of these Governors with toothpaste grins and a new kind of racist populism believe they . . . represent some new kind of liberalism." He was undoubtedly referring to the Governor of Georgia, Jimmy Carter, who, according to him, at the Democratic Governors' Conference in Omaha, Nebraska, asked his fellow Governors to pay tribute to J. Edgar Hoover, "to make the war in Vietnam a non-issue in 1972, and finally, to bring the hillbilly Hitler from Alabama, George Wallace, and the racist Governor of Mississippi, John Bell Williams, back into the Democratic Party. If that is the New South, then we are just one step away from slavery."[10] Despite Bond's unenthusiastic acceptance of Southern politics, however, the South is significantly different politically from what it was when SNCC first began its drive for black political participation in the early to mid 1960's.

There are many other ex-SNCC people engaged in various activities aimed at black liberation. Some have settled into normal, undramatic roles as husbands and wives, mothers and fathers, making a living to take care of their human needs. The whereabouts of many, such as Robert Moses, who received irreparable scars from southern racists, are not known. John Lewis, Chuck McDew, and Ivanhoe Donaldson have assumed leading roles in community affairs where they live. H. "Rap" Brown has had a particularly bad time since his SNCC days (one might add that the reason he became a SNCC member in the first place was that it was rough for a black cat whether he was a SNCC member or not). He was incarcerated for alleged armed robbery, but at this writing is free, still in his own way working for black liberation. John Lewis heads the Voter Education Project, which monitors and facilitates voting in southern states.

To promote or resist change, a social movement in many instances must play a vanguard role. A movement's success or failure centers on its ability to play this role and at the same time not move too far or fast in prompting or resisting the desires of those for whom the movement allegedly speaks. SNCC's entrance into the northern racial scene pushed it to extreme positions mainly because in all of the large northern urban ghettoes there already existed militant black elements. Hence, SNCC had to take a more extreme posture in order to earn a place in the militant camps. The Chicago office of SNCC became extremely militant. "We must hate everything white" may have been an attempt to outmaneuver the Black Muslim and Garveyite positions in the Chicago community.

The outcome was the alienation of the black masses and the loss of active membership. The masses could not relate to the extreme positions because they were not bread-and-butter issues: internal colonialism and the Third World were to them only fuzzy ideals posited by youngsters. In short, SNCC used middle-class, revolutionary, intellectual rhetoric on relatively uneducated poor people who were more concerned with meat to eat now than pie in the sky by and by. The important issues to the black masses were (and still are) jobs, housing, police brutality, education, welfare, health, etc.[11] The masses then and now found it difficult to concentrate on issues that do not produce immediate, tangible results.

SNCC's initial values and ideology, as we shall see in the following chapter, were not significantly different from those of society in general. SNCC merely attempted to bring them to fruition through Black Power. Because it so blatantly exposed the society's shortcomings regarding black people, and at the same time attempted to rouse the black masses to effect their own liberation, constituted authority reacted by tagging Black Power as dangerous and forcing the oppressed blacks to the defense. Thus Black Power lost its meaning and potential effectiveness by being defined in different ways by too many individuals and groups, including elements in the dominant society.

CORE

When Roy Innis became CORE's National Director in 1968, he declared it a separatist/nationalist organization, embracing Garveyism as its guiding philosophy.[12] Like the UNIA, it attempted to establish a relationship between Africans and black Americans by inaugurating an African tour service, by means of which black Americans could make pilgrimages to East Africa, notably Kenya and Uganda.[13] Believing that some black pilgrims would like to become permanent residents, CORE and Idi Amin's government in Uganda struck up an agreement to allow skilled blacks to emigrate to Uganda and take up posts requiring technical and managerial skills. It is called Project Uganda. Only a very few have actually gone. Because of many difficulties, in 1973 Amin asked CORE not to send volunteers because he had to ascertain first how many trained Ugandan technicians and managers living abroad would return before he could make a definite commitment to black Americans. CORE should know, however, according to Amin, "that no change of heart has happened to [him] or any Ugandan towards you and all our brothers and sisters in the Americas."[14] CORE continues its effort to forge this kind of Pan-Africanism.

To further promote African and Afro-American relationships, CORE urged African nations to bestow dual citizenship on all blacks in the Americas. In principle most African leaders agreed that it should be done, but it has not become a reality. For this purpose and others, Innis visited Kenya, Tanzania, Uganda, Somalia, and Liberia. Through the efforts of President Amin particularly, CORE has been accorded special representative status with the Organization of African Unity (OAU), and has official Non-Government (NGO) status with the External Relations Division of the United Nations Office of Public Relations.

CORE's emphasis on establishing relations with Africa is an important aspect of a consistent UNIA-Garvey program; but as it develops these relationships, it continues to involve itself with pressing issues concerning the "nation within a nation" at home. Still following Garveyism, one of these issues is CORE's position on the school integration/desegregation issue. It is similar to Garvey's position on the role of the Ku Klux Klan. Garvey felt the Klan was right to "protect racial purity" because everyone should be proud of his race. Although the proposition logically followed UNIA philosophy, Garvey's appearance before Klan audiences, and vice versa, did not put him in good stead with the masses. Likewise, many have branded CORE's position on school integration as segregation under another guise. Some believe that it is difficult for CORE to claim the title of a "black nationalist organization when it always agreed with George Wallace and other reactionaries."[15] But like the UNIA, CORE reasons that "it is the local school board, the dispenser *and* regulator of money, rewards, good will and other benefits which makes black schools inferior. Under segregation, blacks have been locked into a system over which they have no control, for which they exercise no control, for which they have no responsibility and for which they are powerless to effect meaningful change."[16]

Believing that black and white control of neighborhood schools is essential, CORE's intent was to have black parents control their own schools, as whites do already. It proposed to accomplish this by the creation of what it calls the CORE Unitary School Plan, which called for the rejection of dual (segregated) schools where an essentially white board of education and a white superintendent control a black and white (separate) school system. It also rejected an essentially white school board and superintendent who controlled a unitary system that attempted to foster and maintain racial balance. The CORE plan called for each school district to have separate black and white school boards, each with its own black and white superintendent controlling the schools in their respective districts. This plan differed from the dual system in that (1) each district is unitary, with blacks controlling their district; (2) it allows freedom of choice: black and white children (or their parents) can choose to attend either school; and (3) it eliminates forced bussing.

In April 1972 CORE filed a friend-of-the-court brief appealing a decision by the Federal District Court, Eastern District of Virginia, to the United States Court of Appeals, Fourth Circuit. In *Carolyn Bradley, et al. v. the School Board of Richmond, Virginia, et al.,* the District Court ruled that three separate and unitary school systems—the city of Richmond, and Chesterfield and Henrico counties—had to merge in order to achieve a sort of racial balance, and use bussing to achieve it. The Court of Appeals reversed that decision, arguing that each system was already somewhat integrated, and (1) since Richmond was the only district predominantly black, mergers would, in essence, necessitate setting a quota for blacks; (2) since the state did not draw district lines with the intent to segregate, it constituted *de facto* rather than *de jure* segregation and therefore did not violate the Constitution; and (3) since the districts had different tax bases and jurisdictions, the financing would constitute a burden. Moreover, a district court did not have the jurisdiction to dictate what a state's educational policy should be. Therefore, the decision essentially allowed the districts to implement their own plans as long as they provided for reasonable racial mixture. CORE agreed with the court's decision and argued that its plan should be adopted.

Some argue that CORE's desegregation plan was simply a boon for white racists, who saw it as another way of legally promoting segregation, this time aided and abetted by blacks themselves. Black reaction to the plan on the whole was negative; they, too, saw it as the flip side of a racist coin with segregation imprinted on both sides. Black reaction was divided between a minority of militants who favored the plan and the majority who opposed it. Because CORE has not received a groundswell of support, it has increased the distance between the organization and the masses.

Black Panther Party

The Black Panther Party came into existence in 1966 as a vanguard organization to redress the grievances of the black community by bringing about "revolution through the barrel of a gun." Since then the Party has, at least in rhetoric and action, undergone revolutionary changes. Profane rhetoric is no longer condoned by the national leadership (though individual members may use it); the gun has been replaced by the ballot; "the capitalist system must be destroyed" has been replaced by engagement in electoral politics; and the rabid antireligious emphasis has given way to praise of the institution of religion in the black community.

Apparent changes in the Party organization raise several questions about movement transformation. The first and most crucial is whether the Party has been transformed from a Marxist-Leninist revolutionary organization to a law-abiding reform movement. Could it be that the Party changed its tactics because of societal apprehension and physical coercion by the constituted authority? Was it not expedient to make changes in program and tactics in order to appeal to the black masses who were intially turned off by guns, revolutionary rhetoric, and the incendiary Panther newspaper? Were there individuals in the leadership structure who initially pushed the organization to extreme postures to fit their own needs? The answers to these questions involve gray areas between the external and internal forces operating in the Black Panther orbit. The following discussion attempts to shed some light on them.

It should be noted that the founders of the Black Panther Party, Huey P. Newton and Bobby Seale, were absent, thanks to prison sentences, from day-to-day operations for a considerable period of time. The Party was run by a Central Committee with each member of the committee, including Newton and Seale, having only one vote. Newton makes the point that while he was in prison, he was outvoted in determining Party policy. For example, he opposed the Party's giving up the uniforms they had previously worn, though others felt that in order to relate to the people, uniforms were inappropriate. In his book *To Die for the People* Newton elaborates on what went wrong with the party while he was in prison.

One of the most significant wrongs was the reaction of constituted authority to J. Edgar Hoover's placing the Panthers on the subversive list. As a result, law enforcement agencies throughout the country, at all levels, went on the offensive against them. "The tone for police departments is set in many instances by the FBI, which in numerous ways is both racist and right-wing. . . . It is easy to understand the fact that Panthers are hassled uniformly by police in all parts of the country, when there is clear evidence that the police establishment has developed a monolithically unified stance against them."[17] The Panthers' militant posture, augmented by weapons, made it possible for the authorities to use coercive physical power without having to utilize nonviolent control techniques first.

In addition to constituted authority's verbal condemnation and use of physical coercion, the Panthers' initial extreme posture did not strike a significant chord among the black masses (though it did stimulate much young black blood to run hot!). Their call for revolution has not been the traditional manner through which the black masses have sought redress of their grievances. One may say the Panthers were too far ahead or were operating outside the experiential background of the black masses, or both. Whatever the case, the Panthers initially alienated, then frightened them, making membership in the organization, as they thought, a risky and dangerous undertaking. It was a difficult task to speak for a people who were exhibiting disdain and disagreement.

The only alternatives left were to retrench and concentrate on maintaining the organization or attempt to align with the views of the people. The Panthers chose the latter alternative. In so doing, internal as well as external adjustments were necessary. Internally, the adjustments took the form of expulsions and ideological housecleaning.

That a black revolutionary organization was allowed to exist in the first place was a wonder, but for the organization to have chapters spread throughout the nation was amazing. This external state of affairs contributed to internal tensions and conflicts when chapters were frequently at odds with national headquarters. Ideological and policy disagreements resulted, and the national headquarters was forced to take punitive action against many chapters as a whole and individuals in them. Hence, headquarters constantly published the names of those expelled for being "enemies of the people." In some instances, the exposed "enemies" were infiltrators and counterrevolutionary spies (as might be expected), but in others they were regular members and leaders who did not agree with party policy.

A significant factor in the disagreements was regional differences in approaches to black liberation. Despite their differences, each chapter believed that black oppression is the direct result of white prejudice and discrimination, white racism. Racism, they argued, took on individual and institutional characteristics. Most of the time black reaction to racism is not uniform, either in its ideology or in its strategy and programs,[18] and this lack of uniformity can be found especially in a radical activist movement with chapters or branches throughout the country.

That may be responsible for the national headquarters in Oakland banning its New York chapter for defying it. The expulsion of Michael "Cetewayo" Tabor, Connie Matthews Tabor (husband and wife), and Richard "Dharuba" Moore for "counterrevolutionary" activity may have involved regional as well as ideological differences.[19]

The split between the New York Panther chapter and the Tabors and Moore resulted in a much larger ideological split within the national headquarters itself. The following account points up some of the intricacies. On March 1, 1971, the New York chapter of the Black Panther Party held a press conference at their Harlem office to clarify their position on the expulsion and to announce a reorganization of the national party as they would like it. They began by apologizing for the Party's mistakes, suggesting that they had hindered the black liberation process and often alienated the Party "from our community and the people whom we serve." Specially directed at the Oakland headquarters, they stated that some members of the Central Committee no longer lived in black communities "and instead spent much of their time partying and feasting on $30 meals." Since party policy is formulated at the top, the New York chapter contended that those who criticized the leadership's high living were "purged, branded as pigs, fools, or enemies of the people." In plainer words, they claimed that what happened to Michael Tabor, Connie Matthews Tabor, and Richard Moore, resulted from arbitrary decisions made at the top in the best interest of certain individuals, not the masses.

Because Newton and Seale were in jail and Eldridge Cleaver and Don Cox (members of the Central Committee) were in exile in Algeria, David Hilliard became the leader by fiat. The New York chapter asserted that all others had been silenced by him, pointing out that their criticisms and letters had been ignored by him. (Cleaver fled the country in November 1969 after the California Probation Department ordered his return to prison. He has, however, since voluntarily returned to serve out his sentence.) They then suggested that Hilliard's expulsion of the entire Inter-Communal Section in Algeria (Cleaver, his wife Kathleen, and Cox among others) was the last straw. They charged Hilliard with treason by deliberately deviating "from the principles of the . . . party and its political structure" and for taking party funds for his personal use. Being careful not to implicate Newton, the East Coast chapter suggested that Hilliard had gone so far as to have Newton put on medication in order to control him. As far as they were concerned, they considered Hilliard "purged from the Black Panther Party for life."

Using Cleaver as their cutting edge, the New York chapter then suggested that according to him "counterrevolutionary" Central Committee members ought to be removed. The Central Committee as they saw it should be comprised as follows: "Chairman, Bobby Seale; Minister of Information, Eldridge Cleaver; Field Marshal, Don Cox; and Communications Secretary, Kathleen Cleaver. Ray 'Masai' Hewitt (Minister of Education), and Emory Douglas (Minister of Culture), and Huey P. Newton will be held on trial before the people to be judged on their revolutionary commitment."[20] Though the New York Chapter maintained that their criticisms were not intended to create a split in the Black Panther Party, it in fact did just that.

Newton did not expel David Hilliard, the Chief of Staff, as suggested by the New York chapter, and certainly did not stand a "people's trial." He did, however, expel the New York chapter and those who supported it, including the "International Section" located in Algiers, Algeria, headed by Eldridge Cleaver!

Though the actual Newton/Cleaver split was brought to a head by the New York chapter and the Tabor-Moore expulsions, the ideological rift between Newton and Cleaver went much deeper. On the surface the disagreement came when Cleaver indicated that the expulsions of the New York Panthers were "ill-advised and regrettable" and should not have taken place; he also called for the firing of David Hilliard, who, Cleaver felt, was "responsible for the recent purge, and for 'the party falling apart at the seams.'" Newton, on the contrary, deemed the purges necessary and took personal responsibility for the action. Shortly thereafter, "the Panther newspaper accused Cleaver not only of several 'counterrevolutionary actions,' but of holding his wife Kathleen [Cleaver] prisoner in Algeria." The Cleavers denied the charges and criticized the national party leadership in Oakland: they charged the Oakland leadership with being a right-wing party and said that although Newton founded the party, "it did not give him the right to destroy it" because "the Black Panther Party belongs to the people.'"[21]

The charges and countercharges between Newton and Cleaver were surface manifestations of a much deeper ideological rift. The New York chapter and Hilliard respectively enabled Cleaver and Newton to bring out in the open their ideological disagreements.[22]

Huey Newton has described the period in which Eldridge Cleaver was a major influence in the Black Panther Party as a period of party alienation from the black community. Cleaver has also been called by Newton and Seale the party's hidden traitor. In any case, the dispute gave the Panther leadership an opportunity to "re-align" the party's image and to adopt tactics and behavior to which the black community could relate.

Cleaver was blamed by Seale for alienating black preachers by telling them that the gun, not the Bible, was the path to black liberation. His either/or positions on most issues, contends Seale, alienated many elements in the black community. Seale felt all along that the black church should not have been treated in this manner by the Panthers because by his estimation 40 percent of the black community regularly attend church. To ignore or alien-ate them is absurd. It seemed sensible to Seale to take an activity like the Panther Breakfast for Children Program and relate it to the church. But Cleaver did not seem interested in the Panthers' breakfasts despite the obvious interest of the blacks who regular-ly attended church.

Cleaver, according to Newton and Seale, was interested in raising black consciousness through the written word. In contrast, Newton and Seale felt that a person's consciousness can only be raised so much with words (obviously referring to Cleaver's widely read writings in *Ramparts* and his bestseller, *Soul on Ice*). Seale makes the point that once he was told by an old black man that "poetry might be all right. You all talking about raising my con-sciousness, but you can't raise no hungry man's consciousness. His consciousness is on some food." So Newton and Seale felt that first the person should have his hunger pangs relieved and then perhaps bring on poetry that may "raise his consciousness." After giving a person food and clothing, there is a much better chance that he will read the Panther newspaper he finds in his grocery bag. Seale then made it clear that the Panther Breakfast Program and the grocery-giving was not an end in itself but only a vehicle to remind people of what has to be done to alleviate the dire black condition. And, of course, that the Panthers have the right program to get the job done.

Another area of dispute was originally the Panther uniform—the black beret, black leather jacket, black slacks, "pimp socks" and shined black shoes, and powder-blue shirts with scarfs, or turtleneck shirts. Seale pointed out that to the black community the uniform represented organization and unity, it had symbolic value, as it were, and even elderly blacks would comment, "Lord them young men show is sharp, clean and organized." The symbolism went even further: it attracted young blacks to the organization where they were recruited. Therefore, Cleaver's abandonment of the uniform in favor of "hippie gear" was a mistake, according to Seale, because in the liberation struggle it is necessary to relate to the masses in the most expedient manner. The black masses were not into hippie philosophy or their mode of dress.

Cleaver, on the other hand, "took us more into the radical hippy group of people," and "after about a year and a half or two, the uniform was gone." After Eldridge influenced the abandonment of the uniform, "Party members [were] walking around in big ole boots [and] wild leather jackets. And black people just don't have that conscious relationship to [the hippie dress]."[23]

The upshot of the Panther ideological dispute was that the Party reanalyzed its ideological position and made revolutionary adjustments to the black (and white) community. To begin with, Pan-Africanism has been a thorn in the Panthers' side largely because, seemingly, they couldn't decide whether they were an all-inclusive, class-oriented [Marxist-Leninist] or a black-oriented (nationalist) movement. It should be clear that throughout, there have been shifts in Panther ideology regarding separatism, Marxism-Leninism, Intercommunalism, Pan-Africanism, etc. vis-à-vis black oppression. (In this work, there has been only tangential reference to how the Black Panther Party can be classified as a black separatist movement. To the Panthers the debate is relevant, but to the constituted authority the question is academic. The public at large as well as the constituted authority act as if the Panthers are a separatist (radical) movement. The Congressional hearings, the position taken by the FBI, law enforcement agencies at all levels of government, a majority of the black public (by not supporting and/or joining), the white public, all attest to the *image* the public has of the party: a dangerous black-separatist, radical organization. There is no need to document the image.)

In the initial stages of the Panther organization this confusion involving Marxist-Leninism and black nationalism prompted the movement to minimize the importance of black nationalism (separatism) as well as Pan-Africanism. The Panthers viewed black cultural nationalism[24] as dysfunctional and counterproductive because they used the dialectical class approach rather than racism as the basic underlying cause of black oppression. At other times, when convenient, they did suggest that racism (racist pigs, racist power structure, etc.) was the underlying cause.[25] Over time they realized that any radical black movement that ignored black nationalism as a pervasive force among some elements in especially large urban black communites was doomed to failure. Moreover, Pan-Africanism was regarded by many blacks as the highest form of black nationalism. Hence, the Panthers had to accept black nationalism/Pan-Africanism as a reality in black membership recruitment if they wanted to continue to exist as a relevant organization.

Let us briefly review their prior ideological position. The Panthers, as previously indicated, were initially a self-defense group operating in the Oakland ghetto. They later became Marxist-Leninist, began to view the world as a mélange of communities exploited by capitalists, and therefore became internationalists and intercommunalists. The Panthers' world views alienated militant black nationalists/separatists because they were more concerned with domestic oppression. Many black nationalists believed that joining black Africans in some form of Pan-Africanism was the only form of intercommunalism. But many others regarded the Panthers' new concept of intercommunalism as simply another white philosophy radicalized to include blacks. Hence, the Panthers had to redefine their relationship to Pan-Africanism and black nationalism.

The present Panther position on Pan-Africanism still, somehow, focuses on intercommunalism. Seale indicates that at one time the Panthers were wrong about Pan-Africanism being the highest form of cultural nationalism; that was corrected by Huey Newton's formulation of the concept of intercommunalism because technology has made it possible for all peoples to come into contact with one another, and therefore all peoples are interspersed, interconnected, and interrelated. Because of its resources, Africa is important to what "the racist capitalists develop and produce in communications, travel, and all forms of technology. Black people can be very significantly related to how Africa's control of its resources occurs and how it's going to affect world development." As to whether black people should go to Africa or remain in the United States, Seale suggested that it would be best for them to remain here where blacks live. He does not oppose those who want to go to Africa, but since the United States represents the belly of the whale, blacks should remain here for strategic reasons.[26]

In the Panthers' "new" posture the Party sees electoral politics as a way of further relating to the people. The Panthers have thrown away the gun in order to engage in black-voter registration. In that Oakland is about 50 percent black and 12 percent Chicano (according to Seale), there is a possibility that blacks could vote out the white rulers. As a result, Bobby Seale became a candidate for Mayor of Oakland! With suit and tie, a smile and handshake, nonprofane language, and a rational, nonradical political platform, Seale, Co-Chairman of the Black Panther Party, challenged the incumbent mayor and other candidates. He came in a distant second to the incumbent, yet forced a run-off. Although he lost in the run-off, he ignited the flame of more meaningful participation by blacks in Oakland politics.

In summary, the Cleaver-Newton ideological rift served as a basis for the transformation of the Black Panther Party from a revolutionary organization working outside the system to one now advocating reform measures. Cleaver has returned to the United States and has at this writing served out his original sentence. (He is now also, among other things, an avid follower of Christ, making television spots for white southern Baptists!) Newton, on the other hand, fled to Cuba and also returned to serve out his sentence. The Party is now headed by Elaine Brown. In any case, the Panthers are acting as a different kind of catalytic agent in speaking to black oppression. They are using the system they once damned to attain their reform goals. Whether old conditions that continue to exist will force them back to their earlier revolutionary position outside the system is a question that can only be answered by future events. The next Black Panthers, who may call themselves black mambas, may propose a more drastic solution, and may find a groundswell of support. Or they may not.

The Nation of Islam

The Nation of Islam has maintained its separatist ideology since its inception, but it, too, has made adjustments in its interplay with society at large. Though one could not say in a strict sense that the Nation has been significantly transformed, in the latter seventies it is nevertheless different. In the first place, with the impetus provided by Malcolm X and by younger members too impatient to wait for Allah to take care of the "white devils," it became evident to the Muslim leadership that they could no longer discourage political participation in the "man's" politics. Although the other black movement organizations treated in this work attempted to alter the political and social reality of black oppression by going back and forth on integration and separation themes, the Nation more than others has steadfastly pursued economic and cultural separation at the expense of "things political." This led other movements, especially black nationalists, to criticize the Nation for being all bark and no bite, and that in turn led the Nation, urged by a segment of its membership, to allow political participation. The Muslim entry into politics does not mean that the movement as a whole at its national headquarters or local mosques now endorses or works for candidates. It means only that individual Muslims are free to pursue their own independent political choices.

A second important factor in the Nation's behavior has to do with its past characterization of whites as "white devils." Malcolm X in his latter days cautioned blacks against indicting whites as racists without identifying the underlying cause of racism. He identified the cause of white racism as the capitalist system, and perhaps because of his observation, the Nation now soft-pedals the use of the term "white devil." This downplaying was initiated by the late Elijah Muhammad and continues under the organization's present leadership cadre. (In the 1960's, for example, Louis Lerner, a "blue-eyed devil," printed *Muhammad Speaks.*) The change probably resulted from the embarrassing inconsistency of simultaneously doing business with "the man" and denying his humanity.

A third point in the Nation's adjustment is the emerging relaxation of strict codes of conduct. In the past, Muslims were forbidden to smoke, drink, gamble, or buy on credit; they were not to eat anything from swine—pork ribs, bacon, chops and chitterlings. Muslims could have no social relations with whites; women had to dress in Muslim fashion, wear no lipstick or other makeup, and never be alone in the company of a man other than their husbands. Some Muslims regard these taboos as extreme asceticism, and the attrition rate is high.

Even *Muhammad Speaks* took on a different cast as well as a new name, *Balalia News.* It now seems to speak to community problems, with less emphasis on putting down the blue-eyed devil. In fact it is edited by two black non-Muslims who are concerned not so much with pedogogical problems as with relating to a readership that is about 90 percent non-Muslim. Even the Nation cannot deny relevance.

Another point of significance: the Nation under its new leadership seems to be retrenching on its prior emphasis on establishing a string of nation-wide business enterprises. It has sold many of its establishments around the country, concentrating instead on bolstering its position in Chicago, its headquarters. The shift in the Nation's economic policy no doubt reflects the conventional business approach of Herbert Muhammad, the financial wizard of the Nation's leadership cadre (and the financial manager of Muhammad Ali, current heavyweight champion of the world). In conjunction with its new economic posture, Wallace Muhammad seems to be placing special emphasis on the Nation's reassessment of its primary role and function in relation to the black masses as well as the division of labor in the leadership cadre. That is, Wallace's primary role is to project the Nation's public image, while Raymond Sharrieff and Herbert Muhammad concern themselves respectively with organizational social control and financial matters. Minister Louis Farrakhan, perhaps symbolically fulfilling the role played by Malcolm X, engenders organizational *esprit de corps* by serving as the chief liaison between the Chicago headquarters and the various Mosques around the country.

Finally, the Nation maintains its pragmatic outlook on the black condition, perhaps because it has achieved and played an institutionalized societal role. By declaring its philosophy to be nonracial, placing emphasis on acquiring housing (for Muslims only), stressing the importance of wholesome eating, and attempting to acquire hospitals catering to blacks, the Nation has intentionally or inadvertently aligned its program to fit the needs of the majority of black Americans. With the death of Elijah Muhammad in early 1975 and consequent adjustment to new leadership, the Nation is adjusting remarkably well to change in the organization itself as well as in the general American society. The relationship between organization and society—if the relationship remains dynamic—is certain to cause further adjustment and change.

Republic of New Africa (RNA)

When about 500 black nationalists met in Detroit at the end of March 1968 and signed a declaration of independence for the "black nation," naming itself the Republic of New Africa, it elected then exiled Robert Williams as its president, Milton Henry as first vice-president, and Richard Henry as minister of information. It then called for the establishment of the "black nation" in Mississippi, Louisiana, Alabama, Georgia, and South Carolina.

The RNA created the Black Legionnaires, a military arm (a necessity for any nation) and charged them with the protection of RNA leaders and maintenance of order at RNA functions. The Legionnaires were tested in March 1969 by the Detroit police when the RNA held its first anniversary meeting at the new Bethel Baptist Church in Detroit. After the meeting, Brother Gaidi was preparing to drive away when a gunfight erupted between Legionnaires and Detroit white police. Policemen converged on the church and fired indiscriminately into it. One policeman was killed and several RNA members wounded. It is alleged that the police were trying to assassinate Brother Gaidi, but he escaped. The Henry brothers, along with others, were arrested and subsequently freed by a black Detroit judge.

In June 1969 Brother Gaidi sent President Nixon a note asking for a meeting to negotiate the RNA's demands. Nixon has yet to reply.

In September 1969 Robert Williams returned to the United States after, according to Dunbar, "intricate negotiations with government officials" by Brother Gaidi. The outcome of the negotiations was that Williams was allowed to return to the United States, with only Brother Gaidi and Williams occupying a Boeing 707!

The return of Williams did not bring about the anticipated impetus for the RNA. In fact, he exhibited no enthusiasm for the organization. In December 1969 he resigned as president, indicating that he now believed that "blacks can achieve complete equality only by working within the system." As a result of Williams' resignation, the RNA lost some of its appeal.

Even more crippling was an estrangement between the two Henry brothers. The rift centered on the establishment of RNA territory: Brother Imari was of the opinion that action must replace talk by purchasing land in Mississippi for the RNA; Brother Gaidi thought it premature at least and suicidal at worst to go into hostile Mississippi to establish a nation before the inhabitants were politically educated to their nationhood. Imari was convinced that the Republic needed a 100,000-man defensive force to deter incidents like the New Bethel church attack. Gaidi, on the other hand, felt that the establishment of a large military force was dangerous; it invited confrontation. Gaidi believed, unlike the black youth the RNA was attracting, that painstaking, hard work was necessary in nation-building. You cannot take over by force. He indicated that only through outvoting whites county by county, city by city, state by state, could blacks begin to make fundamental inroads that are realistic in terms of the power relationships.

The outcome of the ideological differences resulted in 1970 in a split in the organization. Gaidi suspended Imari and each brother rallied his respective followers. Meanwhile, Brother Hekima (Tom Norman) temporarily assumed the presidency and arranged a new election. In an election held in March 1970, after conventions in the East (Philadelphia) and Midwest (Grand Rapids, Michigan), with the South abstaining, Imari was elected president (Gaidi did not stand in the election). Imari then claimed to be the organization's legitimate leader. Gaidi dropped out but still claimed he was its legitimate head. He later gave up his RNA name, Gaidi, and his affiliation with the organization.

In May 1970 Imari and a group of his followers moved to New Orleans—part of the organization's national territory—where they opened an RNA office. In the fall of the same year he negotiated a land purchase of twenty acres from a black Mississippi farmer in Hinds County, twenty-five miles outside Jackson.

In 1971 the predictable harassment, provocation, incidents, and charges occurred: Imari and the RNA were found guilty of "taking" the farmer's land after the Mississippi Attorney General, R. F. Sumner, wrote Attorney General Mitchell that the RNA's activities appeared to be an armed insurrection against the state and nation. Mississippi police began arresting RNA members on false charges (any charges) and even Imari himself.

The inevitable confrontation took place on August 1, 1971, between the RNA and FBI agents and local police. With warrants for the arrest of certain RNA members, policemen surrounded the RNA's Jackson headquarters. The RNA members inside were told that they had one minute to come out. When no one appeared, the police fired a shot through a window, which was answered in kind. One police officer was killed and an FBI agent and another policeman were wounded. The seven RNA people inside were no match for the riot guns, an armored vehicle, and tear gas; they surrendered. The person for whom the FBI had a warrant was not in the house. Meanwhile, at another RNA location policemen surrounded the residence of Imari and three other RNA members, who surrendered. There was no shoot-out.

Brother Imari was not at the scene where the officer was killed, but was put in Hinds County Jail in Jackson, Mississippi, charged with being part of a conspiracy to murder, an assault on a federal officer, and violation of a Mississippi "treason" law which carries the death sentence. The other defendants were released on bail, but Imari but was not allowed this privilege.

Brother Imari still directs RNA activity, as evidenced by his missives from his Hinds County maximum security cell (only his family and lawyer are permitted to see him).

What is the ideological perspective of the RNA now that Milton Henry is no longer involved in its activities? In answer to some questions posed by Ernest Dunbar, Brother Imari made the following points:[27]

(1) The break between himself and his brother centered on his desire to begin immediate acquisition of land, while Milton saw that as a future undertaking.

(2) He does not believe that black capitalism is the solution to America's race problem, because he cannot envision the possibility of black people ending poverty or black middle-class frustration by enterprise in the United States.

(3) He believes that whites will never give up anything to blacks until it proves beneficial to whites. Whites in the North can be shown that the peaceful granting of "sovereignty to a black nation in Mississippi is the simplest, cheapest, most logical way for *them* (something they do care about) and end the black depression for us (something they do not really care about)."

(4) Relative to the land dispute involving the Mississippi farmer, Imari said that one does not buy land to establish sovereignty, only to get on with the business at hand. The RNA will conduct a plebiscite in the Kush District (about twenty-five black counties along the Mississippi River from Memphis to the Louisiana border) in order to declare the area's independence. Once free, it will then be a black nation.

(5) How is the RNA, asks Dunbar, to survive in the hostile South? Imari answered that, from the outset, the RNA was aware of the South's hostility, but he was convinced that RNA will succeed. He is also convinced that there is a divine alliance to make the RNA dream a reality. He indicated that New Africa Workers are educating the people to the true meaning of the Kush Nation. "I know this is just a beginning. There are always new questions. How do we *make* the United States accept the results of the plesbiscite? Let's talk about that next time. FREE THE LAND, brother!"

Unlike the Panthers, who went from a revolutionary to a reform posture, the RNA's transformation was in the opposite direction. Its membership has become hard-core separatists, which may account for its lack of mass appeal. A closer look at Robert Williams (as an individual) may shed some light on how this happened, as well as why some people moved from radical to reform positions. We have seen how Brother Imari has moved from a reform to a revolutionary position.

Williams decided to return to the United States from China (he had left Cuba for China when Castro began to show the same racist attitude toward blacks as the typical white Southerner in the United States). Some have indicated that after Williams' vehement anti-American broadcasts while in Cuba and China, his return to the United States without being charged with sedition came in connection with his testimony to "the Internal Security Subcommittee of the Senate Judiciary Committee in March, 1970, perhaps in exchange for promises of no federal prosecution . . ."[28]

Williams has, in fact, radically changed his rhetoric since his return. Perhaps his experience in Cuba made him realize that socialism can be as racist as individual leaders will allow it to be. Castro insisted to Williams that the black man's natural ally was the white working class. "I openly disputed this . . . I had found that whites in the South who helped us were the intelligentsia. The farmers and the millworkers . . . were the ones trying to kill us and standing on the sides jeering."[29] Williams was told by Castro functionaries that Castro could not support black nationalism because it advocated division and self-determination. In short, if Fidel supported black nationalism in America, he would have to consider the heavy concentration of blacks in Oriente Province. What if they wanted self-determination? Williams indicated that he understood the predicament and left Cuba, traveling to the People's Republic of China and finally back to the United States.

Williams' position now, however, seems to have reverted to one of working through the system. He once stated that it was a grave error for militant and just-minded youth to reject struggle in order to join the man's government services, police forces, peace corps, and vital organs of the power structure. His present position, however, is predicated on the concept that "militant change can be more thoroughly effectuated by militant pressure from within as as well as without."[30] Finally, Williams saw the federal government as the only hope for blacks winning equality.

Statements of this sort may lead some to question whether Williams is mouthing instructions from the powers responsible for his return to the United States; it is unusual for a militant to change his mind so rapidly. However, there is another plausible answer: it is difficult for an individual to reject completely his initial and prior societal orientation because of emotional, psychic, and perhaps political reasons. It is possible that Robert Williams, the initial NAACP integrationist from Monroe, North Carolina, has returned to his prior position of working for an integrated society. Or it may be that he really does believe that blacks can gain a degree of equality only through governmental avenues, because otherwise white society at large finds it easy to ignore blacks. Separatists argue that for white America consistently and persistently over time to exert energy for black human decency has neither historical precedent nor contemporary predisposition.

In conclusion: all the movement organizations in differing degrees modified their initial ideological or behavioral positions caused by external and internal change dynamics. Blacks for whom the movements allegedly spoke had differing perceptions of how liberation should be achieved—if they *felt* oppressed in the first place. The general society in which the movements operated also changed. Sometimes it included aspects of a movement's ideas; at other times it forcefully rejected them. Members of the organizations changed their minds about the efficacy of their organization's ideological positions and attempted at best to change or modify the ideologies, at worst to depart from the organization.

11 SEPARATISM: CATALYST FOR CHANGE

We have characterized contemporary black separatist movements as, purposely or unconsciously, agents for change. They propose and attempt to implement political and sociocultural arrangements for black people that may differ from and in some essential ways oppose those of the larger society. Their extreme alternatives are meant either to prompt social change within the system or—being convinced that black liberation is impossible in America because of white racism—to help blacks to accept their own culture and follow their own life styles in their own political, social, and economic institutions. This chapter will analyze the separatist movements in respect to their intent to do one or the other.

The stated Muslim ideology of self-help and economic enterprise differs little from those of the general society. In applying our definition of a separatist movement to them, seemingly they are acting as a catalyst to the general society to influence change to aid the black masses. Hence, Muslim activities are devoted to transforming power relations in the general society to include the black masses.

The members of the Muslim organization are drawn largely from that section of the black population receiving the brunt of white or systemic oppression—the lower level of the socioeconomic scale. Therefore, the Muslim's philosophy of self-help, like Booker T. Washington's, is designed to alter the depraved conditions of that socioeconomic stratum. Both Muhammad and Washington counseled blacks to "depend on self." Both counseled blacks to go into trade and industry. The Muslims have—unsuccessfully in some instances—initiated a program to buy land in the South to raise food (cattle, truck farms, etc.) and to sell it in Muslim-owned restaurants. They have established an Islamic University in Chicago, which brings to mind Washington's Tuskegee Institute. Undertaking these kinds of enterprises is significant in that *both Muhammad and Washington were speaking to and initiating programs ultimately geared to aid lower-class blacks.* Both saw self-help through business and vocational training as the key to self-sufficiency. Any issue of *Muhammad Speaks* shows pictures of black people farming, raising cattle, doing engineering work, engaging in medicine, etc., over the caption "SELF-HELP!"

The difference between Washington and Muhammad lies in the former's open espousal of black self-sufficiency and the latter's covert tactic of achieving the same goal through the system by overtly embracing separatism: Washington counseled blacks to establish separate economic self-sufficiency in the general society; Muhammad did the same, adding Islam, overt racial separatism, and black superiority. Harold Cruse makes the point that the Nation of Islam is the modern "form of Booker T. Washington's economic self-help, black unity, bourgeois hard work, law abiding, vocational training, stay-out-of-the-civil-rights-struggle agitation, separate from the white man, etc., morality." Washington, according to Cruse, "practiced moderate accommodationist separatism while [Muhammad] preaches militant separatism. *But it is still the same separatism whose quality only changes from one era to another.*"[1]

The point should be made that, just as the Muslims' economic program is fashioned after Washington's, it is also closely akin to that of Garvey, since Garvey's program was also fashioned after Washington's. As indicated earlier, Garvey believed in capitalism and the free enterprise system; he rejected Communism and Socialism as the best system for blacks in the United States mainly because he saw no difference between a white Communist or white Socialist. He, like Washington, indicated that the white capitalist was the black man's most expedient ally and that economic programs modeled on the free enterprise system were best because "it is the commercial and financial power of the United States of America that makes her the greatest banker in the world. Hence it is advisable for the Negro to get power of every kind . . . in education, science, industry, politics, and higher government."[2]

The Muslims are indeed following Garvey's advice: they stress scientific expertise, educational excellence (Muslim style), industrial undertakings, and propose a separate black nation. Muslim values, then, reflect those held by Garvey and the U.N.I.A.; Muslim ideology has religion as its foundation for separatism, while Garvey's movement had a back-to-Africa foundation. Both accepted the general society's capitalist economic system as a vehicle for their programs.

The Muslim Program ("What the Muslims Want" and "What the Muslims Believe") shows that they want equality, justice, education, and a stop to police brutality. The total Program is based on "if not, then" propositions; usually implicit in such propositions is a reform intent. Moreover, though the Muslims espouse racial separation, their newspaper, *Muhammad Speaks*, now *Balalia News*, exhibits a consistent tendency to decry any integrationist effort that fails or any injustice blacks receive. (Of course, decrying the failure of integration may be another way of pointing up the futility of possible black acceptance into white-dominated society). Moreover, the paper is pro-Arab and anti-Israeli, which means that it has taken a political stance indicating that the Muslims are indeed concerned with influencing political change. This again is indicative of the Muslims' concern with infusing change-inducing input into the existing system; otherwise, following their rhetoric of noninvolvement, why bother with social change in the system?

Finally, counseled Muhammad, "Observe the operation of the white man. He is successful. He makes no excuses for his failures. He works hard in a collective manner. You do the same."[3]

In short, the Nation of Islam, in the tradition of Washington and Garvey, utilizes the same basic economic framework as the dominant forces in American society. Whether their real values and ideology differ significantly is difficult to tell. What is evident is their apparent acceptance of the same economic system utilized by the "white devils" they ostensibly declare their enemy.

In its transformation from integration to separatism, has CORE changed its values and ideology out of proportion to its original and American values? When CORE endorsed "Black Power" in 1966, unlike SNCC, it continued to develop programmatic alternatives for the black masses. It developed economic, political, and social programs for blacks through black capitalism. Many have equated black capitalism with black power.[4] At the beginning of the current black power era, CORE did, in fact, embrace black capitalism. CORE's values and ideology did not differ significantly from American capitalism, but became in fact its darker brother.

Starting in 1968, however, when Roy Innis became its National Director, CORE began to move away from black bourgeois nationalism à la Floyd McKissick through black capitalism to black nationalism according to Innis. Innis was listed in *Ebony*'s One Hundred Most Influential Black Americans (May 1974). One could say that since *Ebony* is a black bourgeois magazine, its criteria for including Innis leaves little doubt that CORE's values and ideology are somewhere near those held by the American mainstream. (It could also mean that *Ebony* endorses black separatism, but that is very unlikely.)

Finally, CORE's ideology is ostensibly geared to accommodate the black mass in contrast to its former position of bourgeois black nationalism aimed at the "talented tenth." CORE's black nationalist methods and techniques are reminiscent of Washington and Garvey with elements of political activity, community control, and Pan-Africanism. In that Roy Innis is a native of the West Indies (the Virgin Islands), his leadership reflects more of Garvey (also a West Indian) than of Washington. Cruse is again on target when he asserts: "As Innis could not fit Washington and DuBois into his militant trend, he left them out—without explaining how, historically, he can separate Washington from Garvey."[5]

As an organization that is now defunct, SNCC clearly acted as a catalyst in bringing about changes in the way formerly nonmilitant organizations related to the society at large. This was evidenced by the positions taken by heretofore conservative and moderate organizations like CORE; the Urban League; the Black Power Conference in Newark, New Jersey, in 1967; and many other local and regional groups and organizations which endorsed black power.

SNCC's emphasis on Pan-Africanism, independent black political parties, and the exclusion of whites from decision-making roles in black organizations were efforts to effect a black entrance into the arena of political power. Its initial Southern activities were all aimed on including blacks in the political arena, not promoting separation. That is, SNCC first attempted to aid black oppression by engaging in voter registration campaigns; later it attempted to integrate the all-white Mississippi delegation to the Democratic Convention, so as to reflect the 36–40 percent black population in Mississippi. Failing that, it helped to form the Mississippi Freedom Democratic Party (MFDP), still an integrated delegation.

Failing that arrangement, too, SNCC began to advocate all-black political parties, all-black organizations, and ultimately independent black power. The point is clear: SNCC utilized the same tactics the general society condoned in its thrust for black liberation —racial politics. That is, to a large measure ethnic politics still play a significant role in American politics and SNCC's efforts helped blacks to become a strong ethnic factor in the political arena.

SNCC's and the general society's values and ideology closely paralleled, but black people, having no control over the media and relatively little political or economic power, were overcome with white power's determination to negate black power by all means at its disposal.

In the final analysis, SNCC's values and ideology were not significantly different from those of the general society. They merely attempted to implement society's stated values for black people through (separate) black power. Because SNCC exposed society to its contradictions, constituted authority reacted to the exposure by tagging black power as dangerous and forcing the oppressed blacks to the defense. Thus black power lost its meaning and potential effectiveness by too many definitions, until finally the highest representative of constituted authority, former President Richard M. Nixon, defined black power as "black capitalism."

The Black Panther Platform and Program essentially reiterate the ideals and values held by most Americans. Panther leaders often declare that if American ideals were actually implemented on the basis of equality between blacks and whites, there would be no need for the Party to exist. For example, point ten in the Panther's Program is the Preamble to the American Declaration of Independence. But because black people are denied equality and are oppressed in American society, the Panthers initially proposed to change the power relations through "revolutionary black nationalism."

In a word, the Panthers utilized uncommon tactics in attempting to promote commonly accepted American ideals. Black people have not traditionally used armed confrontation as a liberation tactic. Rather, blacks have traditionally used protest, nonviolence, and demonstrations as tactics in reacting against oppression. The Panthers' use of arms in protesting oppression ignited coercive physical oppression from the white power structure and at the same time alienated the bulk of the black masses from the Panthers' Program, because to belong was at best unpopular and at worst dangerous. In order to align the organization's policy with the people's experiential tradition, the Panthers embraced black institutions they formerly disdained: the church, electoral politics, poverty programs, legal counseling, and other nonrevolutionary activity in the black community. Finally, the Panthers, although they embraced most values held by the general society, initially utilized uncommon tactics in attempting to make them apply to the black masses. Currently, Panther sociopolitical behavior does fit the traditional means of black protest to white oppression.

The final example, the RNA, may seem the most radical, but, ironically, its proposal to establish a black nation in the South is tame. Its utopian character stems mainly from the tendency of some Americans to forget that, except when it comes to blacks, community control or states rights are deeply ingrained in American and democratic political philosophy: white Americans, as a matter of course, control their communities and cry wolf when the federal or state government "encroaches" upon "local autonomy." However, when blacks attempt to control *their* communities, the goal becomes nonpositive, "unrealistic," utopian, and "un-American." There would be nothing unrealistic in the establishment of a black community or "nation" in portions of the South where there is a black majority if it were not for two factors: the constituted authority in Mississippi has vowed that the RNA will not succeed there,[6] and the calls of RNA for a black return to these states have not met with much success. There is a significant slowdown in black out-migration from South to North, but Southern rural blacks are still, in significant numbers, moving from Southern rural to Southern urban areas.

Although the RNA's call for a black nation in the South may appear revolutionary, its proposed method of obtaining control is a model of nonrevolutionary conventionality. The initial plan for gaining control over the five states is described below by one of the RNA founders.

> But where in the world can we go? How can we preserve life in this area? Unless we just want to kid ourselves, we've been doing that for over four hundred years and I think we have to stop that.
> We think that we should concentrate on the idea of nationhood within those five states. We see counties in Mississippi that we can take over very easily by a very small movement of people using processes that are not revolutionary. We think Issaquena county, Boliva and Sunflower—all of these can be taken very easily. Issaquena county has fifteen hundred people and voted for a sheriff who is a woman. I can't imagine all those bad revolutionaries when all they have to do is join the black legion, make sure that there is security at the ballot box, walk in fifteen hundred and one people and vote. Vote and make sure the vote is counted. After that, install a black

sheriff who will then deputize thousands of black deputy sheriffs who would then be assigned to a region. Do that, duplicate it over and over again and that's not so far fetched. Green county, Alabama, right now got a group of people sitting down there who are regular, ordinary, used-to-be negroes, wearing shirt and tie, being elected to office—got the whole power of government in their hands. But they are not deluded; they understand that it goes deeper than that. They are going to embark on a program of taking over lands that is not used. Don't you know that in some parts of the country we talk about land. Eastland is getting paid for two-hundred fifty thousand acres of land that are not being planted. And I think that if we control the County Board of Commissioners in some towns it would be a simple matter to enact certain ordinances which will permit land and places, which are not used, to be taken and revert back to the county. And then of course you'll be able to enforce and make certain you have a sheriff, for these are traditional areas of legal authority. If you have a sheriff who is operative in the interest of black nationhood, then it would seem to me that once the county takes the land there ought not to be any problem about that.[7]

There should not, under ordinary circumstances, be any problem with forming a black "nation" by the above-described means. State politics in the American system of government has its roots in county-oriented political input. The difference here is that the RNA is a "radical" black proposal to control local (county) politics.

In summary, the RNA is a catalytic movement organization that proposes to effect change by proposing and working toward establishing black states, hence forcing constituted authority to respond to black needs, values, and goals. But the split in the movement has caused the radical wing of the organization to take premature steps in the direction of its goal.

More evidence suggesting that black separatism is an attempt to force social change in the system rather than a drive toward separation per se was derived by comparing separatist and integrationist views—assuming that integrationist programs approximate the general society's ideals and values. Five issues have been selected: (a) police brutality, (b) military service, (c) self-defense, (d) social and cultural outlooks, and (e) politics and justice. These views on particular issues are derived from the following sources: the Washington "Compromise" Speech; Principles of the Niagara Movement

(DuBois); Declaration of the Right of the Negro Peoples of the World (Garvey); What Do the Muslims Want and What Do the Muslims Believe; Basic Aims of the Organization of Afro-American Unity (Malcolm X's OAAU); Rules and Program of the Black Panther Party. CORE, SNCC, and RNA positions on the selected issues were drawn from various sources other than those indicated above. The comparison is included in the Appendix, below.

Several points can be made. Among the most important is the close similarity of separatists and nonseparatists on most issues ranging from Washington's Atlanta speech to the RNA's Black Nation in the South. Moreover, not only is there consistent similarity on most issues among the different organizations over time but, even more remarkable, there is similarity between *all* the organizations' positions and general American values and social philosophy. For example, black separatist as well as nonseparatist organizations all call for equal justice, better education, an end to police brutality, better housing, etc. Do not all Americans claim these as general American values? Because the separatists demand equality and freedom under the existing system, one could argue that their separatist posture is a tactic to force concessions from the general society. Disregarding their separatist rhetoric, they are only asking more forcefully for what most white Americans take for granted.

Blacks who call themselves separatists and demand the equality, liberty, and justice enjoyed by most Americans are denied these privileges with *inpunity*. Denying legitimacy to blacks who call themselves separatists is generally acceptable to most Americans because separatists in their minds are "extremists" or "militants" or "black revolutionaries." Any black who wants immediate freedom or a Black Nation or community control is depicted as radical, militant, or crazy. But separatists note that equality, justice, and liberty are also denied blacks who claim no allegiance to separatism as their ideology. They therefore conclude that whites are most reluctant to allow blacks to share in the society's social power mechanisms, but will, under pressure, grudgingly concede small bits to "sensible" blacks, namely, those who do not push for self-determination.

Black Separatism as a Critical Alternative

The above discussion was mainly concerned with comparisons between separatist-integrationist ideas and values on the one hand and those of the general American society on the other. How critical that black separatism is as an alternative must be further explored. Those who view separatism as a critical alternative begin with the assumption that black people *as a group* are oppressed without much opportunity to better their situation. Black Americans are victims of internal colonialism, locked into the system without hope of self-determination. Lewis Killian, they argue, has correctly and succinctly summed up white attitudes on black liberation: The most dangerous threat that black America can pose to white America is the desire and demand for self-determination. It then follows that radical proposals for change are necessary for black freedom. But even far-reaching change, such as much of the civil rights package, is sometimes tolerated because it does not pose a threat to the system. Many whites will tolerate and even promote black activities that cause unrest as long as the efforts are directed at reforming the existing system; but when these activities purposely or unintentionally threaten to radically alter the existing system, white participation and promotion turns to opposition.

Separatists argue that examples of white defections from the "black cause" when blacks call for self-determination or systemic change are legion. When SNCC and CORE began to call for black decision-making in predominantly black organizations, most whites could not come to grips with being led by blacks. Most of them left. When blacks then called for self-determination, those who had remained under black leadership—the so-called committed—also left. When blacks began to talk about the reality of internal colonialism and the need not only to change power relations, by changing the system, but also to separate from it, former white support turned to opposition. Many whites argue that blacks forced them to leave the black struggle to blacks alone. This is simply not true. It *is* true that some black people and a few black organizations—the RNA, the Muslims, the Black Panther Party, and later CORE and SNCC—did prefer an all-black membership. But at the same time they asked whites to form organizations in their own communities to aid the black cause. Carmichael, among others, pointed out that since almost all the power to change lay with the white community, whites were in the wrong (black) organizations to promote change. For a short time a few white organizations, particularly the White Panthers and Weathermen, and the New Left in general, did speak to some of the same inequalities that blacks have perennially fought against. But a combination of white apathy or satisfaction and massive governmental campaigns to negate activisim has stilled white efforts at eliminating systemic inequality against blacks. Separatists believe that there is in fact a disturbingly hostile atmosphere of "benign neglect" pervading the white community. Moreover, governmental reactive coercion has greatly minimized black efforts at promoting social movements to ameliorate their oppressed condition.

For whites and some blacks, the civil rights movement did accomplish many of its goals. (1) It succeeded in eliminating most of the legal statutes on which discrimination was based. (2) It revolutionized Southern white politics. The Voting Rights Bill paved the way for black political participation; the number of black elected officials in the South today as compared to the mid-1960's has dramatically increased. (3) Blacks are now employed in places and positions not dreamed of in the early 1960's. (4) Black students are now enrolled in, and many of have graduated from, schools of higher learning which systematically barred them before. The University of Alabama was the first among many. These successes, brought on by the separatist and civil rights movements, have convinced whites and many blacks that the system does work and the American Dream is still alive. Therefore, so the reasoning goes, there is no need for further agitation, especially separatist agitation.

But despite the partial successes of the civil rights movement, white satisfaction that the system works, and the many blacks benefiting from pacification programs and tokenism, there are black people who are not convinced (with abundant evidence to support their position) that things have changed much for the vast majority of black Americans. Many of the unconvinced are ordinary black people who routinely go about their daily lives. Many who question black "progress," in fact, are those who have ostensibly benefited from it. Many black separatists have never believed that black "progress" was anything but a sham and point to tokenism in employment, the white flight to the suburbs, dilly-dallying with equal educational opportunity for blacks, and the "inferior genes" nonsense as evidence to support their position.

Black separatists are concerned with more than bread and butter issues. They are concerned with the total range of black degradation by white America. They believe that the slow effort to persuade whites to look on blacks as fellow citizens and fellow human beings is futile. The separatists claim that only black separation will permit black people the freedom to exemplify their life styles and culture, hence their values, without having to conform to white values, white definitions, and white stereotypes, solely because whites have the (veto) power to define and direct behavior in the existing system dominated by them.

Are separatists serious, then, about the practicality of black self-determination? When asked that question, they respond: Should people be satisfied when they live in a system where their values and life styles and their "peoplehood" are denied and where their minds, bodies, and souls have been spitefully used? Are not freedom, equality, and self-determination basic ends sought by all human beings? Do not most groups wish to form a more perfect union among themselves to promote their own interests? If these things are true, the separatists are serious, and they cite several more reasons why they should be.

Culture

All separatist ideology has emphasized the importance of cultural independence. The emphasis stems from the subordination of black cultural symbolism in the general American cultural arena. Whites tend to deny the existence of a black American culture, claiming it was lost in the process of becoming American. But the separatists argue that blacks should either reject Western culture for their own African heritage or develop their own cultural symbols: The Nation rejects "slaves' names" and Christianity; CORE upholds Garveyism and Africa as its cultural model; RNA rejects European names in favor of African ones and has renamed its potential nation "Kush"; and the Panthers and SNCC indicate an aversion to vapid, jejune middle class values emphasizing selfishness which contributes to the exploitation of one's fellow man.

Separatists point to the components of culture—language, age, sex differences, technology, art, recreation, knowledge and belief, social control, social institutions, observing that each cultural element can be differentiated on a black-white basis. Black culture should therefore not be legitimized by whites. In short, black separatists find it an affront to black dignity even to argue the validity of black culture. They feel their time is better spent promoting self-determination that will permit black people to get on with the business of living their culture rather than arguing with whites about its existence.

Threats to Black Survival

Not only do most whites deny the existence of a viable and authentic black culture, according to separatist philosophy, but there is evidence to suggest that many find the black presence itself threatening. Unlike Native Americans, whose numbers have dwindled from around ten million from the time of the initial white invasion and subsequent subjugation to the present level of less than a million, the black population has steadily increased. But many black people—and not all of them separatists—fear that because whites attempted (with much success) genocide against Native Americans, they are not reluctant to do the same against blacks.

The threat to black survival takes on many guises—economic exclusion, medical experimentation and neglect, and even more blatant forms of limiting the potential of black procreation. Many blacks, including most separatists, go beyond economic exclusion and biological experimentation as examples of dire threats to black survival, suggesting that the danger involves the ultimate threat to group survival: genocide. Those concerned that black genocide by whites might develop into a national policy use two basic arguments: (1) population policies aimed at birth control in the black community are in essence attempts to limit the black political and economic potential, and (2) many governmental policies are in fact aimed at eliminating dignified black survival.

In the first instance, many blacks—especially black males—believe that whites are pushing contraceptives in the black community in order to exterminate black people through family planning and population control. Many black females take a different view, but they, too, are concerned about the possibility of black genocide. Those who would dismiss black concern by labeling the possibility of genocide absurd, hollow, and mostly the rhetoric of black militants aimed at stirring up the ghetto natives, must contend with the fact that the concern is not limited to the black ghetto but pervades the entire black community. According to Dr. Charles V. Willie, "if blacks believe that family planning programs are insidiously designed by whites to exterminate blacks, then blacks will not cooperate with any national population policy which focuses only upon family planning." Willie gives other reasons why blacks are suspicious: (1) "When blacks were nearly one fifth of the total population (18.4 percent) nearly a century and a half ago (1820), whites were concerned neither with the size of the black family nor its structure." The recent concern over the black family—according to Daniel P. Moynihan, because it is not congruent with the rest of the American society—emanates, one suspects, from the fact that a little over a century ago, black people were slaves and posed no threat to white domination.

"Indeed," Willie continues, "during slavery, there were attempts to breed healthy male black slaves with healthy female black slaves, disregarding any family connections and even prohibiting marriage. Neither the size of the black population nor circumstances of family life worried white Americans before black people were free."[8]

(2) The 1960's and 1970's have found black people seeking self-determination through the ballot and other means—by marches and demonstrations, through black caucuses and independent political activity, and, in general, proclaiming freedom now. This black surge for self-determination prompted white Americans to become concerned about the size and the stability of the black family. "Daniel Patrick Moynihan—no doubt inadvertently—tipped off blacks about what was in the minds of whites when he described the situation as 'acute' because of the 'extraordinary rise in Negro population.'" Hence the national call for concern over the black family. The call seems to stem from the rise in the black population from 9.9 percent of the total population around 1920 to 11.4 percent in 1972—no cause for alarm and certainly not an acute increase. But "a population increase of one to two percentage points of the total creates an acute situation and is cause for alarm if the ultimate national goal is to eliminate black people; for such an increase, although small, indicates that they will not go away."

In order to sell such a drastic measure as population control, it must be justified by raising a specter that would become corporeal if the proposed measure (birth control) were not adhered to. Thus the black family, according to Moynihan speaking for the alarmed white community, had become "pathological" and "out of line with other American families" and needed immediate attention because most black families were headed by females rather than males because of divorce and desertion.[9] Dr. Willie continues:

> Back in 1910, 27 percent of black females were members of broken families because their husbands were dead. During that same year, only 6 percent of the black families were broken because of divorce or desertion of the male spouse. Thus, death was four times more frequently a contributor to family disruption than other social causes. I should add that death of the husband was the chief cause for marital breakup for black families compared with desertion or divorce through 1963. Thus, divorce and desertion which were highlighted by Dr. Moynihan as reasons why a national program to stabilize

the black family was needed are newcomers as chief causes of family breakup for black people. It would seem that whites are concerned about the size and stability of the black family now only because the number of black men who are dying prematurely is decreasing and the number of black children born who survive is increasing. If you can understand the basis of the alarm among white liberals about this situation, then you can understand the basis for the charge of genocide which is made by black militants.[10]

Black separatists understand it and take the position that if a national policy focuses only on reproduction, family size, or family planning without considering other socioeconomic factors, black people must not cooperate. To do so would contribute to their own extermination. The separatists (or any keen observer of social class) know that the problem is not excessive black reproduction, for in Western urbanized societies, and particularly the black middle class, *there is an inverse relationship between fertility and socioeconomic status factors:* people of higher income, occupation, and education tend to have fewer children, while the poor have more. The real problem—what a national population policy should focus on—is improving social, physical, and economic conditions for black people. Put another way, the separatists could no longer base their argument against cooperating with "zero population growth" if racist discrimination were eliminated; they could no longer validly argue that whites "blame the victims" by accusing blacks themselves for their plight rather than white racism. But the separatists know that whites are not going to admit that they are responsible for slavery, exploitation, imperialism, or any other residual effect of white racism experienced in black communities. Therefore, when blacks insist that health and wealth must accompany family planning as a national policy, the separatists know they will be in business for a long time to come.[11]

The final important argument used by black separatists is that many governmental policies negate dignified black survival, or any survival at all. Some have believed that the McCarran Act of 1950, which provided for detention camps in a national emergency, was activated during the latter part of the 1960's to detain black revolutionaries. Moreover, others have suggested that these camps, to be located at various places throughout the country, could be used to imprison virtually the whole black population in the event that ghetto revolts took on a national trend. Indeed, still others maintain that the Pentagon has a contingency plan to use the interstate highway system to military advantage in order to take care of any ghetto revolt. Those who dismiss the accusations as idle talk and nonsense, should remember that not long ago Japanese Americans on the West Coast were, in fact, put into detention camps.

Separatists believe that racism is so pervasive that it affects most white Americans, and that white-dominated governments at all levels, especially the federal level, reflect racist policies. They argue, for example, that the Nixon Administration of the recent past which won on the strength of a "law and order" campaign was given free rein to shore up the system. It is only now that we are beginning to discover the numerous violations of the Bill of Rights: illegal wire-tapping, surveillance, bugging, price-fixing, bribery, and obstruction of justice. These were, even for whites, dire threats to democratic government. Blacks can imagine what was in store for them. The Voting Rights Bill was attacked; there was a push for federal support for private (racist) schools; overt racists were nominated for Supreme Court Justices; consideration was given a proposal to remove five- and six-year-old black children from their homes to correctional camps on the basis of tests of their potential for later criminality. One could argue that Nixon and his administration were aberrant, elected in crisis times to cool the nation. That may be true, but aberrant situations with repetition become normality. Separatists argue that the near extermination of Native Americans and the racist detention of around 100,000 Japanese Americans (and not groups of Americans of German ancestry, or even many German Americans who openly supported Hitler) during World War II fall into a "normal" pattern. Their argument is further bolstered by the fact that in 1974 the United States Senate again refused to ratify a United Nations agreement—ratified by 75 other nations including the Soviet Union—outlawing genocide. It failed by a vote of 55 to 36. The failure raises the old question, "Can it happen here?" Separatists answer, "Why not?"

We have argued that black separatism serves as a catalytic agent in the social-change process: it may on the one hand, influence change in the black interest through the system, or, on the other, attempt to establish a separate sociopolitcal alternative outside the established social arrangement. But even separatist extra-systemic activity serves to influence social change in the established social system. Therefore, separatism is simultaneously a catalyst for social change and a critical alternative to it. It could serve to influence for some the realization of a pluralistic society, and for others who desire no contact with whites at least a utopian alternative to their present situation. Finally, separatism is a dynamic and shifting phenomenon, true to its catalytic characteristics. That it is not a viable alternative for most black Americans is one thing, but its long tenure on the American scene is enough to remind us all that its reality is more than a dream for many. It is a critical alternative for blacks who find the American Dream a nightmare.

12 CONCLUSIONS

Though at times black separatism in the United States has caused uneasy concern in the larger community and raised black consciousness, it has never enjoyed mass appeal. In the past as well as today, many blacks who initially embraced and promoted it later abandoned and rejected separatism as unworkable in white-dominated America. Yet the separatist phenomenon persists. At times it quietly slumbers somewhere in the dark recesses of the American character, but it is always ready to burst out, to expose the contradiction between white America's promise of freedom and dignity and the reality of its denial to the majority of black Americans.

The Washington-DuBois-Garvey controversy is relevant to the present black condition. The themes these outstanding men debated in their time—economic self-sufficiency, political emphasis and direction, African emigration, Pan-Africanism, educational strategies, Black Power—are still being debated today. That they are should give pause to those who suggest that a revolutionary change for the better has occurred.

Strategies and tactics for achieving black freedom in the United States were proposed and debated even before Washington, DuBois, and Garvey in the first quarter of the twentieth century. One could argue that the approaches of these three men were expedient refinements of earlier ones of Garnet, Delany, Crummell, Turner, and Blyden, among others. Their statement or restatement of the problem of how to achieve freedom as economic (Washington), educational (DuBois), and national (Garvey) was in each case an ideological prescription for coping with the political, social, economic, educational, and cultural variables related to dignified black survival in a white-dominated society.

Washington emphasized black economic self-sufficiency at any cost through practical, educational endeavors, arguing that socio-political freedom would naturally follow. DuBois initially warned Washington that his obsessive emphasis on economic self-sufficiency without concomitant political and social equality was folly. Garvey, extending Washington's program, advocated a larger and more aggressive economic and political program for blacks on a pan-black scale. DuBois' criticisms of both Washington and Garvey emanated from a well-trained and concerned intellect that led him to believe that black progress would be fostered by the race's "Talented Tenth." His intellectual vantage point may have caused him to misread initially the ideological basis of Washington's and Garvey's appeals, but his ideological disagreement did not cause him to miss the central point, as evidenced by his prophetic statement that the "problem of the twentieth century is the problem of the color line—the relation of the darker to the lighter races of men in Asia and Africa, in America and the islands of the sea." [1] The ideas of these men remain cogent forces for understanding race relations in the United States and on the international scene. [2]

To begin with, DuBois' and Garvey's programs and their socio-political positions were variations on Washington's ideas. In fact, DuBois later admitted that, essentially, he agreed with most of Washington's ideas on most issues. He changed his mind in 1933 about the NAACP's role in the black freedom struggle because its program did not envisage "any direct action of Negroes themselves for the uplift of their socially depressed masses." In 1940, in *Dusk of Dawn,* he concluded that black people must concentrate on economic self-sufficiency, looking to fit themselves "into the new economic organization which the world faces." In the same work he questioned the efficacy of integrated education, arguing that black education for cultural and economic reasons should be different from that of white. Still later, he embraced Washington's ideas of Pan-Africanism and emigrated to Africa, where he died in Ghana in 1963. In short, one of Washington's most persistent critics during his lifetime lived to see events and circumstances leading him to agree with Washington's positions.

Garvey felt that Washington had the best program for the black masses and came to the United States at Washington's behest. Adding decidedly more militancy and some other specifically West Indian ingredients, Garvey, stirring Washington's potion, produced one of the largest black social movements in history.

Garvey undoubtedly was able to accomplish the feat because of the huge black migration from rural to urban America and because of Washington's ideas on economic self-sufficiency.

Washington taught that economic self-determination would eventually afford blacks a choice of interacting with whites on the basis of equality, if they chose to do so at all. Consequently, he attempted to change the existing power relations between black and white urban dwellers by indirectly utilizing black political exclusion to gain economic advantages. That is, he urged blacks not to agitate for political and social equality, but rather, to strive for the kind of vocational education which would in the long run enable them to operate their own businesses. He stressed that in the final analysis economic independence could be achieved only by pursing educational and vocational pursuits in relation to their functional value in the urban marketplace. Washington knew that all blacks who moved from the rural to urban areas would not find jobs.

In addition to labor exclusion, blacks found themselves imprisoned in slum ghettoes. The significance of the ghetto is that it houses the poverty-stricken. For blacks, it was then and remains the physical manifestation of antipathy on the part of urban whites. Blacks who attempted to move into white areas were often met by violence. Urban white racism was a rude awakening for blacks who thought that the city would be a promised land. Their pleasant dreams turned into nightmares; they found that in addition to various manifestations of racism, they were often bewildered by the impersonality and complexity of urban structures. The intricate governmental maze, operated by people the same color as those who oppressed them on plantations and farms, also contributed to their frustations. These rural-oriented, unskilled, and unsophisticated blacks, though they probably never heard the terms, were made aware of *Gemeinschaft* and *Gesellschaft*. The utopian future they envisioned by moving to the city quickly became ideological as a result of white racism. During World War I most were successful in gaining industrial employment, but the end of the war brought economic retrenchment. Blacks lost their jobs to demobilized white soldiers. Organized labor was not much help, and if blacks found work at all, it was often as scabs.

Washington therefore urged blacks to engage in economic activities which would ultimately have the most significant social and political impact. He realized at that time—the late nineteenth and early twentieth centuries—that *political power alone does not significantly affect power relations without the attendant techni-*

cal and economic base. He apparently knew the pitfalls of proposing complete separatism in metropolitan areas, because he emphasized urban programs based not on separatist economics but on proficiency in particular sectors of the urban economy. Washington had a good grasp of what makes the city tick and how best to synchronize the black condition with this urban clock.

Washington's comprehension of the city and what must be done to enhance life in it is relevant to the present. Though during his lifetime roughly 90 percent of the black population resided in the South, he recognized that the black trickle from the rural South could result in a flood of migration to the North. It did.

Separatism and Urbanism, a Contradiction?

Urbanism itself has come to imply a highly complex division of labor, where specialization reaches its most advanced form. Vital to the relationship is the element of interdependence: each part of the urban specialty is necessary to the normal functioning of the metropolitan whole. Politicization of the whole provides incentive for the parts to work for the benefit of the whole. Any segment of the city that does not become an integral and interdependent part of the whole because of its technical, commercial/industrial value eventually suffers by exclusion. Not being a part of the system is not always a neutral state of affairs: systematic contrivance to exclude based on competition is the normal means of determining who or what can be successfully shut out. Total or partial exclusion from participation in the interdependent, politicized urban complex also means that the system operates as a zero-sum game—one sector's loss is another's gain, and vice versa. Exclusion may result in community deterioration (no garbage pick-up, no street cleaning and maintenance, no park upkeep or enforcing of building codes, no street lights, etc.), sociopathic manifestations (alienation, high crime rates, delinquency), and economic dislocations (high unemployment, lack of patronage jobs, unfair tax burdens, menial jobs, and ultimate dependence on social welfare).

Just as the city as a whole is a complex, interdependent entity, so is its economic network. The politicization of its economic network reaches its formal heights in metropolitan government. The informal aspects of economic networks are just as important as the formal ones in that they are often the flip side of the same coin. What happens when the regulated regulates the regulator? Without delving into the question of interurban ecological networks, one may conclude that intraurban economic and political networks are ecologically linked.

This state of affairs should give pause to those who criticize Washington's prescription for black freedom in cities. He realized, first, that urban living dictates that all parts must work together, and, secondly, that working together involves technical and commercial competition, with politics a significant regulating factor. Here his brand of urban separatism takes on a complex character. Groups, like individuals, must possess collective skills and talents vital to the operation of parts valued by the system in order for their withdrawal to have negative consequences for the system as a whole. The group is then in a position to bargain for systemic political and economic changes that maximize their position in the system. It has the opportunity to enhance its indispensability to the system: the more one gets, the more opportunity there is to get more.

Assuming that a group decides to withdraw voluntarily as a functional part of the urban complex, it should follow that the group does not require a symbiotic relationship with the urban system. But withdrawal from the system without the basic requisites for self-sufficiency inevitably has negative consequences, especially when the group declaring independence or separation has no strong base from which to declare its independence. Washington recognized the inherent contradiction of black separatism and the urban system: separatism means withdrawal from the system, yet urbanism creates interdependence of the parts, making the whole operate in the best interest of the parts. This is not to say that pluralism in its social implications cannot operate like separatism. The difference is that pluralist political and economic variables in the symbiotic urban marketplace cannot assume the separatist posture that the social variable can. In fact, the functional importance of political and economic variables may be directly related to the degree of separation that pluralism may assume: the more important or powerful, the greater the possibility of forcing compliance with the desire to be left alone in things social; those less powerful in the hierarchy of power relationships are more vulnerable to outside manipulation.

Washington's prescription for enhancing black participation in the urban power network may be described as economic nationalism, in that he counseled blacks to establish their own businesses and otherwise gain training and experience in vocations that afforded them the opportunity of specialized occupations. In this way they could eventually become important economic cogs in the urban machinery, which would ultimately translate into political and social influence and power. Put another way, a group's economic independence is positively related to the degree in which the total system relies on the group. Washington believed that blacks could gain some control over their lives in urban America by focusing on occupations and skills with the greatest functional economic payoff. He argued that politics was the result of economic phenomena and urged blacks to softpedal purely political activities; political and social power naturally follow economic power. Considering the present state of affairs in this country, and some aspects of the international scene, we argue that Washington's analysis and prescription for urban blacks is still relevant. He felt that the Jewish people in America offered blacks a good example of how to cope with the urban social system.[3] His "Jewish analogy" applied today is instructive to separatists and integrationists alike.

Washington's urban program of "economic separatism" for black America produced payoffs for Garvey, wisdom for DuBois, and success for other non-nationalist black groups—that is the black middle class. I believe that it also contains a message for contemporary black social movements in general and separatist movements in particular, especially since all are urban situated *and* urban oriented: the Nation of Islam was founded in Detroit; CORE was founded in Chicago; the RNA was founded in Detroit; SNCC was founded in Raleigh; and the Black Panther Party was founded in Oakland.

Today, around three quarters of the American population and about the same percentage of blacks live in urban areas: whites live mostly in suburbs and blacks in central cities. The United States is an urban nation. As long as the white population continues to move away from the central city and inhibit the ability of blacks to move out, blacks will continue to be central city people—North and South. Apparently separatists agree with this analysis, for they all, directly or indirectly, fashion their ideas of black freedom around the black urban reality. Imari Obadele (Richard Henry), for example, speaking indirectly of the black urban presence, calls for blacks to leave the cities and move to the Republic of New Africa's Kush district, for he is convinced that blacks can never control their destinies in the cities where they now live. He asks blacks to "give up national claim to the land of the black ghettoes of the North, to which we have nearly as good a claim as to the land in the black belt, in exchange for the full five states."[4] In contrast to the RNA position, CORE calls for black control of black communities, ostensibly because it believes that blacks will continue living en masse in the central cities of most large metropolitan areas. The Nation of Islam has its eighty or so mosques and business enterprises located in the major cities; the Panthers in their heyday also operated from large cities, and prior to its demise SNCC moved its operation to Chicago.

Not only do the separatists pay special attention to the city in its ideological formulation, but many Americans, both black and white, believe that many major cities—at least their central cities —will eventually be politically controlled by blacks.

Accompanying this belief is the notion that the solution to many black problems lies in the political control of cities. The idea may have stemmed from the need to discern a glimmer of hope from somewhere, and black political control of cities where blacks are in the majority was as good as any. But it was nevertheless naive. With the emergence of the idea of metropolitan government (which would nullify black political control of even the central city) and the general failure of black mayors to better the black condition dramatically, more hard-headed thinking is necessary. The first question to be raised is the worth of political control without an accompanying economic base.

Booker T. Washington seems to have understood that agitation for social and political equality without an economic base was putting the cart before the horse. The argument that politics must be controlled *before* economics must consider that the tendency of business today to move to the suburbs is economically motivated and the political ramifications are residual. Black *and* white mayors of large cities with poor central city dwellers must answer the question: What is there left in the central city to control if the economic base is in the suburbs?

Another example can be seen in the Pan-African context. At one time colonial (European) powers controlled Africa politically and economically, but the rise of African nationalism and other forces influenced the powers to leave their territories. Even Portugal, that poor cousin in Europe, decided to leave its rich African possessions. The departures have not significantly altered the objective physical plight of the majority of ex-colonial subjects, because the economic forces are still controlled from without, through neo-imperialism. But if indigenous peoples had political and economic control (which Africans eventually will), they would indeed achieve freedom, even though people can be free and at the same time poor and hungry!

Ideally it would be preferable for black Americans to achieve political and economic gains simultaneously. Just as Washington thought that the political arena must be sacrificed for the economic in order to gain a footing, it is evident today that political and economic control of black destinies must be augmented by other elements necessary for viability in America. Unlike the situation of the Washington era, blacks today can nominally participate in the political system and some economic areas. But the participation thus far has fallen short of initial expectations. It seems that, at this stage, to augment political and economic participation an all-out effort is necessary to orient the skill levels of blacks to the economic realities of urban, technological America. This effort could come through the realization that America is a commercially oriented nation. No group has been successful in America until its members have contributed to the American economy, labor (skilled or semiskilled), technological expertise (organization, bureaucracy), commercial enterprise, or education, while at the same time achieving political means to solidify their economic gains.

Helping blacks to make it in America is an enormous undertaking, because of the complex nature of racism in all its political and economic ramifications. Black separatism should be regarded as one way of coping with this complexity, white flight from the central cities as another. The problems of the cities are not now and not likely to be in the future amenable to purely political solutions through electoral politics. Most everyone agrees that the "new" coalition of rural and suburban political forces controlling state legislatures and the United States Congress will not advocate solutions to central city (black) problems.

Because of the diffusion of real power to the suburban areas, central cities can have all the political representation they can stand, but until there are adequate economic incentives to bolster central city economics, either indigenously or by attracting outside interests, the central city is likely to continue suffering from underdevelopment. Like any dependent colony, the city ghetto will be open to imperialistic predators until it can declare its independence. Even then, as in Africa, it will continue to be dependent upon the suburbs for subsistence because of the location of jobs and the source of real political power. Colonies are abandoned only by force or when they are no longer economically profitable. Both reasons are operative in black-dominated central cities.

From this state of affairs one may conclude that whites are not going to make the necessary economic commitment to deal with central city problems. To them the urban crisis is synonymous with black problems, and they are not going to spend billions of dollars to *begin* dealing with the restoration of urban centers inhabited by poor people (despite the fact that the urban poor are three to one white).

If the present trend continues—and nothing on the horizon suggests it will not—one can conclude that blacks will remain in the central cities, bottled up, with few jobs, low skills, and no economic or social opportunity to better their lot. The colonial nature of the black condition may manifest itself in more separatist movements, destructive hostility, despair, apathy, and internal (perhaps also external) violence. The frustrations created by containment in the ghettoes will squeeze out or burst out. The safest prediction is that those who contributed most to the creation of urban containment will react with righteous indignation to the victims' efforts to extricate themselves. And the separatists, like Brother Imari, who warned against staying in the cities in the first place, can then say, "I told you so!"

Washington's program emphasizing economic priorities are, therefore, still the best prescriptions for bettering of the black condition. By paying particular attention to the political economy of urbanism, groups and individuals can best deal with the reality of their circumstances. In the United States, and perhaps Africa, Kwame Nkrumah's dictum "Seek ye first the political kingdom and the rest will be added" does not hold much water. I must quickly add that often the causal relationship between politics and economics at times places politics first and at others economics. But if I must choose one over the other, economics wins.

Internal Forces

Authoritarianism. One of the prime reasons why separatist organizations have such a high rate of transient members is that the movement requires almost total commitment at the expense of almost everything else in the member's life. Living in such a dynamic society as the United States militates against a high level of commitment, especially when often all the movement can offer is a pie in the sky but no meat to eat now. Loyalty and commitment are much easier to give to a movement that offers immediate, material returns. Hence, reform movements have been more successful than separatist movements in gaining and maintaining black members.

Sex discrimination. Black movements have generally relegated black women to menial positions with males maintaining the important ones for themselves. Not especially enamored over such an arrangement, separatist movements almost automatically exclude by their lack of appeal over one half of their possible members. (At present, however, both the Black Panther organization and the Republic of New Africa have women in leading positions. But it is still true that there is no significant black female membership.)[5]

Criticism of the black bourgeoisie. All separatist movements tend to criticize the black middle class for imitating middle-class white America—for espousing a caricature of middle-class white values, for being what Nathan Hare calls "black Anglo-Saxons" (see, for example, the writings of E. Franklin Frazier). Ironically, and particularly in the light of separatist movements collectively and individually contributing to the resurgence of black consciousness and identity, they should reassess their criticism of the black middle class. They might be surprised at its present outlook and its health.

It may be that a middle-class existence is not as painful to black Americans as many separatists assert. The black bourgeoisie may have inadvertently gained enough race pride and dignity through the Black Power rebellion to live in a normal ethnic fashion without having to ape white society. Frazier should be re-evaluated. It is commonplace to find African art in a black middle-class home and middle-class blacks wearing dashikis and Afros. Many have read the standard "black books" and talk of the "brothers" and "sisters" going to Africa instead of Europe for vacations. The resurgence of black pride and consciousness has benefited the black bourgeoisie and heightened the awareness of the black masses, but the masses have not gained in economic and educational terms in proportion to these middle-class blacks. It is significant that currently there is an increase both *in the number of blacks entering colleges and universities and in the dropout rate of black high school students.* On the surface it would seem that the masses will remain constant in numbers while the black middle class grows larger. The impact of this development on the nature of race relations and on separatism will be of maximum importance in the future. We hazard the following prediction.

Black separatist social movements in the future, envisioning a totally separate black, anti-white nation, will continue to be comprised mostly of poor urban blacks. The leadership, however, will be middle class and the vacillating utopia-seeker type. This, too, has always been the case in Western society in general and black movements in particular. The movement leaders discussed in this book attest to the validity of the generalization.

Pan-Africanism. Pan-Africanism, if it takes the form of emigrationism, will not be economically, politically, or socially feasible: black people cannot return en masse to Africa. Previous attempts in this direction have proved abortive. The example of the Americo-Liberian subjugation of the indigenous people is not lost on African leaders; undertaking enclave-like settlements in any of the African nations would be viewed with suspicion. Thus the individual black American may emigrate—provided he has skills to offer his host native land—but the black mass is culturally and psychologically unprepared to physically return, even if it had the choice—which it does not.

The physical return to Africa is, however, only one facet of Pan-Africanism. The African diaspora is a reality in the same sense as the Jewish diaspora or the European diaspora. Black people are originally from Africa, Jewish people are originally from Israel or Palestine (the Middle East in general), and white people are originally from Europe. Black identification with Africa is no different from "white" identification with Europe and Jewish identification with Israel. In a sense, Europe and Israel serve as role models for white ethnics and Jewish people respectively. The reverse is also true—Europe and Israel view their peoples with pride (especially in the economic realm).

Identification with, and being proud of, the mother land should not, however, become a preoccupation at the expense of gaining power and respect where one presently resides. The black African nations have often expressed sentiment and kinship ties to black Americans, but, at the same time, they suggest that mass emigration to their particular countries would be a cultural and economic disaster. An African diplomat from Ghana, Ebenezer M. Debrah, reflects the thinking of most African leaders. He observes: "If a group of 500 American blacks suddenly came to Ghana, we couldn't absorb them. Africa has problems of housing, employment, and education and, in fact, no African leader encourages a huge back-to-Africa migration." Rather than this, Debrah advocates what he calls "constructive brotherhood."

Pan-Africanism as a constructive force (or brotherhood) among black Americans and Africans is most practical in ways other than a return to Africa. Ambassador Debrah suggests that the "fact that a tenth of the population of one of the world's most powerful nations is black is an asset to Africans and Africans better believe it."[7] (That some blacks are in a position to help shape United States policy in Africa is an asset: Edward Brooke is a Senate expert on Africa, and Representative Charles C. Diggs, Jr., is Chairman of the House African Subcommittee. Robert N. C. Nix is Chairman of the House Foreign Economic Policy Subcommittee.) Blacks in America can help Africans and vice versa in two ways: (1) Blacks in governmental positions could aid black Africa by helping to shape United States policy toward South Africa and Rhodesia. (2) Africans could demand that United States multinational corporations and other United States commercial concerns in Africa have significant black representation in policy-making positions as well as in middle- and lower-level management.

Beyond black representation in white-owned or controlled enterprises, there are, in fact, many skilled black Americans who could aid in African development. Medicine, engineering, business organization and investment are skills sorely needed in Africa.

Black studies. Black studies are desperately needed to help destroy white stereotypes about black people as well as to enhance black social, economic, and political viability. Some rightly argue that many black studies programs as they currently exist do not enhance needed skills both in black America and in Africa. That is, courses which focus solely on the historical and psychological consequences of racism and oppression may help blacks unravel white myths about happy slaves and good masters, but they will not aid in eliminating the good master's great-grandchildren's present oppressive control of international technological and organizational networks. Courses in complex organization, medicine, physics, chemistry, electronics, and mechanical engineering will do much more to eliminate oppression and promote Pan-Africanism. Historical, sociological, spiritual, and psychological myths about black people must be corrected in order to develop positive and true images. But when these investigations and new images become ends in themselves, the danger of neglecting necessary development skills in technical areas increases. Black studies programs or departments must be concerned with the development of both sociocultural and technical skills. Fortunately, black students themselves are beginning to raise questions about black studies courses. S. Jay Walker, Chairman of the Black Studies Program at Dartmouth College, best sums up the emerging black student mood. He writes:

The dashiki-clad shucking and jiving, the revolutionary rhetoric, the signs and symbols: all these are *déja vu* to today's black student. He is no more integration-bound than his brother of the class of 1970, but he has come to realize that he *is* being short-changed; that no matter what society he is going to build for himself, no matter where he is going to build it, he is not going to be equipped by a summa cum laude degree in [such courses as] Preparation of Soul Food. He is unwilling to settle any longer for rhetoric alone; he wants intellectual substance and standards that will allow him to go beyond [white] denunciation into meaningful action.[8]

Black students, some of whom are today's and tomorrow's separatists, must continue to become sophisticated about the phenomenon of separatism and Pan-Africanism. Just as Booker T. Washington, W. E. B. DuBois, and Marcus Garvey, among others who grappled with the question of Pan-Africanism, had to cope with difficulties surrounding its meaning and application under specialized conditions, the question today is no less easy. But despite continuing international, political, and economic domination by white power, African independence and how these new nations relate to the superpowers must be added to the aforementioned list of variables black students must concern themselves with when thinking about Pan-Africanism and cross-national relationships in the black diaspora. They may take their lead from examples set down by black organizations with separatist dimensions.

CORE, for an example, is acutely aware of the past shortcomings of Pan-Africanism and encourages skilled blacks to go to Africa. This is in keeping with the suggestion by African leaders that Afro-Americans and Africans should build their relationships on the basis of substance rather than on an emotional level. That is, relationships built around dashiki and hair style are sure to become meaningless in the future; but commercial and psychological identifications will endure. There is evidence to suggest that the emotional stage is waning: (1) black American businessman are looking to Africa for investment, not in the sense that white Americans look for a share in South African and Rhodesian (Zimbabwean) business that exploits black African labor and natural resources, but investments that will be mutually helpful; (2) black American and African students are developing a more mature outlook on their differences and similarities. This bodes well for the future. It is certain that in time a more meaningful

Pan-African relationship between the black peoples of the African diaspora and black Africans on the African continent will develop.

External Forces

The contemporary black situation is complicated by elite-type, black, upward mobility alongside increasing mass black poverty: a large segment of young, college-educated blacks alongside a huge body of high school dropouts—the highly educated and highly skilled and the low-educated and nonskilled. The pressures brought on by a technological, complex, and cybernated society demand both individual proficiency and group political wisdom. Advances made in both these areas may not be enough to stave off black separatism as an alternative.

What is more important than black skills and proficiency, as it always has been, is the attitude of white Americans toward their black compatriots. With a small increase in equal opportunity in education, employment, housing, and government, the increased competition—resulting from equal opportunity programs—could prompt whites to escalate their resistance to the recent small gains made by blacks. It should be remembered that the Nazis' "final solution" was not aimed at a group of people who were largely unskilled and uneducated. On the contrary, the Nazis resented a highly educated and skilled integrated Jewish population. This should be kept in mind when arguing for black proficiency. Is there reason to believe that too much black competition at the high levels will produce reaction from those who have traditionally even looked down their noses at the low-skilled red-neck? As Wilhelm observes, "After much postponement due to economic dependence on black labor during the last 350 years, the Negro question finally transforms into the Indian question. What is the point, demands white America, in tolerating an unwanted social minority when there is no economic necessity for acceptance? With machines now replacing human labor, who needs the Negro?"[9]

Separatists are not waiting for the question to be posed. Rather, they believe that an ounce of action now is worth a pound of waiting. Black separation may, at this time, appear to many as an unrealized dream by disaffected black radicals who are misreading both black and white sentiments. But whites themselves are, as a matter of course, promoting black separatism by moving to their own suburban enclaves. This is "legitimate" white separation. Theodor Herzel, like the black separatists of today, was told he was whistling in the dark, that his brand of political Zionism was only a pipe dream. Today, millions of Jews (and non-Jews) are paying tribute to his dream. Whether future generations of black Americans will be paying tribute to a black nation dreamed of and forged by today's separatists is unanswerable, but until white America lives up to its stated ideals of justice and equality for black Americans, black separatists will continue the search.

APPENDIX:
VIEWS ON FIVE ISSUES

Police Brutality

Washington:
Though the phrase "police brutality" was not used in Washington's time, brutalizing blacks in sundry and fatal fashions nevertheless occurred. Washington objected to this brutality against black people in various ways. Though the lynching of black people under the "new" Jim Crowism of his time was rampant, Washington always openly condemned it and used his influence as well as his finances to combat legislation which encouraged white brutality against blacks.

DuBois in Principles of the Niagara Movement:
"We repudiate the monstrous doctrine that the oppressor should be the sole authority as to the rights of the oppressed. The Negro race in America stolen, ravished, and degraded, struggling up through difficulties and oppression . . . needs protection and is given mob-violence."

Garvey in Declaration of the Rights of the Negro Peoples of the World:
"In certain parts of the United States of America our race is . . . lynched and burned by mobs, and such brutal and inhuman treatment is even practiced upon our women." "Whereas, the lynching, by burning, hanging or any other means, of human beings is a barbarous practice, and, a shame and disgrace to civilization, we therefore declare any country guilty of such atrocities outside the pole of civilization."

The Nation of Islam:
"We want an immediate end to the police brutality and mob attacks against the so-called Negro throughout the United States."

CORE:
In 1965 CORE organized a march to protest police brutality (in Newark) and Mayor Hugh Addonizio conceded that there was a 'small group of misguided individuals' on the force. The Mayor, however, rejected a demand for a civilian review board. (Allen, *Black Awakening in Capitalist America,* p. 110.)

OAAU:
"We assert that in those areas where the government is either unable or

unwilling to protect the lives and property of our people, that our people are within their rights to protect themselves by whatever means necessary. A man with a rifle or club can only be stopped by a person who defends himself with a rifle or club.

"Tactics based solely on morality can only succeed when you are dealing with basically moral people or a moral system. A man or system which oppresses a man because of his color is not moral. It is the duty of every Afro-American and every Afro-American community to protect its people against mass murderers, bombers, lynchers, floggers, brutalizers, and exploiters."

SNCC:

"Black Power means, for example, that in Lowndes County, Alabama, a black sheriff can end police brutality."(Carmichael and Hamilton, *Black Power*, p. 46.)

Black Panther Party:

"We want an immediate end to police brutality and murder of black people." "We will protect ourselves from the force and violence of the racist police and the racist military by any means necessary." "We believe we can end police brutality in our black community by organizing black self-defense groups that are dedicated to defending our black community from racist police oppression and brutality."

RNA:

"It seems likely that die-hard whites . . . would create situations leading to a general and sustained fight. Our policy, of course, is to delay, if possible, avoid such a turn of events. But the simple, inevitable truth is that, if we are to be free through sovereignty, we will ultimately have to fight." (Obadele, "The Struggle Is for Land," *Black Scholar*, 3 February 1972, 32.)

Military Service

Washington:

The author believes Washington would have ardently supported military service for blacks.

DuBois in Principles of the Niagara Movement:

"We regret that this nation has never seen fit adequately to reward the black soldiers who . . . have defended their country with their blood, and yet have been systematically denied promotions which their abilities deserve. And we regard as unjust, the exclusion of black boys from the military and naval training schools."

Garvey in Declaration of the Rights of the Negro Peoples of the World:

"We declare that no Negro shall engage himself in battle for an alien race without first obtaining the consent of the leader of the Negro People of the World, except in the matter of national self-defense." "We protest against the practice of drafting Negroes and sending them to war with alien forces without proper training, and demand in all cases that Negro soldiers be given the same training as the aliens."

The Nation of Islam:

"We believe that we who declared ourselves to be righteous Muslims, should not participate in wars which take the lives of humans. We do not believe this nation should force us to take part in such wars, for we have nothing to gain from it unless America agrees to give us the necessary territory wherein we may have something to fight for."

CORE:

Prior to Innis' leadership, CORE was a pacifist organization.

OAAU:

Though Malcolm X was personally opposed to military service for blacks, the following excerpt from the OOAU statement does not reflect an opposing position: "The Afro-American veteran must be made aware of all the benefits due him and the procedure for obtaining them. These veterans must be encouraged to go into business together, using G.I. loans, etc."

SNCC:

"A mercenary is a hired killer and any black man serving in this man's army is a black mercenary, nothing else."

Black Panther Party:

"No party member can join any other army force other than the Black Liberation Army." "We believe that black people should not be forced to fight in the military service to defend a racist government that does not protect us. We will not fight and kill other people of color in the world who, like black people, are being victimized by the white racist government of America."

RNA:

"We have . . . tortuously laid the foundations of an army, and units trained in every city (more than two dozen) where the Republic is formally organized."

Self-Defense

Washington:

Ultimate independence through self-help is the best protection against racist aggression.

DuBois:

We refuse to allow the impression to remain that the Negro-American assents to inferiority, is submissive under oppression and apologetic before insults.

Garvey:

We believe that the Negro should adopt every means to protect himself against barbarous practices inflicted upon him because of color.

The Nation of Islam:

"We want our own men and women and our girls to learn to try to protect themselves the best way they can in case of attack." "He will defend us if we believe in Him and trust Him, and we're not going to start fighting with anyone to have Him to defend us. But if we are attacked, we depend on Him to defend us because He has stripped us [of weapons]." (Elijah Muhammad, *Message to the Black Man in America*, p. 319.)

CORE:

The National Director of CORE, Floyd B. McKissick, appearing on "Meet the Press" in August 1966, endorsed self-defense as a CORE tactic.

OAAU:

". . . we assert the Afro-American right of self-defense." "The Constitution of the U.S.A. clearly affirms the right of every American citizen to to bear arms. And as Americans, we will not give up a single right guaranteed under the Constitution. The history of the unpunished violence against our people clearly indicates that we must be prepared to defend ourselves or we will continue to be a defenseless people at the mercy of a ruthless and violent racist mob."

SNCC:

"From our viewpoint, rampaging white mobs and white night-riders must be made to understand that their days of free head-whipping are over. Black people should and must fight back. If a nation fails to protect its citizens, then that nation cannot condemn those who take up the task themselves." (Carmichael and Hamilton, *Black Power*, pp. 52–53.)

Black Panther Party:

". . . organizing black self-defense groups that are dedicated to defending our black community from racist police oppression and brutality."

RNA:

"Our biggest threat comes from white civilian armies, the Ku Klux Klan and those other semi-official forces who for one hundred years have done the dirty work of military oppression in the South. These forces we must be prepared to successfully engage and defeat at all times." (Imari A. Obadele, "The Struggle Is for Land," *Black Scholar*, 3 February 1972, p. 32.)

Social and Cultural Outlooks

Washington:

"We should have so much pride that we would spend more time in looking into the history of the race, more effort and money in perpetuating in some durable form its achievements, so that from year to year, instead of looking back with regret, we can point to our children the rough path through which we grew strong and great." (*Future of the American Negro*, p. 182.)

DuBois in Principles of the Niagara Movement:

"[the Negro] would not Africanize America, for America has too much to teach the world and Africa. He would not bleach his Negro soul in a flood of white Americanism, for he knows that Negro blood has a message for the world. He simply wishes to make it possible for a man to be both a Negro and an American, without being cursed and spit upon by his fellows, without having the doors of opportunity closed roughly in his face." (DuBois, *The Souls of Black Folk*.)

Garvey in Declaration of the Rights of the Negro Peoples of the World:

"We demand complete control of our social institutions without interference by an alien race or races." ". . . that the colors Red, Black, and Green, be the colors of the Negro race."

The Nation of Islam:

"Men everywhere are seeking unity among themselves. Every race of people wants unity with their own kind first." "The original man, Allah has declared, is none other than the black man. From him came all brown, yellow, red and white people." (Muhammad, *Message to the Black Man in America*.)

CORE:

"There is a compelling need to emphasize the socio-psychological aspect of Black Power. We can cry "Black Power" until doomsday [but] until black people accept values meaningful to themselves, there can be no completely effective organizing for the development of black power." (by Roy Innis in Cruse, *Rebellion or Revolution*, p. 199.)

OAAU:

"A race of people is like an individual man; until it uses its own talent, takes pride in its own history, expresses its own culture, affirms its own selfhood, it can never fulfill itself. Our history and culture were completely destroyed when we were forcibly brought to America in chains. And now it is important to know that our history did not begin with slavery's scars. We must recapture our heritage and our identity if we are ever to liberate ourselves from the bonds of white supremacy. We must launch a cultural revolution to unbrainwash an entire people. Our cultural revolution must be the means of bringing us closer to our African brothers and sisters. It must begin in the community and be based on community participation. Afro-American artists must realize that they depend on the Afro-American for inspiration. We must work toward the establishment of a cultural center in Harlem, which will include people of all ages, and will conduct workshops in all the arts, such as film, creative writing, painting, theatre, music, Afro-American history, etc. This cultural revolution will be the journey to our rediscovery of ourselves. History is a people's memory, and without a memory man is demoted to the lower animals. Armed with the knowledge of the past, we can with confidence charter a course for our future. Culture is an indispensable weapon in the freedom struggle. We must take hold of it and forge the future with the past."

SNCC:

"The need for psychological equality is the reason why SNCC . . . believes that blacks must organize in the black community. Only black people can convey the revolutionary idea that black people are able to do things themselves. Only they can help create in the community an aroused and continuing black consciousness that will provide the basis for political strength." (Carmichael, *Stokely Speaks*, p. 27.) "What is Black Consciousness? More than anything else, it is an attitude, a way of seeing the world [and it is] a perpetual search for racial meanings. Black Consciousness . . . forced us [in SNCC] to begin the construction of a new, black value system. A value system geared to the unique cultural and political experience of blacks in this country." (Sellers, *The River of No Return*, pp. 156-57.)

Black Panther Party:

Black power for black people, red power for red people, yellow power for yellow people, brown power for brown people, white power for white people, and all power to the people. Every ethnic groups has particular needs that they know and understand better than anybody else; each group is the best judge of how its institutions ought to affect the lives of its members. (Huey Newton, *Revolutionary Suicide*, p. 167.)

RNA:

". . . to underestimate the potential of a cultural revival, which is only a beginning of a people knowing who they are or all that they can be, would be to deny history. Therefore, the revival of black culture . . . should prove through protracted struggle, to be sufficient as a transitional bridge that would serve to minimize uncertainty, maintain the identity of African people in America and render us less conservative to the nation of land and power. (Yusufu Sonebeyatta [Joseph Brooks], "Ujamaa for Land and Power," *Black Scholar,* October, 1971, p. 20.) "The one redeeming thing about our history in North America has been, as we look back on it, that there have been those few men whose spirits have tingled with the very thought of self-determination and land; whose souls and minds and hearts were truly free—men whose thoughts broke through the barrier of all the intellectual nonsense forced on black men over the years. And, because of those few men, we know today that some fires in human hearts are truly unquenchable—and that the love of family, tribe, and nation will not be extinguished by hundreds of years of torture, mistreatment, rape, robbery, murder, and cruelty." (Private communications from an officer of the RNA.)

Politics and Justice

Washington:
In all things that are purely social we can be as separate as the fingers, yet one as the hand in all things essential to mutual progress. There is no defense or security for any of us except in the highest intelligence and development for all. If anywhere there are efforts tending to control the fullest growth of the Negro, let these efforts be turned into stimulating, encouraging, and making him the most useful and intelligent citizen. There is no escape through law of man or God from the inevitable:

> "The laws of changeless justice bind
> Oppressor with oppressed;
> And close as sin and suffering joined
> We march to fate abrest."

DuBois in Principles of the Niagara Movement:
"... protest ... against the curtailment of citizens political rights." Equal rights in the courts and under the law. We recognize the duty to vote and to obey the laws.

Garvey in Declaration of the Rights of the Negro Peoples of the World:
"Negroes ... should be given the right to elect their own representatives, to represent them in legislatures, courts of law, or such institutions as may exercise control over that particular community." "... the Negro is entitled to even-handed justice before all courts of law and equity in whatever country he may be found."

The Nation of Islam:
We want justice under the laws of the land.

CORE:
"Black people must control all facets of their communities politically, economically, and socially in order to insure that the black community is not subject to injustice and indignities meted out by white people."

OAAU:
"In order for the Afro-Americans to control their destiny they must be able to control and affect the decisions which control their destiny: economic, political and social." "... we'll start ... with a voter-registration drive to make every unregistered voter in the Afro-American com-

munity an independent voter." ". . . organize political clubs to run independent candidates for office."

SNCC:

"If political institutions do not meet the needs of the people, if the people finally believe that those institutions do not express their own values, then those institutions must be discarded." (Carmichael and Hamilton, *Black Power*, p. 176.) "When the Negro community is able to control local offices, and negotiate with other groups from a position of organized strength, the possibility of meaningful political alliances on specific issues will be increased. That is a rule of politics and there is no reason why it should not operate here." (*Stokely Speaks*, p. 42.)

Black Panther Party:

"All black people tried in court by a jury of their peer group or people from their black communities, as defined by the constitution of the United States." "When in the course of human events, it becomes necessary for one people to dissolve the political bonds which have connected them with another, and to assume among the powers of the earth, the separate and equal station to which the laws of nature and nature's God entitle them, a decent respect to the opinions of mankind requires that they should declare the causes which impel them to separation."

RNA:

To assure justice for all; to end color and class discrimination while not abolishing salubrious diversity, and to promote self-respect and mutual respect among all people in the society. (Basic official Document, RNA.)

BIBLIOGRAPHY

"Accomplishments of the Muslims" (pamphlet, n.d.).

Allen, Robert, *Black Awakening in Capitalist America*. New York, Doubleday, 1969.

Aptheker, Herbert, *American Negro Slave Revolts*. New York, Columbia University Press, 1943.

Baker, Ray S., *Following the Color Line: American Negro Citizenship in the Progressive Era*. New York, Harper Torchbooks, 1964.

Baker, Ross, *The Afro-American: Readings*. New York, Van Nostrand Reinhold, 1970.

Bell, Howard H., "Survey of the Negro Convention Movement, 1830-1861," Ph.D. dissertation, Northwestern University, 1953.

Bell, Inge P., *Core and the Strategy of Nonviolence*. New York, Random House, 1968.

Bennett, Lerone, Jr., *Before the Mayflower: A History of the Negro in America*. Baltimore, Penguin Books, 1966.

Bittker, Boris I., *The Case for Black Reparations*. New York, Vintage Books, 1973.

Bittle, William E., and Gilbert Geis, *The Longest Way Home: Chief Alfred C. Sam's Back-To-Africa Movement*. Detroit, Wayne State University Press, 1964.

The Black Panther, 2, No. 4 (August 9, 1969), 12; 2, No. 5 (August 30, 1969), 13; 2, No. 8 (September 27, 1969), 10-11; 4, No. 29 (January 16, 1971), 17; 6, No. 3 (February 13, 1971).

"The Black Scholar Interviews Bobby Seale," *Black Scholar*, 4, No. 1 (1972), 7-16.

"The Black Panther Party Undergoes Major Split," *Black Voice*, 4, No. 4 (March 10, 1971), 1.

Bracey, John H., August Meier, and Elliott Rudwick, *Black Nationalism in America*. Indianapolis, Bobbs-Merrill, 1970.

Brashler, William, "Black on Black: The Deadly Struggle for Power," *New York Magazine*, 8, No. 23 (June 9, 1975), 49.

Breitman, George, ed., *By Any Means Necessary: Speeches, Interviews, and a Letter by Malcolm X*. New York, Pathfinder Press, 1970.

——, *Malcolm X on Afro-American History.* New York, Merit Publishers, 1967.

——, *Malcolm X Speaks: Selected Speeches and Statements.* New York, Grove Press, 1965.

——, *The Last Year of Malcolm X.* New York, Merit Publishers, 1967.

Brisbane, Robert, *The Black Vanguard: Origins of the Negro Social Revolution 1900-1960.* Valley Forge, Pa., Judson Press, 1970.

Brown, Edward, "CORE and Garveyism," *CORE,* 3, No. 3 (Fall/Winter 1973), 41.

Browne, Robert S., "A Case for Separatism," in Robert Browne and Bayard Rustin, *Separatism or Integration: Which Way for America? A Dialogue.* New York, A. Philip Randolph Educational Fund, 1968.

Calista, Donald J., "Booker T. Washington: Another Look," *Journal of Negro History,* 49 (1964), 251.

Cantril, Hadley, *The Psychology of Social Movements.* Garden City, N.Y., Doubleday, Doran, 1945.

Carmichael, Stokely, "Pan-Africanism—Land and Power," *Black Scholar,* 1 (1969), 43.

——, *Stokely Speaks: Black Power to Pan-Africanism.* New York, Vintage Books, 1971.

——, "Toward Black Liberation," *Massachusetts Review,* 3 (1966), 639-651.

——, "What We Want," *New York Review of Books* (September 22, 1966), p. 5.

Carmichael, Stokely, and Charles V. Hamilton, *Black Power: The Politics of Liberation in America.* New York, Random House, 1967.

Clarke, John H., ed., *William Styron's Nat Turner: Ten Black Writers Respond.* Boston, Mass., Beacon Press, 1968.

Cleaver, Eldridge, *Soul on Ice.* New York, McGraw-Hill, 1968.

——, "The Land Question," *Ramparts,* 6 (1968), 51-53.

Cooper, David, ed., *The Dialectics of Liberation.* London, Penguin Books, 1968.

CORE Annual Report, 1973/74.

Cronon, Edmund D., *Black Moses: The Story of Marcus Garvey and the Universal Negro Improvement Association.* Madison, Wis., University of Wisconsin Press, 1955.

Cruse, Harold, *Rebellion or Revolution.* New York, William Morrow, 1968.

——, *The Crisis of the Negro Intellectual.* New York, William Morrow, 1967.

Dimont, Max I., *Jews, God and History.* New York, Signet, 1962.

Draper, Theodore, *Rediscovery of Black Nationalism.* New York, Viking Press, 1970.

DuBois, Shirley, G., *His Day Is Marching On.* Philadelphia, Lippincott, 1971.

DuBois, W. E. B., *Black Reconstruction in America, 1860-1880.* New York, Atheneum, 1972.

——, *John Brown.* New York, International Publishers, 1962.

——, "Segregation in the North," *Crisis,* 41 (1934), 115-117.

——, *The Dusk of Dawn: An Essay toward an Autobiography of a Race Concept.* New York, Schocken Books, 1968.

——, *The Souls of Black Folk.* Greenwich, Conn., Fawcett, 1961.

Dunbar, Ernest, "The Making of a Militant," *Saturday Review* (December 16, 1972), pp. 25-32.

Edwards, Adolph, *Marcus Garvey, 1887-1940.* London, New Beacon Publications, 1967.

Essien-Udom, E. U., *Black Nationalism: A Search for an Identity in America.* New York, Dell, 1964.

Farmer, James, *Freedom—When?* New York, Random House, 1965.

Flynn, John P. "Booker T. Washington: Uncle Tom or Wooden Horse," *Journal of Negro History,* 54 (1969), 262-274.

Foner, Philip S., *The Black Panthers Speak.* Philadelphia, Lippincott, 1970.

———, *The Life and Writings of Frederick Douglass,* Vol. 2. New York, International Publishers, 1950.

Fox, Stephen R. *The Guardian of Boston: William Monroe Trotter.* New York, Atheneum, 1970.

Franklin, John H., *From Slavery to Freedom: Negro Americans.* New York, Vintage Books, 1969.

———, Introduction, *Three Negro Classics.* New York, Avon Books, 1965.

Franklin, Raymond S., and Solomon Resnik. *The Political Economy of Racism.* New York, Holt, Rinehart, and Winston, 1973.

Frazier, E. F., *The Negro in the United States.* New York, Macmillan, 1957.

Frazier, Thomas R., ed., *Afro-American History: Primary Sources.* New York, Harcourt, Brace, and World, 1970.

Garfinkel, Herbert, *When Negroes March: The March on Washington Movement in the Organizational Politics for FEPC.* New York, Atheneum, 1969.

Garvey, Amy J., ed., *Philosophy and Opinions of Marcus Garvey.* New York, Atheneum, 1970.

Garvin, Roy, "Benjamin or 'Pap' Singleton and His Followers," *Journal of Negro History,* 33 (1948), 7-23.

Geyer, Georgie A., "The Odyssey of Robert Williams," *New Republic* (March 20, 1971), p. 14.

Gibson, Richard, *African Liberation Movements: Contemporary Struggles against White Minority Rule.* New York, Oxford University Press, 1972.

Gordon, Eugene, "Negro Novelists and the Negro Masses," *New Masses,* 8 (1933), 16.

De Gramont, Sanche, "Our Other Man in Algiers," *New York Times Magazine* (November 1, 1970), pp. 30-31, 112, 114, 116, 118-119, 126, 128.

Gray, Thomas R., *The Confessions of Nat Turner.* Baltimore, Md., 1831.

Gusfield, Joseph, ed., *Protest, Reform, and Revolt: A Reader in Social Movements.* New York, Wiley, 1970.

Haddad, William F., and Douglas Pugh, eds., *Black Economic Development.* Englewood Cliffs, N.J., Prentice-Hall, 1969.

Hall, Raymond L., ed., *Black Separatism and Social Reality: Rhetoric and Reason.* New York, Pergamon Press, 1977.

Hamilton, Charles V., "An Advocate of Black Power Defines It," *New York Times Magazine* (April 14, 1968), pp. 22-23, 79-83.

Harlan, Louis R., "Booker T. Washington and the White Man's Burden," *American Historical Review,* 71 (1966), 441-467.

Harris, Sheldon H., *Paul Cuffe: Black Americans and the Africa Return.* New York, Simon and Schuster, 1972.

Henderson, William L., and Larry C. Ledebur, *Economic Disparity: Problems and Strategies for Black America.* New York, Free Press, 1970.

Herndon, Angelo, *Let Me Live*. New York, Arno Press, 1969.

Hertzberg, Arthur, ed., *The Zionist Idea: A Historical Analysis and Reader*. New York, Meridian Book, 1960.

Holt, Len, *The Summer That Didn't End*. New York, William Morrow, 1965.

"Huey Newton Talks to the Movement about the Black Panther Party, Cultural Nationalism, S.N.C.C., Liberals and White Revolutionaries," *The Movement* (August 1968), p. 4, pamphlet.

Hughes, Langston, *I Wonder as I Wander*. New York, Hill and Wang, 1956.

Jones, Robert A., *The Nation* (August 11, 1969), p. 102.

Kanet, Roger E., "The Comintern and 'The Negro Question': Communist Policy in the United States and Africa, 1921-1941," paper presented at the 54th Annual Meeting of the Association for the Study of Negro Life and History, Birmingham, Alabama (October 1969), p. 9.

Killian, Lewis M., *The Impossible Revolution? Black Power and the American Dream*. New York, Random House, 1968.

King, Martin Luther, Jr., *Where Do We Go from Here: Chaos or Community*. New York, Bantam Books, 1967.

Lester, Julius, *Look Out Whitey! Black Power Gon' Get Your Mama!* New York, Dial Press, 1968.

——, *Revolutionary Notes*. New York, Grove Press, 1969.

——, "The Angry Children of Malcolm X," in August Meier, Elliott Rudwick, and Francis L. Broderick, *Black Protest Thought in the Twentieth Century*. Indianapolis, Bobbs-Merrill, 1965; 2nd ed., 1971.

Lincoln, Eric., *The Black Muslims in America*. Boston, Beacon Press, 1961.

——, "200 Years of Black Religion," *Ebony*, 30, No. 10 (August 1975), 84-89.

Litwack, Leon, *North of Slavery: The Negro in the Free States, 1790-1860*. Chicago, Ill., University of Chicago Press, 1961.

Llorens, David, "Black Separatism in Perspective," *Ebony*, 23, No. 11 (September 1968), 95.

Lockwood, Lee, ed., *Conversation with Eldridge Cleaver in Algiers*. New York, Delta Books, 1970.

Logan, Rayford, W., *The Betrayal of the Negro: From Rutherford B. Hayes to Woodrow Wilson*. New York, Collier Books, 1965.

Lomax, Louis, *When the Word Is Given*. New York, Signet Books, 1964.

Lynch, Hollis R., ed., *Black Spokesman—Selected Published Writings of Edward Wilmot Blyden*. New York, Humanities Press, 1971.

——, *Edward Wilmot Blyden—Pan Negro Patriot 1832-1912*. London, Oxford University Press, 1970.

McCord, William, *Mississippi: The Long Hot Summer*. New York, W. W. Norton, 1965.

McLaughlin, Barry, *Studies in Social Movements: A Social-Psychological Perspective*. New York, Free Press, 1969.

Major, Reginald, *A Panther Is a Black Cat*. New York, William Morrow, 1971.

Malcolm X, *The Autobiography of Malcolm X*. New York, Grove Press, 1964.

Mannheim, Karl, *Ideology and Utopia*. New York, Harcourt, Brace, 1946.

Mannix, Daniel P., *Black Cargoes: A History of the Atlantic Slave Trade*. New York, Viking Press, 1962.

Marine, Gene, *The Black Panthers*. New York, Signet Books, 1969.

Meet the Press, Washington, D. C., Merkle Press, 1966.

Meier, August, "Booker T. Washington and the Town of Mound Bayou," *Phylon,* 15 (Winter 1954), 396-401.

——, "Negro Class Structure and Ideology in the Age of Booker T. Washington, " *Phylon,* 23 (Fall 1962), 258-266.

Meier, August, and Elliott M. Rudwick, *Core: A Study in the Civil Rights Movement 1942-1968.* New York, Oxford University Press, 1973.

——, *From Plantation to Ghetto.* New York, Hill and Wang, 1966.

Meier, August, Elliott Rudwick, and Francis L. Broderick, *Black Protest Thought in the Twentieth Century.* Indianapolis, Bobbs-Merrill, 1965; 2nd ed., 1971.

Minor, Robert, "After Garvey—What?" *Workers' Monthly,* 5, No. 8 (June 1926), 365.

——, "Death of a Program," *Workers' Monthly,* 5, No. 6 (April 1926), 270.

Muhammad, Elijah, *Message to the Black Man in America.* Chicago, Muhammad Mosque, No. 2, 1965.

Muhammad Speaks, 14 (June 18, 1975), 2.

Myrdal, Gunnar, *The America Dilemma: The Negro Problem and Modern Democracy.* Vol. 2. New York, Harper Torchbooks, 1962.

The New York Times, (April 10, 1971), 24.

——, "Mississippi Bars a Black Nation," (May 9, 1971), 18.

Newton, Huey P., "Address at Syracuse University," manuscript notes by the author (Spring 1971).

——, *Black Liberation News,* 1, No. 5 (November 1969), 7.

——, "Black Panthers," *Ebony,* 24, No. 10 (August 1969), 107-112.

——, "Huey Newton Speaks from Jail," *Motive,* 29 (October 1968), 16-18.

——, "Huey Newton Talks to the Movement about the Black Panther Party, Cultural Nationalism, SNCC, Liberals, and White Revolutionaries," *The Movement* (August 1968), p. 4 (pamphlet).

——, *Revolutionary Suicide.* New York, Harcourt, Brace, & World, 1973.

Nkrumah, Kwame, *Neo-Colonialism: The Last Stage of Imperialism.* New York, International Publishers, 1965.

Nolan, William, *Communism versus the Negro.* Chicago, Henry Regnery, 1951.

North, Joseph, "The Communists Nominate," *New Masses,* 7 (1932), 4.

Obadele, Imari A., "The Struggle Is for Land," *Black Scholar,* 3 (February 1972), 24-36.

Oberschall, Anthony, *Social Conflict and Social Movements.* Englewood Cliffs, N.J., Prentice-Hall, 1973.

Ottley, Roi, "New World A-Coming," in *Inside Black America.* Boston, Mass., Houghton Mifflin, 1943.

Pierce, Chester, "The Black Caucus: Response to Racism in the Mental Health Movement," in Charles V. Willie, ed., *Racism and Mental Health.* Pittsburgh, Univ. of Pittsburgh Press, 1973.

Poinsett, Alex, "CORE Leader Champions Black Separatist Program," *Ebony,* 24, No. 12 (October 1969), 174-176.

Quarles, Benjamin, *The Black Abolitionists.* New York, Oxford University Press, 1969.

——, *The Negro in the Making of America.* New York, Collier Books, 1964.

Record, Wilson, *The Negro and the Communist Party.* Chapel Hill, N.C., University of North Carolina Press, 1951.

Redkey, Edwin S., *Black Exodus: Black Nationalist and Back-to-Africa*

Movements 1890–1910. New Haven, Yale University Press, 1969.

Rotberg, Robert I., ed., *Strike a Blow and Die: A Narrative of Race Relations in Colonial Africa.* Cambridge, Mass., Harvard University Press, 1967.

Rudwick, Elliott M., *Race Riot at East St. Louis.* New York, Atheneum, 1972.

Scheer, Robert, ed., *Eldridge Cleaver, Post Prison Writings and Speeches.* New York, Ramparts Vintage Books, 1969.

Schuchter, Arnold, *Reparations: The Black Manifesto and Its Challenge to White America.* Philadelphia, Pa., Lippincott, 1970.

Scott, Emmett J., *Negro Migration during the War.* New York, Arno Press and the New York Times, 1969.

Seale, Bobby G., *Seize the Time: The Story of the Black Panther Party and Huey P. Newton.* New York, Vintage Books, 1970.

Sellers, Cleveland, *The River of No Return.* New York, William Morrow, 1973.

Sherrill, Robert, "Interview with Milton Henry," *Esquire* (January 1969), p. 73.

Silberman, Charles, *Crisis in Black and White.* New York, Random House, 1964.

Sinclair, John, *Message to the People of the Woodstock Nation,* Ministry of Information, White Panther Party, Ann Arbor, Michigan (1970).

Skolnick, Jerome H., *The Politics of Protest.* New York, Ballantine Books, 1969.

Sonebeyatta, Yusufu [Joseph Brooks], "Ujamaa for Land and Power," *Black Scholar,* 3, No. 2 (October 1971), 13–20.

Spencer, Samuel R., Jr., *Booker T. Washington and the Negro's Place in American Life.* Boston, Little, Brown, 1955.

Stalin, Joseph V., *Marxism and the National Colonial Question.* New York, International Publishers, n.d.

Styron, William, *The Confessions of Nat Turner.* New York, Random House, 1967.

"The Irrepressible Envoy from Ghana," *Ebony,* Vol. 36, No. 1 (November 1970), 74.

Thornbrough, Emma L., "Booker T. Washington as Seen by His White Contemporaries," *Journal of Negro History,* 53 (1968), 161–182.

Toch, Hans, *The Social Psychology of Social Movements.* Indianapolis, Bobbs-Merrill, 1965.

Turner, Ralph H. and Lewis M. Killian, *Collective Behavior.* Englewood Cliffs, N.J., Prentice-Hall, 1957; 2nd ed. 1972.

U.S. Department of Labor, *The Negro Family,* Washington, D.C., Government Printing Office (1965), p. 29.

Vincent, Theodore G., *Black Power and the Garvey Movement.* Berkeley, Ramparts Press, 1971.

———, *Voices of a Black Nation: Political Journalism in the Harlem Renaissance,* Berkeley, Ramparts Press, 1973.

Voting in Mississippi, A Report of the U.S. Commission on Civil Rights, Washington, D.C. (May 1965), pp. 31–39, 56–91.

Wagstaff, Thomas, ed., *Black Power: The Radical Response to White America.* Beverly Hills, Calif., Glencoe Press, 1969.

Walker, David, *Appeal in Four Articles.* New York, Hill and Wang, 1965.

"Wanted by YLP: Luis A. Ferre," *Palante,* Vol. 3, No. 4 (March 5–19, 1971), 24.

Washington, Booker T., *Future of the American Negro.* Boston, Mass., Small, Maynard, 1899.

——, "Up from Slavery," *Three Negro Classics*. New York, Avon Books, 1965.

"We Want Black Power," Chicago Office of S.N.C.C. (1967), leaflet.

Weisbord, Robert G., *Ebony Kinship; African, Africans, and the Afro-American*. Westport, Conn., Greenwood Press, 1973.

——, *Genocide? Birth Control and the Black American*. Westport, Conn., Greenwood Press, 1975.

White, Charles, "Desegregation and the Richmond Story," *CORE*, Vol. 2, No. 3 (Fall 1972), 7.

Wilhelm, Sidney, *Who Needs the Negro?*. Garden City, N.Y., Doubleday, 1971.

Woodward, C. Vann, *Origins of the New South, 1877-1914*. Baton Rouge, La., Louisiana State University Press, 1951.

Wright, Nathan, *Black Power and Urban Unrest*. New York, Hawthorne, 1967.

——, *What Black Politicians Are Saying*. New York, Hawthorne, 1972.

X, Malcolm. See Malcolm X.

"Young Lords Party Position on The Black Panther Party," *Palante*, Vol. 3, No. 3 (February 1971), 2.

Zander, Robert Alex, "Centralized Coordination of Economic Acitivity in Urban Ghettoes: A Case for the Community Development Corporation," Senior Fellowship Thesis, Dartmouth College (Spring 1975).

Zinn, Howard, *SNCC: The New Abolitionists*. Boston, Beacon Press, 1964.

NOTES

1. Introduction

1. John H. Bracey, Jr., August Meier, and Elliott Rudwick, eds., *Black Nationalism in America* (Indianapolis, Bobbs-Merrill, 1970). See esp. pp. xxvi-xxix.

2. See Raymond L. Hall, ed., *Black Separatism and Social Reality: Rhetoric and Reason* (New York, Pergamon Press, 1977).

3. The phenomenon of separatism is not only a social and political reality in American society, but it tends to be the rule rather than the exception in most societies that are not almost completely homogeneous— racially, ethnically, and culturally. Examples of societies experiencing past and present separatist activity include the French and English rift in Canada, the French-Flemish split in Belgium, the Croatian-Serbian conflict in Yugoslavia, Turkish-Greek schism in Cyrus, and the various larger and smaller separatist movements and tendencies in Asia, Africa, and Latin America.

4. Martin Luther King, Jr., *Where Do We Go from Here: Chaos or Community?* (New York, Bantam Books, 1967), p. 28.

5. Ibid., pp. 39–40.

6. Ralph H. Turner and Lewis M. Killian, *Collective Behavior* (2nd ed., Englewood Cliffs, N.J., Prentice-Hall, 1972), pp. 321, 331–333.

7. It is difficult to envision part of the existing social system in the United States being torn off for separate organization and development without having the separation effect changes in the rest of the social system. The "white" South, for example, was prevented by armed force from seceding in 1860. In the same vein, one could argue that, regarding black separation in the contemporary United States, many white Americans would gladly concede to black separation, but just as in 1860, they are afraid to risk the residual effects it would have on the rest of the social, political, and economic system.

8. In many organizations black caucuses have arisen in respone to inadvertent or advertent white racism. Moreover, some black caucuses have resulted in completely separate black organizational development.

Some exampĺes include the Caucus of Black Sociologists (from the American Sociological Association); the African Heritage Studies Association (from the African Studies Association); the National Medical Association (from the American Medical Association). In general, the "black caucus movement" is a response to the reality of black powerlessness in white dominated organizations; hence, in order to cope with the reality of powerlessness, blacks seek to form their own (separate) organization to fulfill their needs and desires. See Chester N. Pierce, "The Black Caucus: Response to Racism in the Mental Health Movement," in Charles V. Willie, ed., *Racism and Mental Health: Essays* (Pittsburgh, University of Pittsburgh Press, 1973).

9. William L. Henderson and Larry C. Ledebur, *Economic Disparity: Problems and Strategies for Black America* (New York, The Free Press, 1970), p. 68.

10. Turner and Killian, *Collective Behavior*, p. 10.

11. Jerome H. Skolnick, *The Politics of Protest* (New York, Ballantine Books, 1969), p. 333.

12. McLaughlin, among others, makes the point that social movements are a "relatively neglected area in social science . . . often regarded as epiphenomena, as the by-product of social and political developments." Barry McLaughlin, ed., *Studies in Social Movements: A Social Psychological Perspective* (New York, The Free Press, 1969), p. 1.

13. For an extended discussion of these member types, see Raymond L. Hall, "Explorations in the Analysis of Black Separatism," in his *Black Separatism and Social Reality*, pp. 13-22.

2. The Roots

1. There is a difference between a *movement* and a *tendency*. Movement is meant in the technical sense of a social movement; a tendency is not a social movement but could very well become one. A tendency represents a general drift in the direction of a social movement but lacks its organizational structure. It may or may not become a developed social movement.

2. Daniel P. Mannix, *Black Cargoes: A History of the Atlantic Slave Trade, 1518-1865* (New York, Viking Press, 1962), chap. 5.

3. See Herbert Aptheker, *American Negro Slave Revolts* (New York, Columbia University Press, 1943).

4. Lerone Bennett, Jr., *Before the Mayflower: A History of the Negro in America, 1619-1964* (Baltimore, Penguin Books, 1966), pp. 37-38 (revised edition).

5. Bracey, Meier, and Rudwick, pp. xxxi, 4-17, 19-20.

6. Ibid., pp. 4-17, 19-20.

7. See E. U. Essien-Udom, *Black Nationalism: A Search for Identity in America* (New York, Dell Publishing, 1964), p. 39

8. C. Eric Lincoln, "200 Years of Black Religion," *Ebony*, 30, No. 10 (August 1975), 84-89.

9. Sheldon H. Harris, *Paul Cuffe: Black Americans and the Africa Return* (New York, Simon and Schuster, 1972), p. 13.

10. Howard H. Bell, "A Survey of the Negro Convention Movement, 1830-1961" (Ph.D. dissertation, Northwestern University, 1953), cited in

Edwin S. Redkey, *Black Exodus, Black Nationalist and Back-to-Africa Movements, 1890-1910* (New Haven, Conn., Yale University Press, 1969), pp. 19-20.

11. "Daniel Coker, 'My Soul Cleaves to Africa,'" in Bracey, Meier, and Rudwick, pp. 46-48.

12. Bracey, Meier, and Rudwick, pp. xxxii-xxxiii.

13. David Walker, *Appeal in Four Articles*, 1829 (New York, Hill and Wang, 1965), pp. 64-65. Italics in the original. Walker's "appeal" was suppressed throughout the South, but later received some assistance from certain abolitionists.

14. Ibid., introduction by Charles M. Wiltse, p. vii.

15. Ibid., p. ix.

16. Quoted in Leon Litwack, *North of Slavery: The Negro in the Free States, 1790-1860* (Chicago, Ill., University of Chicago Press, 1961), p. 238.

17. See Thomas R. Gray, *The Confessions of Nat Turner* (Baltimore, Md., 1831); William Styron, *The Confessions of Nat Turner* (New York, Random House, 1967); and John Henrik Clarke, ed., *William Styron's Nat Turner: Ten Black Writers Respond* (Boston, Mass., Beacon Press, 1968). Thomas Gray interviewed Nat Turner while he was in jail awaiting execution for his deeds. William Styron wrote a historical novel based on the Nat Turner incident which inferred that Nat Turner was a sexually perverted, mentally deranged, unstable, and superstitious misfit. Ten black writers responded by pointing out that Nat Turner was a black revolutionary who "struck a blow for freedom."

18. John Hope Franklin, *From Slavery to Freedom: A History of Negro Americans* (New York, Vintage Books, 1969), pp. 210-212.

19. Bracey, Meier, and Rudwick, p. xxxiv.

20. This address was given at the 1843 National Convention, but the convention, which met in Buffalo, New York, after intense debate voted not to publish the address. Garnet himself published it in 1848 together with Walker's *Appeal*.

21. Henry Highland Garnet, *The Past and Present Condition, and The Destiny of the Colored Race: A Discourse Delivered at the 50th Anniversary of the Female Benevolent Society of Troy, N.Y., February 14, 1848*, in Bracey, Meier, and Rudwick, pp. 115-120.

22. Frederick Douglass, "The Present Condition and Future Prospects of the Negro People." Speech at Annual Meeting of the American and Foreign Anti-Slavery Society, New York, May 1853, in Philip S. Foner, *The Life and Writings of Frederick Douglass, II* (New York, International Publishers, 1950).

23. Frederick Douglass, "Our Elevation as a Race Is Almost Wholly Dependent upon Our Own Exertions," (editorial in the *North Star*, December 3, 1847), cited in Bracey, Meier, and Rudwick, pp. 63-66.

24. Bell, "A Survey of the Negro Convention Movement, 1830-1861."

25. See Bracey, Meier, and Rudwick, pp. 79-110; esp. Document 19 (the National Emigration Convention of 1854).

26. Franklin, pp. 260-270.

27. W. E. B. DuBois, *John Brown*, 1919 (New York, International Publishers, 1962).

28. Ross Baker, ed., *The Afro-American: Readings* (New York, Van Nostrand, Reinhold, 1970), pp. 234-235. Emphasis added.

29. Ibid., p. 237.
30. Edwin S. Redkey, *Black Exodus: Black Nationalist and Back to Africa Movements, 1890-1910* (New Haven, Yale University Press, 1969), p. 21.
31. W. E. B. DuBois, *Black Reconstruction in America, 1860-1880* (New York, Atheneum, 1972), 1934, p. 55.
32. E. Franklin Frazier, *The Negro in the United States* (rev. ed. New York, Macmillan, 1957), pp. 137-138. See especially the painstaking work of DuBois, *Black Reconstruction in America*, chap. X.
33. Frazier, p. 147.
34. Rayford W. Logan, *The Betrayal of the Negro: From Rutherford B. Hayes to Woodrow Wilson*, originally published in 1954 as *The Negro in American Life And Thought: The Nadir, 1877-1901.* (New York, Collier Books, 1965), p. 31.
35. C. Vann Woodward, *Origins of the New South, 1877-1914* (Baton Rouge, La., Louisiana State University Press, 1951), pp. 175-185. See also Franklin, *From Slavery to Freedom*, chaps. 17, 21.
36. Robert G. Weisbord, *Ebony Kinship: African, Africans, and the Afro-American* (Westport, Conn., Greenwood Press, 1973), p. 24.
37. Ibid., p. 25.
38. Frazier, p. 155.
39. Weisbord, p. 27.
40. Roy Garvin, "Benjamin or 'Pap' Singleton and His Followers," *Journal of Negro History*, 33, No. 1 (1948), 7-23.
41. Theodore Draper, *Rediscovery of Black Nationalism* (New York, Viking, 1970), p. 23.
42. Ibid., pp. 36, 40.
43. Redkey, *Black Exodus*, pp. 24-25.
44. One can speculate that the desire of many blacks to join in the fight against the Confederacy was another exhibition of nascent black nationalism.
45. Quoted in Redkey, *Black Exodus*, p. 41.
46. Though Blyden played a significant role in influencing Turner to promote African emigration, I shall not elaborate upon his role largely because—though he was a separatist—he was not a black American and he —unlike Garvey—did not focus his organizational attention in the United States. For a detailed discussion of Blyden see Hollis R. Lynch, *Edward Wilmot Blyden—Pan Negro Patriot 1832-1912* (London, Oxford University Press, 1970); and Hollis R. Lynch, ed., *Black Spokesman—Selected Published Writings of Edward Wilmot Blyden* (New York, Humanities Press, 1971).

3. Separatists in Disguise

1. The discussion of emigration efforts and schemes is based primarily on Edwin S. Redkey's *Black Exodus*, esp. pages 195-250. This work is invaluable to understanding black nationalism and emigration movements from 1890 to 1910.
2. Booker T. Washington, "Up From Slavery," in *Three Negro Classics* (New York, Avon Books, 1965), pp. 29-205.
3. John Hope Franklin, intro. to *Three Negro Classics*.
4. Samuel R. Spencer, Jr., *Booker T. Washington and the Negro's Place in American Life* (Boston, Little, Brown, 1955), p. 163.

5. Emma L. Thornbrough, "Booker T. Washington as Seen by His White Contemporaries," *Journal of Negro History*, 53 (April 1968), p. 162.
6. Washington, "Up From Slavery," p. 182.
7. Eugene D. Genovese, "The Legacy of Slavery and the Roots of Black Nationalism," *Studies on the Left* (November–December, 1966), pp. 14-26, in Thomas Wagstaff, ed., *Black Power: The Radical Response to White America* (Beverly Hills, Calif., Glencoe Press, 1969), p. 139.
8. Washington, "Up From Slavery," p. 141.
9. Booker T. Washington, *Future of the American Negro* (Boston, Mass., Small, Maynard, 1899), pp. 227-228. (Italics added.)
10. August Meier and Elliott M. Rudwick, *From Plantation to Ghetto* (New York, Hill and Wang, 1966), p. 181.
11. Donald J. Calista, "Booker T. Washington: Another Look," *Journal of Negro History*, 49, No. 4 (October 1964), p. 251.
12. Meier and Rudwick, p. 181.
13. T. Thomas Fortune, from an address in "Official Compilation of Proceedings of the Afro-American League National Convention, 1890," in Bracey, Meier, and Rudwick, *Black Nationalism in America*, pp. 212-222.
14. Ibid., pp. 211-212.
15. John P. Flynn, "Booker T. Washington: Uncle Tom or Wooden Horse," *Journal of Negro History*, 54, No. 3 (July 1969), p. 270.
16. Washington, *Future of the American Negro*, p. 182.
17. Ibid., pp. 182-183.
18. August Meier, "Booker T. Washington and the Town of Mound Bayou," *Phylon*, 15 (1954), 400.
19. Franklin, *From Slavery to Freedom*, p. 397.
20. W. E. B. DuBois, *The Souls of Black Folk* (Greenwich, Conn., Fawcett, 1961), p. 49.
21. "Resolutions of the Atlanta University Conference on the Negro in Business," in W. E. B. DuBois, ed., *The Negro in Business* (Atlanta University Publications, No. 4, Atlanta, Ga., 1899), p. 50.
22. "It was this group that was especially instrumental in the burgeoning of the philosophy of racial solidarity, self-help and the group economy, the rationalization of the economic advantages to be found in segregation and discrimination—to use a phrase commonly employed in those days. Washington's National Negro Business League was the platform on which this group expressed its point of view." August Meier, "Negro Class Structure and Ideology in the Age of Booker T. Washington," *Phylon*, 23, No. 3 (1962), 258. (Emphasis deleted.)
23. Washington, "Up From Slavery," p.
24. W. E. B. DuBois, *The Dusk of Dawn: An Essay Toward an Autobiography of a Race Concept* (New York, Schocken, 1968, first published by Harcourt, Brace & World, 1940), p. 201.
25. See Ray Stannard Baker, *Following the Color Line: American Negro Citizenship in the Progressive Era* (New York, Harper Torchbooks, 1964, originally published in 1908 by Doubleday, Page and Company). His insight into the Southern mind relative to education is significant. He observes "the majority view in the South was more or less hostile to the education of the Negro, or, at least, to his education beyond the bare rudiments" (p. 282).
26. Hans Toch, *The Social Psychology of Social Movements* (Indianapolis, Bobbs-Merrill, 1965), p. 238.

27. Stephen R. Fox, *The Guardian of Boston: William Monroe Trotter* (New York, Atheneum, 1970), pp. 21–23.
28. See William E. Bittle and Gilbert Geis, *The Longest Way Home: Chief Alfred C. Sam's Back-to-Africa Movement* (Detroit, Wayne State University Press, 1964).
29. For an excellent discussion of Washington's African involvement, see Louis R. Harlan, "Booker T. Washington and the White Man's Burden," *American Historical Review*, 71 (1966), 441–467. (Quote from p. 464.)
30. Samuel R. Spencer, Jr., *Booker T. Washington and the Negro's Place in American Life* (Boston, Little, Brown, 1955), pp. 191–195.
31. Karl Mannheim, *Ideology and Utopia* (New York, Harcourt, Brace, 1946), p. 184.
32. Harold Cruse, *The Crisis of the Negro Intellectual* (New York, William Morrow, 1967), p. 426.

4. Militant Black Nationalism

1. Edmund David Cronon, *Black Moses: The Story of Marcus Garvey and the Universal Negro Improvement Association* (Madison, Wisc., University of Wisconsin Press, 1955), p. 3.
2. Adolph Edwards, *Marcus Garvey, 1887–1940* (London, New Beacon Publications, 1967), p. 4.
3. Ibid., p. 6.
4. Amy Jacques Garvey, ed., *Philosophy and Opinions of Marcus Garvey* (New York, Atheneum, 1970), p. 126.
5. Ibid.
6. Edwards, pp. 7–8. (Italics added.)
7. Ibid.
8. Robert Brisbane, *The Black Vanguard: Origins of the Negro Social Revolution 1900–1960* (Valley Forge, Pa., Judson Press, 1970), p. 84.
9. Ibid., p. 86.
10. Garvey, p. 129.
11. Edwards, p. 11.
12. Brisbane, p. 87.
13. Cronon, p. 51.
14. Quotes Ibid., p. 52. (Italics added.)
15. Ibid.
16. Brisbane, p. 88.
17. Ibid.
18. Cronon, p. 62.
19. Edwards, pp. 12–13.
20. Cronon, p. 62.
21. Red for the blood blacks have shed, black for pride in color, and green for a new and better life in Africa.
22. Reverend George Alexander McGuire, a well-known Episcopalian priest in Boston, abandoned his church to 1920 to join the Garvey movement. See Brisbane, p. 89.
23. Roi Ottley, "New World A-Coming," *Inside Black America* (Boston, Mass., Houghton Mifflin, 1943), p. 76.
24. Quoted in Brisbane, pp. 89–90.
25. Theodore G. Vincent, *Black Power and the Garvey Movement* (Berkeley, Ramparts Press, 1971), p. 18.

26. Brisbane, pp. 91-92.
27. Ibid., p. 94.
28. Ibid., pp. 95-96.
29. Michael Lewis, "The Negro Protest in Urban America," in Joseph R. Gusfield, ed., *Protest, Reform and Revolt* (New York, Wiley & Sons, 1970), pp. 157-158.
30. George Simon Mwase, *Strike a Blow and Die: A Narrative of Race Relations in Colonial Africa*, ed. Robert I. Rotberg (Cambridge, Mass., Harvard University Press, 1967).
31. Emmett J. Scott, *Negro Migration During the War* (New York, Arno Press and the New York Times, 1969).
32. Elliott M. Rudwick, *Race Riot at East St. Louis, July 2, 1917* (New York, Atheneum, 1972).
33. Marcus Garvey, "The True Solution of the Negro Problem," in Amy Jacques Garvey, ed., *Philosophy and Opinions of Marcus Garvey* (New York, Atheneum, 1970), p. 53.
34. Ibid., p. 37.
35. Garvey, *Philosophy and Opinions*, p. 84.
36. Ibid., p. 19.
37. Brisbane, p. 92.
38. Garvey, p. 93.
39. Edwards, p. 12.
40. Garvey, p. 56.
41. Vincent, *Black Power and the Garvey Movement*, p. 26.
42. Harold Cruse, *Rebellion or Revolution* (New York, William Morrow, 1968), p. 165. (Italics added.)
43. Ibid., p. 205.
44. That Garvey's headquarters and the initial response to his organization was in Harlem can also be attributed to Washington. The Afro-American Realty Company, headed by Phillip A. Payton—a Washington-conceived black organization—was largely responsible for black people "taking over Harlem." See Cruse, p. 204.

5. Subdued Separatism

1. Wilson Record, *The Negro and the Communist Party* (Chapel Hill, University of North Carolina Press, 1951), p. 21.
2. Robert Minor, "Death of a Program," *Workers' Monthly*, 5, No. 6 (1926), 270.
3. Robert Minor, "After Garvey—What?" *Workers' Monthly*, 5, No. 8 (1926), 365.
4. Roger E. Kanet, "The Comintern and 'The Negro Question': Communist Policy in the United States and Africa, 1921-1941," paper presented at the 54th Annual Meeting of the Association for the Study of Negro Life and History (Birmingham, Alabama, October 9-12, 1969), p. 9.
5. William Nolan, *Communism versus the Negro* (Chicago, Henry Regnery, 1951), p. 47.
6. Stalin, *Marxism and the National Colonial Question* (New York, International Publishers, n.d.), pp. 5-10.
7. Record, p. 63.
8. Ibid., p. 72.

9. Joseph North, "The Communists Nominate," *New Masses,* 7 No. 1 (1932), 4.

10. Eugene Gordon, "Negro Novelists and the Negro Masses," *New Masses,* 8 No. 11 (1933), 16.

11. Langston Hughes, *I Wonder As I Wander* (New York, Hill and Wang, 1956), p. 4.

12. Ibid., p. 5.

13. Nolan, p. 30.

14. Record, p. 89.

15. See Angelo Herndon, *Let Me Live,* 1936 (New York, Arno Press, 1969).

16. Benjamin Quarles, *The Negro in the Making of America* (New York, Collier, 1964), p. 206.

17. For an excellent, well-documented analysis of Garveyites' participation in other organizations, see Vincent, *Black Power and the Garvey Movement.*

18. Gunnar Myrdal, *The American Dilemma: The Negro Problem and Modern Democracy,* 1944 (New York, Harper Torchbooks, 1962), Vol. 2, pp. 813-814. See also Michael Lewis, "The Negro Protest in Urban America," in Joseph Gusfield, ed., *Protest, Reform and Revolt: A Reader in Social Movements* (New York, Wiley and Sons, 1970), pp. 149-190; Hadley Cantril, *The Psychology of Social Movements* (Garden City, N.Y., Doubleday, Doran, 1945); and C. Eric Lincoln, *The Black Muslims in America* (Boston, Beacon Press, 1961).

19. Vincent, p. 230.

20. W. E. B. DuBois, "Segregation in the North," *The Crisis,* 41 (1934), 115-117.

21. Essien-Udom, *Black Nationalism,* p. 76. See also Lincoln, *The Black Muslims in America,* pp. 50-56.

22. Draper, *The Rediscovery of Black Nationalism,* p. 70.

23. Ibid., p. 71.

24. Lincoln, p. 11.

25. Draper, p. 75.

26. Elijah Muhammad, *Message to the Black Man in America,* (Chicago, Muhammad Mosque, No. 2, 1965), pp. 24-26.

27. Draper, p. 76.

28. Lincoln, p. 15.

29. Ibid., pp. 16-17.

30. Essien-Udom, p. 80.

31. Lewis M. Killian in his preface to the Atheneum edition of Herbert Garfinkel, *When Negroes March: The March on Washington Movement in the Organizational Politics for FEPC* (New York, Atheneum, 1969).

32. For a detailed analysis of black nationalism after Garvey's deportation, see Theodore G. Vincent, *Black Power and the Garvey Movement,* esp. chap. 9, and "A Note on Researching Black Radicalism," pp. 251-256. See also his subsequent edited work, *Voices of a Black Nation: Political Journalism in the Harlem Renaissance* (Berkeley, Ramparts Press, 1973).

6. Separatist Ideologies, I

1. Essien-Udom, *Black Nationalism,* p. 76.

2. Vincent, *Black Power and the Garvey Movement*, p. 222.
3. Elijah Muhammad, *Message to the Black Man in America* (Chicago, Muhammad Mosque, No. 2, 1965), pp. 53, 103-122.
4. Ibid.
5. *Muhammad Speaks*, Vol. 10, No. 14 (1970), 14-16.
6. Louis Lomax, *When the Word Is Given* (New York, Signet Books, 1964), pp. 108-109.
7. Malcolm X, *The Autobiography of Malcolm X* (New York, Grove Press, 1964-65), pp. 258-259.
8. Ibid., p. 256.
9. George Breitman, ed., *Malcolm X on Afro-American History* (New York, Merit Publishers, 1967), pp. 18-19.
10. See *The Autobiography of Malcom X*, chap. 16.
11. The Muslims now participate in politics. This may be seen as the direct outgrowth of the impact of Malcolm X on the nation. To put it another way, the membership agreed that nonpartisanship is dysfunctional in a system where political, social, and economic factors are so interrelated.
12. Lomax, *When the Word Is Given*, p. 179.
13. *The Autobiography of Malcolm X*, p. 377.
14. Ibid.
15. For a full exposition of the OAAU's program, see George Breitman, ed., *By Any Means Necessary: Speeches, Interviews, and A Letter by Malcolm X* (New York, Pathfinder Press, 1970); and *The Last Year of Malcolm X* (New York, Merit Publishers, 1967).
16. Howard Zinn, *SNCC: The New Abolitionists* (Boston, Beacon Press, 1964), pp. 30-39.
17. Though individuals like Adam C. Powell and Richard Wright, among others, had used it before.
18. Some of the varied definitions of "black power" can be found in the following: Stokely Carmichael, *Stokely Speaks: Black Power Back to Pan-Africanism* (New York, Vintage Books, 1971) (Carmichael's latest book, a compendium of many of his speeches); Carmichael, "What We Want," *The New York Review of Books* (September 22, 1966), p. 5; Carmichael, "Black Power," in *The Dialectics of Liberation*, ed. David Cooper (London, Penguin Books, 1968), pp. 150-174; Carmichael, "We Are Going To Use the Term 'Black Power' and We Are Going to Define It Because Black Power Speaks To Us," in Bracey, Meier, and Rudwick, *Black Nationalism in America*, pp. 470-476; Carmichael and Charles V. Hamilton, *Black Power: The Politics of Liberation in America* (New York, Random House, 1967); Charles V. Hamilton, "An Advocate of Black Power Defines It," *The New York Times Magazine* (April 14, 1968), pp. 22-23, 79-83; Carmichael, "Toward Black Liberation," *Massachusetts Review*, 3 (1966), 639-651; Whitney Young, "Address to a CORE Convention in Columbus, Ohio, July 6, 1968," in *Afro-American History: Primary Sources*, ed. Thomas R. Frazier (New York, Harcourt, Brace, and World, 1970), pp. 487-490; Huey Newton, "Huey Newton Speaks from Jail," *Motive*, 29 (1968), 8-16; Julius Lester, *Revolutionary Notes* (New York, Grove Press, 1969); and Lester, *Look Out Whitey! Black Power Gon' Get Your Mama!* (New York, Dial Press, 1968). There are many other interpretations—pro and con—relative to "black power," but these are the most relevant to this work.

19. Julius Lester, "The Angry Children of Malcolm X," in Meier, Rudwick, and Broderick, *Black Protest Thought in the Twentieth Century*, p. 473.
20. Chicago Office of SNCC, "We Want Black Power" (leaflet, Chicago Office, 1967).
21. Carmichael, *Stokely Speaks*, p. 120.
22. Carmichael and Hamilton, *Black Power*, p. 5.
23. Ibid., pp. 6–22.
24. Carmichael, *Stokely Speaks*, p. 93.
25. August Meier and Elliott M. Rudwick, *CORE: A Study in the Civil Rights Movement 1942–1968* (New York, Oxford University Press, 1973), p. 3.
26. James Farmer, *Freedom—When?* (New York, Random House, 1965), chaps. 4, 7.
27. Ibid., p. 118. (Farmer's italics.)
28. Conversation with Farmer in the summer of 1968 at Syracuse University.
29. Bell, Inge P., *CORE and The Strategy of Nonviolence* (New York, Random House, 1968), p. 187.
30. Allen, Robert, *Black Awakening in Capitalist America* (New York, Doubleday, 1969), p. 132.
31. Ibid., pp. 155–158.

7. Separatist Ideologies, II

1. Bobby G. Seale, *Seize the Time: The Story of the Black Panther Party and Huey P. Newton* (New York, Vintage Books, 1970). Gene Marine, *The Black Panthers* (New York, Signet Books, 1969).
2. Taken from *The Black Panther*, 4, No. 29 (January 16, 1971), 17.
3. Philip S. Foner, *The Black Panthers Speak* (Philadelphia, Lippincott, 1970), pp. xvii–xviii.
4. Ibid.
5. Huey P. Newton, "The Black Panthers," *Ebony*, 24, No. 10 (August 1969), p. 110.
6. "Huey Newton Talks to the Movement about the Black Panther Party, Cultural Nationalism, SNCC, Liberals and White Revolutionaries," *The Movement* (August 1968), p. 4 (pamphlet).
7. Ibid.
8. Sanche de Gramont, "Our Other Man in Algiers," *New York Times Magazine* (November 1, 1970), p. 112.
9. "Huey Newton Talks to the Movement," p. 5.
10. Eldridge Cleaver, "The Land Question and Black Liberation," in Robert Scheer, ed., *Eldridge Cleaver, Post Prison Writings and Speeches* (New York, Vintage Books, 1969), p. 57.
11. Ibid., p. 69.
12. Huey Newton in *Black Liberation News*, Vol. 1, No. 5 (1969), 7.
13. Eldridge Cleaver, "An Open Letter to Stokely Carmichael," in Philip S. Foner, *The Black Panthers Speak*, pp. 105–106.
14. Robert A. Jones, *The Nation* (August 11, 1969), p. 102.
15. *The Black Panther* (August 30, 1969), p. 13.
16. Ibid. (August 9, 1969), p. 12.
17. Ibid., p. 13.
18. "Young Lords Party Position on the Black Panther Party," *Palante*,

Vol. 3, No. 3 (February 1971), (the national organ of the Young Lords Party).

19. "Wanted by YLP: Luis A. Ferre," *Palante*, 3, No. 4 (March 5-19, 1971), 24. (Ferre was the Governor of Puerto Rico who wanted Puerto Rico to become a state. The YLP opposed the idea as "amerikkan imperialism." Puerto Ricans rejected the Ferre-backed referendum on statehood in the November elections, 1972. They voted to keep dominion status—but not Ferre. He was soundly defeated.)

20. See John Sinclair, *Message to the People of the Woodstock Nation* (Ministry of Information, White Panther Party, Ann Arbor, Michigan), 1970.

21. *The Black Panther* (September 27, 1969), pp. 10-11.

22. Huey P. Newton, "Address at Syracuse University" (March 1971), from notes taken by the author.

23. Cleaver in Scheer, pp. 57-72.

24. Draper, *The Rediscovery of Black Nationalism*, pp. 137-138.

25. From Robert Sherrill, "Interview with Milton Henry," *Esquire* (January 1969), p. 73.

26. Parts of the following account of the Henry brothers are taken from Ernest Dunbar, "The Making of a Militant," *Saturday Review* (December 16, 1972), pp. 25-32.

27. Seen in August Meier, Elliott Rudwick, and Frances L. Broderick, eds., *Black Protest Thought in the Twentieth Century* (2nd ed., Indianapolis, Bobbs-Merrill, 1971), pp. 361-372.

28. Robert S. Browne, "A Case for Separatism," in Robert S. Browne and Bayard Rustin, *Separatism or Integration: Which Way for America? A Dialogue* (New York, A. Philip Randolph Educational Fund, 1968), pp. 7-15.

29. Sherrill, pp. 73, 75.

8. Separatist Economic Programs

1. Essien-Udom, *Black Nationalism*, pp. 183-193.

2. Muhammad, *Message to the Black Man in America*, pp. 200-201.

3. Essien-Udom, p. 189.

4. Roy Innis, "Separatist Economics: A New Social Contract," in William F. Haddad and Douglas Pugh, eds., *Black Economic Development* (Englewood Cliffs, N.J., Prentice-Hall, 1969), pp. 50-59.

5. Alex Poinsett, "CORE Leader Champions Black Separatist Program," *Ebony*, 24, No. 12 (1969), 174-176.

6. For the following account of Cleveland CORE's economic proposal I am indebted to William L. Henderson and Larry C. Ledebur, *Economic Disparity: Problems and Strategies for Black America* (New York, Free Press, 1970), pp. 89-97. The authors suggest that CORE's economic philosophy was based on the work of Lewis Kelso and Mortimer Adler, *The Capitalist Manifesto* and *The New Capitalists* (New York, Random House, both 1961).

7. George Breitman, ed., *Malcolm X Speaks: Selected Speeches and Statements* (New York, Grove Press, 1965), p. 10.

8. Ibid., p. 50. (Italics added.)

9. Ibid., p. 226.

10. Ibid., p. 121.

11. Ibid., p. 89.
12. Quotation from Allen, *Black Awakening in Capitalist America*, p. 209.
13. Ibid., p. 211.
14. Carmichael and Hamilton, *Black Power*, pp. 172–173.
15. The 1850's also witnessed the formation of a black political party in New York City. It never had much of an impact, for a number of reasons. Similarly, in 1972 in Gary, Indiana, and in 1974 in Little Rock, Arkansas, some participants in the Black Political Convention called unsuccessfully for a Black Political Party.
16. Eldridge Cleaver, "The Land Question," *Ramparts*, 6 (May 1968), 51–53.
17. Henderson and Ledebur, p. 69.
18. Ibid.
19. "The Black Scholar Interviews Bobby Seale," *Black Scholar*, 4, No. 1 (1972), 10–12.
20. Dunbar, "The Making of a Militant," *Saturday Review*, p. 32. (Italics in the original.)
21. Quoted in David Llorens, "Black Separatism in Perspective," *Ebony*, 23, No. 11 (September 1968), 95.
22. Quotation from private correspondence with Milton R. Henry.
23. See Boris I. Bittker, *The Case for Black Reparations* (New York, Vintage Books, 1973), and Arnold Schuchter, *Reparations: The Black Manifesto and Its Challenge to White America* (Philadelphia, Lippincott, 1970).
24. See "Accomplishments of the Muslims" (pamphlet, n.d.).
25. *Muhammad Speaks*, 14 (July 18, 1975), 2.
26. Ibid., pp. 4, S-1, S-4, 28.
27. William Brashler, "Black on Black: The Deadly Struggle for Power," *New York Magazine*, 8 (June 9, 1975), 49.
28. CORE Annual Report, 1973/74.
29. Ibid.
30. See Robert Alex Zander, "Centralized Coordination of Economic Acitivity in Urban Ghettoes: A Case for the Community Development Corporation," Senior Fellowship Thesis, Dartmouth College (1975).

9. Interrelations and Comparisons

1. Zinn, *SNCC: The New Abolitionists*, p. 41.
2. Ibid., p. 48
3. Ibid., p. 57.
4. Ibid., p. 211.
5. Ibid., p. 213.
6. Ibid., p. 275.
7. Len Holt makes the point that the name COFO dates back to the spring of 1961 when Medgar Evers, an NAACP field secretary, was shot in the back by a white man (who was found not guilty). Dr. Aaron Henry, who headed the Mississippi Freedom Democratic Party, and Carsie Hall, a Mississippi civil rights lawyer, and others formed the group to confer with Governor Ross Barnett to secure the release of a group of Freedom Riders. COFO was formed because it was felt that Barnett would not meet with older civil rights organizations. After the meeting with Barnett, COFO became a nonfunctioning organization. Robert Moses of

SNCC revived COFO in January of 1962. He, too, felt that only a unified effort would yield fruit in the struggle for freedom in Mississippi.

8. Len Holt, *The Summer That Didn't End* (New York, William Morrow, 1965), pp. 30-33.
9. Zinn, p. 263.
10. *Voting in Mississippi:* A Report of the U.S. Commission on Civil Rights, Washington, D.C. (May 1965), pp. 31-39, 56-91.
11. James Farmer in *Freedom—When?* asserts that he felt that to enhance the developing political consciousness of the MFDP it was expedient that he hold his counsel. Zinn pointed out, however, that Aaron Henry wanted to accept the compromise and asked his delegation to do so. The compromise was that two seats at large (not, bear in mind, a part of the "regular" delegation) be designated or added for Aaron Henry and Ed King, and the seating of every member of the racist delegation who were willing to support the national Democratic ticket. Prominent leaders of the civil rights movement argued that the compromise should be accepted. Among them were Martin Luther King, James Farmer, and Bayard Rustin (p. 255). McCord indicates that "the Mississippi white delegation left the convention upon hearing the news [of the proposed compromise.] A month later, they vowed their former loyalty to the Democratic Party. . . . With hardly a single dissent, however, the white Mississippi Democrats announced their support for Senator Goldwater for President." William McCord, *Mississippi: The Long Hot Summer* (New York, W. W. Norton, 1965), p. 117.
12. Farmer, p. 81.
13. *Meet the Press* (Washington, D.C., Merkle Press), Sunday, August 21, 1966, p. 10.
14. Ibid., p. 23.
15. Quoted in Harold Cruse, *Rebellion or Revolution?* (New York, William Morrow, 1968), p. 199.
16. Ibid., p. 200.
17. Bell, *CORE and the Strategy of Non-Violence,* p. 182.
18. Ibid., p. 185.
19. The Abolitionist Movement may be used as a case in point. Abolitionism was not regarded as a significant movement until white abolitionists became involved. Aside from Frederick Douglass, one who cannot be ignored under any circumstance, who were other prominent black abolitionists? There were many. See Benjamin Quarles, *The Black Abolitionists* (New York, Oxford University Press, 1969). Another example is having white presidents or "leaders" of black organizations oriented toward the attainment of equal or civil rights. Imagine Roy Wilkins or Huey Newton "leading" the Italian-American Civil Rights League or the German-American Bund!
20. Robert L. Allen, *Black Awakening in Capitalist America* (New York, Doubleday, 1969), p. 154n.
21. "Cleaver Discusses Revolution: An Interview from Exile," in Foner, ed., *The Black Panthers Speak*, pp. 108-109.
22. Ibid.
23. Meier, Rudwick, and Broderick, *Black Protest Thought in the Twentieth Century*, pp. 387-412.
24. See also observations made by Bell, *CORE and the Strategy of Non-violence*, pp. 46-50, 100, 113, 187-188.
25. Ibid., p. 48.

26. Louis Lomax, *When The Word Is Given* (New York, Signet Books, 1964), p. 89.
27. Ibid., p. 86.
28. See "Manifesto to the White Christian Churches and the Jewish Synagogues of America and all other Racist Institutions." Presentation by James Forman Delivered and Adopted by the National Black Economic Development Conference in Detroit, Michigan, on April 26, 1969," leaflet.
29. Lester, *Revolutionary Notes*, p. 144.
30. Stokely Carmichael, "Pan-Africanism—Land and Power," *The Black Scholar*, Vol. I, No. 1 (1969), p. 38.
31. Carmichael, *Stokely Speaks: Black Power to Pan-Africanism*, p. 188.
32. Cleaver in Scheer, p. 14.
33. Ibid., p. 15.
34. Ibid., pp. 16–17.
35. Ibid., pp. 64–65.
36. Notes taken by me.
37. See Malcolm X, *The Autobiography of Malcolm X* (New York, Grove Press, 1964–65), p. 387. Eldridge Cleaver, *Soul on Ice* (New York, McGraw-Hill, 1968), pp. 50–61.
38. Elijah Muhammad, *Message to the Black Man*, p. 102. (Italics added.)
39. Ibid., pp. 315–316.
40. Huey Newton, "To the R.N.A.," *The Black Panther* (December 6, 1969), in Foner, *The Black Panthers Speak*, pp. 70–73.
41. This speech was made in honor of the impending return of Robert Williams, then president of the RNA. Williams resigned from that honorary position.
42. Lee Lockwood, ed., *Conversation with Eldridge Cleaver in Algiers* (New York, Delta Books, 1970), p. 109.

10. Changes and the Movement Organizations

1. For an excellent discussion of transformation of social movement organizations, see Mayer N. Zaid and Roberta Ash, "Social Movement Organizations: Growth, Decay and Change," in Barry McLaughlin, ed., *Social Movements: A Social-Psychological Perspective* (New York, Free Press, 1969), pp. 461–485.
2. Lewis M. Killian, *The Impossible Revolution? Black Power and The American Dream* (New York, Random House, 1968), p. 109.
3. Ibid., p. 88.
4. Ibid., p. 89.
5. Ibid.
6. Charles Silberman, *Crisis in Black and White* (New York, Random House, 1964), p. 8.
7. Anthony Oberschall, *Social Conflict and Social Movements* (Englewood Cliffs, N.J., Prentice-Hall, 1973), p. 237.
8. Makeba's popularity among whites plunged dramatically after she married Carmichael. Apparently whites find it difficult to differentiate between entertainment and politics when it comes to "militant" blacks.
9. See Kwame Nkrumah, *Neo-Colonialism: The Last Stage of Imperialism* (New York, International Publishers, 1965).

10. Julian Bond, "A Black Southern Strategy," in Nathan Wright, ed., *What Black Politicians Are Saying* (New York, Hawthorne Books, 1972), pp. 139-142.
11. The census data indeed suggests that the age differentials between whites and blacks at the time of death is significant. Although the life expectancy of whites is approaching the mid-seventies, for blacks it is around the mid-sixties. Variables such as housing, food (nutrition), types of employment, mental anguish, etc., should be taken into the life expectancy equation and treated as causal variables in black-white death differentials.
12. See Alex Poinsett, "CORE Leader Champions Black Separatist Program," *Ebony*, 24, No. 12 (1969), pp. 174-176.
13. Edward Brown, "CORE and Garveyism," *CORE*, 3, No. 3 (1973), p. 41.
14. Ibid., p. 55.
15. Charles White, "Desegregation and the Richmond Story," *CORE*, 2, No. 3 (1972), p. 7.
16. Ibid., p. 62.
17. Major, *A Panther Is a Black Cat*, (New York, William Morrow, 1971), pp. 271-272. See also Major's Appendix E, "Chronology" of Panther persecution by police, pp. 296-302.
18. For example, nonviolent resistance remained an operating tactic in the South much longer than it did in the North and on the East and West Coasts. There are other significant differences, such as type(s) of control used by constituted authority. Movements considered by constituted authorities to be dangerous must contend with political surveillance as well as other forms of control techniques, including coercive power. Therefore, what works as a strategy in one part of the country may not work in others.
19. See "Enemies of the People," *The Black Panther*, 6, No. 3 (February 13, 1971), pp. 12-13.
20. "Black Panther Party Undergoes Major Split," *The Black Voice*, 4, No. 4 (March 10, 1971), p. 1.
21. Ibid., p. 1.
22. *New York Times* (April 10, 1971), p. 24.
23. "The Black Scholar Interviews Bobby Seale," *The Black Scholar*, 4, No. 1 (1972), pp. 13-15.
24. One group of cultural nationalism sees whites as the oppressor and does not distinguish between racist and nonracist whites. Moreoever, these cultural nationalists suggest that a black man cannot be an enemy of the people. The Panthers, though believing in black nationalism and black culture, do not believe that emphasizing black culture alone can bring about black liberation. They believe that the system is the oppressor.
25. Seale, *Seize the Time*, esp. pp. 59-84.
26. *The Black Scholar*, 4, No. 1 (September 1972), p. 15.
27. The following account of Brother Imari's position is taken from a letter he wrote to Ernest Dunbar and is published by Dunbar in "The Making of a Militant," *Saturday Review* (December 16, 1972), pp. 25-32.
28. Georgie Anne Geyer, "The Odyssey of Robert Williams," *New Republic*, 164 (1971), p. 14.
29. Ibid.

30. Raymond S. Franklin and Solomon Resnik, *The Political Economy of Racism* (New York, Holt, Rinehart and Winston, 1973), pp. 115–116.

11. Separatism: Catalyst for Change

1. Harold Cruse, *Rebellion or Revolution*, p. 213. (Emphasis mine.)
2. Amy Jacques Garvey, ed., *Philosophy and Opinions of Marcus Garvey*, p. 22.
3. Elijah Muhammad, *Message to the Black Man*, p. 174.
4. Nathan Wright, *Black Power and Urban Unrest* (New York, Hawthorn Publishers, 1967). So did Floyd McKissick.
5. Harold Cruse, *The Crisis of The Negro Intellectual*, p. 429. Cruse also makes the point that West Indians assume a militant posture once in the United States notwithstanding their oppressed condition in their native lands.
6. "Mississippi Bars A Black Nation," *New York Times* (May 9, 1971).
7. Private correspondence with Milton Henry.
8. Charles V. Willie, "Planned Parenthood or Black Genocide: A Position Paper," in Raymond L. Hall, ed., *Black Separatism and Social Reality* (New York, Pergamon Press, 1977), Part VI. Quoted with author's permission.
9. U.S. Department of Labor, *The Negro Family* (Washington, D.C., Government Printing Office, 1965), p. 29.
10. Willie, "Planned Parenthood or Black Genocide: A Position Paper" in Raymond L. Hall, ed., *Black Separatism and Social Reality*.
11. For a provocative discussion of genocide, see Robert G. Weisbord, *Genocide? Birth Control and the Black American* (Westport, Conn., Greenwood Press, 1975).

12. Conclusions

1. W. E. B. DuBois, *Dusk of Dawn*, chap. 7.
2. Shirley Graham DuBois, *His Day Is Marching On* (Philadelphia, Lippincott, 1971), see chaps. 17, 18.
3. Pointing up how Jewish people have utilized the educational system to enhance their position, and how blacks have been denied the use of this avenue, is one way of highlighting the importance of using the system to promote group urban survival. It also highlights a very important point alluded to through the above discussion: becoming an important part of the urban social system requires having a valued commodity (material or knowledge) that, if withheld or withdrawn, would cause the total system unacceptable inconvenience or shut it down altogether. This is not to suggest that the withdrawal of Jewish expertise would shut down the total urban system, but in some, for example New York City where most of the nation's Jews are concentrated, their withdrawal would cause inconvenience to say the least. What if Harlem's two million blacks "withdrew" from participation in the system?
4. Imari Obadele, "The Struggle Is For Land," *The Black Scholar* (February 1972), p. 31.

5. See Brunetta Reid Wolfman, "Black First, Female Second," in Raymond L. Hall, ed., *Black Separatism and Racial Reality*, part VI.
6. "The Irrepressible Envoy from Ghana," *Ebony*, Vol. XXXVI, No. 1 (November 1970), 74, *passim*.
7. Ibid.
8. S. Jay Walker, "Black Studies: Phase Two," in Raymond L. Hall, ed., *Black Separatism and Social Reality: Rhetoric and Reason* (New York, Pergamon Publisers, 1977).
9. Sidney Wilhelm, *Who Needs the Negro?* (Garden City, N.Y., Doubleday, 1971), p. 334.

INDEX

Abolitionists: abolition movement, 25; emigrationism, 24–25; opposition to, 25, 29; platforms, 24, 29, 33; separation, 26, 27
ACS. *See* American Colonization Society
African Blood Brotherhood, 73
African Colonization Church, 14
African Diaspora, 3, 204, 254
African emigration conventions, 40, 41
African Legion, 62, 129
African Methodist Episcopal Church (AME), 34, 35
African nationalism, 67
African Orthodox Church, 62
African People's Revolutionary Party, 204
African Times and Orient Review, 55, 58
African Trading Company, 41
African Union Company, 55
Africans: Christianity, 22; self-determination, 21
Afro-American Council, 48. *See also* Afro-American League
Afro-American League, 47–48
Akim Trading Company, Ltd., 54
Alabama, University of, 234
Al Azhar University (Egypt), 186
Ali, Duse Muhammad, 55, 58
Ali, F. Mohammad (Wali Farrad, Wallace Fard, W. D. Fard), 88–89, 97, 101, 102. *See also* Nation of Islam
Ali, Muhammad, 219
Ali, Noble Drew (Timothy Drew), 87–88, 97–98
Allah, 98, 100–101, 107
Allen, Richard, 23
AME. *See* African Methodist Episcopal Church
American and West African Steamship Company, 41
American Civil Liberties Union, 192
American Colonization Society (ACS), 35, 36; Abraham Lincoln, 29; beginnings, 24; criticism of, 34; resurgence of, 28, 29, 30
American Dental Association, 9
American Medical Association, 9
American Moral Reform Society, 26
American Negro Labor Congress (ANLC), 79
American Sociological Association, 9
Amin, Idi, 207, 208
Anderson, Charles W., 47
ANLC. *See* American Negro Labor Congress
Appeal in Four Articles, 25, 27
Armstrong, General S. C., 42, 43
Ashwood, Amy, 59
Associated Press, 64
Association for the Study of Negro Life and History, 48

Atlanta exposition speech, 44
Atlanta University Conference
  (1899), 50
Attucks, Crispus, 22, 47
Autobiography of Malcolm X, 193–
  194

Back-to-Africa movement: belief
  in, 28–29, 36, 49, 71; criticism
  of, 36; failures, 33, 39, 40, 41,
  54; Liberia, 24, 28, 30, 32, 39,
  40, 41; reasons behind, 29, 32,
  36, 39; separatist modes of, 33.
  See also International Migration
  Society
Back-to-Islam. *See* Nation of Islam
Baker, Ella, 109
Balalia News, 218
Baptist Church of America, 23
Baraka, Ameer, 193
Barry, Marion, 109
Bell, Inge Powell, 174, 175
Bella, Ahmed Ben, 125–126
Bethel Baptist Church (Detroit),
  220
Bilbo, Theodore, 86
Bilbo Negro Repatriation Bill, 86
Black capitalism, 121, 167, 173,
  182, 187, 191; black community,
  162; Eldridge Cleaver, 176–
  177; Marcus Garvey, 61, 63, 71,
  73, 74. *See also* Black Panther
  Party, Capitalism, Congress of
  Racial Equality, Nation of Islam,
  Republic of New Africa, Student
  Non-Violent Coordinating Com-
  mittee
Black churches, 79, 214; African
  Colonization Church, 41; African
  Methodist Episcopal Church
  (AME), 34, 35; African Orthodox
  Church, 62; Baptist Church of
  America, 23; Bethel Baptist
  Church (Detroit), 220; Mother
  Bethel African Methodist Episco-
  pal Church, 23; St. George's
  Methodist Episcopal Church, 23
Black colonization: Ethiopia, 41;
  failure of, 56; Liberia, 41–42
Black community: American econ-
  omy, 248; black capitalism, 162;

black church, 214; black genocide, 35; Black Panther Party,
  124, 163, 211, 212, 214–215;
  black political parties, 28; black
  separatist movements, 164;
  boycotting, 86, 93; central cities,
  246–247; colonization, 28;
  community control, 2, 3, 103,
  104, 179, 180–181, 192; Democratic vote, 83, 84; disenfranchised vote, 111, 171; education,
  38; failure of Communist party,
  77, 79, 84, 85, 93, 150; identity
  with United States, 24, 25, 36,
  37; Jewish community, 135–136;
  New Deal, 84; political exclusion,
  54; post-Civil War period, 38–39;
  self-determination, 21, 36; SNCC,
  113, 115, 116, 117, 170, 206–
  207; as a swing vote, 28; urban-
  ization, 67, 72, 243, 248; voter
  registration, 113, 169; voting
  rights, 27, 30, 31, 51, 85. *See also*
  Congress of Racial Equality.
Black convention movement, 26,
  27, 48; Colored National Convention of 1853, 28; Convention
  of 1843, 27; Convention of 1847,
  27; Convention of 1920, 61,
  62–63, 66; Convention of 1921,
  64
Black Cross Nurses, 62
Black culture, 2, 27, 134. *See also*
  Black community
Black Eagle Flying Corps, 62
Black Economic Research Center
  (New York City), 134
Black family, 236–238
Black genocide, 35, 120, 134, 135,
  152, 176, 236–239, 254
Black House, San Francisco, 125
Black journals. *See under* names of
  publications
Black Legion, 129–130, 136–137,
  219–220
Black Liberation Army, 164
Black middle class, 67, 86, 135,
  153, 155, 246, 250; black organ-
  izations, 76; Black Panther Party,
  153; black separatism, 164;
  Communist Party, 78, 79, 80;

Black middle class (*cont.*)
Malcolm X, 108; Nation of Islam, 102; united against oppression, 91

Black Muslims. *See* Nation of Islam

Black Nation, 167

Black nationalism: appeal of, 179; definition, 1, 2, 3; Floyd McKissick, 227–228; Marcus Garvey, 66; W. E. B. DuBois, 87, 93; white reaction, 179

Black newspapers: *African Times and Orient Review*, 55, 58; *Balalia News*, 218; *Boston Guardian*, 53; *Crisis*, 65, 68; *Crusader*, 63; *Defender* (Chicago), 63; *Freedom's Journal*, 24–25, 26; *Michigan Chronicle*, 131; *Muhammad Speaks*, 140, 160–161, 183, 218, 226, 227; *Negro World*, 60, 62, 68, 81; *New York Age*, 47–48; *The North Star*, 33; *Our Own*, 58; *Rights of All*, 25, 26; *The Voice of the People*, 40

Black Panther Party: alliances, 127–128; appeal of, 138, 176; banning of New York chapter, 212–213; black church, 214; black community, 124, 163, 211, 212, 214–215; black middle class, 153; Black Panther symbol, 113, 124; black power concept, 152, 187; black separatism, 123, 194–195; Bobby Seale, 113, 123, 124, 127, 210, 210, 212–214, 216–217; capitalism, 187, 192, 195; changes within, 211–212, 222; Communist Party, 128; community control, 124–125, 127; CORE, 123, 175–177; economic program, 151–154, 159, 163–164; Eldridge Cleaver, 125, 189, 190, 201; founding of, 113, 123, 124, 200, 209–210, 246; Huey Newton, 113, 123, 125, 189, 201, 210, 212, 213; ideology, 7, 8, 123, 125–126, 128, 151, 217, 229–230, 235; internal colonialism, 126, 128; leadership, 124, 190, 201, 210, 212; Lowndes County Freedom Organization, 124; Malcolm X, 193–194; Marxist-Leninist position, 150, 152, 188, 215–216; membership, 125, 127, 128, 129, 163, 211, 216; Nation of Islam, 123, 191–194; origins, 187; Pan-Africanism, 215–216; Panther Breakfast for Children Program, 214; reparations, 152, 158–159; Richard Nixon, 127, 191, 229; RNA, 194–195; SDS, 128; self-defense, 124, 125, 175, 176, 177, 194; SNCC, 123, 124, 127, 176, 187–191; socialism, 126–127; split in Party, 212–217; Stokely Carmichael, 188, 190; tactics, 8; uniform, 210, 214–215; United Black Fund, 154; voting registration, 153–154, 216–217; white membership, 233

Black Panther Party for Self-Defense, 124. *See also* Black Panther Party

Black power: Black Panther Party, 152, 187; constituted authority, 229; CORE, 117, 118, 119, 121, 176, 181–182, 227; definition, 134, 203; development of, 173; Eldridge Cleaver, 127, 213–215, 217; Floyd McKissick, 117, 181; inception of, 127; Malcolm X, 9, 116; Nation of Islam, 186; SNCC, 9, 115, 116, 127, 184, 186, 201, 207. *See also* Carmichael, Stokely; Congress of Racial Equality; Hamilton, Charles V.; Student Non-Violent Coordinating Committee

Black Power Conference (1967), 228

Black Power Movement, 114

Black separatism: appeal of, 241; as an alternative, 56, 254–255; black community, 164; Black Panther Party, 123, 194–195; capitalism, 157–158; Communist Party, 75, 77, 78, 79, 85; competition among movements, 167; contemporary history, 4, 94;

Black separatism (*cont.*)
criticism of black bourgeoisie,
250; definition, 2, 3, 12-13;
development of, 29, 33, 108;
historical roots, 18, 85, 86;
Huey Newton, 194-195; ideology, 108, 166-167; membership, 250-251; Pan-Africanism,
251-254; political equality, 247-
248; reasons for, 23, 29, 32, 35;
sex discrimination, 250; support
of, 35; theoretical considerations,
9-11; urban program, 245-246;
urbanism, 244-249; white capitalism, 157-158; white reaction,
29
Black separatist movement: as an
alternative, 232-235, 240; black
community, 164; black survival,
235-239; catalyst for change,
231-232, 239-240; cultural
independence, 235; definition,
225; values, 232. *See also* Separatist movement
Black Star Line, 61, 63-64, 75
Black studies, 9, 252-254
Black United Front, 189-190. *See
also* Black Panther Party, Carmichael, Stokely
Black Zionism, 76, 78. *See also*
Zionism
Blyden, Edward W., 35, 36, 37, 54,
56, 71, 241
Bolsheviks, 77
Bond, Julian, 9, 110, 205-206
Boston Guardian, 53
Boston Massacre, 22
Bourgeois reformism, 1, 2. *See also*
Black nationalism
Boynton Case, 168
Briggs, Cyril, 63, 73, 75
Brooke, Edward, 252
Brown, Elaine, 217
Brown, H. "Rap", 9, 116, 148,
188, 201, 206
Brown, James, 6
Brown, John, 29
Brown, Oscar C., 86
Brown vs. Topeka (1954), 93-94
Browne, Robert S., 134-136
Bulis, J. C., 40

Bunche, Ralph, 91
Butler Bill (1892), 35, 36, 41

California, University of (Berkeley), 174
Capitalism, 159-160, 162, 165; of
Black Panther Party, 187, 192,
195; black separatism, 157-158;
Marcus Garvey, 75; Stokely
Carmichael, 149. *See also* Black
capitalism
Carey, Gordon, 168
Carmichael, Stokely: African
People's Revolutionary Party,
204; Black Panthers, 188, 190;
call for black power, 6, 152, 170,
187, 191, 205; on capitalism,
149; on colonialism, 115-116;
constituted authority, 169;
expelled from SNCC, 189, 204;
Huey Newton, 190-191; Marxism, 150; Pan-Africanism, 204;
Parchman Mississippi Penitentiary, 168; power, 233; self-
defense, 173; SNCC, 5, 9, 110,
112, 148, 151, 172, 189, 200-
201, 204-205. *See also* Black
Power, Student Non-Violent
Coordinating Committee
Carter, Jimmy, 206
Castro, Fidel, 137, 223
CDC. *See* Community development
corporation
Central Intelligence Agency, 191
Century magazine, 55
Chaney, James, 6, 111
CHAP. *See* Committee to Help Aid
Prisoners
Chapman, Samuel, 39-40
Charles, Ray, 110
Chilembwe, John, 66
China, and RNA, 137
Chiriqui Project for Colonization,
30
Christian Pacifist Fellowship of
Reconciliation, 121. *See also*
Fellowship of Reconciliation
Civil Rights, erosion of, 38
Civil Rights Bill (9164), 200
Civil Rights Movement, 97, 107,
108-112, 117, 234. *See also*

Civil Rights Movement (*cont.*)
Congress of Racial Equality,
Student Non-Violent Coordinating Committee
Civil War, 24, 28, 30-31, 32, 34,
37, 137; black soldiers, 47;
slavery, 29, 35, 152
Clark, James, 173
Cleaver, Eldridge: black capitalism, 176-177; Black Muslims,
192, 193; Black Panther Party,
125, 189, 190, 201; black power,
127; in exile, 212; Huey Newton,
213-214, 217; internal colonialism, 126, 152; reparations, 193;
RNA, 195; SNCC, 188; split in
Black Panther Party, 213-215,
217; Zionists, 129
Cleaver, Kathleen, 213
COFO. *See* Council of Federated
Organizations
Collective behavior theory, 9-11,
17
Colleges and universities: Al-Azhar
University (Egypt), 186; University of Alabama, 234; University of California, Berkeley, 174;
Cornell University, 177; Fairleigh
Dickinson University, 134;
Fisk University, 109; University
of Islam, 88, 140; Lincoln University, 80, 130, 132; Morehouse
College, 119; University of North
Carolina Law School, 119;
University of Ottawa, 131; San
Francisco Law School, 124; Shaw
University (Raleigh, N. C.), 109;
Temple University, 131; Yale
University School of Law, 130
Colonization: black community,
28; British interests, 36; French
interests, 36; Haiti, 30; Isthmus
of Panama, 30; Liberia, 36;
rejection of, 30; Third World,
115-116. *See also* Chiriqui Project for Colonization, Internal
colonialism, Liberia
Colored National Emigration
Association, 40
Columbus, Christopher, 101
Committee to Help Aid Prisoners

(CHAP), 162-163
Communist Party: appeal to black
intellectuals, 76, 79-80, 81, 129;
beginnings in U. S., 75-76; black
church, 79; black middle class,
78, 79, 80; Black Panther Party,
128; black separatism, 75, 77, 78,
79, 85; black/white workers, 75,
76, 79, 85; Comintern Congress
(1928), 77, 81; Communist
International (Comintern), 75-76, 78, 81, 85; failure in black
community, 77, 79, 84, 85, 93,
150; Marcus Garvey, 73, 75, 76,
78, 85, 93, 226; National Negro
Congress, 91, 92; Negro nation,
77, 78, 79; policy proposals, 77-79, 82-83; publicity campaigns,
81, 82; UNIA, 76-77
Community development corporation, (CDC), 145
Community Self-Development
Act, 146, 147
Compromise of 1850, 28, 29, 33
Compromise of 1877, 32, 38
Congress of Racial Equality
(CORE): African-Afro-American
relationship, 207-208; Baltimore
National Convention, 119, 120;
black capitalism, 119, 120, 121,
227-228; black community, 142-143, 147, 172, 176, 181, 182,
183, 184, 208-209, 247-248;
Black Panther Party, 123, 175-177; black power, 117, 118, 119,
121, 126, 181-182, 227; changes
within, 118, 121, 227-228;
Cincinnati convention (1968),
120; Cleveland Economic Proposal, 144-145; Committee to
Help Aid Prisoners (CHAP), 162-163; community programs, 4,
162-163; cultural model, 235;
direct-action tactics, 167, 170,
172; economic philosophy, 142-148, 150, 154, 157, 159, 162-163; Floyd B. McKissick, 119-120, 161, 172, 182, 210;
founded, 92, 93, 94, 108, 116,
118, 246; Freedom Rides, 92-93;
ideology, 7-8, 116-117, 135,

Congress of Racial Equality (*cont.*)
200, 228; integration, 117, 118,
178; internal colonialism, 162;
James Farmer, 92, 110, 117–119,
121, 168; 172, 177, 178, 181,
182; magazine *CORE*, 162, 163;
Malcolm X, 181; membership, 92,
97, 118, 119, 120, 121, 167, 168,
176, 183–184; Nation of Islam,
118, 177–183; National convention (1966), 177, 181; National
convention (1968), 176; New
York City Board of Education,
120–121; Pan-Africanism, 121,
207, 253; Project Uganda, 207;
RNA, 123, 183–184; Roy Innis,
118, 120–121, 122, 142, 145–
147, 173, 207, 227–228; school
desegregation plan, 208–209;
SNCC, 121, 167–175; tactics,
109, 110, 111, 167; Unitary
School Plan, 208–209; W. E. B.
DuBois, 228; white member-
ship, 5, 233
Conshankin, Bishop, 86
Coolidge, President Calvin, 66
CORE. *See* Congress of Racial
Equality
Cornell University, 177
Cornish, Samuel E., 24, 25, 26
Costa Rica, 30
Cotton States Exposition (1895),
43; Speech, 38, 43–44, 231
Council of Federated Organiza-
tions (COFO), 111, 171
Cox, Courtland, 148
Cox, Don, 212, 213
CP, CPUS. *See* Communist Party
Crisis, 65, 68
Crummell, Alexander, 28, 241
Crusader, 63
Cruse, Harold, 57
Cuffee (Cuffe), Paul, 24, 56
Cultural nationalism, 1, 2, 125,
167; Marcus Garvey, 70, 71.
See also Black nationalism

Daddy Grace, 86
Daley, Mayor Richard J., 161
Darrow, Clarence, 81
Davis, Benjamin, Jr., 79

Deacons for Defense and Justice,
180
Deane, Captain Harry, 41
Debrah, Ebenezer M., 251–252
Declaration of Independence, 8
Defender (Chicago), 63
Delany, Martin R., 28, 33–34, 36,
37, 54, 241
Democratic National Convention:
(1964), 4–5, 111, 112–113,
171–172, 173, 228; (1968), 205
Dennis, Dave, 171
Department of Health, Education,
and Welfare, 163
Department of Justice, 110, 169
Department of Labor, 163
Depression, 80, 85, 86, 93
Diggs, Charles C., Jr., 252
Domino, "Fats," 110
Donaldson, Ivanhoe, 173, 206
Douglas, Emory, 213
Douglass, Frederick, 27, 28, 29, 33,
38; (ship), 61
Draper, Theodore, 33
Dred Scott Decision of 1857, 29
Drew, Timothy. *See* Ali, Noble
Drew
DuBois, W. E. B.: black national-
ism, 87, 93; Booker T. Washing-
ton, 47, 49–50, 51, 52, 53, 54,
242; Congress of Racial Equality,
228; early years, 52; educational
philosophy, 50, 51, 113; emigra-
tionism, 54; Marcus Garvey, 65,
68, 72; NAACP, 50, 51, 53, 69,
73, 87, 242; Niagara Movement,
51, 53, 231–232; Pan-Africanism,
253; Pan-Negro Congress, 54;
philosophy, 87, 242; popularity
with militants, 57; Republic of
New Africa, 191
Dunbar, Ernest, 222
Dusk of Dawn, 87, 242. *See also*
DuBois, W. E. B.
Duvalier, "Papa Doc," 125
Dylan, Bob, 6

Ebony magazine, 125, 228
Economic nationalism, 1, 2. *See
also* Black nationalism, Congress
of Racial Equality

Education. *See* Black studies
Ellis, W. H., 41
El-Shabazz, El-Hajj Malik. *See* Malcolm X
Emancipation Proclamation of 1863, 25, 30, 42
Emigrationism: abolitionists, 24–25; Booker T. Washington, 54, 55, 253; Butler Bill, 35; Caribbean, 29; decline of, 30; despair over, 32, 37; early black efforts, 23–24, 34, 35, 38, 40–42, 56; failures of, 33, 36, 70; from the South, 33; Latin America, 29; Liberia, 30, 64; low profile of, 49, 54; opposition to, 25; reasons for, 38, 56; re-emergence of, 32; sentiments for, 57; slavery, 24, 30; W. E. B. DuBois, 54. *See also* Back-to-Africa movement, Garvey, Marcus; International Migration Society, Pan-Africanism
Emigration organizations: African Trading Company, 41; American and West African Steamship Company, 41; Colored National Emigration Association, 40; Liberian Colonization Society, 40; Liberian Emigration Clubs, 39; Liberian Trading and Emigration Association of the United States, 41; New York and Liberia Steamship Company, 41
Equal Rights League, 30
Essien-Udom, E. U., 89, 141
Ethiopia, black colonization, 41
Ethiopian Peace Movement, 86
European Common Market, 155
Evers, Medgar, 169

Fair Employment Practices Commission (FEPC), 91
Fairfield Herald (South Carolina), 31
Fairleigh Dickinson University, 134
Fard, Prophet Wallace. *See* Ali, F. Muhammad
Fard, W. D. *See* Ali, F. Muhammad
Farmer, James: internal colonialism, 15; Malcolm X, 180;

National Director of CORE, 92, 110, 117–119, 121, 168, 172, 177, 178, 181, 182; Freedom Rides, 169; Nixon administration, 177, 182, 183
Farrad, Wali. *See* Ali, F. Muhammad
Farrakhan, Louis, 219
Father Divine, 86
Federal Bureau of Investigation, 130
Federal Housing Act, 146
Fellowship of Reconciliation (FOR), 92, 118, 121, 167
FEPC. *See* Fair Employment Practices Commission
Firestone family, 73
Firestone Rubber Company, 65
Fisk University, 109
Flummer, Daniel J., 39, 40, 41
FOI. *See* Fruit of Islam
FOR. *See* Christian Pacifist Fellowship of Reconciliation
Ford, James W., 79, 83
Forman, James, 110, 116, 148, 151, 186, 188, 205
Fortune, T. Thomas, 47
Fourteenth Amendment, 31
Frazier, E. Franklin, 250
Free African Society, 23
Free Speech Movement, 174
Freedman's Bureau, 32
Freedom Now Party (1963–64), 4
Freedom Rides, 92–93, 110, 167, 168, 169
Freedom—When?, 117, 179. *See also* Farmer, James
Freedom's Journal, 24–25, 26
Fruit of Islam (FOI), 88, 105, 129, 182. *See also* Nation of Islam
Fugitive Slave Law, 28, 33

Gaidi. *See* Henry, Milton R.
Gaither, Tom, 168
Garnet, Henry Highland, 27, 28, 241
Garrison, William Lloyd, 25, 29
Garvey, Amy Jacques, 57, 65
Garvey, Marcus, 37, 191; African Legion, 129; appeal of, 60, 66–67, 76, 84; black capitalism, 61,

Garvey, Marcus (*cont.*)
63, 71, 73, 74; Black Convention
of 1920, 61, 62–63, 66; Black
Convention of 1921, 64; black
land, 126; Black Star Line, 61,
63-64, 75; Booker T. Washington, 57, 59, 63, 66, 71, 72, 242–
243; call for black nationalism,
66; capitalism, 75; as charismatic
leader, 69–70, 74; Communist
Party, 73, 75, 76, 78, 85, 93,
226; CORE's ideology, 228;
critics of, 61, 64, 65, 68, 73, 75;
as cultural nationalist, 70, 71;
death of, 66; early life, 58–59,
70; economic philosophy, 63,
141, 142, 148, 149; Elijah
Muhammad, 97; failure in Liberia, 65; following, 60, 62, 74;
founding and growth of Universal Negro Improvement Association, 59, 60; in Harlem, 59–60;
ideology, 84, 226–227; Ku
Klux Klan, 68, 208; legal problems, 63–64, 65, 74; Nation of
Islam, 97, 98, 226–227; National
Club, 58; Negro Declaration of
Rights, 62, 66, 232; Negro
Factories Corporation, 63, 71,
73, 75; *Negro World*, 60, 62,
68; Noble Drew Ali, 88, *Our
Own*, 58; Pan-Africanism, 67–68,
70, 72, 121, 253; as Provisional
President of Africa, 62, 64; race
purity, 65, 67, 68–69, 76, 83;
reasons for failure, 65, 70–71,
73–74; Tuskegee Institute, 57,
59; union workers, 75; Univer-
sal Negro Improvement Associa-
tion, 68, 70, 71, 101, 227;
waning career, 65, 66, 70, 86;
W. E. B. DuBois, 65, 68, 72;
The Watchman, 58
Garveyism, 86, 93, 177, 206, 207,
208
Genius of Universal Emancipation,
25
Ghana, 54, 132
Ghana-Mali-Songhai era, 125
Ghandi, Mohandas, 92
GOAL. *See* Group on Advanced
Leadership

Goldwater, Barry, 170
Goodman, Andrew, 6, 111
Green power, 73–74
Grimke, Archibald, 54
Group on Advanced Leadership
(GOAL), 131–132

Haiti, 29, 30
Hamid, Suli Abdul (Bishop Con-
shankin), 86
Hamilton, Charles V., 115, 150–
151
Hampton, Wade, 34
Hampton Institute, 42, 43
Hare, Nathan, 250
Harlem, 86, 108, 120–121, 143,
172, 183, 200; Marcus Garvey in,
59–60; UNIA in, 59–60
Harlem Shadows, 81
Harlem Renaissance, 66, 79, 80,
81, 83, 93
Harper's Ferry, 29
Hartigan, Neil, 161
Hayes, Garfield, 81
Hayes, Rutherford B., 32
Haywood, Harry, 79
Hekima, Brother (Tom Norman),
221
Henry, Aaron, 171
Henry, Milton R. (Brother Gaidi
[Obadele]), 129–133, 136–
137, 155–156, 201, 219, 220–
222. *See also* Republic of New
Africa
Henry, Richard B. (Brother
Imari A. Obadele), 129–133,
154–155, 201, 219, 220–222,
246, 249. *See also* Republic of
New Africa
Herndon, Angelo, 82
Herzel, Theodor, 254–255
Hewitt, Ray "Masai", 213
Hilliard, David, 212, 213
Holt, Len, 167
Homestead Act, 146
Honduras, 30
Hoover, Herbert, 83–84
Hoover, J. Edgar, 206, 210
Hughes, Langston, 80–81
Huiswood, Otto, 75, 77

Hutton, Bobby, 125

IFCO. *See* Interreligious Foundation for Community Organizations
ILD. *See* International Labor Defense
IMS. *See* International Migration Society
Imari, Brother. *See* Henry, Richard B.
Industrialization, 67
Innis, Roy: community control, 143–144; CORE's economic platform, 145–147; CORE's new directions, 118, 227–228; National Director of CORE, 120–121, 122, 142, 173, 207, 228; promotion of African-Afro-American relationships, 208
Institutional racism, 115
Integration movements, 4
"Inter-communalism," 128–129
Internal colonialism: Black Panther Party, 126, 128; community control, 143; CORE, 162; Eldridge Cleaver, 126, 152; Huey Newton, 127, 128; James Farmer, 15; Malcolm X, 148–149; separatist economic programs, 157, 158, 165, 233; SNCC, 115, 185; Stokely Carmichael, 116, 150. *See also* Colonization
International Labor Defense (ILD), 81–82; *See also* Communist Party
International Migration Society (IMS), 39, 40, 57. *See also* Back-to-Africa movement, Emigrationism
Interreligious Foundation for Community Organizations (IFCO), 205
Islam, University of, 88, 140

Jackson, Jesse, 161
Jackson, Jimmy Lee, 5
Jews, 135–136, 148, 151, 155, 186–187, 246, 255; Jewish model of Booker T. Washington, 49. *See also* Black Zionism
Johnson, Lyndon B., 5, 200
Jones, Absalom, 23
Journal of Negro History, 48–49

Kansas Exodus, 33
Kansas-Nebraska Act of 1854, 29
Kennedy, John F., 106–107, 199–200
Kennedy, Robert F., 146
Kenyatta, Jomo, 67
King, C. B., 169
King, Ed, 109
King, Edwin, 171
King, Dr. Martin Luther, Jr.: as a leader, 186; ideology, 6, 105–106, 166; March on Washington, 4; "Meredith Mississippi Freedom March," 5; Montgomery Bus Boycott, 109; murder of, 201; rise of, 94
King, Slater, 169
King of Mecca, 98, 99
Ku Klux Klan, 4, 31, 51, 65, 67, 68, 105, 180, 208

League for Nonviolent Civil Disobedience to a Segregated Army, 130
League of Struggle for Negro Rights (LSNR), 79, 80
Leonard, Freddy, 168
Lerner, Louis, 218
Lewis, John, 9, 110, 111, 116, 148, 168, 169, 206
Lewis, William H., 47
Liberia, 65, 70–71; Back-to-Africa movement, 24, 28, 30, 32, 39, 40, 41; black colonization, 41–42; colonization, 36; emigrationism, 30, 64; UNIA, 64–65
Liberia Colonization Society, 40
Liberian Emigration Clubs, 39
Liberian Exodus Joint Stock Steamship Company, 32, 34
Liberian Temple, 41
Liberian Trading and Emigration Association of the United States, 41
Libia, 160

Lincoln, Abraham, 29-30
Lincoln Plan, 30
Lincoln University, 80, 130, 132
Little, Malcolm. *See* Malcolm X
"Little Richard," 110
Lockheed, 160
Logan, Rayford, 53
Lombard, Rudy, 118
Lonnie X, 181
Lowndes County Freedom Organization, 5, 112, 113, 124, 151, 172, 184
L'overture, Toussaint, 47
LSNR. *See* League of Struggle for Negro Rights
Lundy, Benjamin, 25

McCarran Act (1950), 238
McDew, Chuck, 206
McKay, Claude, 80, 81
McKissick, Floyd B.: background and philosophy, 119-120; black bourgeois nationalism, 227-228; black capitalism, 121; black power, 117, 181; CORE, 119-120, 161, 172, 182, 201; McKissick Enterprises, 177, 182
Makeba, Miriam, 190, 204
Malcolm X (E-Hajj Malik El Shabazz, Malcolm Little): black middle class, 108; Black Panther Party, 193-194; Black power, 9, 116; CORE, 181; death, 108, 132; early background, 90-91; economic program, 117; Elijah Muhammad, 105, 107; federal government, 169; integration, 178; internal colonialism, 148-149; James Farmer, 180; Nation of Islam, 104, 107, 177, 179, 184, 193, 217, 219; Organization of Afro-American Unity, 189; ouster from Muslims, 107, 184, 192; Pan-Africanism, 204; philosophy, 105-108, 122, 123; RNA, 191; separate state, 132; rise to prominence, 4, 94, 104; SNCC, 184, 185, 186; separatism, 97, 193; white racism, 218
Malcolm X Society, 132-133, 201
Mangoumbel, Moussa, 55

March on Washington (1963), 4, 110-111, 168-169, 199
March on Washington Movement (MOWM), 91-92, 93
Marshall, Thurgood, 202
Marxism-Leninism, 73, 127, 128, 151, 175, 190, 194; position of Black Panther Party, 150, 152, 188, 215-216
Menelek, King of Abyssinia, 41
Meredith, James, 5
MFDP. *See* Mississippi Freedom Democratic Party
Message to the Black Man in America, 140, 192
MGT. *See* Moslem Girls' Training
Michigan Chronicle, 131
Migrationism, 36, 67
Miller, Kelly, 54
Mississippi Freedom March (1966), 5, 6, 112
Mississippi Freedom Democratic Party (MFDP): Democratic National Convention (1964), 4-5, 111, 112-113, 171-172, 173, 228; founding of, 112; SNCC, 151, 170, 184
Mitchell, John, 221
Montgomery Bus Boycott, 94, 109
Moore, Richard "Dharuba," 212
Moorish-American Science Temple, 87
Morehouse College, 119
Morgan, Clement, 54
Morgan, J. P., 61, 73
Morgan, Senator John T., 41
Moses, Robert, 9, 110, 171, 206
Moslem Girls' Training (MGT), 88
Mother Bethel African Methodist Episcopal Church, 23
Movement Organization, 9, 12
MOWM. *See* March on Washington Movement
Moynihan, Daniel P., 236, 237
Muhammad, Abkan, 185-186
Muhammad, Elijah (Elijah Poole): background, 89; black community, 103-104; constituted authority, 89-90, 169; Chicago, 161; death, 162, 219; Fard's messenger, 101; Marcus Garvey,

Muhammad, Elijah (*cont.*)
97; land question, 102, 139;
Malcolm X, 105, 107; Muslim
religion, 98, 108; nation-within-
a-nation, 139–140, 178; Booker
T. Washington, 226, 227; white
devils, 100, 194, 218
Muhammad, Herbert, 219
Muhammad, Wallace, 162, 219
Muhammad Speaks, 140, 160–161,
183, 218, 226, 227
Mussolini, 71

NAACP. *See* National Association
for the Advancement of Colored
People
Nation of Islam (Black Muslims):
appeal, 102, 103, 179, 192;
black community control, 103,
104, 179, 180–181, 192; black
middle class, 102; Black Panther
Party, 123, 191–194; black
power, 186; Booker T. Washington, 226; changes in ideology,
217–219, 227; in Chicago, 206,
219; Christianity, 2, 104, 235;
constituted authority, 89;
CORE, 118, 177–183; economic
philosophy, 139–142, 154, 157,
159, 160–161, 162; Eldridge
Cleaver, 192, 193; founding,
87–89, 92, 93, 97, 246; Fruit
of Islam (FOI), 105, 182; Huey
Newton, 193; ideology, 4, 7, 97,
101–102, 122, 194, 200, 225;
integration, 106, 178; Malcolm X,
104, 107, 177, 179, 184, 192,
193, 217, 219; Marcus Garvey,
97, 98, 226–227; membership,
90, 102, 132, 225; membership
requirements, 103, 161, 162;
nation-within-a-nation, 160;
origins, 97–101; politics, 107;
program, 227, 232; recruitment,
102; reparations, 158–159, 186;
RNA, 123; SNCC, 184–187;
territorial separatism, 107, 135,
193; Three Year Economic
Savings Program, 140; white
devils, 101, 103, 105, 184–185,
218; white membership, 162,
233. *See also* Malcolm X, Elijah
Muhammad, *Muhammad Speaks*
National Association for the
Advancement of Colored People
(NAACP): as lobbyist, 84; constituted authority, 73; Council of
Federated Organizations, 171;
integration of military, 130;
membership, 67, 76, 79, 164;
Robert Williams, 133, 224; role
in black freedom struggle, 6, 12,
92, 186, 242; "Scottsboro Boys",
81; sit-in movement, 109; SNCC,
202; Temporary Student Non-
Violent Coordinating Committee,
110; W. E. B. DuBois, 50, 51,
53, 69, 73, 87, 242
National Black United Front, 204
National Black Economic Develop-
ment Conference (1969), 205
National Club, 58
National Colored Teachers Associa-
tion, 55
National Committees to Combat
Fascism, 127
National Community Corporation
Certification Board, 146–147
National Conference for a United
Front Against Fascism, 127
National Movement for the Estab-
lishment of a Forty-Ninth State,
86, 93
National Negro Business League, 50
National Negro Congress 1935
(NNC), 91, 92
National Student Association, 110
National Urban League (NUL), 76
Negro Declaration of Rights, 62,
66, 232
Negro Equal Rights League
(NERL), 53, 67
Negro Repatriation Bill (1939), 86
Negro Factories Corporation, 63,
71, 73, 75
Negro World, 60, 62, 68, 81
New Deal, 84, 85–86, 93
New Left, 174–175, 233
New York Age, 47–48
New York and Liberia Steamship
Company, 41
New York City Board of Educa-

New York City (*cont.*)
tion, 120–121, 183
New York Magazine, 161
New York State Suffrage Association, 28
New York Times, 178
Newton, Huey: Black Muslims,
193; Black Panther Party, 113,
123, 125, 189, 201, 210, 212,
213; black separatism, 194–195;
Eldridge Cleaver, 213–214,
217; internal colonialism, 127,
128; personal background, 125;
revolutionary nationalism, 125,
187; Stokely Carmichael, 190–
191
Niagara Movement (1905), 51, 53,
231–232
Nicaragua, 30
Nix, Robert N. C., 252
Nixon, Richard M: administration,
239; black power, 127, 191, 229;
James Farmer, 177, 182, 183;
Republic of New Africa, 136,
220; reparations, 136; Thurgood
Marshall, 202
Nkrumah, Kwame, 204, 249
NNC. *See* National Negro Congress
Norman, Tom (Brother Hekima),
221
North Carolina, University of, Law
School, 119
North Star, The, 33
Northern Student Movement, 202
Not without Laughter, 80
NUL. *See* National Urban League

OAAU. *See* Organization of Afro-
American Unity
OAU. *See* Organization of African
Unity
Obadele, Brother Gaidi. *See* Henry,
Milton R.
Obadele, Brother Imari. *See* Henry,
Richard B.
O'Boyle, Archbishop Patrick, 111,
169
Office of Economic Opportunity,
163, 200
Opportunity magazine, 83
Organization of African Unity

(OAU), 208
Organization of Afro-American
Unity (OAAU), 108, 148, 149,
180, 189, 232. *See also* Malcolm
X
Ottawa, University of, 131
Owen, Chandler, 75

Pan-African Cultural Festival
(1969), 190
Pan-Africanism, 167; African
development, 55; Black Panther
Party, 215–215; black separatism,
251–254; CORE, 121, 207, 253;
definition, 3; impracticality of,
251–252; Malcolm X, 204;
Marcus Garvey, 67–68, 70, 72,
121, 253; new directions, 253–
254; SNCC, 115, 185, 191, 228;
Stokely Carmichael, 204; UNIA,
68, 207; W. E. B. DuBois, 253
Panama, 30
Pan-Negro Congress (1900), 54
Parchman Mississippi Penitentiary,
168
Parker, Charlie, 110
Parker, John J., 84
Parks, Rosa, 109
Patterson, William L., 81
Peck, James, 168
Pennsylvania Central railroad, 160
People United to Save Humanity
(PUSH), 161
Plessy vs. Ferguson, 39
Political nationalism, 3. *See also*
Black nationalism, SNCC
Political parties: Democratic, 4,
31, 32, 83, 84, 111, 149, 206;
Peace and Freedom, 189; Popu-
list, 38; Republican, 28, 31, 32,
83, 149; Socialist, 73, 76
Poole, Elijah. *See* Muhammad,
Elijah
Poor, Salem, 2
Progressive Era, 38, 56
Project Uganda, 207. *See also*
CORE
Prosser, Gabriel, 26, 106
Protestant ethic, 144, 179
PUSH. *See* People United to
Save Humanity

Quaker Friends of Reconciliation, 118. *See also* Fellowship of Reconciliation

RAM. *See* Revolutionary Action Movement
Ramparts, 214
Randolph, A. Philip, 68, 73, 75, 91-92, 93, 130
Reconstruction, 38, 113, 200; black participation, 31, 34, 37; economy, 32; end of, 53; politics, 32, 34; white fears, 31
Redmond, Charles L., 27
Reeb, James, 5
Religious nationalism, 1, 2. *See also* Nation of Islam
Reparations: Black Panther Party, 152, 158-159; Eldridge Cleaver, 193; Malcolm X Society, 133; Nation of Islam, 158-159, 186; Richard M. Nixon, 136; RNA, 136, 137, 155, 156, 158-159; separatist economic programs, 159, 164; SNCC, 151, 158-159, 205
Republic of New Africa (RNA), 7; Black Legion, 129-130, 136-137, 219-220; black nation, 123, 128, 153; Black Panthers, 194-195; changes in ideology, 220-221, 222; and China, 137; constituted authority, 220, 221, 230, 231; CORE, 123, 183-184; culture, 235; economic program, 154-157, 159, 164; Eldridge Cleaver, 195; founded, 97, 129, 133, 219, 246; ideology, 8, 129, 134, 230-231; KUSH Nation, 222; leadership, 129, 133, 134, 219-220, 221, 246; Malcolm X, 191; membership, 220, 222; Nation of Islam, 123; organized, 123, 129, 133, 183, 191; reparations, 136, 137, 155, 156, 158-159; Richard Nixon, 136, 220; Robert F. Williams, 97, 129, 133, 191, 219, 220; Robert S. Browne, 134-135; SNCC, 123, 191; split within movement, 220-222; W. E. B. DuBois, 191; white membership,

223
Reston, James, 178
Revolutionary Action Movement (RAM), 4, 169
Revolutionary black nationalism, 1, 2, 97, 125-126, 187; Robert Williams, 4. *See also* Black Panther Party
Revolutionary War, 22, 137
Riots (1964-1966), 5, 200, 201-202
Rizzo, Frank, 173
RNA. *See* Republic of New Africa
Robber Barons, 57
Roberts, Benjamin, 27
Rockefeller family, 73
Roosevelt, Franklin D., 83, 84, 91
Roosevelt, Theodore, 47
Rural Development Incentive Act, 146, 147
Russwurm, John B., 24
Rustin, Bayard, 92, 130, 167, 168, 173

Sacco-Vanzetti case, 81
St. George's Methodist Episcopal Church, 23
Salem, Peter, 22
Sam, Chief Alfred C., 54
San Francisco Law School, 124
Saturday Evening Post, 80
Schwerner, Michael, 6, 111
SCLC. *See* Student Christian Leadership Conference
Scott, Emmett J., 72
Scott, Stanley, 161
Scottsboro case, 81-82
SDS. *See* Students for a Democratic Society
Seale, Bobby: Black Panther Party spokesman, 124, 127, 210; changes in Black Panther Party, 210, 212-214, 216-217; ideology, 193; as mayoral candidate, 153-154; organization of Black Panther Party, 113, 123
Sellers, Cleveland, 148
Selma March (1965), 5
Separatist movement, 7, 139, 164-165, 199, 206, 224. *See*

Separatist movement (*cont.*)
  also Black separatism, Black
  separatist movement
Separatist typologies, 12-17, 251
Shabazz, Betty, 125
Shaw University (Raleigh, N. C.),
  109
Shuttlesworth, Fred, 109
Sierra Leone, 22, 24, 39
Silver, Horace, 110
Sinclair, William, 54
Singleton, Benjamin "Pap," 33, 37
Sit-in movement (1950), 108-109,
  110, 117, 167, 174, 200
Slavery: British, 22; Civil War, 29,
  35, 152; emigrationism, 24, 30;
  free blacks, 22, 27; the North,
  27, 29, 30, 31; slave revolts, 26,
  27; white America, 21-23
SNCC. *See* Student Non-Violent
  Coordinating Committee
Social movement theory, 9, 11-12
Socialism, 138, 148, 150, 157, 159,
  160. *See also* Black Panther Party,
  Congress of Racial Equality,
  Malcolm X, Nation of Islam,
  Republic of New Africa, Student
  Non-Violent Coordinating Com-
  mittee
Soul on Ice, 125, 214
Soul Students Advisory Council
  of Merritt College, 123-124
Southern Christian Leadership
  Conference (SCLC), 12; demise,
  174; emergence of, 109-110;
  growth, 110; split with SNCC, 5
Southern Education Fund, 100
Stalin, Joseph, 77
Stalinism, 78
Student Non-Violent Coordinating
  Committee (SNCC), 4, 7, 12;
  black bourgeoisie, 114; black
  community, 113, 115, 116, 117,
  170, 206-207; black community
  control, 113, 115, 116; Black
  Panther Party, 123, 124, 127,
  176, 187-191; black power, 9,
  115, 116, 127, 184, 186, 201,
  207; black vote, 111, 113, 119;
  change in ideology, 200, 203;
  civil rights movement, 94, 97;

constituted authority, 229;
  CORE, 121, 167-175; Council of
  Federated Organizations, 171;
  demise of, 202-203, 204;
  economic program, 149, 151,
  154, 159; Eldridge Cleaver, 188;
  emergence of, 108-112, 167,
  246; Freedom Rides, 93, 110;
  ideology, 112, 122, 135, 229,
  235; internal colonialism, 115,
  185; John Lewis, 111; Lowndes
  County Freedom Organization,
  112, 113; Malcolm X, 184, 185,
  186; membership, 185, 188-189,
  203, 204; Mississippi Freedom
  Democratic Party, 151, 170, 184;
  NAACP, 202; Nation of Islam,
  184-187; Pan-Africanism, 115,
  185, 191, 228; political participation, 206, 228-229; reparations, 151, 158-159, 205; Republic of New Africa, 123, 191; split
  with SCLC, 5; Stokely Carmichael, 5, 9, 110, 112, 148,
  151, 172, 189, 200-201, 204-
  205; *The Student Voice*, 110;
  tactics, 110-114; voter registration, 228; white membership,
  233. *See also* Temporary Student
  Non-Violent Coordinating Committee
Students for a Democratic Society
  (SDS), 128, 174
Sumner, R. F., 221

Tabor, Connie Matthews, 212
Tabor, Michael "Cetewayo," 212
Taft, William Howard, 47
Temple University, 31
Temporary Student Non-Violent
  Coordinating Committee
  (TSNCC), 109-110, 167. *See also*
  Student Non-Violent Coordinat-
  ing Committee
Terrell, Robert H., 47
Territorial separatism, 1, 2. *See also*
  Nation of Islam, Republic of
  New Africa
Third World, 105; colonization,
  115-116
Thompson Tank, 169

Thornbrough, Emma, 44
Thuku, Harry, 67
To Die for the People, 210
Trotter, William Monroe, 38, 52–
53, 54, 67
Truman, Harry, 130
TSNCC. *See* Temporary Student
Non-Violent Coordinating Com-
mittee
Turner, Bishop Henry McNeil,
34–37, 39, 40, 41, 54
Turner, Nat, 47, 106
Turner, Nathaniel, 26
Tuskegee Institute, 43, 44, 51, 57,
59, 72, 226. *See also* Washington,
Booker T.
Tyson, J. Sheriff, 168

Uganda, 121
"Ujamaa," 3, 137–138, 157
UNIA. *See* Universal Negro Im-
provement Association
United Arab Republic, 141
United Black Fund, 154
United Communist Party, 76
United States Air Force Infor-
mation Office, 131
United States Commission on
Civil Rights, 171
United States Constitution, 23, 35
102
United States Supreme Court, 38,
46, 84, 167, 168
United Transatlantic Society, 33
Universal Africa Motor Corps, 62
Universal Negro Improvement
Association (UNIA): administra-
tion of, 65, 70, 71, 97; Black Star
Line, 61, 64; business enterprises,
63; Communist Party, 76–77;
decline of, 66; founding of, 59,
60; growth of, 60, 62; in Harlem,
59–60; ideology, 101, 102, 208,
226–227; Liberian government,
64–65; Marcus Garvey, 68, 70,
71, 101, 227; Pan-Africanism,
68, 207
Up from Slavery, 59. *See also*
Washington, Booker T.

Vesey, Denmark, 26, 106

Vietnam War, 137, 200, 206
Voice of the People, The, 40
Voter Education Project, 206. *See
also* Lewis, John
Voting Rights Bill, 113, 234, 239

Wagner, Mayor Robert (NYC), 170
Walker, David, 25–26, 27
Walker, S. Jay, 252–253
Wallace, George, 206, 208
*War in America: The Malcolm
X Doctrine*, 133
War on Poverty, 200, 203
Ward, Samuel Ringgold, 28
Washington, Booker T.: African
Union Company, 55; Cotton
States Exposition speech, 43–
44, 231; criticisms of, 49–50,
51–52, 53; death of, 55, 56,
67; W. E. B. DuBois, 47, 49–
50, 51, 52, 53, 54, 242; early
years, 42–43; economic pro-
gram, 67, 121, 141, 142, 149,
151, 244, 249; education, 45,
46, 50, 51–52, 113; Elijah
Muhammad, 226, 227; emigra-
tionism, 54, 55, 253; Hampton
Institute, 42, 43; ideology,
55–57, 225–226, 228; influ-
ence, 43, 44, 47, 48, 51, 52,
55; Jewish model, 49; Marcus
Garvey, 57, 59, 63, 66, 71,
72, 242–243; politics, 44, 46,
47, 48, 50, 51; separatism,
44, 45, 46, 47, 48, 49, 56;
Tuskegee Institute, 43, 44,
49, 51, 57; as Uncle Tom, 48;
Up from Slavery, 59
Watts, 172, 200
Weathermen, 233
Wells-Barnett, Ida, 54
White, George H., 53–54
White Panther Party, 128, 233
White separatism, 254
Wiley, George, 118
Wilkerson, Doxey A., 79
Williams, John Bell, 206
Williams, Robert F.: background,
94, 133–134; change in rhet-
oric, 223, 224; constituted
authority, 169; founding of

Williams, Robert F. (*cont.*)
  RNA, 97, 129, 133, 191;
  NAACP, 133, 224; president of
  RNA, 219; resignation from
  RNA, 220; revolutionary black
  nationalism, 4
Wilson, Woodrow, 53
Woodson, Carter, 48, 68
Workers' Party, 76
World War I, 34, 55, 66–67, 72, 243
World War II, 90, 93, 130

Wright, Richard, 80, 81

Yakub, 98–99, 100
Yale University School of Law,
  130
Young Lords Organization (Young
  Lords Party), 126

Zinn, Howard, 168–171
Zionists, 129. *See also* Black
  Zionism